New Directions in Cognitive Grammar and Style

Advances in Stylistics
Series Editors: Dan McIntyre, University of Huddersfield, UK, and Louise Nuttall, University of Huddersfield, UK

Editorial Board:
Jean Boase-Beier, University of East Anglia, UK
Beatrix Busse, University of Heidelberg, Germany
Szilvia Csábi, Independent Scholar
Yaxiao Cui, University of Nottingham, UK
Manuel Jobert, Jean Moulin University, Lyon 3, France
Lorenzo Mastopierro, University of Nottingham, UK
Eric Rundquist, Pontifica Universidad Católica de Chile, Chile
Odette Vassallo, University of Malta, Malta
Peter Verdonk, University of Amsterdam (Emeritus), The Netherlands
Chantelle Warner, University of Arizona, USA

Titles in the series include:
Chick Lit: The Stylistics of Cappuccino Fiction, Rocío Montoro
Corpus Stylistics in Principles and Practice, Yufang Ho
Crime Fiction Migration, Christiana Gregoriou
I.A. Richards and the Rise of Cognitive Stylistics, David West
Mind Style and Cognitive Grammar, Louise Nuttall
Narrative Retellings, Marina Lambrou
Oppositions and Ideology in News Discourse, Matt Davies
Pedagogical Stylistics, Michael Burke, Szilvia Csábi, Lara Week and Judit Zerkowitz
Style in the Renaissance, Patricia Canning
Stylistic Manipulation of the Reader in Contemporary Fiction, Sandrine Sorlin
Sylvia Plath and the Language of Affective States, Zsófia Demjén
Telecinematic Stylistics, Christian Hoffmann and Monika Kirner-Ludwig
Text World Theory and Keats' Poetry, Marcello Giovanelli
The Stylistics of Poetry, Peter Verdonk
World Building, Joanna Gavins and Ernestine Lahey
World Building in Spanish and English Spoken Narratives, Jane Lugea

New Directions in Cognitive Grammar and Style

Edited by
Marcello Giovanelli, Chloe Harrison and Louise Nuttall

BLOOMSBURY ACADEMIC
LONDON • NEW YORK • OXFORD • NEW DELHI • SYDNEY

BLOOMSBURY ACADEMIC
Bloomsbury Publishing Plc
50 Bedford Square, London, WC1B 3DP, UK
1385 Broadway, New York, NY 10018, USA
29 Earlsfort Terrace, Dublin 2, Ireland

BLOOMSBURY, BLOOMSBURY ACADEMIC and the Diana logo
are trademarks of Bloomsbury Publishing Plc

First published in Great Britain 2021
This paperback edition published in 2022

Copyright © Marcello Giovanelli, Chloe Harrison,
Louise Nuttall and Contributors, 2021

Marcello Giovanelli, Chloe Harrison and Louise Nuttall have asserted their right under the Copyright, Designs and Patents Act, 1988, to be identified as Editors of this work.

For legal purposes the Acknowledgements on p. xiv constitute an extension of this copyright page.

All rights reserved. No part of this publication may be reproduced or transmitted in any form or by any means, electronic or mechanical, including photocopying, recording, or any information storage or retrieval system, without prior permission in writing from the publishers.

Bloomsbury Publishing Plc does not have any control over, or responsibility for, any third-party websites referred to or in this book. All internet addresses given in this book were correct at the time of going to press. The authors and publisher regret any inconvenience caused if addresses have changed or sites have ceased to exist, but can accept no responsibility for any such changes.

A catalogue record for this book is available from the British Library.

A catalog record for this book is available from the Library of Congress.

ISBN: HB: 978-1-3501-1111-0
       PB: 978-1-3501-9693-3
       ePDF: 978-1-3501-1112-7
       eBook: 978-1-3501-1113-4

Series: Advances in Stylistics

Typeset by Integra Software Services Pvt Ltd.

To find out more about our authors and books visit www.bloomsbury.com and sign up for our newsletters.

Contents

List of figures		vii
List of tables		x
List of contributors		xi
Acknowledgements		xiv
1	Introduction *Marcello Giovanelli, Chloe Harrison and Louise Nuttall*	1

Part I Cognitive Grammar in literary contexts

2	Re-cognizing Free Indirect Discourse *Peter Stockwell*	17
3	The dynamicity of construal, embodied memory and (mental) time travel in Mohsin Hamid's *Exit West* *Anne Holm*	35
4	Construal, blending and metaphoric worlds in Francis Harvey's 'The Deaf Woman in the Glen' *Nigel McLoughlin*	51
5	Guilty grammar: See-saw perspective and morality in a poem by E.E. Cummings *Louise Nuttall*	75

Part II Cognitive Grammar in non-literary contexts

6	'28 Palestinians die': A Cognitive Grammar analysis of mystification in press coverage of state violence on the Gaza border *Christopher Hart*	93
7	'Hmmm yes, but where's the beef?' Cognitive Grammar and the active audience in political discourse *Sam Browse*	117
8	Modelling intentionality in Cognitive Grammar *Matthew Voice*	135

Part III Cognitive Grammar in multimodal contexts

9	'Subject and object and the nature of reality' in *Are You My Mother? Richard Finn*	157
10	'All the figures I used to see': Using Cognitive Grammar to grapple with rhythmic and intertextual meaning-making in Radiohead's 'Pyramid Song' *Clara Neary*	181
11	Allocating meaning across the senses: Cognitive Grammar as a tool for the creation of multimodal texts *Alison Bown*	201

Part IV Cognitive Grammar in educational contexts

12 From theoretical to pedagogical grammar: The challenges of writing a textbook on Cognitive Grammar *Marcello Giovanelli and Chloe Harrison* 221

13 Recontextualizing Cognitive Grammar for school teaching *Ian Cushing* 241

14 Towards a concept-driven pedagogy: A model of linguistic knowledge *Sally Zacharias* 261

15 Coda *Marcello Giovanelli, Chloe Harrison and Louise Nuttall* 281

Index 284

Figures

2.1	FID as a deflection across world-boundaries	24
2.2	Vantage Point for 'in front of' and 'behind' (after Langacker 2008: 76)	25
2.3	Attentional windowing of narratorial control	26
2.4	Attentional windowing of character control	26
2.5	Attentional windowing of free indirect discourse	27
2.6	Attentional windowing of character-to-character free indirect discourse	29
4.1	Expected attentional arrangement of spaces (derived from Langacker 2008: 58)	56
4.2	Expected attentional arrangement of spaces (derived from Stockwell 2009)	57
4.3	Representation of re-attending the target through the blend	58
4.4	Conceptual arrangement of opening stanza	60
4.5	Map of input spaces into the WOMAN AS LANDSCAPE blend	64
4.6	WOMAN AS RAVEN blend	65
4.7	Agent-patient relationships in WOMAN IS BADGER metaphor	66
4.8	Trajector-landmark alignment of WOMAN IS BADGER metaphor	67
4.9	Conceptual arrangement of close of poem	68
4.10	Vertical conceptual arrangement of final part of poem	68
4.11	Text-world projections of blends as sub-worlds and world-building elements for mega-blend	69
5.1	Image schema activated for prepositional phrase 'up ... out of' (based on Evans and Green 2006: 182)	81
5.2	Objective and subjective construal in asymmetrical viewing arrangements	83
6.1	Canonical event model: Two-participant action chain	98
6.2	Active transitive versus passive construction	99
6.3	Absolute intransitive	102
6.4	Agentless passive construction	103
6.5	Scanning	103
6.6	Agent-instrument profile	105
6.7	Patientless active construction	106
6.8	'Soldiers had opened fire after rioting'	107
6.9	Directional prepositions	108
6.10	Image taken from the *Wall Street Journal*	109

6.11	Path profiling	110
6.12	Video still from *The Guardian*	110
7.1	The immediate scope of 'desk ornament'	122
7.2	Focusing in the clause	123
7.3	The composition of 'wealth creator'	126
7.4	Respecifying the 'wealth creators'	127
7.5	Multi-process reconstrual of 'wealth creators'	128
8.1	Modelling intentional and superventional processes in SFL (adapted from Simpson 1993: 89)	137
8.2	Planes of intention in relation to an example canonical event	141
8.3	Connecting intentions hierarchically across discourse	150
9.1	Optimal viewing arrangement in *Fun Home* (Bechdel 2006, quoted in Pleyer and Schneider 2014: 49)	158
9.2	Egocentric viewing arrangement in *Fun Home* (Bechdel 2006: 44, quoted in Pleyer and Schneider 2014: 47)	158
9.3	Usage event grounding in comic books	162
9.4	Narrative and depictive viewing arrangements	164
9.5	Depiction and narration of telephone call (Bechdel 2012: 229)	168
9.6	Depiction and of re-enacting telephone call (Bechdel 2012: 233)	168
9.7	Multiple depictive and narrative perspectives (Bechdel 2012: 234)	169
9.8	Complex modal predication and basic implicit predication	171
9.9	Depictive grounding focusing on $_c$Alison's conceptualizing activity	173
9.10	$_c$Alison as discursively grounded conceptualizer	175
9.11	Relative reality conceptions	176
9.12	Focusing on $_c$Alison's reflection	176
10.1	*Oooh, ooh, ooh*	191
10.2	Line 1: *Jumped in the river and what did I see?* and Line 5: *All my lovers were there with me*	193
10.3	Line 2: *Black-eyed angels swam with me* and Line 6: *All my past and futures*	194
10.4	Line 3: *A moon full of stars and astral cars* and Line 7: *And we all went to heaven in a little row-boat*	195
10.5	Line 4: *And all the figures I used to see* and Line 8: *There was nothing to fear, nothing to doubt*	195
11.1	Chapter Two of *Loss of Grasp*: Meeting in the Restaurant	212
12.1	A more traditional geometric diagram representing types and instances (from Giovanelli and Harrison 2018: 109)	232
12.2	A metaphorical illustration of summary scanning (from Giovanelli and Harrison 2018: 68)	232

13.1	An action chain	245
13.2	The CLAUSE STRUCTURE IS ENERGY TRANSFER visual metaphor	251
13.3	Energy transfer embodied	254
14.1	Generic discourse-world of the classroom	266
14.2	Langacker's reality-irreality continuum (based on Langacker 1991: 242)	273

Tables

3.1 Properties of Lyric Narration versus Narrative Urgency	41
4.1 Representation of Blended Elements in WOMAN IS STONE Metaphor	61
4.2 Representation of Blended Elements in WOMAN IS THORN Metaphor	62
4.3 Representation of Blended Elements in the WOMAN IS BONES Metaphor	63
14.1 The Linguistic Knowledge Framework	269

List of contributors

Alison Bown is a writer and sound designer working across games, cinema and theatre audio. She completed her interdisciplinary PhD at Bath Spa University and University of Bath across computer science and digital writing. Her research methodology is practice-led and focuses on the ways that language and sound can be braided together within creative texts, particularly interactive texts. She is also interested in user interaction and its impact on narrative transportation. By using linguistics to develop an understanding of the cognitive processes employed within the mind of player readers, she hopes to develop techniques useful to writers moving into the digital domain.

Sam Browse is a former Senior Lecturer in English Language. He is the author of *Cognitive Rhetoric: The Cognitive Poetics of Political Discourse* (John Benjamins, 2018) and has published widely on cognitive grammar, Text-World Theory and political discourse. His research brings together ideas from classical rhetoric, cognitive stylistics and cognitive and social psychology to examine how audiences interpret the language of politics. He now puts his academic expertise into practice in the British Parliament as a Senior Assistant to a Labour Party politician.

Ian Cushing is Lecturer in the Department of Education at Brunel University, UK. He has a broad range of teaching and research interests, including English education, critical language policy, ideologies about language in educational contexts and grammar pedagogies. He has published a number of journal articles and book chapters in these areas. His doctoral research involved the theorization, application and evaluation of a cognitive stylistic pedagogy for secondary school English teachers, drawing on Text World Theory and Cognitive Grammar. He continues to work closely with teachers.

Richard Finn is a researcher in the School of English at the University of Sheffield, UK. His interests focus on communicating experiences of mental illness, multimodality, comic books and cognitive linguistics.

Marcello Giovanelli is Senior Lecturer in English Language and Literature at Aston University, UK. He has research interests in applications of Text World Theory and Cognitive Grammar to literary discourse and in pedagogical stylistics. Recent books include *Text World Theory and Keats' Poetry* (Bloomsbury, 2013), *Teaching Grammar, Structure and Meaning* (Routledge 2014), *Knowing about Language* (with Dan Clayton, Routledge, 2016) and *Cognitive Grammar in Stylistics: A Practical Guide* (with Chloe Harrison, Bloomsbury, 2018). He has published widely on cognitive stylistics and applied linguistics in major international journals.

Chloe Harrison is Lecturer in English Language and Literature at Aston University, UK. Her research interests include cognitive stylistics (and specifically the application of Cognitive Grammar for literary-linguistic analysis), re-reading and contemporary fiction. She has a number of publications in these areas, including two recent books: *Cognitive Grammar in Contemporary Fiction* (Benjamins, 2017) and *Cognitive Grammar in Stylistics: A Practical Guide* (with Marcello Giovanelli, Bloomsbury, 2018). She is also Treasurer for the International Association of Literary Semantics.

Christopher Hart is Professor of Linguistics at Lancaster University, UK. His research investigates the connection between language, cognition and action in social and political contexts of communication. He is the author of *Critical Discourse Analysis and Cognitive Science: New Perspectives on Immigration Discourse* (Palgrave, 2010) and *Discourse, Grammar and Ideology: Functional and Cognitive Perspectives* (Bloomsbury, 2014). He is editor of *Cognitive Linguistic Approaches to Text and Discourse: From Poetics to Politics* (Edinburgh University Press, 2019) and *Researching Discourse: A Practical Guide* (Routledge, 2020).

Anne Holm is Senior Lecturer in English Literature at Linnaeus University, Sweden. She earned her PhD at the University of Tampere, Finland, in 2014. Her dissertation explored embodied metaphors in Dylan Thomas's writing. Her research interests include stylistics, embodiment in literature, Conceptual Metaphor Theory and applications of Cognitive Grammar to literary analysis. At the moment she is researching metaphors of displacement in migrant literature.

Nigel McLoughlin is Professor of Creativity and Poetics at the University of Gloucestershire, UK. He has published five collections of poetry, the latest of which is *Chora: New and Selected Poems* (Templar Poetry, 2009). He has also written on creative writing pedagogy, the creative process and cognitive poetics in relation to poetry. He was editor of *Iota* poetry journal for seven years and was awarded a National Teaching Fellowship in 2011.

Clara Neary is Senior Lecturer in English Language at the University of Chester, UK. Working in cognitive stylistics, she is particularly interested in conceptual metaphor theory, cognitive grammar and narrative point of view and has applied these and other stylistic techniques to a range of literary genres, including Victorian poetry and contemporary Indian literature in English. She is also interested in the expansion of stylistic enquiry into genres such as music and autobiography.

Louise Nuttall is Senior Lecturer in English Language and Linguistics at the University of Huddersfield, UK. Her research centres on cognitive stylistics and reader-response research with a focus on how minds are represented and responded to across text-types. She is the author of *Mind Style and Cognitive Grammar: Language and Worldview in Speculative Fiction* (Bloomsbury, 2018) and co-editor of *Cognitive Grammar in Literature* (with Chloe Harrison, Peter Stockwell and Wenjuan Yuan, John Benjamins, 2014).

Peter Stockwell is Professor of Literary Linguistics at the University of Nottingham, UK, and a Fellow of the English Association. He has published twelve books and over eighty articles in stylistics, sociolinguistics and applied linguistics, including *Texture: A Cognitive Aesthetics of Reading* (Edinburgh University Press, 2009), *Cognitive Poetics* (Routledge, 2002 and 2020) and *The Language of Surrealism* (Palgrave, 2017). He co-edited *The Cambridge Handbook of Stylistics* (Cambridge University Press, 2014), *The Language and Literature Reader* (Routledge, 2008) and *Contemporary Stylistics* (Continuum, 2007).

Matthew Voice is Associate Lecturer at De Montfort University, UK where he teaches functional and cognitive approaches to language and linguistics. His research is concerned with the development of cognitive linguistic frameworks in relation to critical and literary discourse analyses, with current projects focusing in particular on the language of drone warfare.

Sally Zacharias is Lecturer in Educational Linguistics and Teacher Education in the School of Education at the University of Glasgow, UK. Her research interests draw on cognitive frameworks and discourse studies to investigate the development of abstract concepts in pedagogical settings. Her fields of research include cognitive diversity, metaphor, intercultural understanding and science communication. She delivers language awareness sessions for pre-service subject teachers.

Acknowledgements

The editors and publisher gratefully acknowledge the permission granted to reproduce the copyright material in this book:

ARE YOU MY MOTHER?: *A Comic Drama by Alison Bechdel*. Copyright © 2012 by Alison Bechdel. Used by permission of Houghton Mifflin Harcourt. All rights reserved.

'The Deaf Woman in the Glen' used by permission of Dedalus Press (www.dedaluspress.com).

'Dawn', from *Collected Poems Volume 1* by William Carlos Williams. Used by permission of Carcanet Press.

Image taken from the *Wall Street Journal*, used by permission of Said Khatib/Agence France-Presse/Getty Images

'Me up at does'. Copyright © 1963, 1991 by the Trustees for the E. E. Cummings Trust, from *Complete Poems: 1904–1962* by E. E. Cummings, edited by George J. Firmage. Used by permission of Liveright Publishing Corporation.

'Pyramid Song' by Radiohead, used by permission of Warner Chappell Music

Screenshot from *Loss of Grasp*, used by permission of Serge Bouchardon

Video still from *The Guardian*, used by permission of Guardian News and Media Ltd.

Every effort has been made to trace copyright holders and to obtain their permission for the use of copyright material. The publisher apologizes for any errors or omissions in the above list and would be grateful if notified of any corrections that should be incorporated in future reprints or editions of this book.

1

Introduction

Marcello Giovanelli, Chloe Harrison and Louise Nuttall

1. Cognitive Grammar and cognitive linguistics

Ronald Langacker's Cognitive Grammar, the subject of the chapters in this book, is one of a number of language frameworks that form part of the broader field of cognitive linguistics, a field that starts from the central premise that 'language is assumed to reflect certain fundamental properties and design features of the human mind' (Evans and Green 2006: 5). The increasing interest in discourse and text analysis informed both by cognitive linguistic methods and by the relationship between literary study and cognition more generally has led to what is now a fully formed and established cognitive stylistics (e.g. Gavins and Steen 2003; Stockwell 2009, 2020; Gibbons and Whiteley 2018; Giovanelli and Harrison 2018) that draws on the best knowledge about language and the mind in the service of exploring how texts are created, received and evaluated. Cognitive Grammar is now an established analytical method within the field. This book showcases the latest work using Cognitive Grammar in stylistics.

Cognitive linguistics covers a range of approaches and frameworks that nonetheless share key or 'primary commitments' (Lakoff 1990: 40) and are distinguishable from more formal and decontextualized approaches to language study typified, for example, in generative linguistics. First, there is a 'generalization commitment', which dictates that there is a systematic set of principles that govern all aspects of language and, therefore, key organizational principles can account for language at its different levels (lexis, syntax, phonology and so on). Second, a 'cognitive commitment' operationalizes language within the frame of general cognition, itself viewed as embodied and shaped by our interaction with the physical world via unique 'species-specific anatomical and neurological structures' (Tyler 2012: 28). Embodiment thus provides both affordances and limitations in terms of how we perceive and represent the world. Indeed Mandler (2004) argues that our early sensorimotor experiences and interactions with the environment as young infants give rise to basic image schematic patterns (see also Johnson 1987) from and within which basic meanings such as movement, containment and force are understood. Embodiment is therefore also indicative of 'experiential realism' (Lakoff 1987: iv), a counter to an objectivist approach to reality in the sense that language may be understood not as providing a direct representation of the world but rather one that is subjectively and intersubjectively constructed.

Cognitive linguistics has two main areas of study, 'cognitive semantics and cognitive (approaches) to grammar' (Evans and Green 2006: 48), the latter area consisting both of Langacker's grammar and a group of construction grammars (e.g. Goldberg 1995; Croft 2001). Within cognitive semantics, topics and concepts such as categorization (e.g. Lakoff 1987), encyclopaedic knowledge and schemas (e.g. Schank and Abelson 1977; Fillmore 1982; Schank 1982), image schemas (Johnson 1987; Mandler 2004), force dynamics (e.g. Talmy 1988) and metaphor (e.g. Lakoff and Johnson 1980; Lakoff and Turner 1989) provide an extensive theoretical basis for approaches to grammar that emphasize how linguistic forms are inherently meaningful in their own right. These two areas are therefore both closely interrelated and interdependent.

2. The parameters of Cognitive Grammar

Langacker's theory of Cognitive Grammar adheres to the primary commitments of cognitive linguistics, outlined in the previous section, and also proposes some central ideas that characterize its distinctive theoretical approach to language. This section will provide a brief overview of these key ideas, but for a more detailed account of the theory see Langacker (1987, 1991, 2008); and for the application of the theory framed through a stylistics perspective, specifically, see *Cognitive Grammar in Stylistics: A Practical Guide* (Giovanelli and Harrison 2018).

First, Cognitive Grammar is a usage-based model, which explains the use of language events in terms of *constructions* (Langacker 2008: 161). A construction is a pairing between form and meaning which creates a unit of language. Consider, for example, the following sentence: *Millie's stocking is above the fireplace.* This construction is made up of discrete symbolic units: there is a named actor, signalled through the proper noun 'Millie'; the stative verb 'is' suggests an ongoing situation; and particular entities that populate the location can also be identified ('stocking' and 'the fireplace'). More generally, these individual units can also work to evoke particular mental templates regarding how constructions should be understood. For example, in this sentence the preposition 'above' encodes a spatial relationship, suggesting the physical location of the stocking in relation to the fireplace. Of course, the lexical choices further evoke mental templates: the combination of 'stocking' and 'fireplace' in this construction may call up schematic knowledge, such as that relating to Christmas. In these ways, any linguistic construction can be regarded as inherently meaningful, encoding a particular understanding or interpretation of experience in the world, as signalled through both single instances of language and the combination of units in larger constructions.

Any account of Cognitive Grammar similarly begins with *construal*, which is one of the most important concepts in the theory and which underpins many of the other ideas. Any linguistic construction imposes a particular construal of the proposed content. Simply put, construal is 'our manifest ability to conceive and portray the same situation in alternate ways' (Langacker 2008: 43). As producers of language, as both writers and speakers, we have a set of choices available to us regarding how we represent, or construe, our experiences of the world. For example, we can choose the level of detail with which we describe something (*specificity*), we can choose which part of a scene to pay the most attention to (*focus*), and we can also choose whether to foreground our narrative voice (*perspective*) (Langacker 2008: 33–78). Cognitive Grammar provides a framework through which we can analyse different construals, and the effects such choices have for the directing of attention and for literary or textual interpretation more generally. While the original application of the theory explores, in particular, the construal presented by linguistic producers (writers, speakers), construal also occurs in linguistic reception, as a process similarly experienced by readers and listeners (see Hart 2011; Harrison 2017a, b). Idiosyncratic schematic knowledge held by a reader or listener may impact on how a linguistic construction is interpreted and the significance a reader or listener attributes to particular linguistic choices. This dual nature of construal makes it an attractive concept for stylisticians: it provides the theoretical apparatus through which to analyse linguistic choice, on the one hand, and reader-centred meaning, on the other. Consequently, it is intuitive and psychologically grounded, while also offering the linguistic rigour which is at the heart of all stylistic analysis.

Scaling up from smaller linguistic constructions, Cognitive Grammar can also account for clausal structures. In Cognitive Grammar clauses can be considered in terms of *action chains*, which describe how energy and motion are transferred between entities within a linguistic construction (Langacker 2008: 355). In a prototypical clause, there is an *agent* (energy source) who (wilfully) initiates an action, and a *patient* (energy sink) that experiences a change of some kind as a result of the action. Of course, in texts clausal structures are often more complex, and Cognitive Grammar provides a tool-kit through which participant roles can be further differentiated, depending on how the entity or participant functions in a particular clause. This tool-kit allows researchers to further designate the role for each clausal participant; whether it is one which involves physical movement (*mover*) or a cognitive process (*experiencer*); or whether the clausal participant inhabits a static location (*zero*) or performs a role of transferring energy between two other entities (*instrument*). Cognitive Grammar's action chain model has obvious similarities with Systemic-Functional Grammar's transitivity framework (Halliday 1971), and these points of contact between the two theories are drawn out in detail in Nuttall (2018: 52–4).

These descriptions of constructions, construal and clausal archetypes emphasize the importance of schematic templates in our understanding and use of language. Text producers and receivers draw on these prototypical structures to construe and interpret instances of language in the world. Despite its usage-based classification, however, the early work of Langacker explored contrived instances of language to help illustrate the theory with an emphasis on manufactured examples from spoken discourse and the relationship between interlocutors in a spoken event, over written discourse and writer-reader relationships. Equally, original applications of Cognitive Grammar explored constructions of language that are below and up to the level of the clause. More recently, however, linguists across disciplines, from Critical Discourse Analysis (e.g. Hart 2014; Browse 2018a) to second language acquisition (e.g. Matsumoto 2008;

Arnett and Jernigan 2014), have started to apply Cognitive Grammar for the analysis of clausal and larger discourse-level structures and to a range of instances of language in broader contexts. It is this versatility and scalability of Cognitive Grammar that also make it an appealing choice for literary linguistic research. The next section identifies some of the leading applications of the theory in contemporary stylistic research.

3. Cognitive Grammar and stylistics

Six years ago, two of us co-edited and each of us contributed chapters to the first book-length treatment and application of Cognitive Grammar in stylistics. *Cognitive Grammar in Literature* (Harrison et al. 2014) contained stylistic analyses of a range of narrative fiction and poetic texts. Although the book captured the innovative work that was being carried out in the field at the time, its analytical scope was restricted to the analysis of literary texts. In the following years, the majority of researchers drawing on Cognitive Grammar have maintained this focus and used literature and literary contexts as starting points both to consolidate existing analyses and applications of Cognitive Grammar and to develop new innovations and directions for the framework.

One such development has been the integration of Cognitive Grammar into more traditional areas of stylistic scholarship. For example, Nuttall (2018) reconceptualizes 'mind style' (Fowler 1977; Semino 2002), drawing extensively on the notion of construal to analyse the ways that characters' world-views are linguistically realized and the processes by which readers form and articulate their impressions of particular fictional minds (see also Nuttall 2015, 2019 for further discussion). Indeed the study of mind style has provided ample opportunities for researchers to integrate concepts from Cognitive Grammar more generally and other studies have examined the ways in which, for example, narratorial reliability is both linguistically realized and interpreted by readers. This particular focus appears in studies of characterization in contemporary fiction by, for example, Harrison (2017b) on dementia, Giovanelli (2018) on alcohol-induced amnesia and Harrison (2019) on disorientation and claustrophobia. More broadly, Cognitive Grammar has informed a number of other areas of literary study (see Stockwell 2009, 2020). For example, Harrison (2017a) offers a book-length study of four contemporary novels that incorporates close textual analysis with reader-response analyses. Reader-oriented work is also at the centre of research by Nuttall and Harrison (2019, 2020) who examine the ways in which readers reconceptualize perspective across re-readings of literary fiction. Taking a comparative narratological approach, Giovanelli (2019, 2020) analyses the processes of literary revision and memory across different genres in the war writing of Siegfried Sassoon, and Esmaeili and Amjad (2016) examine the ways in which readers' attention is directed across traumatic episodes in Gustav Hasford's novel *The Short-Timers*.

These new directions in the stylistic application of Cognitive Grammar in literary contexts have coincided with an increasing exploration of non-literary discourse. Indeed some of the most innovative work inspired by Cognitive Grammar has been, in keeping with the eclectic range of interests in stylistics more broadly, in non-literary spheres. Browse (2018a), for example, explores political discourse by taking a methodological approach combining more traditional discourse analytical work with more recent advances in critical cognitive linguistics. Using a reader-oriented empirical approach, he demonstrates the importance of considering the participatory role of the audience in the reception of political discourse and provides a series of frameworks for analysis that explicitly import and reconceptualize approaches that have usually been reserved for the analysis of literary texts (see also his chapter in this volume). A critical cognitive linguistics is also well served by the work of Christopher Hart, another contributor to this book. In his analysis of media discourse, Hart (2010, 2013, 2014) highlights how Cognitive Grammar and concepts arising from cognition more generally may be used to draw attention to the kinds of representations of both immigration and violence that appear across different forms of newspaper reporting.

A further recent innovative use of Cognitive Grammar outside of literary criticism has been within pedagogical contexts. Although there is a strong tradition of second language (L2) researchers using Cognitive Grammar in theoretical and experimental ways, and recontextualizing these into pedagogical practices (e.g. De Knop and De Rycker 2008; Holme 2009; and, for an overview, Giovanelli and Harrison, this volume), there have historically been fewer instances of this kind of work in first language (L1) research. More recently, however, the potential Cognitive Grammar offers L1 language and literary pedagogy has become apparent. For example, in a book-length study of the affordances of cognitive linguistics in L1 English teaching more generally, Giovanelli (2014) demonstrates how clause-level analysis informed by Cognitive Grammar can provide ways for students to critically consider the kinds of representations of individuals, groups and ideologies that appear in news media. Giovanelli also demonstrates how students can draw on a range of 'embodied learning activities' (2014: 43), including gesture and the simulation of energy transfer through role-play to examine the effects of particular grammatical constructions in texts. In addition, Cushing (2019) argues that the inherent meaningfulness of linguistic forms that is at the heart of Cognitive Grammar means that it should be an attractive model for the classroom and demonstrates how Cognitive Grammar can be integrated into the study of poetry (see also his chapter in this volume). In these ways, a pedagogical stylistics or 'grammatics' (Halliday 2002: 416) emerges which, drawing on Cognitive Grammar concepts, enables teachers to utilize theoretical ideas in innovative ways.

Taken together, these recent directions using Cognitive Grammar demonstrate both the flexibility of the framework and how researchers from across different fields within applied linguistics more broadly (literary linguistics, critical discourse analysis, educational linguistics) have seen and articulated the value of integrating Cognitive Grammar into their methodologies and analytical methods. This flexibility is equally apparent in the way that much of this work has incorporated Cognitive Grammar approaches into existing frameworks (e.g. Harrison 2017b; Nuttall 2018) so as to complement and generally improve their analytical power, or else to replicate established studies to show the alternative exploratory potential that a Cognitive Grammar approach may offer (e.g. Browse 2018b). As Langacker (2014: xiv) himself notes in the foreword to *Cognitive Grammar in Literature*, 'the extensive CG application to literature will require and inspire significant elaboration of the framework'. It is clear that developing Cognitive Grammar into other discourse types and fields of enquiry will further inspire researchers and will open up exciting future areas of research.

4. Chapters in this book

All of the chapters in this book were first presented as papers at the *Cognitive Grammar in Stylistics* Symposium that we organized at Aston University in 2018 (the exception is Hart's chapter which covers a different data set from his original paper but does draw on a similar analytical approach, and Alison Bown's chapter which was submitted after attendance at the conference). Following the symposium, and in making preparations for this book, our authors' refined chapters seemed to fit naturally into four distinct parts and so we have organized the book in order to reflect what we perceive as major strands in Cognitive Grammar scholarship: first, the development of existing concepts in stylistics related to the study of literary texts; second, the development of existing concepts related to the study of non-literary texts; third, the development of Cognitive Grammar to examine multimodal discourse; and fourth, a focus on Cognitive Grammar in pedagogical and practitioner-based contexts. Although we have organized the chapters in this way, we also hope that reading across the sections will enable readers to see multiple connections between the applications of Cognitive Grammar that this book showcases.

The first four chapters explore the application of Cognitive Grammar in literary contexts. In Chapter 2, Peter Stockwell considers a cornerstone of traditional stylistic analyses, the speech and thought representation model, and proposes a new, psychologically grounded method for analysing free indirect discourse. Drawing on wider principles of cognitive linguistics, Stockwell explores how fictional minds are modelled by readers as a process of deictic deflections across text-world boundaries. His discussion demonstrates, in particular, how the Cognitive Grammar concepts of vantage point positioning, windowing and perspective can be applied to describe readers' attentional experience of the free indirect discourse phenomenon. Although Stockwell illustrates this new approach through a number of literary examples (from *Madame Bovary* and *Ulysses*, to *Emma* and *Lolita*), he argues that free indirect discourse occurs across both fiction and non-fiction texts, and that it elicits a range of interpretative and experiential effects such as sarcasm, parody, and emotional and ideological alignment, among others.

In Chapter 3 Anne Holm carries out an extended analysis of Mohsin Hamid's (2017) contemporary speculative fiction novel, *Exit West*, which is centred on the experience of being a refugee and questions what it means to be disconnected from one's past and memories. Holm demonstrates how conventional memory metaphors such as LIFE IS A JOURNEY and LIFE IS A STORY are countered by particular stylistic choices in the novel: modality, representations of action chains and embodied metaphors of disconnection. Her analyses of sections of the novel draw out these conflicting style choices by exploring instances of opposing metaphoric mappings of time (e.g. Moving Time vs. Moving Ego), and contradicting representations of movement (e.g. absent event trajectories vs. the presence of dynamic life story metaphors). Holm notes how such choices work together to challenge readers' construal, and subsequent interpretative experience, of this text. She argues that this novel displays a disruption of sequentiality and narrative order, which in turn foregrounds the narrator's struggle with feelings of displacement.

Chapter 4 similarly examines representations of complex metaphors and their framing through an account of construal phenomena. In this chapter Nigel McLoughlin integrates concepts from Text World Theory (Werth 1999; Gavins 2007) and Conceptual Blending (Fauconnier and Turner 2002) alongside key ideas from Cognitive Grammar, to produce a holistic analytical model. The poem under consideration, 'The Deaf Woman in the Glen' (Harvey 2007), activates a containment schema in the title, which is then elaborated on through other trajector-landmark constructions in the text. McLoughlin demonstrates how this schema is developed through a series of metaphors which represent a target space that is highly schematic in the first sentence, but more richly specified in the second. The chapter concludes by identifying how a Cognitive Grammar analysis can be enriched through integration with Blending Theory specifically and argues that such a conceptual apparatus enables researchers to examine how linguistic constructions bring about a refocusing of attention. This process allows readers to apprehend complex metaphors more successfully by re-visualizing the target domain in reference to features of the source domain.

Louise Nuttall draws together a discussion on reader interpretation and an account of Cognitive Grammar's subjective/objective construal in Chapter 5. Nuttall argues that E. E. Cummings' poem 'Me up at does' presents parallel perspectives (of the speaking poetic persona and the mouse) to which readers are invited to attribute mental states. Nuttall proposes that this process of mind attribution, or 'mind-modelling' (Stockwell 2009; Stockwell and Mahlberg 2015), can be framed through an account of shifting levels of subjective and objective construal in the poem. She further outlines how this experience of dual perspective accounts for readers' ethical responses to the text, as it elicits feelings of identification with the speaker and sympathy for the mouse. This analysis has implications for wider discussions about perspective-taking and ethical alignment in fiction.

In Chapters 6 and 7 in Part 2, each of the authors builds on their considerable existing research to provide illuminating Cognitive Grammar accounts of non-literary discourse, in tandem with a strong political focus. In Chapter 6, Christopher Hart examines mystification, the effect that results from the downplaying of agency within a clause so as to obscure or omit perceived intentionality for actions and events. Hart focuses on press reports of state violence on the Gaza border, providing a rigorous and convincing account of the various ways in which mystification is enacted and the ideological effects of various construal patterns. Hart explores, from a Cognitive Grammar perspective, what Lui and O'Halloran (2009) call 'intersemiotic parallelism', the ways by which visual images used in news reports cohere with mental representations cued by the language of a text in order to make visible the various ideologies at play. In Chapter 7, Sam Browse also examines particular ideological forces by synthesizing Cognitive Grammar, Text World Theory and active audience theory (Hall 1980) to explain the ways that audiences react to and position themselves relative to political texts. Using a 'think aloud' method to capture reader responses to the speeches of two political party leaders, Browse demonstrates how a renewed focus on the reception-end of texts, which he argues is missing from conventional critical discourse analysis, can provide insights into how an audience's knowledge stores or 'models of reality' interact with the linguistic forms in the text to construe a 'proffered meaning', which may be adopted, or resisted and 'reconstrued'.

Matthew Voice's analysis in Chapter 8 examines characterization and intentionality, demonstrating how the mapping of inferences can both influence and be influenced by linguistic choices which present particular construals of events. Voice argues that the analysis of mind-modelling alongside a consideration of inferred intentionality can help effectively scale up an application of Cognitive Grammar, enabling analyses of both sentences and more macro-discourse structures and patterns.

In the first chapter in Part 3, Richard Finn builds on a previous Cognitive Grammar analysis of viewing arrangements in Alison Bechdel's *Fun Home* (Pleyer and Schneider 2014). While *Fun Home* is considered a biographical account of Bechdel's father, *Are You My Mother?* instead focuses on Bechdel's mother and on their relationship, and also contains a meta-commentary on Bechdel's process of writing the book. Finn explores how the language and pictorial narration in this multimodal text move between subjective and objective viewing arrangements, and he examines how these movements can be traced to other linguistic phenomena such as the representation of deictic shifts and grounding across modes of discourse. Finally, Finn argues that the consideration of conceptualizers as discourse 'participants' and 'enactors' (Werth 1999; Gavins 2007) can help differentiate between enactors as objects of conceptualization and discursive participants in the text. Such conclusions have significance for the exploration of subjectivity in multimodal media as well as other types and modes of storytelling.

In Chapter 10, Clara Neary also utilizes Cognitive Grammar in a multimodal context, this time in conjunction with the cognitively oriented 'musical grammar' (Zbikowski 2017). Neary builds on her previous work (Neary 2019) to examine the means by which 'Pyramid Song', a song by the alternative Rock band Radiohead, deviates from musical and lyrical patterns established in their previous work. Using a multimodal analysis of the ways that meaning is formed both musically and lyrically, Neary both develops emerging work examining the interrelationship of music and lyrics using cognitive poetics (e.g. Voice and Whiteley 2019), and explicitly captures some of what she perceives as the key interpretative effects of the song on a listening audience. In Chapter 11, Alison Bown's examination of multimodality also brings together Cognitive Grammar and musical grammar, this time to explore how writers of multimodal interactive texts might make use of some fundamental Cognitive Grammar concepts to inform the creative process. Bown draws on her own experience as a sound designer and writer to suggest that writers may benefit from the insights that Cognitive Grammar permits 'into the ways that readers interact with texts and process their contents'. In doing so, Bown argues that being mindful of various construal phenomena provides an opportunity for writers to think about the creative decisions they make in terms of how they draw on different semiotic systems to position their readers in various ways. To illustrate her points, Bown provides detailed Cognitive

Grammar-inspired analyses of two multimodal texts and some practical ways that writers might use the model in their own planning and writing.

The three chapters which form the final part of the book examine the ways in which knowledge about language (and specifically Cognitive Grammar) might be useful in educational contexts. To this extent, they all confirm the value of Cognitive Grammar to the applied linguist as much as to the theoretical one. In Chapter 12, Marcello Giovanelli and Chloe Harrison reflect on writing their recent undergraduate textbook *Cognitive Grammar in Stylistics: A Practical Guide* (Giovanelli and Harrison 2018), in which they reconfigure and recontextualize Langacker's model for a novice audience. Acknowledging that Langacker's publications are largely research and reference texts rather than pedagogical ones, Giovanelli and Harrison argue that the need for a Cognitive Grammar textbook is overdue and that Cognitive Grammar can provide a powerful tool for reframing our way of thinking about language and pedagogy. Providing specific examples of activities from their textbook, they demonstrate the various ways in which Cognitive Grammar can support students to engage with different text types (literary, non-literary, multimodal and so on) as well as arguing that insights from the classroom may also be useful for Cognitive Grammar as a theory itself. In this way, Giovanelli and Harrison maintain the commitment stylisticians have historically had to viewing the relationship between stylistics and pedagogy as 'symbiotic'. A similar commitment to Cognitive Grammar as a valuable pedagogical tool is evident in Chapter 13, written by Ian Cushing. In his chapter, Cushing draws on his extensive research working with secondary schoolteachers in England to demonstrate how Cognitive Grammar might support the teaching of poetry, in this instance to much younger learners. Cushing's chapter outlines how he worked with participating teachers to devise a series of poetry lessons and activities, which were underpinned by key Cognitive Grammar principles. His chapter describes both the ways in which teachers were encouraged to use Cognitive Grammar to think about the kinds of activities they planned and delivered and the extent to which a concept-driven pedagogy (see Giovanelli 2014) drawing on, for example, embodiment and energy transfer, enabled students to explore key aspects of the poem and to reflect on their interpretations in novel ways. Indeed Cushing argues that the kind of linguistic knowledge that is afforded by Cognitive Grammar should be available to all teachers of English; his chapter therefore ends with a call for greater cognitive linguistic awareness in teacher education more generally.

In Chapter 14, Sally Zacharias also addresses linguistic knowledge in the secondary classroom, in this case through an exploration of how Cognitive Grammar (and cognitive linguistics more broadly) can provide a rigorous framework for analysing and understanding the nature of classroom discourse and the ways in which the social and physical environment may affect the development of students' conceptual thinking. Like other chapters in this volume that emphasize the importance of context in text analysis, Zacharias's work is illuminating in the way that she stresses the applied potential of the model. For example, like Browse, Zacharias argues that drawing on Text World Theory's notion of the discourse-world extends Cognitive Grammar's potential to analyse 'dynamic, socially embedded patterns of language-in-use'. Like Bown and Cushing, she proposes that Cognitive Grammar offers a radical way of rethinking language awareness education for practitioners in their day-to-day activities. In Zacharias's chapter, Cognitive Grammar therefore is conceived as an *applied* Cognitive Grammar in the most enabling sense.

In the chapters that follow, our contributors have drawn largely from Langacker's model, which presents the most detailed and unified framework currently available. References to Cognitive Grammar (as distinct from other cognitive grammars) are therefore taken from Langacker (1987, 1991, 2008). In all chapters, key Cognitive Grammar ideas are italicized on first mention. Overall, we believe that the chapters in this volume provide an up-to-date account of some of the exciting new directions researchers are taking in using and developing Cognitive Grammar to examine various aspects of authorial style, reader response, theoretical, thematic and generic concerns, pedagogical approaches and practitioner concerns. We are confident that the current volume thus provides an overview of how far the field has come since 2014 and offers a platform from which further innovations and developments may follow.

References

Arnett, C. and H. Jernigan (2014), 'A Cognitive Grammar Account of Case for L2 Students of German', *GFL*, 15 (1): 68–93.

Browse, S. (2018a), *Cognitive Rhetoric: The Cognitive Poetics of Political Discourse*, Amsterdam: John Benjamins.

Browse, S. (2018b), 'From Functional to Cognitive Grammar in Stylistic Analysis of Golding's *The Inheritors*', *Journal of Literary Semantics*, 47 (2): 121–46.

Croft, W. (2001), *Radical Construction Grammar: Syntactic Theory in Typological Perspective*, Oxford: Oxford University Press.

Cushing, I. (2019), 'A Textured and Sensory Grammar for the Experience of Reading', *English in Education* (online first).

De Knop, S. and T. De Rycker (2008), *Cognitive Approaches to Pedagogical Grammar: A Volume in Honour of René Dirven*, Berlin: Mouton de Gruyter.

Esmaeili, P. and F.A. Amjad (2016), 'Textual Properties and Attentional Windowing: A Cognitive Grammatical Account of Gustav Hasford's *The Short-Timers*', *Journal of Literary Semantics*, 45 (2): 161–74.

Evans, V. and M. Green (2006), *Cognitive Linguistics: An Introduction*, Edinburgh: Edinburgh University Press.

Fauconnier, G. and M. Turner (2002), *The Way We Think: Conceptual Blending and the Mind's Hidden Complexities*, New York: Basic Books.

Fillmore, C. (1982), 'Frame Semantics', in The Linguistic Society of Korea (ed.), *Linguistics in the Morning Calm*, 111–37, Seoul: Hanshin Publishing Co.

Fowler, R. (1977), *Linguistics and the Novel*, London: Methuen.

Gavins, J. (2007), *Text World Theory: An Introduction*, Edinburgh: Edinburgh University Press.

Gavins, J. and G. Steen (2003), *Cognitive Poetics in Practice*, London: Routledge.

Gibbons, A. and S. Whiteley (2018), *Contemporary Stylistics: Language, Cognition, Interpretation*, Edinburgh: Edinburgh University Press.

Giovanelli, M. (2014), *Teaching Grammar, Structure and Meaning*, London: Routledge.

Giovanelli, M. (2018), '"Something Happened, Something Bad": Blackouts, Uncertainties and Event Construal in *The Girl on the Train*', *Language and Literature*, 27 (1): 38–51.

Giovanelli, M. (2019), 'Construing and Reconstruing the Horrors of the Trench: Siegfried Sassoon, Creativity and Context', *Journal of Literary Semantics*, 48 (1): 85–104.

Giovanelli, M. (2020), 'Siegfried Sassoon, Autofiction and Style: Retelling the Experience of War', in M. Lambrou (ed.), *Narrative Retellings: Stylistic Approaches*, 113–127, London: Bloomsbury.

Giovanelli, M. and C. Harrison (2018), *Cognitive Grammar in Stylistics: A Practical Guide*, London: Bloomsbury.

Goldberg, A. (1995), *Constructions at Work: A Construction Grammar Approach to Argument Structure*, Chicago, IL: Chicago University Press.

Hall, S. (1980), 'Encoding/Decoding', in S. Hall, D. Hobson, A. Lowe and P. Willis (eds), *Culture, Media, Language*, 128–38, New York: Routledge.

Halliday, M. (1971), 'Linguistic Function and Literary Style: An Inquiry into the Language of William Golding's *The Inheritors*', in S. Chatman (ed.), *Literary Style: A Symposium*, 330–68, Oxford: Oxford University Press.

Halliday, M. (2002), 'On Grammar and Grammatics', in J. Webster (ed.), *On Grammar: Vol 1 of the Collected Works of M.A.K. Halliday*, 348–417, London: Continuum.

Hamid, M. (2017), *Exit West*, London: Hamish Hamilton.

Harrison, C. (2017a), *Cognitive Grammar in Contemporary Fiction*, Amsterdam: John Benjamins.

Harrison, C. (2017b), 'Finding Elizabeth: Construing Memory in *Elizabeth Is Missing* by Emma Healey', *Journal of Literary Semantics*, 46 (2): 131–51.

Harrison, C. (2019), 'A "Half-remembered Quality": Experiencing Disorientation and Claustrophobia in *The Goldfinch*', in C. Hart (ed.), *Cognitive Linguistic Approaches to Text and Discourse: From Poetics to Politics*, 37–53, Edinburgh: Edinburgh University Press.

Harrison, C. and L. Nuttall (2019), 'Cognitive Grammar and Reconstrual: Re-experiencing Margaret Atwood's "The Freeze-Dried Groom"', in L. Stewart-Shaw and B. Neurhor (eds), *Experiencing Fictional Worlds*, 177–97, Amsterdam: John Benjamins.

Harrison, C. and L. Nuttall (2020), 'Re-reading as Re-telling: Re-evaluations of Perspective in Narrative Fiction', in M. Lambrou (ed.), *Narrative Retellings: Stylistic Approaches*, 217–234, London: Bloomsbury.

Harrison, C., L. Nuttall, P. Stockwell and W. Yuan (eds) (2014), *Cognitive Grammar in Literature*, Amsterdam: John Benjamins.

Hart, C. (2010), *Critical Discourse Analysis and Cognitive Science: New Perspectives on Immigration Discourse*, Houndmills, Basingstoke: Palgrave Macmillan.

Hart, C. (2013), 'Event-construal in Press Reports of Violence in Political Protests: A Cognitive Linguistic Approach to CDA', *Journal of Language and Politics*, 12 (3): 400–23.

Hart, C. (2014), *Discourse, Grammar and Ideology: Functional and Cognitive Perspectives*, London: Bloomsbury.

Harvey, F. (2007), 'The Deaf Woman in the Glen', in F. Harvey (ed.), *Collected Poems*, 35–6, Dublin: Dedalus Press.

Holme, R. (2009), *Cognitive Linguistics and Language Teaching*, Basingstoke: Palgrave Macmillan.

Johnson, M. (1987), *The Body in the Mind: The Bodily Basis of Meaning, Imagination and Reason*, Chicago, IL: Chicago University Press.

Lakoff, G. (1987), *Women, Fire and Dangerous Things: What Categories Reveal about The Mind*, Chicago, IL: Chicago University Press.

Lakoff, G. (1990), 'The Invariance Hypothesis: Is Abstract Reason Based on Image Schemas?', *Cognitive Linguistics*, 1, 39-74.

Lakoff, G. and M. Johnson (1980), *Metaphors We Live By*, Chicago, IL: Chicago University Press.

Lakoff, G. and M. Turner (1989), *More Than Cool Reason: A Field Guide to Poetic Metaphor*, Chicago, IL: University of Chicago Press.

Langacker, R. W. (1987), *Foundations of Cognitive Grammar, vol. I: Theoretical Prerequisites*, Stanford: Stanford University Press.

Langacker, R. W. (1991), *Foundations of Cognitive Grammar, vol. II: Descriptive Application*, Stanford: Stanford University Press.

Langacker, R. W. (2008), *Cognitive Grammar: A Basic Introduction*, Oxford: Oxford University Press.

Langacker, R. W. (2014), 'Foreword', in C. Harrison, L. Nuttall, P. Stockwell and W. Yuan (eds), *Cognitive Grammar in Literature*, xiii-xiv, Amsterdam: John Benjamins.

Lui, Y. and K. O'Halloran (2009), 'Intersemiotic Texture: Analyzing Cohesive Devices between Language and Images', *Social Semiotics*, 19 (4): 367-88.

Mandler, J. (2004), *Foundations of Mind: Origins of Conceptual Thought*, New York: Oxford University Press.

Matsumoto, N. (2008), 'Bridges between Cognitive Linguistics and Second Language Pedagogy: The Case of Corpora and Their Potential', *SKY Journal of Linguistics* 21: 125-53.

Neary, C. (2019), '"Please Could You Stop the Noise": The Grammar of Multi-modal Meaning Making in Radiohead's "Paranoid Android"', *Language and Literature* 28 (1): 41-60.

Nuttall, L. (2015), 'Attributing Minds to Vampires in Richard Matheson's *I Am Legend*', *Language and Literature*, 24 (1): 24-39.

Nuttall, L. (2018), *Mind Style and Cognitive Grammar: Language and Worldview in Speculative Fiction*, London: Bloomsbury.

Nuttall, L. (2019), '"Real" Mind Style and Authenticity Effects in Fiction: Represented Experiences of War in *Atonement*', *Style*, 53 (2): 215-35.

Pleyer, M. and C. Schneider (2014), 'Construal and Comics: The Multimodal Autobiography of Alison Bechdel's *Fun Home*', in C. Harrison, L. Nuttall, W. Yuan and P. Stockwell (eds), *Cognitive Grammar in Literature*, 35-52, Amsterdam: John Benjamins.

Schank, R.C. (1982), *Dynamic Memory*, New York: Cambridge University Press.

Schank, R.C. and R.P. Abelson (1977), *Scripts, Plans, Goals and Understanding: An Inquiry into Human Knowledge Structures*, Hillsdale, NJ: Lawrence Erlbaum.

Semino, E. (2002), 'A Cognitive Stylistic Approach to Mind-style in Narrative Fiction', in E. Semino and J. Culpeper (eds), *Cognitive Stylistics: Language and Cognition in Text Analysis*, 95-122, Amsterdam: John Benjamins.

Stockwell, P. (2009), *Texture: A Cognitive Aesthetics of Reading*, Edinburgh: Edinburgh University Press.

Stockwell, P. (2020), *Cognitive Poetics: An Introduction*, 2nd edn, London: Routledge.

Stockwell, P. and M. Mahlberg (2015), 'Mind-modelling with Corpus Stylistics in *David Copperfield*', *Language and Literature*, 24 (2): 129-47.

Talmy, L. (1988), 'Force Dynamics in Language and Cognition', *Cognitive Science* 12, 49-100.

Tyler, A. (2012), *Cognitive Linguistics and Second Language Learning: Theoretical Basics and Experimental Evidence*, New York: Routledge.

Voice, M. and S. Whiteley (2019), '"Y'All Don't Wanna Hear Me, You Just Wanna Dance": A Cognitive Approach to Listener Attention in OutKast's "Hey Ya!"' *Language and Literature*, 28 (1): 7–22.

Werth, P. (1999), *Text Worlds: Representing Conceptual Space in Discourse*, London: Longman.

Zbikowski, L. (2017), *Foundations of Musical Grammar*, New York: Oxford University Press.

Part One

Cognitive Grammar in literary contexts

2

Re-cognizing Free Indirect Discourse

Peter Stockwell

1. The nature of FID

Of all the forms in which the speech, thought and writing of others can be presented textually, free indirect discourse (FID) has come to be widely regarded as the most literate, the most literary, the most complex, and has become the most discussed. This sustained level of interest and contentious debate seems to indicate an object of study that has not really ever been precisely delineated, and a set of theoretical perspectives that so far have failed to frame the concept adequately. In this chapter, I propose a means of understanding FID that is consistent with our current best knowledge of language and mind, and I also use this new perspective to account for prior models of FID.

The simplest description of FID is that it is a presentation of a character's speech or thought entwined within the commentary of a narrator or another character. It is typically manifest in the third person, and it is often possible to identify what the character might have actually said or thought even though not all of their words are directly presented. FID is the overarching term for free indirect forms of *speech* presentation (FIS) and *thought* presentation (FIT), and even situations in which a character's *writing* is mediated by a narrator (FIW), for example if they are writing a letter or note. Given that the different forms of FID often involve a narratorial level and a character level, the style has been most associated with literary prose fiction. Although all periods of literature contain examples of FID, it is a form that is particularly novelistic, and so can be seen to have increased in usage from the mid-eighteenth century onwards in Europe (see Simpson 1993; Rundquist 2017).

The term seems to have first been used by Bally (1912) as *style indirect libre*, translated as 'free indirect style', and observed most profusely in nineteenth-century French novels such as Gustave Flaubert's *Madame Bovary*, published in 1856. The technique is ubiquitous in this novel, but here is a particular example:

Elle abandonna la musique. Pourquoi jouer? qui l'entendrait? Puisqu'elle ne pourrait jamais, en robe de velours à manches courtes, sur un piano d'Érard, dans un concert, battant de ses doigts légers les touches d'ivoire, sentir, comme une brise, circuler autour d'elle un murmure d'extase, ce n'était pas la peine de s'ennuyer à étudier. Elle laissa dans l'armoire ses cartons à dessin et la tapisserie. A quoi bon? à quoi bon? La couture l'irritait.

— J'ai tout lu, se disait-elle.
(Flaubert, *Madame Bovary*, 1971: 65)

[She gave up her music. Why play? Who would listen? Since she could never, in a short-sleeved velvet gown, on an Erard piano, in a concert, running her delicate fingers over the ivory keys, feel, like a breeze, circling around her a murmur of ecstasy, it was hardly worth bothering herself with practising. She left in the cabinet her drawing books and embroidery. What's the use? what's the use? Sewing annoyed her.
'I have read everything', she said to herself.]

My translation here is literal to the syntactic order, and so captures the stream of Emma's thoughts in that long sentence in the middle of the excerpt, where she delays the main verb (*sentir*, feels) bringing the sensuality of the dress, and short sleeves, and the expensive piano, and her delicate fingers and the touch of the ivory keys into prominence before the clause completes. She also delays the direct object (*un murmure d'extase*, a murmur of ecstasy) until after the delicate comparison with the breeze circling around her. The first sentence of the excerpt is clearly the narratorial voice. The first two exclamatory questions then clearly mark a move into her consciousness, and could be free direct thought, without any reporting verb such as '*Why play?' she thought*, although the tense-ending of *entendrait* ('would') perhaps signals a preparatory transition into FID. The final sentence looks at first like direct speech, marked in the original with a long dash and a reporting verb (I have anglicized the punctuation in the translation), but the reflexive reporting verb shows that it is really direct thought. Between the narratorial framing, though, the middle passage conveys Emma's own wishes and desires entwined with the narrator's presentation. Although the sensual thoughts are hers, the syntactic arrangement is of course the narrator's: it is the narrator who delays the verb and foregrounds the delicacy of her desire. There is a neat double-function in the simile 'comme une brise', where the ecstatic feeling immediately after 'sentir' is Emma's, but the syntactic sequencing that makes the audience's murmur 'like a breeze' is the narrator's, such that it is hard to distinguish the two minds. This is FID.

It should be clear even from this single example that the different forms of discourse presentation in prose fiction can be arranged on a spectrum from a very vague narratorial assertion that speech or thought happened, right through to verbatim direct speech or thought without any narratorial marking such as speech marks or reporting verbs at all. In the middle of this continuum, FID then has ill-defined boundaries, at least in purely linguistic terms. In the original classic stylistic treatment of the notion, Leech and Short (1981: 325) claim that free indirect speech 'is, as it were, a free form "purporting" to be Indirect Speech'. The choice of 'purporting' here, with its 'scare quotes' and distancing marker 'as it were', is instructive of their sense that there is a wilful pretence or veiled proposition in operation. My own proposal, set out in the chapter, is that FID is indeed a cognitive discourse feature, which essentially requires an integrated sense of stylistic patterning and the mind that expresses it.

Definitions of FID have focused on one of four aspects: formal *identification*, *fidelity*, *mode* and *voice*. First, there has been a long tradition, particularly within literary linguistics, to identify FID as a form of speech and thought presentation delineated by linguistic features. Leech and Short (1981), mentioned above, are the best example of this. Their continuum places different forms on a range from the narrative report of speech through indirect speech and free indirect speech to direct speech and free direct speech. The key differences between these are expressed by their linguistic patterns. Direct speech, for example, contains a reporting verb, quotation marks and the verbatim reported material (*'I'll come back here tomorrow'*, *she said*). Indirect speech contains a reporting verb followed by a subordinate clause that contains the spoken material which is 'backshifted' for tense and deixis (*She said that she would return there the following day*). Free forms omit the narratorial reporting verbs, or the graphological markers. These forms appear to be 'free' of narratorial intervention, as if the character is being allowed to speak directly for themselves. By contrast, forms at the other end of the spectrum display an apparent narratorial control. Free indirect forms, in this scheme, seem to make the narratorial control relatively transparent, with a sense of direct access to conscious speech or thought. Since speech is externalized and thought is internalized, FIS conveys a literary sense of an author/narrator mediating the character's speech, whereas FIT conveys a sense that telepathy into a character's consciousness feels natural (Leech and Short 1981; see also Cohn 1978 and Semino 1997).

This stylistic approach to FID has been highly productive, and a rigorous advance on earlier, impressionistic identifications of the phenomenon (see McHale 1978 for an early survey). However, its primary focus on the stylistic manifestation of FID serves to de-emphasize the cognitive dimension, even though that sense of consciousness is always implicit in such approaches. Furthermore, the stylistic account relies on a continuum of forms that are banded together into categories of free direct speech, direct speech, indirect speech and so on. A purely linguistic approach cannot justify the bandings, bundles of features nor distinctions, since the fuzziness or blending at the edges of each category is a signal that the continuum is dependent on cognitive interaction and interpretative identification. The impressionistic sense that FIS feels different from IS at least captured this delineation, though without the linguistic rigour.

We can return a cognitive dimension explicitly to the stylistic account. Leech and Short (1981: 325) give the example of an imagined original Direct Speech form and its FIS conversion. The free indirect sentence *He would return there to see her again the following day* can be imagined to have derived from a direct form, such as *He said, 'I'll come back here to see you again tomorrow'*. We can trace the 'backshifting' of elements between these two sentences as follows:

He said	< deleted >	[ ]
I'	< personal deictic shift >	He
ll	< textual (modal) deictic shift >	would
come back	< spatial / relational deictic shift >	return
here	< spatial deictic shift >	there
to see	< copied >	to see
you	< personal deictic shift >	her
again	< copied >	again
tomorrow	< temporal / relational deictic shift >	the following day

In this case, we can see that there are mainly personal, temporal and spatial deictic shifts, but all of these are realized in relation to a located speaker, such that as readers we have to adjust our perspective from one location to another. The shifts from 'come back' to 'return' and from 'tomorrow' to 'the next day' are movements along a spatial or temporal line, but are also relational shifts in the sense that they encode a different social register. Although 'to see' and 'again' are copied across between the two, in fact they are only superficially unchanged: in fact, these two phrases have to conceptually agree with the surrounding deictic shift, so they cannot really be said to be unchanged in situated meaning. 'He said', of course, is deleted from the transformation, since the FID version has been relocated to the nearer, narrated deictic position, and the reference to the more distant deictic point where 'he' is 'I' is no longer needed. We can describe these deictic positions in terms of ontological levels, or 'worlds', in Text World Theory terms (see more in the next section below).

Second, discussions of FID, and discourse presentation more generally, have pursued the notion of the *fidelity* of the presented form to the apparent source utterance. In other words (as in the example just given), how close is the textual record to the actual words or thoughts that might have been spoken or thought? This is further complicated by the fact that (for example in the sentence from Leech and Short above) a range of FID forms are available: perhaps a more prototypically FID form might have been *He would come back here to see her again tomorrow*, which is a little bit more faithful to the original direct speech form. Of course, in the case of literary fiction, there is no actual original form, since the entire scenario is fictional, and in fact the textual representation is instantly its own first origin, although the claim to verisimilitude remains. Aside from this fictionality problem, the notion even of an apparent original utterance to which the textual form is faithful is problematic, since every textual form is an artifice. Even the freest form of direct speech in a novel is unlikely to be an accurate phonetic transcription of an imagined original speech, complete with accent and intonation included. And even dialectal representations are usually stereotyped or 'cleaned-up' for textual clarity (see Hodson 2014). For less free forms of discourse along the spectrum, the problem is also one of disentangling the surface form (which is the author/narrator's choice) and the character's underlying choices: the latter can only be reconstructed by interpreting the character's apparently original meaning from the narratorial filtering and then guessing at the form of the utterance that might have realized this proposition (fictionally speaking, of course!). This is clearly absurd (as Fludernik 1993 also observes).

Short, Semino and Wynne (2001) address this problem by differentiating between the pragmatics of a *report* and that of a *representation*. In a news report, for example, it is often important to be precise in reproducing the exact words that were uttered; at other times it is sufficient merely to represent what the person's meaning was in order to present them fairly. True fidelity to the source utterance applies to the former but not the latter, and Short et al. argue that it is usually pragmatically possible to tell which is which in context. Again, this is more complex in the case of literary fiction, where the context is textually contained and the imagined original is instantiated by the representation itself. News reports do not generally include FID (though see Redeker 1996; Blinova 2012), and there is usually little confusion between the reporter's voice and the people in the news. In literary fiction, there is a question of who is responsible for the fidelity of the presentation, and this is not easily ascribable especially with FID. Are all examples away from free direct speech instances of increasingly bad faith on the part of the narrator? One way of thinking about fidelity that is consistent with cognitive linguistics would be to regard it as a prototype effect, with a form of textual representation being regarded as a good or relatively less good example of its imagined original. Of course, this would also require not only a pragmatic but also a cognitive framing, as adopted later in this chapter. In short, the sense of whether a piece of represented discourse seemed 'authentic' or not would be a matter for the reader's sense of plausibility and feeling of immersion in the world of the fiction, such that a prior, origin utterance could be imagined.

The *mode* of discourse presentation, as suggested above, has been located historically in the rise of the novel, particularly the post-Austen novel, reaching its most experimental style in the 1890s and into literary modernism. This too, however, seems to be a best prototype, because examples of FID can be found in very early novels, such as in the work of Henry Fielding, and even earlier literature such as Chaucer and the Gawain-poet (see Pons-Sanz 2019). Literariness seems to offer good opportunities for FID principally because of its ontological shifts when it is fictional, or when a lyric or narrative poem involves dramatic monologue, or when a staged piece of drama presents a disjunction between the world of the text and the world of the audience. Again, however, literariness is not an essential mode: as mentioned above, FID can occur in news reports, and can be found in everyday conversation (see Tannen 1989; Toolan 2001; Mildorf and Thomas 2017). Although Banfield (1982) and Ehrlich (1990), among many others, suggest that FID requires a written form, it is often found in conversational banter, ridicule, sarcasm and gossip. This widespread set of contexts aligns well with the cognitive linguistic principle that linguistic practice is a continuum and there is no need for a 'special' theory of any part of language, such as literariness.

The final type of definition of FID has circled around the notion of *voice*. It seems obvious that FID involves a sense of the mind or consciousness of an author, narrator or character, in addition to an exclusively linguistic focus. Banfield (1982) attempts to reconcile the stylistic description of discourse presentation with the cognitive effect, with a focus on the sense of a single voice. She takes a literal view of FID, noting that it cannot be disentangled into different voices, so in fact there is no voice at all, only an expression, unuttered, of a character's subjectivity. In fact, any attempt to distinguish two voices analytically can only serve to render them into their component parts which are by definition no longer FID. For her, then, FID can only occur in context and intact, and since in practice the linguistic string that appears as FID is in fact not literally spoken by any single person within the text, Banfield describes FID as an 'unspeakable sentence', an utterance of a single voice who does not actually exist anywhere outside the text in hand. Of course, to be even more literal, this is not strictly true, since the FID was literally created in an author's mind, and is literally read (silently or aloud) by a reader. However, even this lends credence to Banfield's otherwise mystical notion that FID sentences actually reflect the thoughts of a character but are speakerless, and are therefore examples of non-narration (and no-narrator) within a narrative (see also, for a similar single-voiced view, Ehrlich 1990, and, by contrast, Fludernik 1993, whose single voice is the narrator's).

Banfield was responding to the notion that FID could be regarded as a 'dual voice' (Pascal 1977; Mey 2000), as possessing 'bivocality' (Bakhtin 1973) or 'polyvocality' (McHale 1978). In this view, there are two discernible voices in FID, typically a character's speech or thought which is then 'blended' with the narrator's writing. The bundle of features that can characterize FID as outlined above from Leech and Short (1981) provides a complex set of possible permutations for this blend. Given this, it should be stylistically possible to disentangle the linguistic traces of the two voices, or at least to assign values in the utterance to one or other voice, even if some features might be ambivalent or do double service. Schlenker (2004), for example, distinguishes between the context of thought and the context of utterance in the FID blend: so lexicalizations like referential indexicals and demonstratives come from the context of thought, while choices of tense and aspect and pronominals (as grammaticalizations) come from the context of utterance. Lexicalizations depend on the position and intention of the speaker (their thoughts) whereas grammaticalizations depend on the situation and meaning of the utterance itself. Similarly, Maier (2015) proposes a view of FID as a 'mixed quotation' which can be analytically broken down to assign some original elements to the character and then other elements are 'unquoted' and assigned to the narrator. In both these cases, the key factor is a differentiation between the ontological levels of narrator and character, which are then given responsibility for particular parts of the utterance.

An analytical approach to such examples might be able to discern the two voices, but it is not at all certain that this is a natural, common effect: Bray (2007) outlines an experiment with non-academic readers which suggests that they do not perceive two voices in some passages of Jane Austen's FID. The problem with the dual mind argument is not Banfield's transcendental mindless narration, but rather that there is no correlate of a 'blended' mind in the rest of the language system. Again, it is a principle of cognitive linguistics that all practices of language are in continuity with each other. You cannot blend a mind in reality, so you cannot have a special case of one in literary fiction.

The mind is the unit of consciousness. While there is a little theoretical wriggle-room in Palmer's (2004, 2010) notion of 'social minds' (where the collective thoughts or gossip of a village or group, for example, can be represented singularly), this still constitutes a mind that is inextricably connected to its language practice. A social mind is simply a zoomed-out mind, but it is still a mind: we can still model the collective consciousness of a group of people as if it were a singularly wilful entity.

My problem on the one side with the single voice argument is that it impossibly presumes an utterance without a mind and on the other side with the dual voice argument is that it implausibly presumes a blended mind. Neither of these is psychologically acceptable, and both fly in the face of a basic cognitive linguistic principle: language and mind are inseparable. The resolution seems to me to rest in an understanding that there are at least two minds involved in FID, but they can be arranged in layers or in proximity to the reader. Delfitto, Gaetano and Reboul (2016), for example, propose a sense of different ontological levels of a 'Higher Experiencer' and a 'Lower Experiencer', where the main readerly effect is 'empathic identification'. In a development of the Bakhtinian approach, Sotirova (2004, 2005, 2010) suggests that there is a 'dialogism' between these different levels. It is indeed essential theoretically to preserve a sense of the ontological layers between reader/author, narrator and different instances of characters, while also recognizing the effects that arise when one mind is accessed via another.

2. Free Indirect Discourse as deflection and windowing

So far I have invoked some principles of cognitive linguistics that should inform this discussion. They are:

- minds are the units of consciousness;
- there is a continuity between all settings of language;
- there is a continuity between language and other aspects of embodied experience;
- perspective, conceptual positioning and viewpoint are key to construal.

The first principle here means that we cannot separate stylistic patterning from a readerly sense of the mind which must have articulated that pattern – whether this is an actual person at our ontological level (an author), or a fictional mind within the world of the text (narrator and characters). The two central principles mean that we cannot produce a special theory that only accounts for literary reading; we must draw on our general theory of language, while presuming that literature works by exploiting our ordinary cognitive capacities and the workings of language overall. The last principle above means that we must look to the cognitive linguistics of situatedness for solutions to understanding FID. In what follows I will draw on Cognitive Grammar (Langacker 1995, 2008, 2009), force dynamics and attentional windowing (Talmy 2000, 2007, 2008; Harrison 2014), and Text World Theory (Werth 1999; Gavins 2007). My thinking aligns with the recent use of cognitive grammatical approaches to explore literary reading (see Stockwell 2009, 2014; Nuttall 2018; Giovanelli and Harrison 2018). My argument is that FID is fundamentally and schematically a perspectival phenomenon, and so it is most amenable to a linguistic approach grounded in spatial metaphor and positioning (Stockwell 2013).

In his recollections *in memoriam* for his colleague Geoff Leech, Mick Short described how Geoff met his wife:

> Geoff and Fanny met around the time of Geoff's BA graduation and he proposed to her within a week, saying, when she accepted his proposal, that he was glad he didn't now have to go to any more dances!
>
> (Short 2014: 10)

I would like to argue that the last part of this can be construed as an example of FIS. The original DS form would probably be: *'I'm glad I now don't have to go to any more dances!'* An IS form might be: *He said that he was pleased that he no longer had to go to any more dances*. Aside from the backshifting of personal and temporal deixis, I have also included here a shift in textual deixis to lift the register slightly with 'pleased' and 'no longer'. This latter form is very close to the example in the excerpt above, which in fact moves on from a narrative report of a speech act ('he proposed'), and an introductory reporting verb 'saying'. I think it is plausibly not a simple case of IS because of the temporal 'now' and the exclamation mark. If these belong to the deictic centre of Mick, then it is IS, but if (I think a more natural construal) they both belong to Geoff's deictic centre, then the excerpt ends in FIS.

What we have here is not a blended, unuttered voice, nor a dual voice of 'MickGeoff', but a simple report of a past utterance: Geoff's words deflected through Mick. The deflection occurs across deictic shifts, and can be represented as a traverse of world-boundaries, as presented in the text-world diagram in Figure 2.1.

To understand the nature of this excerpt, the reader (in this case, me) has to shift my attention towards Geoff, who is at one remove temporally and epistemically (in a switched EPS world) from the ontological level of Mick, who is telling the tale. It is easy for me to understand that Geoff's sentiments are being deflected through Mick. The

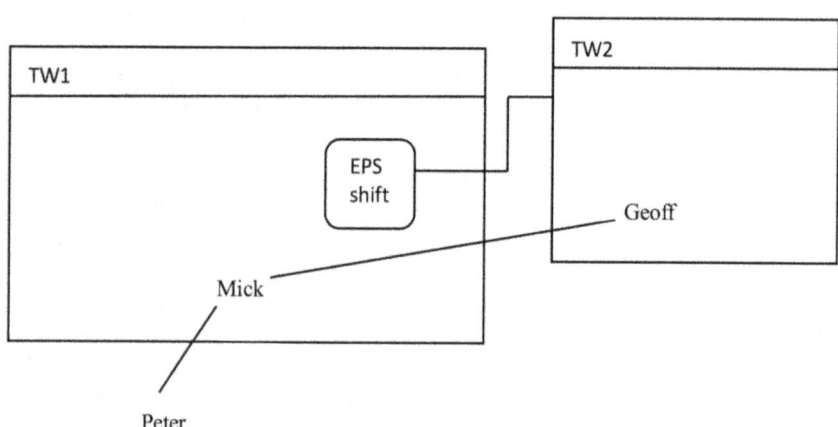

Figure 2.1 FID as a deflection across world-boundaries.

thread that connects my attention across the world-boundaries involves casting my mind through Mick to Geoff. This mind-cast is deflected in the course of FID.

The analytical procedure, then, for understanding FID is firstly to identify the mind-cast and its route: who are the minds involved, and for which parts of the discourse are each of them responsible. The effect can be highly immersive during actual reading: the analytical decomposition is a matter for later reflection, I think. In this case, I can hear Geoff's intonation and my attention is there deictically in the past where Geoff met his wife. In fact, that world level (TW2 in Figure 2.1) is remote from me and the participant Geoff is inaccessible to me. The power of the slippage from narrative to FIS means that I hardly notice that I have been momentarily taken somewhere else.

> These narrative tricks [like FID] are only possible if the reader is successfully lulled into the false sense that they are positioned within a participant-accessible text-world, when in fact they are experiencing an enactor-accessible modal-world reflecting the narrator's perspective and inner thoughts.
>
> (Gavins 2007: 131)

Each text-world boundary that is crossed attentionally here is a deictic shift, marked by the text and available for readerly construal. In cognitive linguistics, understanding that FID is dependent on deictic shifting means that it fundamentally depends on identifying the *vantage point* of the discourse (Langacker 2008: 76). Concepts and relationships between concepts are necessarily viewed from a position and objects located in a 'line of sight': the difference, for example, between *in front of* and *behind* involves a diametric switch of vantage point in relation to the two objects in scope (the focused trajector and the landmark ground) (see Figure 2.2). Including prepositional phrases, Vantage Points are generally realized by deictic markers.

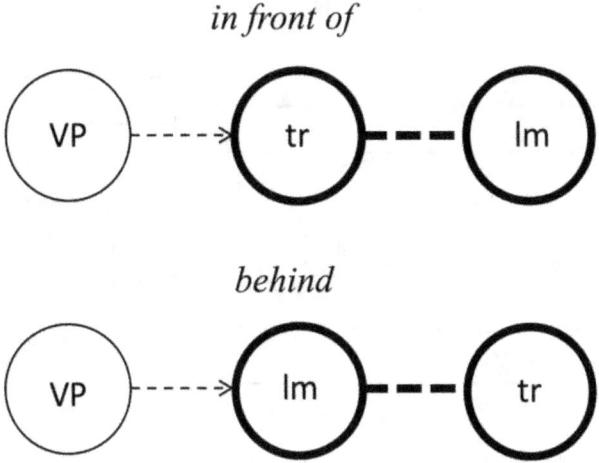

Figure 2.2 Vantage Point for 'in front of' and 'behind' (after Langacker 2008: 76).

Furthermore, a text can encourage a reader to profile one object rather than another: in other words to pay more attention to the trajector or the landmark. One way of encouraging a profiling of the trajector would be to increase its textual size with a great deal of pre- and post-modification, for example. Compare: *The chair was in front of the table* with *The rickety wooden chair that was literally on its last legs was in front of the table*. The Vantage Point can be profiled along its trajectory, to focus on one object or the other, or of course the attentional window can be zoomed out to encompass the entire process (see Talmy 2007, 2008).

We can combine the cognitive grammatical framework of attentional windowing with the text-worlds approach I have been using so far to think about FID and other types of discourse presentation. If a reader is encouraged to profile the narratorial discourse only (as in Figure 2.3), then the effect is a Narratorial Report or Indirect Speech. If the profiling is windowed more towards the character, then it appears as if that character has free control over their own discourse (as in Figure 2.4) in the form

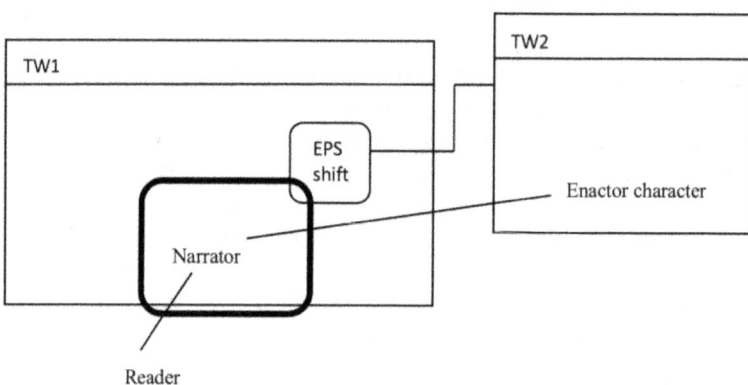

Figure 2.3 Attentional windowing of narratorial control.

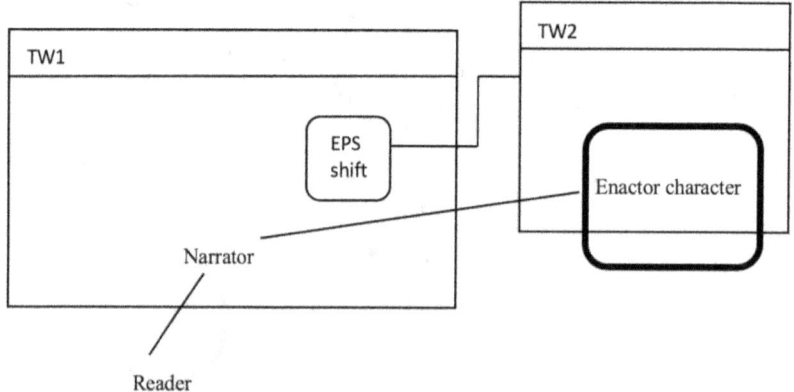

Figure 2.4 Attentional windowing of character control.

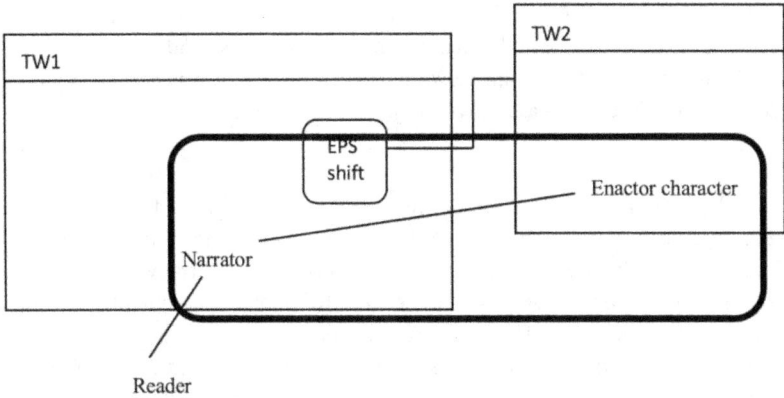

Figure 2.5 Attentional windowing of free indirect discourse.

of Direct Speech or Free Direct Speech. Lastly, if the attentional windowing zooms out to encompass both narrator and character across a world boundary, then the effect is Free Indirect Discourse (as in Figure 2.5). Here, there is a profiling of the deflection itself.

To summarize so far: FID is a deflection across world-boundaries; FID is a fundamentally perspectival phenomenon; mind-casting is the mechanism for FID; FID depends upon identifying the nature of the Vantage Point; the stylistic presentation of discourse within a text is a matter of attentional windowing.

3. Revisiting the classics of FID

The procedure for a cognitive poetic analysis of FID, then, is as follows.

1. Identify the Vantage Point in relation to TR and LM (usually narrator and character, although it could be one character speaking about another, or an authorial intervention in the narrative);
2. Pick out the windowing construal;
3. Identify the deictic centre realizations (for two windowed enactors, this is FID);
4. Track the relationships between the two minds;
5. Explore the shifts along the deictic braid;
6. Describe and interpret the effect of the overall mind-cast.

In the rest of this chapter, I will apply this procedure to several of the classic examples from celebrated previous discussions of FID. First, here is an excerpt from James Joyce's (1922) *Ulysses*, quoted by Upstone (2017) as a prime example of FID:

> He kicked open the crazy door for the jakes. Better be careful not to get these trousers dirty for a funeral. He went in, bowing his head under the low lintel. Leaving the door ajar, amid the stench of mouldy lime-wash and stale cobwebs he undid his braces. Before sitting down he peered through a chink up at the next-door window. The king was in his countinghouse. Nobody.
>
> (Joyce 1922: 66)

The FID here lies in the deflection between reader and the character Leopold Bloom via the Joycean narrator. We follow Bloom into his toilet not only psychologically but spatially too (*in–under–amid–down–up at–in*) and sensorially. This is a simple deflection through the narrator, with the effect I think of empathetic identification. It could nearly be Free Direct Thought, but the persistence of 'he' and the idiosyncratic Joycean narratorial voice so far, I think, keeps the attentional window zoomed out to sustain the FID. Figure 2.5 captures the schematic for this passage.

Although this Joyce extract exhibits empathy, a common effect of FID is irony. In fact, this might even be its prototypical function. This passage is from Jane Austen's *Emma* (1815), quoted by Flavin (1991) as an example of how characterization works in the novel's narrative technique.

> 'Nonsense! He does not care about Jane Fairfax. In the way of love, I am sure he does not. He would do any good to her, or her family; but –"Well," said Mrs. Weston, laughing, 'perhaps the greatest good he could do them, would be to give Jane such a respectable home.'
>
> 'If it would be good to her, I am sure it would be evil to himself; a very shameful and degrading connexion. How would he bear to have Miss Bates belonging to him? – To have her haunting the Abbey, and thanking him all day long for his great kindness in marrying Jane? – "So very kind and obliging! – But he always had been such a very kind neighbour!" And then fly off, through half a sentence, to her mother's old petticoat. "Not that it was such a very old petticoat either – for still it would last a great while – and, indeed, she must thankfully say that their petticoats were all very strong."'
>
> 'For shame, Emma! Do not mimic her. You divert me against my conscience. And, upon my word, I do not think Mr. Knightley would be much disturbed by Miss Bates....
>
> (Austen 1815: 176)

The excerpt shows Emma ridiculing Miss Bates. The character adopts the Austen-narrator's own FID technique, and is scolded for it by Mrs Weston. She embeds echoic ridicule and sarcasm within Direct Speech inside her own dialogue. This undercuts some of the empathy a reader might have established for Emma. In mimicking Miss Bates' actual voice, the echo can be seen as Free Indirect Speech from the vantage point of the participants at the same world level (Emma and Mrs Weston), but it is schematically an example of Direct Speech by Emma for the reader at the top world level. Either way, it seems to me that the attentional windowing here is embedded in the novel, and is an example not of narrator-character deflection but a more complex

Re-cognizing Free Indirect Discourse

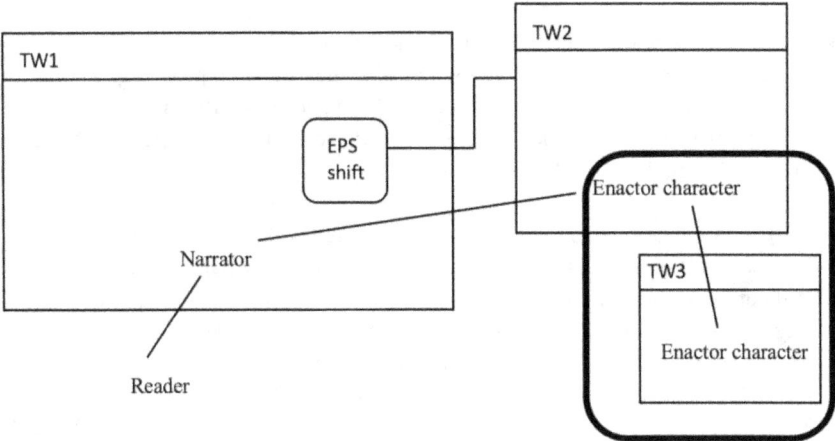

Figure 2.6 Attentional windowing of character-to-character free indirect discourse.

scheme. Here, a reader has to cast their mind along the braid through the usual narrator and into the enactor Emma, and then a further deflection to the enactor Miss Bates. The FID within Emma's Direct Speech is windowed for attention (see Figure 2.6).

An example is used by Leech and Short (1981: 264) to show that FID can also appear, non-prototypically in the first-person mode. This is from Vladimir Nabokov's (1955) *Lolita*:

> Hardly had the Farlows gone than a blue-chinned cleric called – and I tried to make the interview as brief as was consistent with neither hurting his feelings nor arousing his doubts. Yes, I would devote all my life to the child's welfare. Here, incidentally, was a little cross that Charlotte Becker had given me when we were both young. I had a female cousin, a respectable spinster in New York. There we would find a good private school for Dolly. Oh, what a crafty Humbert!
> (Nabokov 1955: 100)

Leech and Short point out that the pronoun choice must be consistent with the primary discourse situation (here, 'I', 'me' and 'my'): in our terms, this means that the personal deixis must be consistent with the world-level in attentional focus. The sentence beginning 'Yes, I would devote all my life...' is clearly FIS. The function of the FID here is aimed towards an effect of persuasion or alignment between reader and the internal narrator. There is a temporal deictic shift outwards to the imagined moment of the novel's utterance ('and I tried to make the interview [...] brief'). Even though this is FIS, it is quite easy to recover the apparent DS here, so in schematic terms the windowing of the mindcast would be leaning towards the Humbert character, zooming in towards the right side of a text-world structure like Figure 2.5. This delicacy within the notion of the attentional window reminds us that the window is a dynamic and responsive shifting profile, rather than a static and bounded space.

In all of the examples above, the FID occurs in excerpts and in even longer contexts where the texture of the style is variable. Sometimes the stylistic markers are extremely subtle, but I still think that even highly transient cues are often picked up by readers. Here, for example, is a complex excerpt from Brian Aldiss and Roger Penrose's (1995) polemical science fiction work, *White Mars*. In this case, I have marked up the initial boundaries of the discourse types:

> [IT] Java Joe explained to me that he had thought much about this wonderful place, Crome, while passing his motions. [FIS] He saw it all as a metaphor – although he did not know that particular word. [NRT] From this vision of the good house his suggestion had evolved. [PN] Here he paused, searching my face with that good-natured gaze of his. [NRS] I prompted him to go on.
> ' [DS] "Us shits," he said, "should be kept separate…"…'
>
> (Aldiss and Penrose 1995: 225)

What complicates this is that the entire excerpt is embedded within the direct speech of another character, Crispin Barcunda, who is recounting his meeting with Java Joe (hence the paragraph-initial speech marks). Setting this aside, the narrative report of speech (NRS) that characterizes the whole of the foregoing chapter shifts in the first line of the excerpt to indirect thought. The sentence beginning 'He saw it all as a metaphor' is most easily interpreted as FIS, I think, with Java Joe being deflected via Crispin Barcunda, and then outwards to the novel's narrator to the reader. However, the comment '– although he did not know that particular word' refocuses the attentional window on Crispin, and moves this sentence towards Narrative Report of Thought (NRT). My own reading felt the texture of this as jarring, until I managed to disentangle the embedded deflections. The next line is what Toolan (2001) calls Pure Narration (PN), but the trajectory of the Vantage Point is manipulated deictically by 'that good-natured gaze'. A major effect of this complex texture and attentional repair is to distance the crew-member's inarticulacy from the philosophical register of the novel as a whole. In this case, FID serves a thematic purpose.

The last example is from Toolan's (2001) book on narrative. He quotes an excerpt from James Joyce's story 'Eveline' (1914), showing that the texture of the discourse presentation is 'highly fluid, even volatile' (Toolan 2001: 140). The following moves from NRT, to PN, to FIT in each sentence respectively:

> She felt her cheek pale and cold and, out of a maze of distress, she prayed to God to direct her, to show her what was her duty. The boat blew a long mournful whistle into the mist. If she went, tomorrow she would be on the sea with Frank, steaming towards Buenos Ayres.
>
> (Joyce 1914: 48)

Toolan notes that the middle PN sentence is almost entirely impersonal, except for the word 'mournful', and this, I think, serves to prepare a reader for a profiling window towards the FIT that follows.

Toolan also includes a note on a literary critical dispute around the following sentence from the previous page of 'Eveline':

> As she mused the pitiful vision of her mother's life laid its spell on the very quick of her being – that life of commonplace sacrifice closing in final craziness.
>
> (Joyce 1914: 47)

Hart (1969: 51) says that Eveline's words here show her inability to love and her inarticulate reliance on 'tawdry clichés'. Chatman (1978), by contrast, accuses Hart of confusing character viewpoint and narratorial voice here. Chatman argues that the narrator is parodying a pulp-literature style by using words that would not be in Eveline's vocabulary. We can understand this dispute in terms of attentional windowing. Hart has profiled the narrator and character in a broad FIT window; Chatman has profiled a narrower narratorial window, reading the sentence as NRT. The consequences of this differential windowing amount to the differences in their overall interpretations.

4. Effects and uses of FID

It has struck me that almost all prior discussions of FID have treated it primarily as a stylistic feature, or primarily as a feature of consciousness, whereas the obvious solution is to regard it properly as a heteronomous phenomenon that involves the integration of both of these two partial perspectives. FID is an experience between text and cognition, and so is best described, understood, analysed and used to frame interpretation all within the remit of cognitive poetics. Not only can we identify the nature and quality of FID, and other forms of discourse representation; we can use our analytical understanding to explore the textural differences and unique qualities of reading literary works.

Through this chapter, I have briefly set out how a view of FID as a deictic deflection and attentional windowing can address different interpretative and experiential effects. The prototypical feeling arising from FID is probably irony, though here there are several sub-divisions within that notion that shade into sarcasm, parody, ridicule, mimicry and even more subtle subliminal effects such as snark, wryness, poignancy as well as gentle affection, echoic solidarity, and emotional and ideological alignment. The last of these is perhaps a function of the persuasive effect that FID can have: aligning a reader with a character's thinking, without the text appearing overtly polemical nor didactic. There is, of course, also a plausibility effect of FID. Characters appear to have their own lives, even within the artificial fiction of the narrative. Characterization is thus also a function of FID. And finally, the feeling of immersion in the world or worlds of a text is both an effect and an enabling circumstance of FID (see Eckardt 2014).

Although the emphasis throughout this chapter has been on literary instances of FID, it should be clear that the phenomenon is one that is not exclusively and peculiarly literary, nor even fictional. In retaining the cognitive linguistic commitment to treating the language system as a consistent domain, I am not denying the particular power of literary works to affect many of these experiences most powerfully. Indeed, I think that moving towards a better overall understanding of the nature and texture of FID allows us to see how subtle and complex our human capacity for engaging our attention and imagination can really be.

Acknowledgements

Note: I would like to thank Violeta Sotirova for her insightful comments on an earlier draft of this chapter.

References

Aldiss, B. and R. Penrose (1995), *White Mars, or The Mind Set Free*, London: Little, Brown.
Austen, J. (1815), *Emma*, London: John Murray.
Bakhtin, M. (as V.N. Voloshinov) (1973), *Marxism and the Philosophy of Language*, New York: Seminar Press.
Bally, C. (1912), 'Le Style Indirect Libre en Français Moderne', *Germanisch-Romanische Monatsschrift*, 4: 549–56 and 597–606.
Banfield, A. (1982), *Unspeakable Sentences*, Boston: Routledge & Kegan Paul.
Blinova, O. (2012), 'The Notion of Free Indirect Discourse and Its Use in Contemporary Journalism', *Humanities and Social Sciences Review*, 1: 1365–71.
Bray, J. (2007), 'The "Dual Voice" of Free Indirect Discourse: A Reading Experiment', *Language and Literature*, 16: 37–51.
Chatman, S. (1978), *Story and Discourse*, Ithaca: Cornell University Press.
Cohn, D. (1978), *Transparent Minds: Narrative Modes for Presenting Consciousness*, Princeton: Princeton University Press.
Delfitto, D., F. Gaetano and A. Reboul (2016), 'The Semantics of Person and *de se* Effects in Free Indirect Discourse', *SpringerPlus*, 5 (1): 1451.
Eckardt, R. (2014), *The Semantics of Free Indirect Discourse: How Texts Allow Us to Mind-Read and Eavesdrop*, Leiden: Brill.
Ehrlich, S. (1990), *Point of View: A Linguistic Analysis of Literary Style*, London: Routledge.
Flaubert, G. (1971), *Madame Bovary*, Paris: Garnier Frères [original 1856].
Flavin, L. (1991), 'Free Indirect Discourse and the Clever Heroine of *Emma*', *Persuasions: Journal of the Jane Austen Society of North America*, 13: 50–7.
Fludernik, M. (1993), *The Fictions of Language and the Languages of Fiction: The Linguistic Representation of Speech and Consciousness*, London: Routledge.
Gavins, J. (2007), *Text World Theory: An Introduction*, Edinburgh: Edinburgh University Press.
Giovanelli, M. and C. Harrison (2018), *Cognitive Grammar in Stylistics: A Practical Guide*, London: Bloomsbury.
Harrison, C. (2014), 'Attentional Windowing in David Foster Wallace's "The Soul Is Not a Smithy"', in C. Harrison, L. Nuttall, P. Stockwell and W. Yuan (eds), *Cognitive Grammar in Literature*, 53–67, Amsterdam: Benjamins.
Hart, C. (1969), 'Eveline', in C. Hart (ed.), *James Joyce's Dubliners: Critical Essays*, 48–52, New York: Viking.

Hodson, J. (2014), *Dialect in Film and Literature*, London: Macmillan.
Joyce, J. (1914), 'Eveline', in *Dubliners*, 25–9, London: Grant Richards.
Joyce, J. (1922), *Ulysses*, Paris: Sylvia Beach.
Langacker, R.W. (1995), 'Viewing and Cognition in Grammar', in P.W. Davis (ed.), *Alternative Linguistics: Descriptive and Theoretical Modes*, 153–212, Amsterdam: John Benjamins.
Langacker, R.W. (2008), *Cognitive Grammar: A Basic Introduction*, New York: Oxford University Press.
Langacker, R.W. (2009), *Investigations in Cognitive Grammar*, Berlin: Mouton de Gruyter.
Leech, G. and M. Short (1981), *Style in Fiction*, London: Longman.
McHale, B. (1978), 'Free Indirect Discourse: A Survey of Recent Accounts', *PTL: A Journal for Descriptive Poetics and Theory of Literature*, 3: 249–78.
Maier, E. (2015), 'Quotation and Unquotation in Free Indirect Discourse', *Mind and Language*, 30: 345–73.
Mey, J.L. (2000), *When Voices Clash. A Study in Literary Pragmatics*, Berlin: Mouton de Gruyter.
Mildorf, J. and B. Thomas (eds) (2017), *Dialogue Across Media*, Amsterdam: John Benjamins.
Nabokov, V. (1955), *Lolita*, Paris: Olympia Press.
Nuttall, L. (2018), *Mind Style and Cognitive Grammar*, London: Bloomsbury.
Palmer, A. (2004), *Fictional Minds*, Lincoln: University of Nebraska Press.
Palmer, A. (2010), *Social Minds in the Novel*, Columbus: Ohio State University Press.
Pascal, R. (1977), *The Dual Voice*, Manchester: Manchester University Press.
Pons-Sanz, S. (2019), 'Speech Representation as a Narrative Technique in *Sir Gawain and the Green Knight*', *The Review of English Studies*, 70 (294): 209–30.
Redeker, G. (1996), 'Free Indirect Discourse in Newspaper Reports', *Linguistics in the Netherlands*, 13 (1): 221–32.
Rundquist, E. (2017), *Free Indirect Style in Modernism: Representations of Consciousness*, Amsterdam: John Benjamins.
Schlenker, P. (2004), 'Context of Thought and Context of Utterance: A Note on Free Indirect Discourse and the Historical Present', *Mind and Language*, 19 (3): 279–304.
Semino, E. (1997), *Language and World Creation in Poems and Other Texts*, London: Longman.
Short, M. (2014), 'In Memory of Geoffrey Leech (1936–2014)', *European English Messenger*, 23 (2): 9–13. Available online: http://essenglish.org/messenger
Short, M., E. Semino and M. Wynne (2001), 'Revisiting the Notion of Faithfulness in Discourse Report/(Re)presentation Using a Corpus Approach', in A. Combrink (ed.), *Poetics, Linguistics and History*, 484–509, Potchefstroom: Potchefstroom University Press.
Simpson, P. (1993), *Language, Ideology and Point of View*, London: Routledge.
Sotirova, V. (2004), 'Connectives in Free Indirect Style: Continuity or Shift?' *Language and Literature*, 13 (3): 216–34.
Sotirova, V. (2005), 'Repetition in Free Indirect Style: A Dialogue of Minds?' *Style*, 39 (2): 123–36.
Sotirova, V. (2010), 'The Roots of a Literary Style: Joyce's Presentation of Consciousness in *Ulysses*', *Language and Literature*, 19 (2): 131–49.
Stockwell, P. (2009), *Texture: A Cognitive Aesthetics of Reading*, Edinburgh: Edinburgh University Press.
Stockwell, P. (2013), 'The Positioned Reader', *Language and Literature*, 22 (3): 263–77.

Stockwell, P. (2014), 'War, Worlds and Cognitive Grammar', in C. Harrison, L. Nuttall, P. Stockwell and W. Yuan (eds), *Cognitive Grammar in Literature*, 19–34, Amsterdam: Benjamins.

Talmy, L. (2000), *Toward a Cognitive Semantics, Vol. 1: Concept Structuring Systems*, Cambridge: MIT Press.

Talmy, L. (2007), 'Attention Phenomena', in D. Geeraerts and H. Cuyckens (eds), *The Oxford Handbook of Cognitive Linguistics*, 264–93, Oxford: Oxford University Press.

Talmy, L. (2008), 'Aspects of Attention in Language', in P. Robinson (ed.), *Handbook of Cognitive Linguistics*, 27–38, London: Routledge.

Tannen, D. (1989), *Talking Voices: Repetition, Dialogue and Imagery in Conversational Discourse*, Cambridge: Cambridge University Press.

Toolan, M. (2001), *Narrative: A Critical Linguistic Introduction*, 2nd edn, London: Routledge.

Upstone, S. (2017), *Literary Theory: A Complete Introduction*, London: Hachette.

Werth, P. (1999), *Text Worlds: Representing Conceptual Space in Discourse*, Harlow: Longman.

3

The dynamicity of construal, embodied memory and (mental) time travel in Mohsin Hamid's *Exit West*

Anne Holm

1. A cognitive stylistic approach to narrating the experience of displacement

Mohsin Hamid's *Exit West* (2017) tells the story of a young couple who flee civil war in their unnamed home country through a magical doorway. Although the novel can be classified as speculative fiction, the world it projects is eerily easy to conceive of, and supernatural elements are limited to the doorways that are opening up in different parts of the world, allowing people to migrate in search for safety. This chapter investigates the ways in which the protagonists' loss of contact with their past is presented as a 'felt' displacement, in part as a result of the unusual method of relocation. The portals make the novel's depiction of having to leave one's home behind quite unique: they cut out the experience of the perilous get-away as they cut the protagonists off from their pasts and throw them into an unknown future. Hamid uses various narrative techniques in portraying the ruptures to the couple's – and others' – reality, for instance omniscient narration, metaphor and temporal shifts. In my reading, this stylistic diversity is key to construing the protagonists' struggle to start over and come to terms with the past.

Hamid has dealt with similar themes in his earlier work, drawing on his own Pakistani background, but opted not to specify the initial setting in *Exit West*. In a 2017 interview he says the following about his thinking behind the choice: 'We move through time throughout our entire lives. The city of our childhood doesn't exist when we are forty, fifty, seventy years old. Whenever you meet someone who is elderly, you are meeting someone who is a migrant.' This idea of being a migrant through time, expressed also explicitly in the novel, is rooted in two major conceptual metaphors: LIFE IS A JOURNEY and LIFE IS A STORY (Lakoff and Turner 1989: 60–1; Kövecses 2002: 65). These metaphors are very prominent, and often intertwined, in life writing, but they are also frequently employed in fiction dealing with memory and remembering. In this chapter they will be analysed from an embodied perspective, focusing on how the journeying on the level of plot connects to narrativizing the experience of migration and displacement. Significantly, since embodied experience can to an extent be seen as universal (Yu 2008: 247; Kövecses 2005), it offers a means of creating resonance in the processing of vicarious experiences, as Hamid's point about being a migrant through time also suggests.

In exploring how such metaphoric patterns are mapped when engaging with the text, I draw on the notion of dynamicity as an aspect of construal in Cognitive Grammar (Langacker 2008: 79). This involves paying attention to how conceptualizations unfold when unpacking realizations of conceptual metaphors. Furthermore, I employ an enactivist approach to discussing mental imagery from a readerly perspective: literary style is viewed as 'a stimulus-driven, bottom-up process' (Burke 2013: 199) and taken to evoke simulation of experiences with an embodied basis. Although the assumption of the embodied mind underlies Langacker's theoretical model, and other linguistic and literary applications of Cognitive Science, the way in which the body figures in processing linguistically encoded experiences is something that requires further investigation, in Cognitive Grammar and cognitive approaches more generally. In the case of *Exit West*, I argue that attention to the construal of linguistic realizations of embodied metaphors ultimately reveals how the novel both builds on and brings into question the modern notion of time as unrepeatable and irreversible.

2. Embodied metaphors, retrospect and simulation

As a result of overwhelming empirical evidence from Cognitive Science, the mind is assumed to be embodied. In Cognitive Linguistics, embodiment refers to the way in which language is bound to our bodily interaction with the world (Fauconnier and Turner 2002: 377). Bodily experience provides the basis for understanding things like movement along a path and the boundedness of spaces, and these image schemas give rise to many metaphorical extensions (e.g. Johnson 1987), for instance deeming the human body a world in itself, containing our cognitive resources. Such metaphors are considered groundlaying in our thinking, interaction with one another and creative contexts (Lakoff and Johnson 1980; Lakoff and Johnson 1999). Because of certain patterns of embodied experience being widely shared, recognizing and unpacking realizations of embodied metaphors often produces a sense of tangibility and familiarity in the mapping process. That said, a distinction should be made between primary and complex metaphors as regards the potential for such universality: culture-specific layers may be added in complex metaphors building on embodied primary metaphors (Lakoff and Johnson 1999: 60).

The embodied foundation of the intersecting metaphors LIFE IS A JOURNEY and LIFE IS A STORY is strongly sequential due to the underlying PATH schema, at least when it comes to narratives that are not especially experimental in their structure. The JOURNEY metaphor typically suggests dynamicity as well – a sense of transition that is often absent from the experiences themselves (Lakoff and Johnson 1980: 95), and indeed often the linguistic expression as well. For example, we might talk about overcoming obstacles as if they were mountains we managed to climb. In addition to transition, the presence of the FORCE schema may also suggest change, as in the metaphor CHANGE IS MOTION (Dancygier and Sweetser 2014: 45). In realizations that overlap with the LIFE IS A STORY metaphor (see Kövecses 2002: 64–5) the effect is quite often one of physical achievement that adds drama and contributes to character development, like in this passage from *Exit West*: 'she almost felt that if she got up and walked home at this moment there would be two Nadias, that she would split into two Nadias, and one would stay on the steps reading and one would walk home' (Hamid 2017: 154–5). The feeling of change and inner conflict the character is experiencing is expressed in a physical split resulting in two diverging storylines, and further on the reader discovers that the feeling comes to define the character's path. Significantly, the LIFE IS A STORY metaphor typically adds coherence and causal links to events (Lakoff and Johnson 1980: 172–3), although in reality we tend to view the role of chance and our (occasional) lack of control in how events take their course as a fact of life.

This kind of projected movement has often been analysed in literary texts under the rubric of the MIND IS A BODY MOVING IN SPACE metaphor (e.g. Turner 1996; Bradburn 2011; see also Sweetser 1990), but due to the self-reflective nature of Hamid's novel, I prefer to discuss these tendencies as overlaps of LIFE IS A JOURNEY and LIFE IS A STORY instead. For the sake of convenience, I will refer to the combination as the 'Dynamic Life Story' metaphor. As Kai Mikkonen points out in his analysis of the metaphor of narrative as travel, travelling offers 'a basic model for "viewing" space and events within time', but also a way of 'understanding time by enacting in time something that seems like an inevitable pattern of events: a correlation between the structuring of the text and that of the world' (2007: 300). Indeed, time is an important aspect of mapping metaphorical life journeys. Lakoff and Johnson make a distinction between two dynamic conceptualizations, TIME IS A MOVING OBJECT and TIME IS STATIONARY AND WE MOVE THROUGH IT (1980: 43–5; see also Grady 1997; Evans 2003). These pervasive conceptualizations, though by no means universally applicable (see for example Sullivan and Bui 2016), place the past behind the conceptualizer and the future ahead, but the latter metaphor specifically projects a horizontally extended path (Evans 2003: 202), containing the 'metaphorical entailments' A JOURNEY DEFINES A PATH and THE PATH OF A JOURNEY IS A SURFACE (Lakoff and Johnson 1980: 91). The former entailment, goal-orientedness, is particularly strongly present in the LIFE IS A STORY metaphor as well, while the latter allows for complex elaborations of the idea of the temporality of space within a narrative.

In terms of memory, a notable consequence of viewing life as a journey, and life as a story in relation to it, is that the past (whether fictive or real) may appear as a place one can simply revisit. However, Evans (2003: 202) observes that horizontal motion trajectories in conceptualizing time and space are arguably a cultural construct, and Jens Brockmeier (2008) points out that memories are not contained in storage rooms that can be entered – the metaphor does not capture how memory retrieval works. While the notion of experientiality in cognitive narratology (e.g. Fludernik 1996) accommodates non-sequential mental representations of a world, it is also worth considering how the representation is constructed (instead). As sociologist Matti Hyvärinen writes, 'telling about a life, a past, an individual occasion, is always an active, purposeful, and constructive move' (2017: ix). In my analysis I suggest that Hamid builds on conventional spatio-temporal trajectories in *Exit West*, but in a way that consciously moves away from simple sequentiality.

When it comes to processing these metaphors, the enactivist approach to cognition offers further tools for unpacking their embodied nature. Taking its roots in the work of Francisco Varela, Evan Thompson and Emily Rosch (1991), enactivism views cognition as the enaction of one's surroundings (see also Di Paolo and Thompson 2014; Noë 2012). Mental processes and situated embodied action are closely linked: 'Rather than being a mere receptive medium, human perception is a sensorimotor skill whereby the embodied action of the perceiver makes the world available to experience' (Polvinen 2016: 28). Literary applications of enactivism have drawn attention to the active reading of narrative as a temporal process (Popova 2015) and to how emphasis on the reader's engagement with the experiential qualities of texts allows for more nuanced analyses of their what-it's-likeness (Caracciolo 2014). Both Popova and Caracciolo also address the role of metaphor in such active interaction with texts. I draw on Caracciolo's idea of mental imagery in particular: building on Barsalou's (1999), Gallese's (2005) and Zwaan's (2008) work, among others, Caracciolo (2014: 95) argues that the simulation of a bodily perceptual experience in a literary text involves the activation of 'memories of past interactions with the world', or 'experiential traces'. Metaphorical language 'picks up two experiential traces and weaves them together into a new, surprising, and sometimes unsettling expression' (Caracciolo 2014: 108). The hard-to-grasp qualities of an experience may thus be enacted by way of association.

As regards simulation of the embodied sequentiality of LIFE IS A JOURNEY, and LIFE IS A STORY by extension, Raymond Gibbs has argued that the JOURNEY metaphor 'primes' the conceptualizer for physical movement in space even in the case of abstract realizations (2006; 2013; see also Gibbs and Matlock 2008). As Caracciolo (2018) states, we understand action verbs, spatial descriptions and embodied metaphors by running internal simulations of the actual ways of carrying these out. This also links to the concept of subjective movement (Langacker 1991; see also Langacker 2012a) or fictive motion (Talmy 2000; Matlock 2004; Richardson and Matlock 2007; Yuan 2014). In the context of literary study, Caracciolo and others (e.g. Rice 2007; Troscianko 2010) have proposed that imagery can be seen as embodied in itself due to recreating sensimotor patterns. However, simulations are not activated across the board when coming into contact with imagery (Kuzmičová 2014: 279): running a simulation does not produce a mental image of what is being simulated in an automated fashion. According to Kuzmičová (Kuzmičová 2014: 280), not enough attention has been paid to 'what it is *like*, in terms of experience, to have these images and what they are really images of'. With a view to this, it is also worth considering in what way being aware of engaging with a literary text affects simulations. Merja Polvinen builds on Alva Noë's (2012) notion of the duality of perceptual experience in arguing that 'our sense of a high-resolution perception is dependent on our understanding of the significance of our own enactive processing of the fiction as fiction' (2016: 30). If perception consists of simultaneously experiencing the world and the way it is presented in experience, as Noë posits, then enactment of literary imagery must also encompass the way in which simulation is prompted (or not).

3. The dynamicity of construal and lyric narration

Reminiscent of the duality of perceptual experience as outlined by Noë, Langacker's definition of meaning includes both the conceptual content and the way that content is construed (2008: 43). When conceptual content is encoded into a linguistic expression, a particular construal is imposed. Although Langacker (2008: 55) stresses that Cognitive Grammar does not claim meanings are necessarily visually or spatially based, he uses the metaphor of a scene and a certain way of perceiving it to illustrate how construal works. Among the four main phenomena that pertain to construal Langacker (2008: 73) describes perspective as referring to how a scene is viewed from a particular vantage point, resulting in a particular viewing arrangement. Such an arrangement requires that the participants in the communicative situation – in a literary context the writer and the reader – are connected through grounding (Harrison 2017: 33). This can be related to the reader's enactment of imagery involving embodied sequentiality. As Langacker (2008: 74) points out, rather than viewing a scene from a fixed location, 'the viewer is often conceived as being in motion', and a fictional viewer being conceived as moving can in turn be connected to what Anežka Kuzmičová terms 'enactment-imagery', summarized as 'vicarious experiencing proper of the referential contents' (2014: 282).

In Kuzmičová's analysis of enactment-imagery, as distinct from 'description-imagery', the reader's own position in relation to the storyworld is emphasized, and an inner stance entailing the activation of the senses is at the centre (2014: 282). The definition makes for an illuminating parallel to Langacker's notion of subjective versus objective construal. When a scene is construed with maximal objectivity, the viewer is paying full attention to the scene and there is little awareness of the viewer and their circumstances (Langacker 2008: 77). This correlates with how enactment-imagery works: although characterized by the reader's active engagement with the text, Kuzmičová (2014: 283) stresses that in reading there is an effortless feel to enactment-imagery, and a certain sense of medium transparency is required. By contrast, the outer stance in Kuzmičová's (2014: 283) definition of description-imagery can be paralleled with a viewing arrangement in which the subject of conceptualization is in focus. In Langacker's discussion of simulation, however, degrees of transparency can be compared to how simulated experience is 'attenuated' in relation to engaged experience – simulations are always partial and often less detailed (2008: 536–7).

As has already become apparent, Langacker's notion of conceptualization is at its core profoundly dynamic. Put simply, language is something that happens (2012b: 531). An important feature of construal is its temporality: 'As an aspect of construal, dynamicity pertains to how a conceptualization develops and unfolds through processing time' (Langacker 2008: 79). By processing time Langacker means the temporality of mental processing, while conceived time refers to time as an object of construal. These two come together interestingly in processing realizations of the Dynamic Life Story metaphor in reading *Exit West*: actual time travel and mental time travel co-exist in a way that is reminiscent of Bakhtin's (1981) chronotope, the inseparability of time and space. While narratologists have traditionally privileged time over space (Ryan 2014), both within storyworlds and as regards processing them, Langacker's model is essentially four-dimensional. Although Langacker contrasts nouns and verbs in terms of their expansiveness, time can be a factor in profiling nouns as well; in addition to nouns like 'minute' and 'hour', time may act as the domain of instantiation in the case of a noun like 'beep' in that the duration of the sound is part of it (Langacker 2012a: 202). That said, the construal of motion events involves 'a *conceptual layering*, whereby movement through space occurs through time, rather than movement through time occurring through space' (Langacker 2012a: 202). This would correspond with the 'Moving Ego' (Evans 2003: 57) mapping of time (TIME IS STATIONARY AND WE MOVE THROUGH IT), and arguably contrasts with what is termed 'subjective time' in cognitive psychology, defined as 'the time of the body, the perception of change, and related to bodily processes' (Wittman 2016: 132). Generally, change, or comparison between states, is what lies at the core of Lakoff and Johnson's discussions of time metaphors as well (1980; see also Evans 2003: 15).

Bringing to mind the enaction of referential content, Langacker writes that 'recalling or imagining an event involves a partial simulation of the real-time sequential experience of observing it' (2012a: 205). This would be an example of sequential scanning; alternatively summary scanning is a process 'whereby structures experienced sequentially are superimposed, as in a multiple-exposure photograph' (2012a: 206). Although with verbs the former is predominant, summation also 'has the dynamic properties of ordering and directionality' (2012a: 206). For example, grammatical operations imposed upon a verb may 'override' its sequentiality and render its content to be viewed holistically (2012a: 207), as in the nominalization of a verb. In Langacker's example '[f]rom here the fall to the valley floor is about 600 feet' the successive locations on the path of conceptualization define the motion event. However, arriving at a holistic view, by attending to different facets of the scene in a process that unfolds through time, may be a particularly complex operation in literary contexts and calls for more detailed investigations of how a 'full configuration' (2012a: 207) is reached and available for further analysis.

While dynamicity pertaining to profiling events has obvious relevance to the cognitive stylistic analysis of narrative texts, I argue that the dynamic properties of processing a (seemingly) static scene also deserve attention with regard to narrativizing hard-to-grasp experiences in instances of what I label as lyric narration. This does not only rely on metaphors – they are indeed pertinent in all kinds of contexts – but rather a narrative mode that builds on the Dynamic Life Story metaphor. Here I draw on Paul Simpson's idea of narrative urgency (2014; see also Harrison 2017: 35–6), a (non-exhaustive) list of stylistic markers that help involve the reader in a particularly action-intense passage of a narrative and tie them to the motivations and goals of the protagonist. Because lyricality is often employed in reflective passages of narration, it only makes sense that it does not predominantly involve narrative urgency. In contrast to Simpson's markers (2014: 7–8), I hypothesize that lyric narration might, to varying degrees, have the following properties:

Table 3.1 Properties of Lyric Narration versus Narrative Urgency

Narrative Urgency	Lyric Narration
Simple sentences	Long sentences lacking grammatical rigour
Physical actions rather than mental processes	Prominence of (embodied) mental processes
Categorical rather than modalized statements	Prominence of modality
Close to synchronized duration of events and narration	Discourse time exceeding story time
Free forms of speech and thought	Free forms of (speech and) thought
Ellipsis	Extended description, parallelism and use of associative sound patterns

Many of the properties relate to the salient portrayal of a fictional mind, for example where thought representation is more prominent than speech, which is in line with a reflective mode of narration. As such, the list of characteristics may evoke Genette's definition of a descriptive pause (1980: 94) that amounts to a 'nonexistent diegetic duration', but while lyricality can be said to have a strong descriptive element to it, I would like to extend its narrative function to diegetic progression as well. Werner Wolf (2007), for example, has criticized the pairing of existents/description and events/narration by putting emphasis on the fundamentally transmedial nature of the descriptive – something I would suggest is evoked in lyric narration that involves sensory input (and its enactment).

Among classical narratologists, Gerald Prince's definition of description, as static as it is, includes 'happenings', and can be related to what Langacker writes about the dynamics inherent to the process of summation:

> The representation of objects, beings, situations, or ... happenings in their spatial rather than temporal existence, their topological rather than chronological functioning, their *simultaneity rather than their succession*. (Prince 1987: 19, emphasis added)
>
> As we scan through a complex scene, successively attending to various facets of it, the elements apprehended at each stage are summed, or superimposed. In this way a detailed conception is progressively built up, becoming active and available as a *simultaneously accessible whole for a certain span of processing time*.
> (Langacker 2008: 83, emphasis added)

In terms of analysing the stylistic diversity in *Exit West* and the ways in which the novel invites embodied reader involvement, I will focus on the relationship between processing eventfulness and 'stylistic gestalt' (Harrison 2017: 32). I argue that dynamicity as the enactment of embodied imagery is relevant across the board, though to different degrees. This is in contrast to Kuzmičová's conception of description-imagery: according to Kuzmičová, such imagery creates a felt impact of slowing down and thus 'lacks the experiential richness of enactment-imagery' (2014: 283–4). In fact, I would say that some of the experiential richness may follow from the effect of slowing down, as per Reuven Tsur's characterization of the cognitive resonance of poetry: 'One of the major functions of poetry is promoting heightened awareness, either awareness of the reality perceived, or of the cognitive mechanisms that enable us to perceive reality' (1992: 375). While on the one hand Tsur's account echoes the classic stylistic concept of defamiliarization (Shklovsky 1965), its scope is considerably broader and accommodates attention to the enactment of embodied imagery.

It should be noted, however, that the main distinction between enactment-imagery and description-imagery in Kuzmičová's categorization is the presence or absence of an experiencer in the scene, resulting in an inner or outer stance of processing content respectively. These can, in turn, be equated with Langacker's subjective and objective construal. The position from which a scene is viewed and any changes to that position are crucial, particularly as regards complex realizations of the JOURNEY metaphor. As Kai Mikkonen points out, 'events and movements impose a structure on space, the orientation provided by the traveling individual and his or her experiencing point of view' (2007: 289). The structure thus given to space, even in metaphorical applications of journeying, also extends to temporality via the path projected across it. The experiencing point of view may even become more resonant through manipulations of expected trajectories, as Barbara Dancygier observes in her analysis of Jonathan Raban's travel narratives: 'blends which reverse trajectors and landmarks or present space as time offer a fresh, personal description of the experience. Such blends seem to be constructed to allow the writer to tell his story from a personal, experiential viewpoint. They do not actually change the story being told, but they do change the perspective from which it is told' (2005: 114). With instances of the kind of lyric narration outlined above, however, the perspective may be fairly implicit, or subjected to the pre-eminence of an omniscient narrator.

4. (Mental) time travel in *Exit West*

The kind of stylistic diversity I have alluded to is established at the very beginning of *Exit West* as we are introduced to the two main characters:

> In a city swollen by refugees but still mostly at peace, or at least not yet openly at war, a young man met a young woman in a classroom and did not speak to her. …
> It might seem odd that in cities teetering at the edge of the abyss young people still go to class – in this case an evening class on corporate identity and product branding – but that is the way of things, with cities as with life, for one moment we are pottering about our errands as usual and the next we are dying, and our eternally impending ending does not put a stop to our transient beginnings and middles until the instant when it does.
>
> (Hamid 2017: 1–2)

I would like to zoom in on two things here: manifestations of the Dynamic Life Story metaphor and their relation to the perspectives the reader is asked to adopt throughout the passage. First, the narrator takes the role of the omniscient storyteller by voicing a profound knowledge of how life is – that our life trajectories ultimately are linear but that we do not know how long our lifelines are. Interestingly, the narrator's conjecturing relies on the two opposite metaphoric mappings of time, Moving Time and Moving Ego, which call for different perspectives for processing the conceptual content presented. Although only implicitly about time, the phrase 'cities teetering at the edge of the abyss' can be read as a metonymical realization of the Moving Ego mapping: the embodied representation of an entire city as 'teetering' on the verge of destruction suggests that the city's inhabitants, the protagonists included, are headed towards an event that will permanently change their lives. Conceptualizing the threat of such an event by observing a fictional agent's prospective trajectory, through objective construal, could be seen to pave the way for the reader to become invested in the characters' fate, even if the metonymical phrasing is quite generic. Furthermore, the last clause in the quoted passage ('our eternally impending ending …') is a realization of the Moving Time (TIME IS A MOVING OBJECT) mapping in that the end point of a person's timeline seems to be an active agent in motion. There is, then, a collision of these two perspectives in what is a spatio-temporal portrayal of death looming, and the reader is implicitly asked to reconcile the perspectives upon reading on.

Second, the way this collision is presented also brings into focus how the narrative about to unfold is framed in an awareness of such sequentiality as imposed. The prominence of the narrator's point of view denies the characters any agency at this point, and there is an almost pandering tone to some of the word choices – for instance people are said to just 'potter about', not knowing of the approaching end. Moreover, despite the reference to the specific events about to take place, there is a strong sense of schematicity to the passage: the setting and the characters are presented as generic through the use of indefinite articles ('a city', 'an evening class', 'a young man', 'a young woman'), and their story, then, as just another love story. The narrator also uses heavily modalized expressions ('it might seem odd') and the generic pronoun 'we', adding to this feeling. This 'we' surfaces in the novel on several occasions, for instance in this passage that similarly has a foreboding tone: 'when we migrate, we murder from our lives those we leave behind' (Hamid 2017: 94). Interestingly, Hamid explicitly states in the interview referred to earlier that '*Exit West* personalizes and universalizes the idea of migration; it is personal for the two people in the novel, and universal because there are echoes of it in ourselves.' The interplay between inviting an embodied response to the implied life-changing event and narrative schematicity then finds motivation in rendering the theme of migration in readerly terms.

After the schematic framing of the storyworld, the events that bring the two main characters together begin to unfold. A relationship develops between Nadia and Saeed, although they have not become deeply committed yet when the war breaks out. Nevertheless, they decide to flee together upon hearing of the existence of the magical doorway. The description of passing through the portal recalls the opening through references to beginnings and endings, but the narration follows the perspective of the characters closely:

> Drawing close she was struck by its darkness, its opacity, the way that it did not reveal what was on the other side, and also did not reflect what was on this side,

and so felt equally like a beginning and an end [...] It was said in those days that the passage was both like dying and like being born, and indeed Nadia felt a kind of extinguishing as she entered the blackness.

(Hamid 2017: 98)

The reader is merely shown the opacity of the experience as it strikes Nadia. The vague sense of 'extinguishing' suggests that she can now physically feel the past being 'murdered'. While temporal expansiveness (Langacker 2012a: 197) is created through the initial verb phrases ('drawing close', 'struck'), there is a considerable lack of specificity in the depiction of the actual transit, for instance in the passive '[i]t was said' and the qualifier 'a kind of'. Because of the reader being required to fill in such gaps, this arguably results in an effect of time slowing down in reading, activating a more lyric mode of narration, as outlined in Table 3.1: there is little for the reader to cling onto, particularly very little action. At the same time, the embodied notion of something simultaneously beginning and ending invites enactment of the common experience of time as movement, or perceived change. The conceptual content may then perhaps initially be construed objectively, creating an awareness of Nadia's transition, but a shift to a more subjective construal takes place to allow for picturing 'how things look through the eyes of the traveler' (Langacker 2008: 537). The reader would then be required to draw on familiar experiential traces regarding time as movement, resulting in the character's movement and observations becoming more 'implicit as features of the (imagined) viewing situation' (Langacker 2008: 537).

The narrative aspect of journeying becomes more prominent when the initial shock of relocation has been dealt with and the characters start looking ahead and towards the past. Nadia and Saeed arrive at Mykonos first, but face difficulties settling there, and after a while they decide to leave through another portal that has opened up, this time ending up in London. Nadia and Saeed each have their own ways of coping with the challenges they face. In this key passage, Saeed experiences a connection with his countrymen and is for a moment reminded of the journey's start:

> One afternoon he was there at prayer time, and he joined his fellow countrymen in prayer in the back garden, under a blue sky that seemed shockingly blue, like the sky of another world, absent the airborne dust of the city where he had spent his entire life, and also peering out into space from a higher latitude, a different perch on the spinning Earth, nearer its pole than its equator, and so glimpsing the void from a different angle, a bluer angle, and as he prayed he felt praying was different here, somehow, in the garden of this house, with these men. It made him feel part of something, not just something spiritual, but something human, part of this group, and for a wrenchingly painful second he thought of his father.

(Hamid 2017: 148)

Perhaps the most noticeable stylistic feature of the passage, evoking the notion of lyric narration, is that it consists of two long sentences broken up with multiple commas, creating a distinct rhythm in reading. The parts are arguably apprehended as separate profiles connected through 'unmarked' coordination (see Nuttall 2014: 90), meaning that there is no particular asymmetry marking the sequence. This is further complemented by alliteration (repeated 's' sounds) and parallelism: the word 'blue', first linked with the sky on looking up whilst praying, is used several times, and there are also many comparative expressions, drawing the reader's attention to Saeed's present existence in contrast with the past. Narrative duration exceeds the duration of the events, which was earlier identified as a marker of lyric narration (see Table 3.1): there are no apparent events but we are instead given Saeed's observations and reflections on the situation. Moreover, this focus on mental processes, another distinguishing feature of lyric narration, has a markedly physical feel to it due to the sensory input ('blue', 'glimpsing the void', 'a different angle'). Overall, the conceptual content is subjectively construed as Saeed's thinking process is placed onstage.

On the other hand, even though event trajectories are largely missing from the passage, I would argue there is a certain dynamicity to how the descriptive elements are summed in processing the conceptual content. This is related to the Dynamic Life Story metaphor. Towards the end of the passage, the memory of home appears as a momentary painful flinch, not something to return to: Saeed's father is now dead, and Saeed has found it difficult to mourn for him due to the distance and the lack of contact between them after his departure. Thus the moment in which his thoughts seemed to be roaming freely collides with an obstacle on the 'timeline', and the past is instead presented 'in' subjective time, through a realization of physical change. It is also noteworthy how this disruption to Saeed's reflections on his situation is present on the clausal level: the phrase 'for a wrenchingly painful second' is the first example of conceived time in the passage after the initial '[o]ne afternoon', and it is quite specific at that. It interrupts the slow feel of the narrative duration by zooming in on an abrupt reminder of reality, specifically the reality of our time on this earth being finite. But, its duration is also limited and the narrative moves forward – an example of the Dynamic Life Story metaphor that could be interpreted as providing a way of coping.

Furthermore, the horizontal sequentiality of the PATH schema is challenged with the VERTICALITY schema in the way that the realization of life being different in this new place is presented: first in the implied looking up at the sky and then in the expressions 'peering out into space from a higher latitude', 'a different perch on the spinning Earth' and 'nearer its pole than its equator'. While all of these have an experiential basis in the character's situation and surroundings – Saeed is looking up at the sky, and he is also further up north in London than he was in his home country – as linguistic expressions they amount to a cumulative effect of zooming in and out, thus connecting to the metaphorical idea of the change in angle (cf. UNDERSTANDING IS SEEING). At the same time, because of the sentence structure lacking a clearly defined path and the metaphoricity present, the sensory verbs 'peering' and 'glimpsing' cannot be seen as profiling clear, dynamic trajectories, and the experience is also said to be confined to this particular space, the garden. It remains unclear what lies ahead for the protagonist. This is further reinforced by the deictic expressions in the passage ('here', 'this house', 'these men').

Finally, the interior perspective is reinforced by the movement seemingly outside of it. Although the narrator is not present in the same way as in the opening of the novel, there is a distinct sense of literariness to the passage (cf. LIFE IS A STORY). This is tied to the markers of lyric narration proposed earlier (see Table 3.1). The long sentences produce an effect of slowing down reading, while simultaneously creating a sense of breathlessness. This is the case whether reading out loud or simulating reading out loud; the summation of elements requires effort on the reader's part. The transparency of the medium, which according to Kuzmičová is a condition for enactment-imagery, is therefore not fulfilled here, but I would argue that the dynamicity of processing the metaphorical trajectories amounts to a 'felt' conceptualization of the scene. In addition, the PART-WHOLE relationship that is built up in the passage – being part of a group of 'countrymen', glimpsing 'the world' from a particular vantage point – recalls the metonymical personification of the initial setting from the opening of the novel, and thus not only reminds us of Saeed's journey but also contains echoes of the powerful narratorial framing. The reader then becomes aware of *both* 'the reality perceived' and 'the cognitive mechanisms that enable us to perceive reality', as per Tsur's characterization of poetry. Rather than distancing the reader from the conceptual content, their coexistence in the reading process heightens the resonance of the passage.

5. Conclusion

In this chapter I have illustrated how the enactment of conceptual content pertaining to the Dynamic Life Story metaphor creates dynamicity in reading Hamid's *Exit West*. Although the PATH schema that underlies the megametaphor (Werth 1999) imposes sequentiality onto conceptualizing the protagonists' journey, the temporality of processing such linguistic encodings was found to challenge the notion of a simple linear trajectory. This corresponds to what Langacker writes about the complexity of the process: 'It occurs on multiple *time scales*, ranging from the coordination of articulatory gestures, on the smallest scale, to the apprehension of extended discourse, on the largest. Recall, projection, and backtracking represent other departures from strict linearity' (2012b: 561). I have demonstrated that shifts in terms of what is perceived as onstage in particular scenes create noteworthy readerly effects, but the alternating harmony and contrast between conceived time and processing time in particular brought into focus how the characters' escape through time travel obstructed a 'horizontal' mental connection to the past. 'Recall' does not correspond with 'retrieve' in this constellation: subjective time, the perception of change, emphasizes a momentariness and the impossibility of reliving a particular past occurrence.

My discussion also demonstrated that the literariness of the Dynamic Life Story metaphor heightens the reader's processing of conceived time (travel) as a theme in the novel. As Kai Mikkonen writes, travel as a narrative element provides a 'model for negotiating the relationship between the process of experience and narrative order, the difference between the shape of experience and the shape of narrative' (2007: 301). Although I would argue that the shape of the narrative in *Exit West* mirrors the shape of the experiences depicted in many important respects, the active negotiation of the relationship between experientiality and narrative order (and duration) is at the core of the novel's stylistic strategies of engaging the reader. While Saeed as a narratorial conceptualizer attempts to recollect things that are 'outside the ground' with respect to the viewing arrangement in the prayer scene (cf. Harrison's [2017: 37] analysis of retrospection in McEwan's *Enduring Love*), the narrator occasionally provides platforms that invite the reader to view things past and yet to occur on a hypothetical, stylized timeline.

The analysis also discussed the role of lyric narration in conveying the protagonists' inner struggles to come to terms with the experience of displacement. The focus was on stylistic markers of interiority, for instance long sentences, parallelism and metaphorical directionality drawing attention to mental processes. Even though the discussion did not directly address projected realities created through modality, implied motion trajectories were shown to add to the portrayal of Saeed's realization of an altered view on life in a new situation. While the hypotheticality of the directionality can clearly be inferred from the context, I argue that the enaction of the conceptual content is prompted nevertheless and that it complements the literary feel of the passage. Further investigations of the dynamicity inherent to processing such embodied portrayals of mental mechanics could provide valuable insights into how particular construals, especially of a poetic nature, enable the enaction of a world in contexts that require complex simulations.

References

Bakhtin, M. ([1938] 1981), *The Dialogic Imagination: Four Essays*, Austin: University of Texas Press.
Barsalou, L.W. (1999), 'Perceptual Symbol Systems', *Behavioral and Brain Sciences*, 22: 577–660.
Bradburn, E. (2011), '1620–1700: Mind on the Move', in D. Herman (ed.), *The Emergence of Mind. Representations of Consciousness in Narrative Discourse in English*, 132–58, Nebraska: University of Nebraska Press.
Brockmeier, J. (2008), 'Austerlitz's Memory', *Partial Answers*, 6: 347–67.
Burke, M. (2013), 'The Rhetorical Neuroscience of Style: On the Primacy of Style Elements during Literary Discourse Processing', *Journal of Literary Semantics*, 42 (2): 199–215.
Caracciolo, M. (2014), *The Experientiality of Narrative: An Enactivist Approach*, Berlin: De Gruyter.
Caracciolo, M. (2018), 'A Walk through Deep History: Narrative, Embodied Strategies, and Human Evolution', *Costellazioni*, 2 (5): 123–46.
Dancygier, B. (2005), 'Blending and Narrative Viewpoint: Jonathan Raban's Travels through Mental Spaces', *Language and Literature*, 14 (2): 99–127.
Dancygier, B. and E. Sweetser (2014), *Figurative Language*, Cambridge: Cambridge University Press.
Di Paolo, E. and E. Thompson (2014), 'The Enactive Approach', in L. Shapiro (ed.), *The Routledge Handbook of Embodied Cognition*, 68–78, London: Routledge.
Evans, V. (2003), *Structure of Time: Language, Meaning and Temporal Cognition*, Amsterdam: John Benjamins.

Fauconnier, G. and M. Turner (2002), *The Way We Think. Conceptual Blending and the Mind's Hidden Complexities*, New York: Basic Books.
Fludernik, M. (1996), *Towards a 'Natural' Narratology*, London: Routledge.
Gallese, V. (2005), 'Embodied Simulation: From Neurons to Phenomenal Experience', *Phenomenology and the Cognitive Sciences*, 1: 23–48.
Genette, G. ([1972] 1980), *Narrative Discourse: An Essay in Method*, Ithaca: Cornell University Press.
Gibbs, R.W. (2006), 'Metaphor Interpretation as Embodied Simulation', *Mind & Language*, 21 (3): 434–58.
Gibbs, R.W. (2013), 'Walking the Walk While Thinking about the Talk: Embodied Interpretation of Metaphorical Narratives', *Journal of Psycholinguistic Research*, 42 (4): 363–78.
Gibbs, R.W. and T. Matlock (2008), 'Metaphor, Imagination, and Simulation: Psycholinguistic Evidence', in R.W. Gibbs (ed.), *Cambridge Handbook of Metaphor and Thought*, 161–76, New York: Cambridge University Press.
Grady, J. (1997), *Foundations of Meaning: Primary Metaphors and Primary Scenes*, Doctoral dissertation, U.C. Berkeley.
Hamid, M. (2017), *Exit West*, London: Hamish Hamilton.
Harrison, C. (2017), *Cognitive Grammar in Contemporary Fiction*, Amsterdam: John Benjamins.
Hyvärinen, M. (2017), 'Foreword', in B. Schiff, A.E. McKim and S. Patron (eds), *Life and Narrative: The Risks and Responsibilities of Storying Experience*, ix–xxii, Oxford: Oxford University Press.
Johnson, M. (1987), *The Body in the Mind. The Bodily Basis of Meaning, Imagination, and Reason*, Chicago: University of Chicago Press.
Kuzmičová, A. (2014), 'Literary Narrative and Mental Imagery: A View from Embodied Cognition', *Style*, 48 (3): 275–93.
Kövecses, Z. (2002), *Metaphor: A Basic Introduction*, Oxford: Oxford University Press.
Kövecses, Z. (2005), *Metaphor in Culture: Universality and Variation*, Cambridge: Cambridge University Press.
Lakoff, G. and M. Johnson (1980), *Metaphors We Live By*, Chicago: University of Chicago Press.
Lakoff, G. and M. Johnson (1999), *Philosophy in the Flesh: The Embodied Mind and Its Challenge to Western Thought*, New York: Basic Books.
Lakoff, G. and M. Turner (1989), *More Than Cool Reason. A Field Guide to Poetic Metaphor*, Chicago: University of Chicago Press.
Langacker, R.W. (1991), *Foundations of Cognitive Grammar, Vol. II: Descriptive Application*, Stanford: Stanford UP.
Langacker, R.W. (2008), *Cognitive Grammar: A Basic Introduction*, Oxford: Oxford University Press.
Langacker, R.W. (2012a), 'Linguistic Manifestations of the Space-Time (Dis)analogy', in L. Filipovic and K. Jaszczolt (eds), *Space and Time in Languages and Cultures*, 191–215, Amsterdam: John Benjamins.
Langacker, R.W. (2012b), 'Elliptic Coordination', *Cognitive Linguistics*, 23 (3): 555–99.
Matlock, T. (2004), 'Fictive Motion as Cognitive Simulation', *Memory & Cognition*, 32: 1389–400.
Mikkonen, K. (2007), 'The "Narrative Is Travel" Metaphor: Between Spatial Sequence and Open Consequence', *Narrative*, 15: 286–305.

'Mohsin Hamid on *Exit West* and the Politics of Fiction', February 2017. Available online: https://www.penguin.co.uk/articles/in-conversation/interviews/2017/feb/interview-mohsin-hamid-exit-west/, accessed (10 September 2018).

Noë, A. (2012), *Varieties of Presence*, Cambridge and London: Harvard University Press.

Nuttall, L. (2014), 'Constructing a Text World for *The Handmaid's Tale*', in C. Harrison, L. Nuttall, P. Stockwell and W. Yuan (eds), *Cognitive Grammar in Literature*, 83–99, Amsterdam: John Benjamins.

Polvinen, M. (2016), 'Enactive Perception and Fictional Worlds', in P. Garratt (ed.), *The Cognitive Humanities. Embodied Mind in Literature and Culture*, 19–34, London: Palgrave Macmillan.

Popova, Y. (2015), *Stories, Meaning, and Experience: Narrativity and Enaction*, London: Routledge.

Prince, G. (1987), *A Dictionary of Narratology*, Lincoln: University of Nebraska Press.

Rice, C. (2007), 'Fictive Motion and Perspectival Construal in the Lyric', in I. Jaén and J. J. Simon (eds), *Cognitive Literary Studies: Current Themes and New Directions*, 183–98, Austin: University of Texas Press.

Richardson, D. C. and T. Matlock (2007), 'The Integration of Figurative Language and Static Depictions: An Eye Movement Study of Fictive Motion', *Cognition*, 102: 129–38.

Ryan, M. (2014), 'Space', in P. Hühn et al. (eds), *The Living Handbook of Narratology*, Hamburg: Hamburg University. Available online: http://www.lhn.uni-hamburg.de/article/space, accessed (28 March 2019).

Shklovsky, V. ([1917] 1965), 'Art as Technique', in L.T. Lemon and M.J. Reis (eds), *Russian Formalist Criticism: Four Essays*, 3–24, Lincoln and London: University of Nebraska Press.

Simpson, P. (2014), 'Just What Is Narrative *Urgency*?' *Language and Literature*, 23 (1): 3–22.

Sullivan, K. and L.T. Bui (2016), 'With the Future Coming Up behind Them: Evidence That Time Approaches from behind in Vietnamese', *Cognitive Linguistics*, 27 (2): 205–33.

Sweetser, E. (1990), *From Etymology to Pragmatics. Metaphorical and Cultural Aspects of Semantic Structure*, Cambridge: Cambridge University Press.

Talmy, L. (2000), *Toward a Cognitive Semantics, Vol. 1: Concept Structuring Systems*, Cambridge: MIT Press.

Troscianko, E. (2010), 'Kafkaesque Worlds in Real Time', *Language and Literature*, 19 (2): 151–71.

Tsur, R. (1992), *Toward a Theory of Cognitive Poetics*, Amsterdam: North Holland.

Turner, M. (1996), *The Literary Mind: The Origins of Thought and Language*, New York and Oxford: Oxford University Press.

Varela, F.J., E. Thompson and E. Rosch (1991), *The Embodied Mind: Cognitive Science and Human Experience*, Cambridge: MIT Press.

Werth, P. (1999), *Text Worlds: Representing Conceptual Space in Discourse*, London: Longman.

Wittmann, M. (2016), *Felt Time: The Psychology of How We Perceive Time*, Cambridge, MA: MIT Press.

Wolf, W. (2007), 'Description as a Transmedial Mode of Representation: General Features and Possibilities of Realization in Painting, Fiction and Music', in W. Wolf and W. Bernhart (eds), *Description in Literature and Other Media*, 1–87, Amsterdam: Rodopi.

Yu, N. (2008), 'Metaphor from Body and Culture', in R.W. Gibbs, Jr. (ed.), *The Cambridge Handbook of Metaphor and Thought*, 247–61, Cambridge: Cambridge University Press.

Yuan, W. (2014), 'Fictive Motion in Wordsworthian Nature', in C. Harrison, L. Nuttall, P. Stockwell and W. Yuan (eds), *Cognitive Grammar in Literature*, 177–93, Amsterdam: John Benjamins.

Zwaan, R. (2008), 'Experiential Traces and Mental Simulations in Language Comprehension', in M. De Vega, A.M. Glenberg and A.C. Graesser (eds), *Symbols and Embodiment: Debates on Meaning and Cognition*, 165–80, Oxford and New York: Oxford University Press.

4

Construal, blending and metaphoric worlds in Francis Harvey's 'The Deaf Woman in the Glen'

Nigel McLoughlin

1. Introduction

In this chapter I develop a framework drawn from Cognitive Grammar and Conceptual Integration (Blending) Theory to analyse how complex metaphorical blends achieve their effects in Francis Harvey's poem 'The Deaf Woman in the Glen' (Harvey 2007: 35-6). The poem was selected as one of the one hundred best Irish poems of the twentieth century (Duffy and Dorgan 1999) but has received very little critical attention. Moya Cannon (2013: 1) described it as showing how a character can be 'so much part of the bone and nerve of their landscape'. The analysis that follows explores how the construal relations and blending structure in the poem achieve this effect.

In the following sections I outline in brief the main theoretical structures in Blending Theory, and the main concerns of construal in Cognitive Grammar, before exploring the attentional relationship between source and target spaces according to Langacker's (2008) approach and the arrangement suggested by Stockwell's (2009) ideas on attentional salience and focus. I integrate these positions with regard to the base function of metaphor, to bring the target into clearer focus by using the qualities of the source. The poem is presented in its entirety in advance of the analysis for ease of reference. After using the framework to analyse the poem, I discuss the major patterns that emerge in theoretical terms and conclude with an assessment of the usefulness of the approach and how the overall meaning that emerges through the close reading of the poem is supported, both with regard to Cannon's observation above, and in developing a fuller reading and interpretation of the poem.

2. Conceptual Blending Theory

Conceptual Blending Theory or Conceptual Integration Theory (hereafter Blending Theory) was developed in the 1990s by Fauconnier and Turner (1996, 1998, 2002) from previous work in Conceptual Metaphor Theory (Lakoff and Turner 1989) and Mental Spaces Theory (Fauconnier [1985] 1994) to explain the dynamics of meaning construction through conceptual integration processes. The basic structure of Blending Theory posits that four mental spaces are required for conceptual integration to occur. These are two 'input spaces' which represent the concepts to be combined and their internal structural and framing relationships, the 'generic space' which represents the abstract commonalities between the two input spaces, and the 'blend space' where these concepts are combined using framing and structural representations which may be derived from one or both of the input spaces (Fauconnier and Turner 2002: 40–2). This basic structure of four mental spaces can be expanded as necessary where additional input spaces are required, so there may be blends which can serve as further input spaces, or the blend may depend on roles, structures and frames that come from three or four separate input spaces (see for example Fauconnier and Turner's (2002: 292–5) discussion of Death as the Grim Reaper).

The common structure and roles within the composition of both input spaces are represented in the 'cross-space mapping' between them, and this mapping is used to project the correspondences into the blend space. In the blend space emergent structure arises from processes of composition, completion and elaboration (2002: 48). 'Composition' is the process of bringing together the separate elements in the blend such as the enactors present and the roles that they fill to create relationships between them that are not in the original input spaces. 'Completion' draws into the blend the organizing frames that structure the elements schematically in a context, thus providing a richer and more complete scenario, while 'Elaboration' allows the blend to 'run', including likely inferences and consequences of the new blended situation, creating further structure which may emerge in that process.

The transfer of framing structure during completion can operate in blends in four different ways (2002: 120–35). The first of these are 'simplex networks', where framing structure is transferred from one of the input spaces, while the other input space has no framing structure. For example, in the conceptualization of 'Richard II was the grandson of Edward III' one input space which is the familial relationship structure is transferred into the blend, while the other input space has only individuals who will fill slots in that familial relationship structure. The second type are 'mirror networks' where all of the spaces share the same organizing frame structure. Fauconnier and Turner (2002: 59–62) exemplify this type with the 'Debate with Kant' blend, where a modern philosopher's disagreements with Kantian philosophy can be conceptualized as positioning both protagonists in a contemporary arena where the debate can happen face to face. The debate frame is being used to structure all of the spaces. In the input spaces, there is no debate *per se*, but there are assertions and counter-assertions which can be taken as one side of a debate, and so when put together in the blend these claims and counter-claims create what we can construe as a debate. The third type is a 'single-scope blend'. In this type, while each input space has its own organizing frame, only one of those frames is transferred into the blend. Fauconnier and Turner's example (2002: 126–8) relates to business and boxing, where actions in the business world are described using the scenario of a boxing match and its concomitant parlance.

The final type of blend is a 'double-scope network'. As we might expect, here both input spaces possess their own frame structure, and both frame structures project, sometimes to differing degrees, to organize the framing structure of the blend space. Sometimes the frames in the input spaces clash when being projected into the blend, as can be seen in Fauconnier and Turner's (2002: 131–4) discussion of 'digging your own grave'. Here the blend takes structure from the death and burial frame, but since the act of digging a grave does not cause death, the cause-effect alignment comes from the 'unwitting failure' input (2002: 133). In this case, when the grave has been dug, the person who digs it unwittingly becomes the occupant, because they cannot extricate themselves.

The blend space is also a space of 'compression'. The relationships mapped between the input spaces, referred to as '"outer-space" links', are compressed in the blend into '"inner-space" relations' (2002: 92–3). The relationships being compressed are referred to as 'vital relations' (2002: 93). These are time, space, identity, role, representation, change, intentionality, analogy and disanalogy, part-whole relations and cause-effect relations. For instance, in Fauconnier and Turner's (2002: 63–5) 'Regatta' example, the temporal outer-space link is between Northern Light sailing in 1853 and Great American II sailing in 1993. This 140-year span is compressed in the blend to create a scenario where both vessels sail the same course at the same time in a race with the later vessel 4.5 days ahead. Similarly, if one were to say that 'The Pope was Italian for 500 years, until he became Polish in 1978', this compresses a series of individuals who have filled that role into a single person, a compression into uniqueness in the blend. The overall effect, in line with the stated goals of blending (see Fauconnier and Turner 2002: 346), is to create a blend where the vital relations are strengthened through being portrayed at 'human scale', by compressing 'what is diffuse', moving 'from many to one', to offer a 'global insight', or 'come up with a story'. This usually means that there will be scaling down from many to one for events and roles, and time scale is collapsed or foreshortened. But this is not always the case: a model of the solar system and a model of an atom can both be the same size.

Fauconnier and Turner (2002: 325–34) assert a number of principles for how blends are constrained and governed. The over-arching principle is the Integration Principle which states that the process should '[a]chieve an integrated blend' (2002: 328). The others suggest mechanisms by which this first principle can be achieved. The Topology Principle (2002: 327) says that the topology of inputs and outer-space links should be reflected by the topology of the inner-space relations of the blend. A Pattern Completion Principle (2002: 328) suggests that existing patterns can be used as further inputs and that completing frames should have relations capable of being compressed. The Maximization of Vital Relations Principle (2002: 330) suggests that vital relations be maximally represented in the blend and reflected in the outer-space relations between the inputs. Furthermore, these should be intensified where possible (Intensification of Vital Relations Principle). The Web Principle (2002: 331) suggests the unitary nature of the blended complex between input and blend spaces and that this should maintain the web of connections between input spaces and blend space in any manipulation of the blend. However, input spaces can also 'be modified by reverse mapping from the blend' (2002: 49) which can strengthen or complete the integrated complex. The Unpacking Principle (2002: 332) suggests that the entire network should be recoverable from the blend, and the Relevance Principle (2002: 333) suggests that elements in the blend should be relevant to, and capable of creating links to other spaces and enabling the blend to run, while at the same time, any important relations between the input spaces should demonstrate compressed versions in the blend. Sometimes there will be tension within the blend whereby all of the governing principles cannot be completely satisfied. In such cases there may be 'flaws in the blend' (2002: 342) which, in their example, lead to difficulties fully processing the fact that in order to eject a floppy disk, one used to have to drag it into the trash, which is a violation of the web principle.

3. Cognitive Grammar

The underlying principle of Langacker's approach in developing Cognitive Grammar (1987, 1991, 2008, 2009) is that 'lexicon and grammar form a gradation consisting solely in assemblies of symbolic structures' (2008: 5). As part of the process of creating meaning, assemblies of structures and the structures assembled are also capable of creating *construal*. Construal is seen as operating in four main ways: the first is *specificity*, which considers how detailed the presentation of the state of affairs is (2008: 55).

The second axis along which construal varies is that of *focus* (2008: 57–65). This derives from the selection of material with regard to what is presented as being foregrounded, what remains in the background and how components make up more complex structures. As components are assembled into more complex symbolic assemblies, *elaboration sites* (abbreviated to 'e-sites') in one component are filled by elements of the other component (2008: 198–9). This is suggestive of the cross-domain mapping process in blending. For example, the assembly 'tall building' consists of a component 'tall' that profiles a height above some notional norm, and an entity that fills out that profile as the *trajector* that possesses the quality. When these are brought together, the component 'building', which profiles a thing, attaches to the e-site for the trajector role that is unfilled in the 'tall' component. These elaboration sites are schematic elements and can be multiple in more complex expressions which have a number of components integrating into a larger assembly (2009: 12–17).

Focus also relies on the scope of what is presented. Here the important distinction is between immediate scope and maximal scope. If one refers to 'a knee', in immediate scope is 'the leg' because KNEE (small capitals are used to denote conceptual structures) relies on LEG as part of what defines it – it is the major joint in the leg. The maximal scope is the BODY, because the leg is also defined as part of a body. What is in immediate and maximal scope can change, so HOUSE is in immediate scope for 'front door', while STREET is in maximal scope, but STREET is in immediate scope for 'house', and TOWN is in maximal scope.

The third major constituent of construal is *prominence* (2008: 66–73). This specifies the entity in attentional prominence, or what is *profiled* against the *base* (2008: 66). For example, 'foot' shares the same immediate scope (LEG) as 'knee' does, and the same maximal scope (BODY), but the element which is profiled against that base is different. Likewise, 'leave' profiles the beginning of a process that can be brought into profile in its entirety by 'go'. One may think of this as an attentional 'window' (2008: 428) which captures a section of the entire process for direct focus. The second aspect of prominence is *trajector-landmark alignment* (2008: 66), where the trajector is the entity in primary focus, and the *landmark* is the entity in secondary focus. This is the difference between 'the picture is above the mantelpiece' and 'the mantelpiece is below the picture'. Both refer to the same spatial arrangement, but the item being specified in terms of its location, and therefore the primary focus, is different in each, while in each case the item being used as secondary focus is a landmark by which we can find the location of the thing sought. The second example seems odd, because it is more usual for the trajector to be the moveable item being located in terms of the fixed item, rather than vice-versa. These can be temporally located as well as physically located. The passive voice changes the trajector-landmark alignment of the active construction because the primary focus has moved. In the active, the trajector is usually the *agent*, and the landmark the *patient*, while the passive focuses on the effect on the patient thereby making it the primary focus (2009: 114).

The final aspect of construal is *perspective* (2008: 73–85), which examines the *viewing arrangement* (2008: 73) with respect to the relationship between who is doing the viewing and the thing being viewed. Related to this is the idea that an arrangement can be *subjectively* or *objectively* construed (2008: 77). This examines the asymmetry between what is being viewed and the viewers. When an entity is presented with no explicit mention of being viewed, it is said to be objectively construed. The viewers in this arrangement are therefore 'offstage' and outside of attention, and may not be considered at all; they are subjectively construed. In the temporal aspect of perspective, an arrangement can be said to be *summarily scanned* if it is conceptualized as a snapshot apprehended in its entirety (2008: 83), or *sequentially scanned* if the conceptual effect of the arrangement includes a series of different stages visualized over time throughout the process (2008: 111).

With regard to metaphor, Langacker says the following, which has direct implications for how the input spaces in metaphor work in attention as the blend space is formed:

> The source domain of a metaphor has a kind of precedence vis-à-vis the target domain. Usually more concrete or more directly anchored in bodily experience, the source domain provides a conceptual background in terms of which the target domain is viewed and understood. Viewing the target against this background results in a hybrid domain or blended space ... We can also say, with equal validity, that the source and target domains jointly constitute the background from which the blended conception emerges. Not only does the blend inherit selected features of both the source and the target but it is also foregrounded in the sense of being most directly coded linguistically.
>
> (Langacker 2008: 58)

In Langacker's description above, the prominence of the input spaces is not equal. The source space is relatively less prominent and defocused in comparison to the

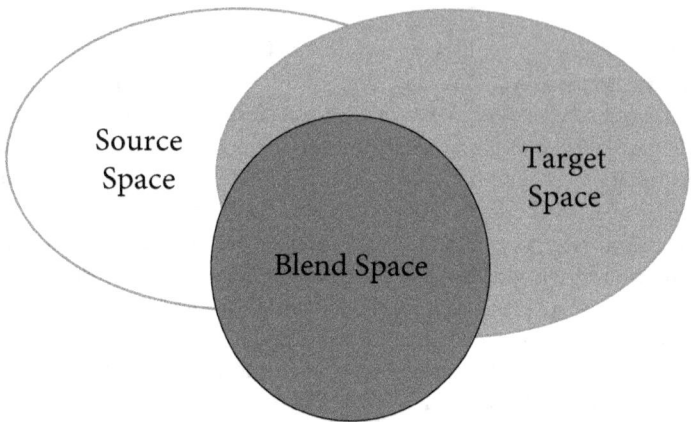

Figure 4.1 Expected attentional arrangement of spaces (derived from Langacker 2008: 58).

target space. The source space serves as background. The target space therefore acts like a trajector in relation to the landmark (source space). The blend space emerges as attentionally more prominent than both, and is therefore focused against a background of both target and source spaces. The generic space is not mentioned, and must therefore be completely backgrounded in attention, so as to be outside the viewing frame presented. Langacker's proposed arrangement may be diagrammatically represented as Figure 4.1. Because this is a dynamic operation that changes both conceptual focus and prominence over time, it may be helpful to track the attentional movements through Stockwell's model of attentional resonance.

Stockwell's (2009: 20–6) model was developed from ideas around attentional figures, and aims to elucidate the processes involved as literary figures enter attention, are maintained in attention, and lose attentional focus through 'occlusion' (2009: 22), attentional decay or 'neglect' (2009: 21), or attention 'shifts' (2009: 25). In Stockwell's terms, although the target is normally encountered first, it is usually attentionally the least salient, because it tends to be non-specific, inactive or abstract. The source of the metaphor on the other hand is usually specific, active and more detailed in its description. So, according to Stockwell's model the source space should attentionally occlude the target space, which would then become attentionally backgrounded. This is clearly in line with Blending Theory in the case where the frame and structure of the source space are being used to structure the blend. Although in double scope blends this arrangement may be a little more contentious, one would still expect the source space to be attentionally privileged because it is conceptually better specified through being more detailed and more conceptually accessible. It is less abstract than the target space generally is. The blend is usually cognitively foregrounded since it is cognitively more interesting because it is novel, or aesthetically distant from the norm (2009: 25). Therefore, the attentional arrangement described as Stockwell's model would imply is the arrangement in Figure 4.2:

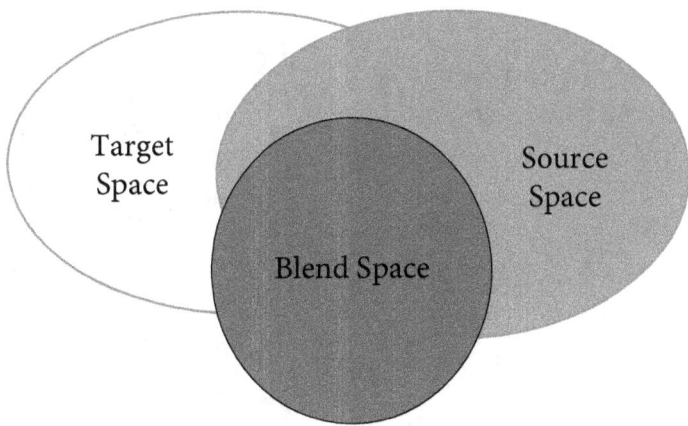

Figure 4.2 Expected attentional arrangement of spaces (derived from Stockwell 2009).

In his discussions of foregrounded and backgrounded text-worlds, Browse (2014, 2016) draws on Stockwell's attentional resonance model to describe similar arrangements, in relation to a resonant qualities inherent in both backgrounded underspecified target worlds, and foregrounded detailed source worlds of epistemically shared metaphor worlds in Ishiguro's *Never Let Me Go* (2014: 69–82), which leads him to posit 'conceptual oscillation' (81) between these spaces. His discussion of foregrounding in extended metaphor in discourse around the 2008 crash (2016: 18–37) also visualizes these spaces as 'more or less foregrounded by the linguistic forms of the metaphor' (2016: 25) leading to a refocussing of attention between them. However, because Browse is concerned with the toggling effect on text-worlds, he does not examine the effect of the blend.

Both the arrangements in Figures 4.1 (from Langacker's description) and 4.2 (from applying Stockwell's model) show that the blend space is the most attentionally salient, not least because it is conceptually emergent, and novel, but it also has an interesting effect on the target space. It has the potential, through the cross-space mappings that give rise to it, to activate potential e-sites. These arise from unfilled slots in the schematic structure being reverse mapped from the blend to the target space. These can in turn help create emergences, through the process of being filled, or elaborated, as the blend is run. This is the purpose of metaphor, of course, to allow us to better visualize the target, in more detail, and often to embody or physicalize it through bringing it within human scale.

Because the creation and running of a blend is an emergent process, I think that at different points in the process both the arrangements shown in Figures 4.1 and 4.2 are true. Initially, the target is attended, then the source space occludes it due to its more detailed, interesting and specific representation, then the blend emerges from the combination of the spaces, backgrounding both of them, which is the arrangement in Figure 4.2, and to borrow Browse's term, there may be 'conceptual oscillation' between them. The cross-space mapping and reverse mapping processes can also

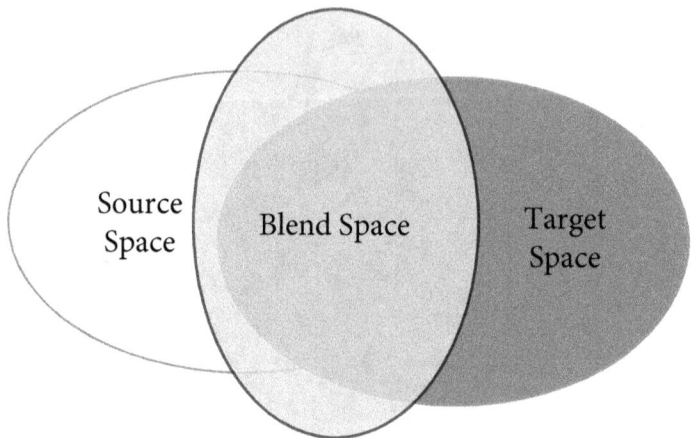

Figure 4.3 Representation of re-attending the target through the blend.

draw attention back to the target, and allow the target to come forward in attention again, giving an arrangement rather like the one Langacker suggests (see Figure 4.1). However, I would argue that the target is viewed through the blend, because the focus of the metaphor becomes the new way of seeing the target. Therefore, the attentional salience of both blend and target is high and the source is backgrounded. In Figure 4.3 below, I represent this as a transparency of the blended space.

In the Analysis section that follows, I will examine how construal, particularly trajector-landmark alignment, helps to structure the blends in the poem, presented in full below. I will show how cross-space mapping and reverse mapping from the blend to the target space create empty e-sites which can be filled from contextual knowledge to elaborate the blend. The analysis will also address how candidate meanings are activated in the target space for the submerged metaphors suggested by the blend, effectively refocussing the target through the lens of the blend.

4. Analysis

The Deaf Woman in the Glen

for Robert Bernen

> In her own silence
> in the silence
> of the glen she is
>
> a stone accepting
> rain, a thorn bent
> under the weight

of the wind, a heap
of bleached bones
in the gullet

of a dry burn. She has
hair whiter than
Scardan has in

winter; feldspar is
the pink grained
in the granite

of her cheeks; clouds
shadow the unplumbed
peat-brown

of her eyes and, perched
on this outcrop
of rock outside her

door and native
to her station as
the raven to its

crag, she is
locked in this
landscape's fierce

embrace as
the badger is whose
unappeasable jaws only

death unlocks from
the throat of rabbit
or rat and

moves, free yet
tethered, through
Time's inexorable weathers

in her solitary orbit
of the silent spaces
under the haunches

of her mountains and
the grey distended
udder of the sky.

Francis Harvey

The title of the poem activates a CONTAINMENT schema where the trajector (THE DEAF WOMAN) is contained in the landmark (THE GLEN). This also serves to ground the anaphoric references in the first stanza 'her' and 'she'. The first stanza also creates a viewing arrangement whereby the viewer visualizes a double containment. The woman is contained 'in her own silence' but this is similarly nested within 'the silence of the glen'. This also splits the space of silence into two *dominions*, or spaces of conceptual influence (Langacker 2008: 242), the silence belonging to the deaf woman and the silence belonging to the glen. These two spaces are brought into focus serially moving from the woman to the glen, which conceptually creates the effect of an outward zoom from the initial immediate scope of THE WOMAN'S SILENCE to the maximal scope of THE SILENCE OF THE GLEN. The effect of the title and first stanza can be diagrammatically represented as in Figure 4.4.

The idea of the woman being in possession of silence is reflective of the Irish construction used to express being in a state of silence – that it is rendered 'i do thost', literally 'in your silence' and the English syntax follows that Irish idea. This is neatly paralleled by 'the silence of the glen', through which the two dominions of silence are linguistically marked by possession.

'She is' at the end of the first stanza can be read as though the syntax has been reversed, or, if the stress is read as falling on 'is', as a bold, bare, statement of existence. However, it is attached to the complement clause that begins stanza two across the stanza break. This gives a short period, during which the reader must perform a reverse sweep saccade, which allows the initial interpretation to emerge, before the continuation of the complement, or more exactly three complement clauses, each of which serve as a metaphor and blend.

In the first of these blends, 'she is // a stone accepting rain', the target of the metaphor (SHE) is in an otherwise unstructured input space, while the source of the metaphor

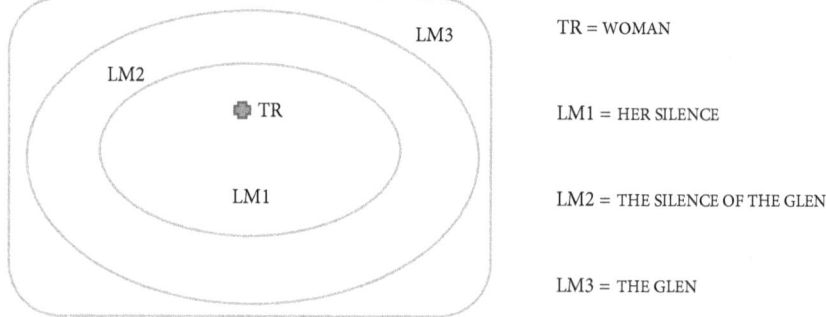

Figure 4.4 Conceptual arrangement of opening stanza.

exists in an input space which is structured by the relationship of the stone to rain. The stone fills the role of trajector because it is the most salient, while its landmark (RAIN) fulfils the role of thing being accepted. The progressive, while profiling a process, is summarily scanned because it makes prominent the ongoing process with the beginning and ending of the process outside the immediate scope (Langacker 2008: 65). This medial windowing creates the conceptual equivalent of a snapshot of the process at one point. Through the atemporal nature of the relationship as it is construed, this creates a sense of timelessness in the process. It can be taken to signify that the stone has been accepting rain throughout its existence and will continue to do so. Following Coulson's (2006: 190) example, the spaces can be represented in Table 4.1 below.

This is a simplex blend where an unstructured space provides an entity in the blend, and the structure for the blend comes entirely from the source space. However, the arrangement brought out through the cognitive grammar analysis demonstrates how the blend reflects back to the target space and elaborates it. This reverse mapping implies e-sites at the schematic level, which specify the action and landmark relationship in the target space, suggesting elements that are potentially there but unfilled. In other words, it offers a submerged metaphor and creates a need to fill in the metaphoric targets for the source RAIN, and the process that relates them. We can use contextual knowledge to fill the empty e-sites in the structure. So 'rain' may be read as being metaphorically equivalent to adversity (into each life a little rain must fall) and therefore this attaches a stoic quality to the woman who is able to weather adversity with the unchanging quality of stone. This compresses the atemporal relation between stone and rain, which may persist for millennia into a single human lifetime, thereby bringing the blend back to the human scale, and offering a restriction on the elements that may fill the e-sites in the target space to those that may operate in relation to the woman within her life.

This is followed by two further metaphors: the first of these is structured as a reduced relative clause in the passive: 'a thorn' (visualized from contextual knowledge to be a blackthorn or hawthorn tree) that is 'bent under the weight of the wind'. The passive reverses the normally expected trajector-landmark relationship, so that the thorn is more salient, because we focus on what has happened to it rather than the agent that caused it. The process is also construed from the point of completion, and this terminal windowing creates a *complex atemporal relation* (Langacker 2008: 117) which is summarily scanned and focused on the completed action. So, again in our blend, the trajector, process and landmark roles align to structure the blend. Here the

Table 4.1 Representation of Blended Elements in WOMAN IS STONE Metaphor

Generic Space	Input Space (Target)	Input Space (Source)	Blend Space	Emergence
Trajector	SHE	STONE	WOMAN AS STONE	WOMAN
Action	-	ACCEPTING	ACCEPTING	ACCEPTS/PERSISTS THROUGH
Landmark	-	RAIN	RAIN	ADVERSITY

metaphoric equivalence drawn between the woman and the thorn tree is back-filled by our contextual knowledge that thorn trees in exposed areas tend to bend away from the direction of the prevailing wind as they grow. This means that the branches also face away from the adverse prevailing conditions creating more weight on the leeward side. This in turn gives them a distinctive shape which is both a result of the conditions and an adaptation to them in order to survive. This creates an emergence from the blend, again by filling the e-sites in the target space derived from the cross-space mapping of the structure provided by the source space and reverse mapping from the blend as it is run. These relationships are mapped in Table 4.2.

Likewise, in the third metaphor the woman is 'a heap / of bleached bones / in the gullet // of a dry burn'. The HEAP OF BONES acts as trajector while THE GULLET OF THE BURN becomes the landmark within which they are positioned. This is an atemporal relation, and another summary scan, as it focuses on a state rather than a process. Again, the woman occupies the trajector role in the target input space and the structure from the source space is used to structure the blend. Similarly, by cross-space mapping, and reverse mapping, e-sites are activated in the target space as the blend is run. This again implies a metaphoric equivalent in the target space for the woman being 'in the gullet of a dry burn', allowing us to fill in a target for that submerged metaphor. Drawing on contextual knowledge that bones in a gullet signify that something has been eaten, we may fill in the relationship with an inference that the woman is being consumed by her environment and that this process is advanced. The dry burn may signify that the bones have died of thirst. This is complicated by the potential physical attribute of being skeletally thin in the woman's old age, so the overall image is that the ageing woman has been reduced to a skeletal version of her former self through the harshness of years spent in the glen, but that too is metaphorically consistent with a process of consumption in its broadest sense. These relationships are displayed in Table 4.3.

At this point in the poem the images begin to become more elaborate, and are sometimes suggestive of metaphor rather than being directly metaphoric in relation of target and source. In the first of these, 'she has // hair whiter than / Scardan has in // winter' a comparison is made where an equivalence is suggested between the woman and the Scardan waterfall on the attribute of whiteness of hair. Here we construe the 'hair' of the waterfall as the water that falls down it which is normally white from being

Table 4.2 Representation of Blended Elements in WOMAN IS THORN Metaphor

Generic Space	Input Space (Target)	Input Space (Source)	Blend Space	Emergence
Trajector	SHE	THORN	WOMAN AS TREE	WOMAN
Action	-	BENT	BENT	ADAPTED AND SHAPED
Landmark	-	WEIGHT OF WIND	WEIGHT OF WIND	TO AND BY HER HARSH ENVIRONMENT

Table 4.3 Representation of Blended Elements in the WOMAN IS BONES Metaphor

Generic Space	Input Space (Target)	Input Space (Source)	Blend Space	Emergence
Trajector	SHE	HEAP OF BLEACHED BONES	WOMAN AS SKELETAL REMAINS	WOMAN
State	-	IN	IN	CONSUMED
Landmark	-	THE GULLET OF A DRY BURN	THE GULLET OF A DRY BURN	ARID AND PREDATORY LANDSCAPE

aerated as it falls. This may appear to be particularly white in winter when the water flow increases and there may be frost around the course of the waterfall as well. This also reactivates the BLEACHED BONES from the previous metaphor through the quality of whiteness.

The metaphor that follows is more complex and is best shown in a spatial diagram (see Figure 4.5), as it requires several target and source spaces that themselves stand in relation to each other as they feed into the overall blend. Initially, the stanza causes a garden path effect in the reading, because the reduced relative clause 'the pink [that is] grained' can be initially misread as a compound adjective, particularly since the noun is formed from what is normally an adjective ('pink'). On first reading this may trip the reader into the question 'the pink-grained what?' Attentionally, it is quite striking; it slows the reader, and makes them re-read, drawing particular attention to the image. The alignment of the structure in the blend comes from the common trajector-landmark relationships in the source and target spaces of the blend. In one input space, designated the source space below, 'feldspar' (TR) is grained in 'the granite' (LM) and in the target space 'the pink' (TR) is grained in 'her cheeks' (LM). This produces a double scope blend where one input space is structured by a GEOLOGY frame, and the other by a HUMAN BODY frame.

However, in terms of trajector-landmark alignment, both input spaces have the same basic structure, and share the same relation between them based on the action of graining. Direct equivalence is therefore suggested between the two trajectors and the two landmarks. This provides an underpinning structure of conceptual relations in the blend that facilitates the structural mapping and makes explicit the compression from geological scale feldspar in granite to human scale pink in the cheek. This is further complicated in this case because it is suggestive of a zoom outwards from immediate to maximal scope – in the source space from THE PINK FLECKS IN THE CHEEK to THE WHOLE CHEEK, and in the target space from FELDSPAR to THE GRANITE material that contains it. This may direct us to a further conceptual zoom towards the maximal scope of GRANITE, because granite is part of, and is contained by, the rocky landscape of the glen, while the cheek being part of a woman may direct us to the further metaphoric association that THE WOMAN IS THE LANDSCAPE. This may be supported through reactivation of the previous metaphor of WOMAN AS STONE in stanza 1.

In Figure 4.5, the arrows signify this move from part to whole to the implied greater whole as part of the shift from immediate to maximal scope. The concepts activated in the greater whole are not explicitly present in the poem, and are shown as dashed boxes. These are emergences from the blend. The previous metaphor of WOMAN IS STONE is associatively reactivated through the equivalence between THE WOMAN'S CHEEK and GRANITE, and also supports the wider scope of the blend to include LANDSCAPE and BODY. This is still a compression whereby an entire landscape is reduced to human scale through this equivalence. The relationships between the input spaces may be mapped as in Figure 4.5.

The surface form of this metaphor suggests that the speaker of the poem is attempting to describe the feldspar in the granite in terms of the pink in the woman's cheek. This conforms to the usual 'Target is Source' form of metaphor. However, this metaphor is reversible in the sense that we have a clear idea of the nature of feldspar and granite which serves to provide us with a visual representation of the pink cheeks of the woman, so in that sense the FELDSPAR-GRANITE relation serves as the source to map the appearance of the pink cheeks of the woman. Therefore, I analyse this metaphor as being in the form 'Source is Target'. The 'Source is Target' version of the

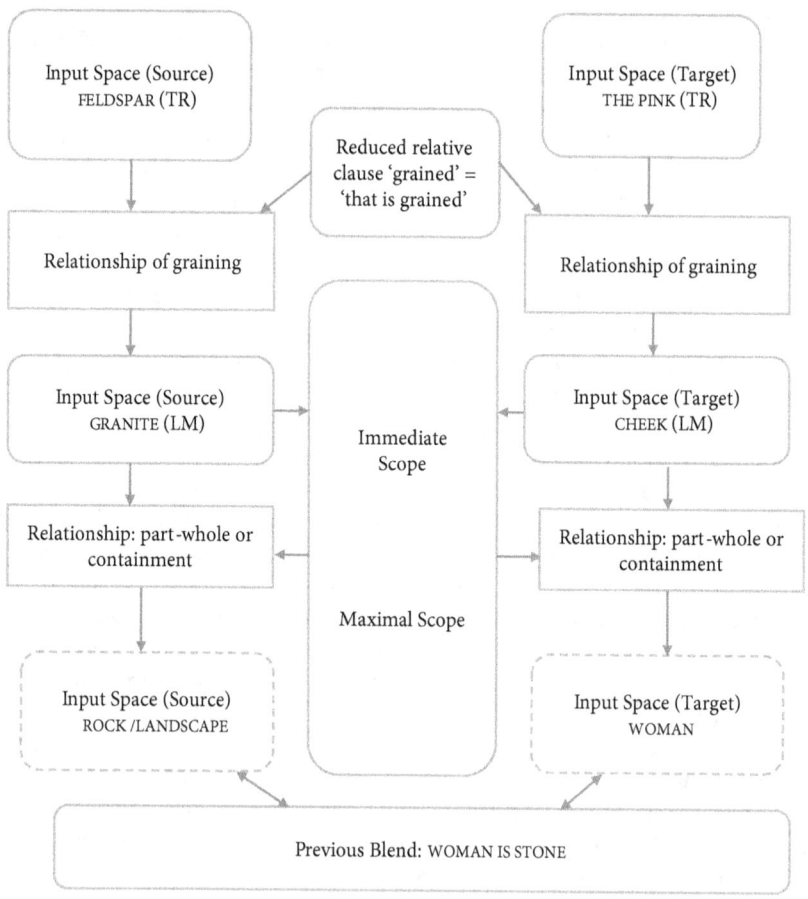

Figure 4.5 Map of input spaces into the WOMAN AS LANDSCAPE blend.

metaphor seems more prominent due to the more specific description of FELDSPAR and GRANITE in the source space being both more attentionally salient and having more potential to transfer those specific attributes onto the more schematic targets of PINK and CHEEK. This makes the pink more specific in terms of shade and texture, and lends the cheek a specific granite-like quality.

This is followed by an image 'clouds / shadow the unplumbed / peat-brown // of her eyes' in which equivalence is drawn between bog holes, suggested by the quality of being peat-brown and unplumbed, and her eyes. Actual clouds can shadow a bog, but what shadows her eyes are metaphorical clouds, in a positional sense, as in eyebrows, or in a clouding sense may be visualized as cataracts, which cloud and whiten the iris of the eye from their normal (in this case dark brown) colour. This reinforces the metaphor of the WOMAN AS LANDSCAPE through part-whole relations.

This is followed by another complex set of relations across the two stanzas beginning with 'and, perched'. Here a blend is constructed between the woman and a raven through the sense of belonging to their environment, grounded through the attribution of perching to the woman. This creates a set of inputs as shown in Figure 4.6.

In this blend the trajector-landmark alignment in the input spaces supports the blend through the shared action of perching on various landmarks. This in turn is supported by the explicit point of comparison regarding both the woman and the raven being equally 'native' and adapted to their 'station'. The adjectival nature of 'perched' evokes a birdlike quality in the woman, and draws her conceptually closer to the raven she is equivalent to. Because of this equivalency of action and equivalency of suitedness to the landscape, this allows a WOMAN IS RAVEN metaphor to emerge when

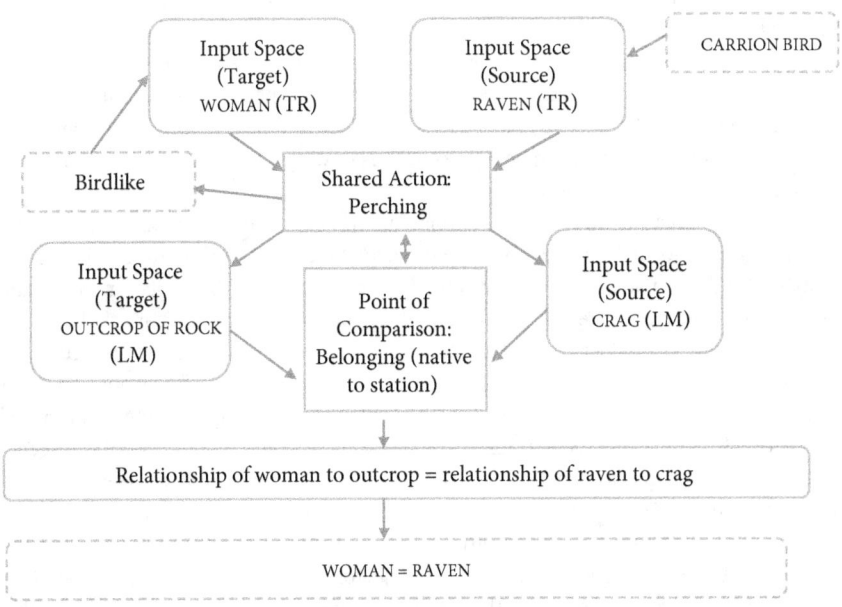

Figure 4.6 WOMAN AS RAVEN blend.

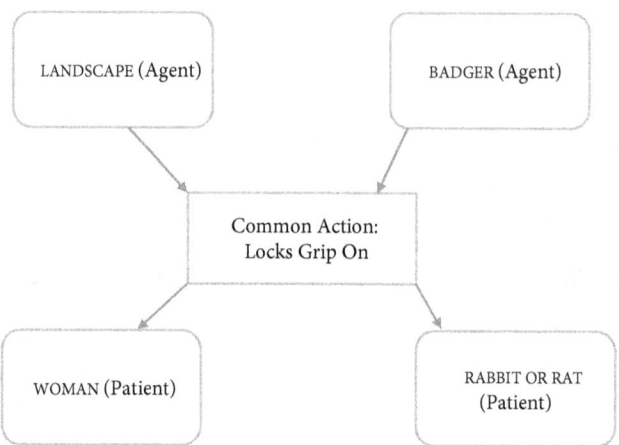

Figure 4.7 Agent-patient relationships in WOMAN IS BADGER metaphor.

the blend is run. The stanza break after 'outside her' is also evocative of a CONTAINMENT schema as it allows the meaning that she is surrounded by rock to fleetingly operate before the sense continues with regard to the rock's position 'outside her door'.

In the second half of the long sentence that forms the second half of the poem, the comparison moves to an image of the woman being 'locked' in the 'landscape's fierce embrace' in the same way a badger is trapped by the fact that its jaws lock on to its prey. In terms of the agent and patient roles in the comparison, the woman is in the patient role, receiving the 'embrace' of the landscape in the target space, while the badger is the agent of locking onto its prey in the source space. Therefore, the complex metaphor does not align, because the agents of the respective actions are LANDSCAPE and BADGER, which would suggest equivalence between them in their respective roles in the action. The *action chains* (Langacker 2008: 355–6) do align however, because the direction of energy transfer can be represented as flowing from agent to patient in both input spaces as shown in Figure 4.7.

However, because the woman's position is expressed through the passive construction 'is locked' this reverses the trajector-landmark alignment. In the passive construction, the patient is focused and therefore becomes the trajector, while the agent of the action occupies the landmark role as the secondary focal participant in the relation. While Langacker asserts that the agent is defocussed in passive constructions (2009: 14), here I consider it still a focal participant because it is foregrounded in an attentionally salient possessive construction, rather than being relegated into a 'by' clause or left out entirely. While this now has the effect that the direction of the agent-patient relationships is structurally misaligned in the input spaces, the trajector-landmark roles are aligned, so that when the input spaces are blended WOMAN and BADGER are aligned in the blend. One may deduce from this example that the structure of the input spaces in terms of trajector-landmark alignment is therefore more facilitatory for constructing the blend than the agent-patient relationships. This arrangement is mapped in Figure 4.8 below.

Francis Harvey's 'The Deaf Woman in the Glen' 67

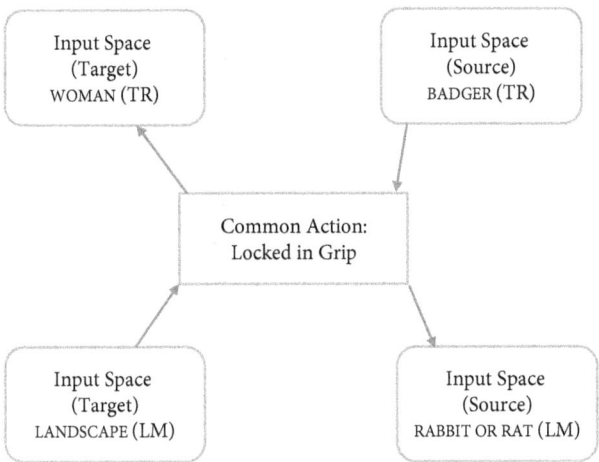

Figure 4.8 Trajector-landmark alignment of WOMAN IS BADGER metaphor.

The agent-patient relations and the action chains now run in opposite directions in the input spaces, and the action chains create tension in the blend because of this misalignment. The blend has elements of both action chains, with energy moving from landmark to trajector in the case of the woman, and from trajector to landmark in the case of the badger. This does not appear to preclude the blend from running however. In fact, the action chain structure from the source space affords the possibility of reading 'embrace' as being a mutual activity in the target space, transferring the agentive qualities of the BADGER back to the WOMAN in the target space through cross-space mapping. So not only is this woman locked in the landscape's embrace, but her grip on the land will also only be 'unlocked' by death. This creates the image of mutual possession, and mutual fierceness as an emergence from the blend.

In the closing part of the poem the woman is represented as being 'free yet / tethered' as a badger is free to move its body around a focal point where it is locked onto its prey, describing an arc, or a circular path around this focus, made explicit in the poem as being 'through / Time's inexorable weathers // in her solitary orbit'. This creates an image of a trajector in orbital movement, suggesting a zoom out to the planetary orbits, moving freely around their star, yet tethered to it by the force of gravity. The focus of the orbit is the landmark, 'silent places', which reactivates the conceptual arrangement of the start of the poem, where the woman is within her silence, and within a greater silence of the glen. The separation of these silences is maintained. This concentric arrangement now returns with the addition, as shown in Figure 4.9, of the orbit of the woman around both of these spaces. In effect, HER ORBIT now describes the boundary of what contains them, which is analogous to the boundary described by THE GLEN in the opening CONTAINMENT schema. This too creates a conceptual equivalence between HER ORBIT and THE GLEN. Emerging from this relationship is the image that she is both contained by and contains the glen. This also re-evokes the similar abstracted conceptual arrangement of mutual embrace developed through the WOMAN IS BADGER

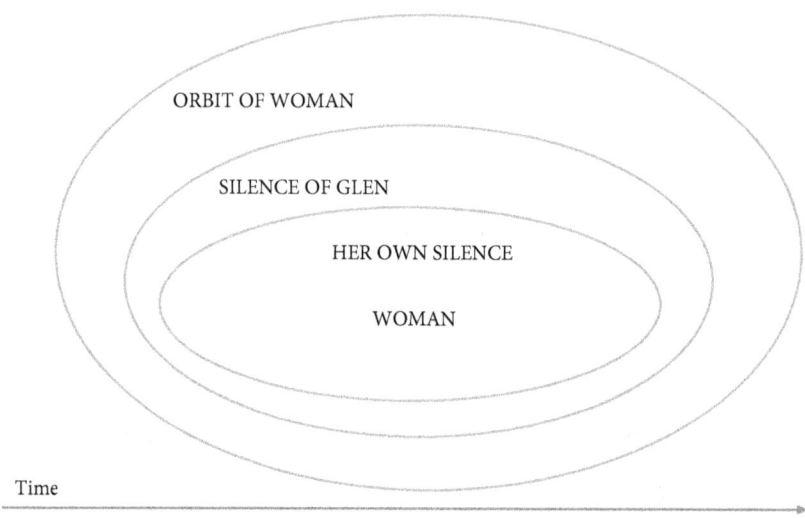

Figure 4.9 Conceptual arrangement of close of poem.

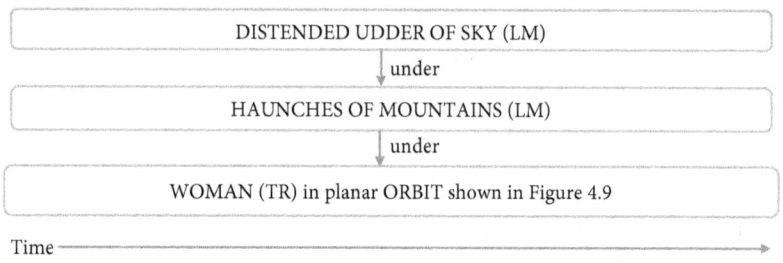

Figure 4.10 Vertical conceptual arrangement of final part of poem.

metaphor above, because being 'in an embrace' is also based upon a CONTAINMENT schema. This paradox also conceptually allows a physical representation of the relationship the poem has been working towards through its blends, the woman and the landscape are unified and inseparable, they belong to each other, and can each be visualized through the qualities and relations of the other.

While this conceptual arrangement is active, another set of images brings out trajector-landmark arrangements where the woman as trajector moves both around the landmark of 'silent places' in an orbital fashion and under the landmarks of 'haunches of her mountains' and the 'grey distended udder of the sky'. Conceptually we can evoke a planar orbit as shown in Figure 4.9 above, but the preposition 'under' works on a vertical axis, so the movement is represented both horizontally and vertically as in the arrangement in Figure 4.10.

All three of the spaces above are also themselves blend spaces – the uppermost from a blend of the distended udder and sky, which combines a source space representing a convex entity (UDDER) in metaphoric relation with SKY, which is normally viewed as concave. From this we may create a blend where the sky 'hangs down' on the mountains, perhaps as low cloud or mist, possibly activating 'milky' from the dominion of 'udder' when distended or full of milk. It may also evoke nourishment as a quality of the sky by spreading activation. Likewise, 'the haunches of her mountains' is also a blend, between the physical body part HAUNCHES and MOUNTAINS. Here the possessive may be taken to signify a part-whole relationship, whereby the mountains are equivalent to the haunches of the woman as landscape, evoked by extension of the other blends in the poem, or it may be read as possessive, so that the woman owns the mountains, which look like haunches. In both cases haunches are represented as forming part of the dominion of woman.

The entire poem works towards a mega-blend whereby THE WOMAN IS THE LANDSCAPE and vice-versa. The conceptual effect is to create a mental representation of the woman made up of various parts and qualities of landscape, in the same way Giuseppe Arcimboldo used fruit and vegetables to create the man in his painting *Vertumnus*. This 'Arcimboldo effect' is also conceptually reversible, so as the woman can be seen as being constructed of elements of landscape, so the landscape too takes on qualities associated with her, most explicitly with regard to 'hair' and 'haunches'. This can also be visualized in terms of Text World Theory (Werth 1999; Gavins 2007). Each of the metaphors creates a 'blended world' (Gavins 2007: 129), focalized by the speaker from an 'empty text world' (Lahey 2004: 26), representing 'epistemic modal-worlds' (Gavins 2007: 110) that signify the speaker's belief in the similarity or metaphoric equivalence expressed. Because they are projected by the focalizing consciousness into a world where the propositions are assumed to have truth value, these worlds themselves act as 'world-building elements' (Gavins 2007: 36) with the global text-world of the

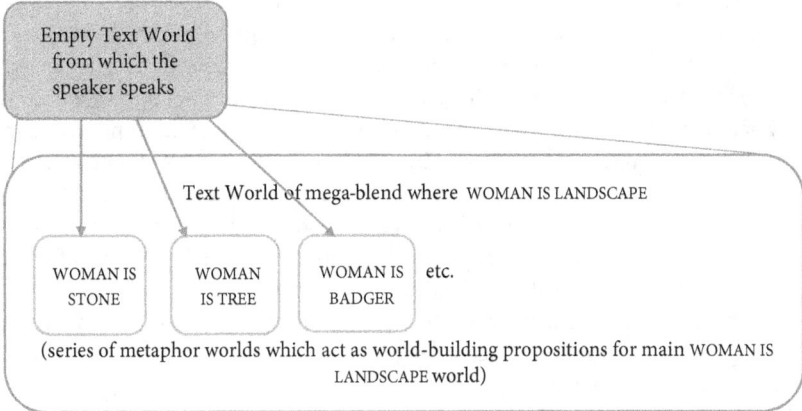

Figure 4.11 Text-world projections of blends as sub-worlds and world-building elements for mega-blend.

mega-blend inhabited by the WOMAN AS LANDSCAPE. These metaphoric blended worlds are true 'sub-worlds' (Werth 1999: 213; Gavins 2007: 52) because they are projected into the global text-world as world-building elements to build the larger conceptual state of affairs represented by the mega-blend, also being epistemically focalized by the speaker. This might be diagrammed as seen in Figure 4.11.

5. Discussion

The analysis of the poem demonstrates a number of common features that recur throughout the poem. First, the poem is based on a CONTAINMENT schema, which is initiated through the trajector-landmark arrangements of the first stanza, and returns to explicit attention in the final images of the poem. It is conceptually reactivated in attention at several points in the body of the poem through the repeated use of the preposition 'in' which takes as its landmark at various points, 'the gullet of a dry burn' that contains the bones, 'winter' which contains the image of the waterfall and 'granite' which contains the feldspar equated to the pink in her cheeks. The preposition 'outside' also helps re-evoke this conceptual arrangement through the positioning of the 'door' and by extension, through its immediate scope, the house, within the rocky landscape. The preposition 'in' also recurs in the latter part of the poem where the woman is 'in' the embrace of the landscape. The recurrence of this image keeps the CONTAINMENT schema active in attention as each blend in turn is focused upon.

Second, the poem is made up of only two sentences. In the first sentence a series of metaphors are presented in which the target space is highly schematic and under-specified, consisting only of the trajector 'she', while the source spaces are presented as relations in which a trajector is offered in direct equivalence to the 'she', but structured in relation to a landmark. The relation and landmark structure have no equivalence in the target spaces, and therefore serve to structure the blend space. The cross-space mapping brings across the instantiated structure from the source space. In this way we visualize the woman in the position of the trajector in the source space: a woman as stone accepting rain. Reverse mapping from the blend space to target space, which must be more schematic, therefore affords the potential to evoke the missing structure in the target space resulting in e-sites being created for the equivalent processes and entities. These e-sites must be elaborated from the reader's contextual knowledge and constrained by the abstracted structure mapped from the blend space. This has the effect of creating submerged metaphoric equivalents for both the process and non-aligned entities in the source space, which, because the reader is a co-participant in creating them, leads to the potential for many differently instantiated metaphoric readings. This affords a 'double-vision' (Gavins 2007: 152). For example, in the first metaphor the woman is conceptualized both as a stone accepting rain and, in my reading, as a stoic inhabitant resigned to what the harsh environment can throw at her.

The second sentence of the poem is more complex, and specific, in terms of the structures presented in both spaces. However, the source space is still richer in terms of the specificity of the images presented, while the target space remains comparatively schematic. The structures in both input spaces mirror each other in terms of trajector-landmark alignment and the abstract structure of profiled relations. This means that while the two input spaces are structured by different frames, the underpinning commonality in terms of trajector-landmark alignment creates equivalences across the blend through cross-space mapping. The alignment facilitates processing of which participants stand in metaphoric relation to their equivalents in the other input spaces. This is particularly demonstrated where agent-patient roles do not correspond in the input spaces, but the trajector-landmark alignment does. This alignment appears to be more critical than the agent-patient role alignment in allowing the correct cross-space mapping, and facilitates the running of the blend.

Sentence two is very long, leading to increased processing difficulty. However, this is mitigated by the fact that each blend creates an attentional window, attended serially with concomitant reduced focus on the macrostructure, in a similar fashion to how Langacker (2009: 338) suggests individual clauses are focused in preference to the entire sentence. The individual blends are profiled, becoming trajectors against the landmark of the wider sentence structure. This creates a piecemeal attentional focus on each blend in the sentence in serial arrangement, thereby helping to facilitate and foreground the 'Arcimboldo effect' through maintaining attentional focus on individual blends, and therefore features, of the whole. This focuses the woman as a collection of features that can be attended to in the same way that individual fruit or vegetables can be isolated from their positions in the anatomical arrangement that makes up the features of face and body in paintings like *Vertumnus*. The woman becomes a conceptually liminal and uncanny creature, focused more clearly as a collection of conceptual parts, while the whole is more schematically rendered. Part of this schematicity is supported by the 'open' targets of the metaphors in the first three to four stanzas of the poem. She is underspecified as woman, and conceptually specified only through landscape-based blends. This supports her conceptual representation as inseparable from the landscape.

6. Conclusion

From the study presented above, two main conclusions may be drawn. First, the application of Cognitive Grammar, in particular the analysis of construal, can be fruitfully combined with Blending Theory, as a stylistic framework for analysis. Analysis of the profile relations and windowing functions can elucidate the detail of how blends use these to facilitate cross-mapping and reverse mapping to structure blends. This analytical framework further demonstrates a mechanism, compatible with both theories, whereby features of the blend are mapped back on to the target space in order to refocus attention on the target space and to create a double vision. This shows how the target is re-visualized and seen differently through the blend. This is in line with the purpose of metaphor more broadly, which is to make the target of the metaphor more clearly apprehendable through the use of features of the source.

Second, the framework allows a principled, rigorous and replicable means for analysing poetic metaphor, and poems that create overarching conceptual effects, such as the 'Arcimboldo effect' described in the analysis of the poem, that are not otherwise approachable in detail through other cognitive stylistic means. The analysis of this poem has demonstrated how the woman is 'literally, bonded to' her land (Cannon 2007: 2). The poem creates the conceptual effect of the woman being only apprehendable through the landscape that she inhabits, and foregrounds her inherent liminality as an entity that is not apprehendable as a discrete being. She is conceptually inseparable from the landscape that both contains her and is contained by her.

References

Browse, S. (2014), 'Resonant Metaphor in Kazuo Ishiguro's *Never Let Me Go*', in C. Harrison, L. Nuttall, P. Stockwell and W. Yuan (eds), *Cognitive Grammar in Literature*, 69–82, Amsterdam: John Benjamins.

Browse, S. (2016), 'Revisiting Text World Theory and Extended Metaphor: Embedding and Foregrounding Extended Metaphors in the Text-Worlds of the 2008 Financial Crash', *Language and Literature*, 25 (1): 18–37.

Cannon, M. (2007), 'Introduction', in F. Harvey (ed.), *Collected Poems*, 1–3, Dublin: Dedalus Press.

Cannon, M. (2013), 'Introduction: Clarity with Mystery', in D. Potts (ed.), *In This Landscape's Fierce Embrace: The Poetry of Francis Harvey*, 1–3, Newcastle Upon Tyne: Cambridge Scholars Publishing.

Coulson, S. (2006), 'Conceptual Blending in Thought, Rhetoric, and Ideology', in G. Kristiansen, M. Achard, R. Dirven and F.J. Ruiz de Mendoza Ibáñez (eds), *Cognitive Linguistics: Current Applications and Future Perspectives*, 187–210, Berlin: Mouton de Gruyter.

Duffy, N. and T. Dorgan (1999), *Watching the River Flow: A Century in Irish Poetry*, Dublin: Poetry Ireland.

Fauconnier, G. ([1985] 1994), *Mental Spaces*, Cambridge: Cambridge University Press.

Fauconnier, G. and M. Turner (1996), 'Blending as a Central Process of Grammar', in A. Goldberg (ed.), *Conceptual Structure, Discourse, and Language*, 113–30, Stanford: CSLI Publications.

Fauconnier, G. and M. Turner (1998), 'Principles of Conceptual Integration', in J-P. Koenig (ed.), *Discourse and Cognition*, 269–83, Stanford: CSLI Publications.

Fauconnier, G. and M. Turner (2002), *The Way We Think: Conceptual Blending and the Mind's Hidden Complexities*, New York: Basic Books.

Gavins, J. (2007), *Text World Theory: An Introduction*, Edinburgh: Edinburgh University Press.

Harvey, F. (2007), 'The Deaf Woman in the Glen', in F. Harvey (ed.), *Collected Poems*, 35–6, Dublin: Dedalus Press.

Lahey, E. (2004), 'All the World's a Subworld: Direct Speech and Subworld Creation in "After" by Norman McCaig', *Nottingham Linguistic Circular*, 18: 21–8.

Lakoff, G. and M. Turner (1989), *More Than Cool Reason: A Field Guide to Poetic Metaphor*, Chicago: University of Chicago Press.

Langacker, R.W. (1987), *Foundations of Cognitive Grammar, Vol. 1: Theoretical Prerequisites*, Stanford: Stanford University Press.
Langacker, R.W. (1991), *Foundations of Cognitive Grammar, Vol. 2: Descriptive Application*, Stanford: Stanford University Press.
Langacker, R.W. (2008), *Cognitive Grammar: A Basic Introduction*, New York: Oxford University Press.
Langacker, R.W. (2009), *Investigations in Cognitive Grammar*, Berlin: Mouton De Gruyter.
Stockwell, P. (2009), *Texture: A Cognitive Aesthetics of Reading*, Edinburgh: Edinburgh University Press.
Werth, P. (1999), *Text Worlds: Representing Conceptual Space in Discourse*, London: Longman.

5

Guilty grammar: See-saw perspective and morality in a poem by E.E. Cummings

Louise Nuttall

1. Introduction

The following is a poem published in 1963 by the American poet E.E. Cummings:

> Me up at does
>
> out of the floor
> quietly Stare
>
> a poisoned mouse
>
> still who alive
>
> is asking What
> have i done that
>
> You wouldn't have
>
> (Cummings 2016: 828)

For stylisticians, the poetry of E.E. Cummings offers an interesting case study for showcasing the core theoretical and practical underpinnings of stylistics. Often chosen as examples for pedagogical demonstrations of stylistic analysis in student textbooks and teacher handbooks (e.g. Leech 1969; Short 1996; Simpson 2004; Jeffries and McIntyre 2010; McIntyre and Jeffries 2017), Cummings's poems exhibit a distinctive, unconventional style, the grammatical makeup of which contributes significantly to their interpretation. In explanations of its language, Cummings's poetry has seen the application of a number of frameworks, from transformational-generative grammar (Fairley 1975) and SPOCA grammar (Short 2005) to cognitive linguistic models of knowledge schemas and metaphor (Van Peer 1987; Burke 2007). For those working at the forefront of stylistics, Cummings's poetry has offered 'an ideal test case for the applicability of newly developed linguistic theories' (Van Peer 1987: 597).

While Cognitive Grammar is far from newly developed – set out in the work of Ronald Langacker (1987, 1991, 2008, 2009) and richly applied in discussions of style (Stockwell 2009; Harrison et al. 2014; Harrison 2017; Giovanelli and Harrison 2018; Nuttall 2018) – its adoption as a theoretical and methodological basis for textual analysis remains, at present, on the periphery of stylistics. By applying Cognitive Grammar to a short poem by Cummings, this chapter seeks to specify the central contribution that this framework offers stylistics as a basis for understanding textual interpretation.

The dominant approach in existing stylistic analyses of Cummings's poems is to look for patterns of foregrounded linguistic choices as a means of accounting for their interpretation. This approach typically identifies cohesive patterns of 'deviation' and 'parallelism' (see Short 1996: 36) across multiple language levels within individual poems (e.g. Burke 2007; McIntyre and Jeffries 2017) or across collections of his poems (e.g. Cureton 1979; Gómez-Jiménez 2017). This analytical approach offers a way in to Cummings's poems in the face of the non-standard structures and images that they typically present. Such an analysis of the poem '(Me up at does)', for example, might observe the prominent parallelisms in this poem's layout at the level of graphology: its mirrored top and bottom halves in the arrangement of its short stanzas, the capitalized pairs of words 'Me' and 'You'/'Stare' and 'What' that are aligned by this layout, and the contrasting deviation of the lower-case pronoun 'i'. Moving on to syntax, this analysis might further compare the top and bottom halves of the poem, the top half of which is highly non-standard, or deviant, in contrast to the more standard syntax of the mouse's question in the second half (see analysis in Section 3). Based on such co-existing patterns across the poem, and their 'congruence of foregrounding' at different linguistic levels (Leech 1985: 50), this kind of traditional stylistic analysis could support an interpretation of the poem as inviting us to compare the speaker and the mouse who speaks back at him, and as reflecting in its form the fundamental similarity – or mirror image – implied by its closing rhetorical question.

Although systematic and linguistically grounded, this method of decoding the poem one language level at a time is rather divorced from the actual experience of online interpretation. Noting a similar 'bottom-up' analytical method in existing work on Cummings's poetry in 1987, Van Peer argued:

> The central problem of interpretation, as illustrated in various approaches to his work, remains as interesting as it is unsolved. Part of the reason for this state of affairs, I should like to suggest, is that insufficient attention has been paid to the dynamic nature of literary understanding.
>
> (597)

Drawing on Schema Theory (Schank and Abelson 1977), Van Peer argued for an approach that recognizes the 'top-down' role of pre-existing knowledge structures during text processing and their complex two-way interaction with the linguistic cues foregrounded by the text. Some twenty years later, Burke (2007) proposed a similarly integrated 'cognitive-linguistic-stylistic' approach to a poem by Cummings, drawing on Cognitive Metaphor Theory (Lakoff and Johnson 1980) and related work on image schemas (Johnson 1987). Continuing this discussion a further ten years later, and benefiting from significant advances in cognitive linguistics in this time, this chapter models the dynamic process of interpretation using Cognitive Grammar.

2. Guilt, grammar and iconicity

One feature of '(Me up at does)' that this analysis seeks to explain is the interpretation of its syntax as reflecting a particular set of emotions in the speaker. In an analysis of this poem as part of an online course for students of stylistics, Short (2005) states:

> The disrupted grammar of the first part of the poem is effectively a kind of grammatical symbolism – it helps to represent the disjointed, uncomfortable effect on the persona of the poem, who has found the dying mouse (which he, presumably, has poisoned). This helps to remind us of the feelings of guilt we have if we kill pests in this way.

This interpretation is seen also in Fairley (1975: 90), who describes the 'jumbled' sequencing of words and phrases in the poem as suggesting the 'agitated condition of the speaker'. More broadly, the interpretation of Cummings's syntax as 'iconic', or as reflecting the worldview it describes, is one often found in response to Cummings's poetry in general (e.g. Cureton 1981). Considering another poem by Cummings, McIntyre and Jeffries (2017: 169) suggest that its deviant syntax can be seen to reflect 'a version of our thought processes when we are experiencing extremes of emotion'. This effect is best described as 'diagrammatic iconicity', or a perceived, indirect parallel between an aspect of conceptual structure (e.g. knowledge or experience) and the formal structure (e.g. the sequence) of the language which represents it (Fischer 2014: 382; see also Nänny and Fischer 1999). This kind of interpretative parallel is often identified in literary texts, in which the ability of linguistic structure to reflect the emotions and thought processes of a writer/speaker as a form of 'experiential iconicity' (Enkvist 1981; Tabakowska 1999) is associated with a range of emotional and aesthetic effects (Müller 1999; Burke 2001; Jeffries 2010; Fischer 2014). For Leech and Short (2007: 189), such iconicity is said to produce an emotive 'enactment' of the reflected experiences in readers of the text. However, the processing underpinning this perceived comparison and its emotive impact on a reader are less clearly delineated in these accounts (see also Burke 2001; Freeman 2009).

In his analysis of '(Me up at does)' Short (2005) argues that its 'force' arises from the perceived disruption to a grammatically normal version of its syntax, which he re-arranges, or 'normalis[es]', like so:

> A poisoned mouse who, still alive, is asking 'What have I done that you wouldn't have?' stares quietly up at me.[1]

While making no direct claims about our online processing of the poem, Short does suggest that we 'to some degree "re-cast"' its grammar in 'our struggle to come to terms with it' (2005). Comparably, describing the puzzle-like nature of Cummings's poems more broadly, Runcie (2013) describes 'the tiny thrill of realising your own language is leading you up the garden path [...] You just have to piece each bit together as it arrives, ending up with a complete, pristine thought that you've helped to make'. Finally, in a pedagogical context, McIntyre and Jeffries (2017) recommend that students rewrite the non-standard structures of the poem they analyse as a means of interpreting its grammar and its relation to meaning. It is only by revealing fully 'the nature of the non-standardness', they argue, that its effects can be understood (2017: 168–9).

In the analysis that follows, I use Cognitive Grammar as a means of explaining the foregrounded language of Cummings's poem and its iconic interpretation by readers. As I shall argue, this framework not only offers a means of accounting for perceived degrees of 'non-standardness' in embodied terms, but also models the dynamic way in which such unconventional structures are processed, or 'piece[d] together' (Runcie 2013), online during reading. It is the distinctive nature of this processing, specifically the poem's manipulation of cognitive mechanisms of attention, scanning and simulation, that I argue results in an enactment of the discomfort and guilt that it expresses.

3. Processing unconventional forms

Applying Cognitive Grammar, deviant and normalized, standard and nonstandard forms all represent different *construals*, or alternative representations of the same experience (Langacker 2008: 43). In this model, the perceived well-formedness and conventionality of a linguistic expression are understood in terms of the extent to which its construal is canonical, or prototypical, in relation to our embodied experiences as human beings. One dimension of construal relevant to this poem is *prominence*: the choice of which entity to pay most attention to as part of a description, or the arrangement of its conceptualization in terms of foreground and background (2008: 66). Any linguistic expression describing the relationship between two or more entities is said to impose a *trajector-landmark alignment* upon them, with one entity – the *trajector* – given primary focal prominence as 'the entity construed as being located, evaluated, or described' (2008: 71), and the other construed as secondary – the *landmark*. The Cognitive Grammar concept of a prominent trajector explains the meaningful difference in expressions such as (i) and (ii):

(i) The cheese (*tr*) on the counter (*lm*)
(ii) The counter (*tr*) under the cheese (*lm*)

In clauses, the trajector is typically the grammatical subject. By grounding our understanding of the subject in embodied processes of attention, Cognitive Grammar provides an explanation for the conventional ordering of syntactic components in languages, and the types of entities which typically occupy such positions. Just as our attention typically lands first on the most prominent entity when physically viewing a scene, a movement from trajector to landmark, e.g. subject–verb–object in English, is said to reflect a 'natural path of mental access' when processing sentences (2008: 372). In addition, the features of entities which stand out attentionally in perception can be seen to motivate our choice of subject as part of a linguistic construal. In perception, these features include animacy or movement, human or human-like qualities, definition or delineation, as well as other salient qualities of 'figures' such as size, colour and volume (Stockwell 2002: 15; Wagemans et al. 2012). Applied to a linguistic construal, in simplified terms following Langacker (1991: 306–9), a prototypical subject – a prominent trajector – might be seen therefore to be the entity which is most *agentive, empathetically recognizable, definite* and (more broadly) *figural*, as illustrated by the following list:

1) *agency*
(active or energetic participants (agents) are better subjects than passive recipients of action (patients))
       (a) The dog chased the ball
       (a') The ball was chased by the dog

2) *empathetic recognizability*
(entities that are like us – human or human-like – are better subjects than those that are not, e.g. animals, objects or abstractions)
       (b) I am in love
       (b') Love is all around me

3) *definiteness*
(specific, definite referents are better subjects than non-specific, indefinite ones)
       (c) Jacob is a baby
       (c') A baby is Jacob

4) *figural qualities*
(entities that are brighter, bigger, louder etc. are better subjects than those that are not)
       (d) The fire is on the horizon
       (d') The horizon is under the fire
       (see also Stockwell 2009: 25 for an extended list of figural qualities)

Crucially, these features are situational 'motivations' (Langacker 2008: 368) as opposed to criteria for the choice of subject. Sentences (a') to (d') are not ungrammatical, but rather less conventional and will seem subtly deviant to speakers of English.[2] These motivations can be ignored to create unprototypical trajectors, the results of which may be poetic, as in (b') – a lyric from the 1995 hit song 'Love Is All Around' by Wet Wet Wet – or defamiliarizing, as in (d'). As a further example of the latter, the defamiliarizing quality of (e') below may be attributed to its choice of the less agentive, empathetically recognizable, definite and figural entity as trajector:

>   (e') <u>Cheese</u> behind the screaming child

In some situations, where multiple entities are similar in terms of these features, there may be no inherent motivation to attend to either as primary focal participant over the other.

>   (f) <u>The cheddar</u> is next to the gouda
>   (f') <u>The gouda</u> is next to the cheddar

In this last example, the choice of subject depends entirely on the cheese of interest to the speaker. Ultimately, the choice of which entity to cast as trajector is always a subjective matter of construal, that is, dependant on the communicative and conceptual goals of a speaker/writer, and one which can be manipulated to achieve a range of stylistic effects.

Applied to '(Me up at does)' this model can begin to explain the nature of its syntactic deviation in the first half of the poem. By beginning with 'Me', our attention is invited to land first on the implied speaker of the poem as the trajector and starting point for our processing of this scene. With no verb to indicate a participant role in a process here, 'Me''s agency is left temporarily unclear. Meanwhile, this 'Me' is empathetically recognizable as an assumed human speaker, but not particularly definite or figural in other senses since we are given no indication of its referent beyond the implied voice of E.E. Cummings himself. On reaching the verb 'Stare', the agency of 'Me' now needs to be resolved. While some readers may interpret 'Me' as the agent of this action, the preposition 'up' together with the object-form of the pronoun (as opposed to 'I') strongly invites a reading of the human 'Me' as the patient, or passive recipient of another participant's action.

On reaching the other profiled participant in this relationship – 'a poisoned mouse', our attention is invited to shift to this participant, whose isolated presentation in a separate one-line stanza causes it to stand out as a figure graphologically, and whose agency, empathetic recognizability and definiteness also increase as the poem continues. The mouse's agentive role in 'Stare' is further developed by 'asking'; its empathetic recognizability increases due to its personification by 'who' and its apparent ability to speak, while its definiteness increases through its pre- and post-modification 'poisoned' and 'still who alive', despite the initial indefinite article.

From 'a poisoned mouse' onwards, therefore, readers must reassess the trajector/landmark alignment of this sentence's construal. Contrary to its word order, we are invited to recognize 'a poisoned mouse' as the primary focal participant (or trajector) in its conceptualization, with 'Me' as the landmark. For Langacker (2008: 80), this reassessment brought about by the unconventional word order involves a process of *backtracking* to repair our conceptualization of this scene. Since the 'natural path' of mental access to a conceived situation prototypically begins with the trajector, the delayed subject of this poem requires that readers 'undo[…] or redo[…] what has already been accomplished' (2008: 490) to restore this path in their attentional scanning of the situation. In this respect, a Cognitive Grammar analysis would seem to match, and describe more closely, the nature of the 're-cast[ing]' (Short 2005) or 'piece[ing] together' (Runcie 2013) that is arguably undertaken by readers of this poem.

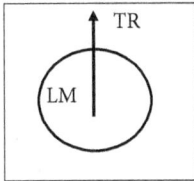

Figure 5.1 Image schema activated for prepositional phrase 'up ... out of' (based on Evans and Green 2006: 182).

Other aspects of the poem serve to disrupt processing in different ways. Together, the prepositions 'up' and 'out of' can be said in cognitive linguistic terms to activate an underlying 'image schema', or basic cognitive model, of the spatial movement they represent (Johnson 1987; Evans and Green 2006: 179). This image schema consists of an abstract entity (the trajector) moving in relation to a container (the landmark) and can be represented as in Figure 5.1.

Arising through our sensory experiences of containment and movement since infancy, this knowledge schema can be said to include a sense of the physical qualities of the containers to which the movement 'out of' typically applies: such as being permeable, transparent or containing an exit point. These embodied norms offer an explanation for the strangeness of the construction 'out of the floor', which in this context seems supernatural or ghostly, suggesting the mouse's line of sight is somehow passing through a solid object.

In addition, related work in cognitive linguistics suggests that our comprehension of language involves a *mental simulation* of the experiences described (Barsalou 1999, 2009; Langacker 2008: 536). Specifically, linguistic descriptions of movement have been shown to re-activate parts of the motor cortex associated with the actual bodily movements (Hauk et al. 2004) and to create difficulty in simultaneously carrying out those movements in a conflicting direction (Glenberg and Kaschak 2002; Fischer and Zwaan 2006). This has been seen to apply even where the described movement is 'fictive', as in the movement along a line of sight associated with vision, e.g. staring (Matlock 2004; see also Talmy 2000). Significantly for the present analysis, Richardson and Matlock (2007) found that comprehension of such 'fictive motion' sentences affected participants' physical eye movements when examining a path. Applied to this poem and its vertical layout, the movement being described by this prepositional construction might be seen to invite readers to simulate this upwards movement during its processing, and perhaps even re-read it physically, up the page. By directing attention back upwards to 'Me', this construction conflicts with the downwards scanning invited by the poem's graphology, instead contributing to the backtracking invited by its syntax.

Other constructions in the poem contribute to the poem's upwards/backwards tugging of attention. For some readers, the word 'Stare', made figural by its capitalization and the unconventional synaesthesia of its modification by 'quietly', may loosely activate the meaning of its homophone 'stair', primed by previous conceptualization of 'out of the floor' and the poem's stair-like layout. Similarly, the unconventional word order of 'still who alive' invites a momentary activation of the alternative meaning of 'still' as an adjective (meaning stationary), with its associations of death primed by 'poisoned', before inviting readers to backtrack and reinterpret it as modifying 'alive'. Applying Cognitive Grammar, the multiple meanings activated by such instances of semantic/syntactic deviation and their role in interpretation can be modelled in terms of their effects for readers' dynamic activation and reactivation of potential meanings along a path of scanning, or *reference point chain*, during reading (Langacker 2008: 83).

Finally, the mouse's final question, though standard or conventional syntactically speaking, further complicates our processing of this situation. Unlike the first half of the poem, the word order here conforms to a natural path of mental access, with our attention invited to land first on 'i', who as a speaking/questioning mouse is agentive, empathetically recognizable and now better delineated than the unspecified human listener, and hence a prototypical choice of trajector. As in the first half of the poem, however, our attention as readers is once again invited to shift to the other participant, 'You', the capitalization and graphological separation of which (at the start of an isolated line/stanza) lend it a figural quality in contrast to the lower case, mid-line 'i'. The lack of punctuation here also causes this final line to read like a statement as opposed to a question; the direct address of the second person 'You' implicating us personally (and definitely) as readers, and, through negation, leading us to conceptualize the very actions and agency it denies. Through this construal, then, this 'You' participant can be seen to draw attention as a prominent trajector, this time in a process of doing that is left implicit in the closing line.

Overall then, it is possible to identify a basic pattern in our processing of this poem and the profiled relationship at its core. Parallel to the mirrored layout of the top and bottom halves of the poem, a mirroring can be seen in our attention to the situation it describes. Beginning with attention to the human speaker of the poem, our attention as readers is drawn to the mouse buried at its centre, before ultimately being drawn back to the human speaker/hearer with whom we are invited to identify. Through the choices made in their linguistic construal, and the backtracking, simulation and attentional shifts they invite, these two entities are engaged in a struggle for prominence as part of our conceptualization.

According to Runcie (2013), Cummings's poems reveal the influence of riddles or jokes on his work, specifically 'their tendency to interpret something one way and then change direction'. An analysis of this poem using Cognitive Grammar has explained the linguistic choices which encourage this change of direction, and has modelled the cognitive mechanisms involved in its experience during reading.

4. See-saw perspective

Another way of describing this processing using Cognitive Grammar is in terms of *perspective*. As a further dimension of construal, perspective concerns the vantage point from which a situation is conceived, and the degree to which the conceptualizer is attended to as part of this conceptualization. To describe the latter, Langacker distinguishes between *subjective* and *objective* construal (2008: 77). To take this poem as an example, a situation such as a man watching a dying mouse could be

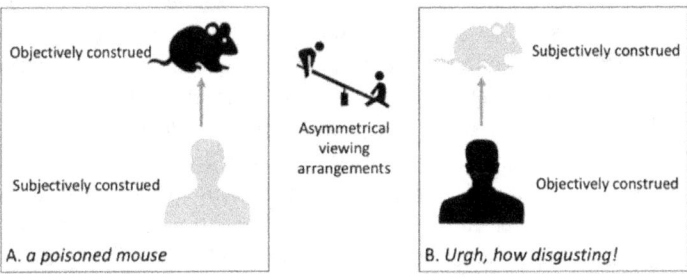

Figure 5.2 Objective and subjective construal in asymmetrical viewing arrangements.

linguistically construed in two alternative ways (see Figure 5.2). First, attention may be focused entirely upon the mouse with minimal indication of the position, attitude or identity of the viewer (e.g. 'a poisoned mouse'). In this case, we can describe the mouse as objectively construed and the man as subjectively construed. Alternatively, attention may instead be focused entirely on the viewer and their vantage point (e.g. 'Urgh, how disgusting!'). In this case, the man is now objectively construed (the focus of our attention), and the mouse is subjectively construed in the background.

For shorthand, in stylistics, we can refer collectively to the first arrangement (A in Figure 5.2) as an 'objective construal' of the situation overall, and the second (B in Figure 5.2) as a 'subjective construal' (see also Giovanelli and Harrison, this volume). These two construals, or *viewing arrangements*, reflect two ends of a cline and the maximum degree of 'asymmetry' between the viewer and the viewed in terms of attention (Langacker 2008: 77). However, these asymmetrical arrangements are the exception rather than the norm. Language users typically divide attention to some extent as part of a construal using *grounding elements* (2008: 260) such as deixis and modality to indicate the perspective of a conceptualizer alongside description of what is conceived (e.g. 'that disgusting poisoned mouse is just beneath my feet'). The way in which attention is divided in these – more common – cases of construal is described in Cognitive Grammar in terms of a competition between the two, whereby the more attention is given to one entity (e.g. the viewer) the less attention can be given to the other (e.g. the viewed). While Cognitive Grammar claims to align with no particular psychological theory of attention (Langacker 1987: 115), this model of attention as a 'limited resource' which must be 'allocated' or shared between entities (Langacker 2008: 365; see also work in psychology by Kahneman 1973; Navon and Gopher 1979; Styles 2006: 153–91) can be seen to underpin its accounts of prominence and perspective:

> When one participant is left unspecified, the other becomes more salient just through the absence of competition. On the other hand, augmenting the salience of one participant diminishes that of others (in relative terms) even when they are fully specified.
>
> (Langacker 2008: 384)

Essentially, in this model, our attention to the different entities construed as part of a situation is a bit like a see-saw; as attention to one goes up, the other goes down. What this means theoretically, of course, is that there must be instances in which attention is divided more equally between the two, in a symmetrical viewing arrangement.

This would seem to be the case in Cummings's poem. While the scene we are being invited to conceptualize here involves a subjectively construed human ('Me') looking down at an objectively construed mouse ('a poisoned mouse'), the grammar of the poem simultaneously invites an objective construal of this persona ('You') from the subjective vantage point of the mouse beneath them ('i'). Essentially, we are led to place ourselves in the shoes of both human and mouse while reading. The combination of both perspectives in the poem, enacted through the conflicting upwards and downwards scanning invited in readers, can be seen to add up to a division of attention in two opposing directions as part of its conceptualization. Alongside the backtracking encouraged by the unconventional word order, the invitation to divide our attention between these two perspectives is another potential source of difficulty for readers of this puzzle-like poem.

5. Mind-modelling and moral judgement

So far, this analysis has offered an account of readers' dynamic online interpretation of this poem and the unconventional structures it presents. While admittedly lengthy relative to the short poem in question, by modelling the processes that take place in the mind of a reader step by step, this analysis offers a basis for explaining the iconic interpretation of the poem and its emotional impact.

By inviting readers to consider two perspectives side by side during reading, the poem can be said to encourage readers to 'mind-model' (Stockwell 2009; Stockwell and Mahlberg 2015) both the speaker and the mouse. Drawing on the general cognitive capacity known as 'perspective-taking', 'mentalizing' or 'theory of mind' (Baron-Cohen et al. 1985; Malle and Hodges 2005; see also 'mind attribution' in Nuttall 2018), the presentation of these points of view invites us to attribute rich mental states to these characters that go beyond those explicitly indicated by the text itself. This is reflected in interpretations of the poem that describe both an identification with the speaker and sympathy for the mouse, such as that of Short (2005; Section 2), and that below:

> Yeah, the poor mouse just wanted to eat, yet he is murdered by 'you'. Makes you stop and think about the carelessness we use in throwing around sanctity for life. This animal can live b/c [sic] it is cute, this one dies b/c [sic] it is annoying, or it is tasty.
>
> (Lo Justin 2004)

Furthermore, drawing on our Cognitive Grammar analysis, the specific way in which readers are invited to process these competing perspectives, by shifting between them attentionally through scanning, backtracking and mental simulation, might be seen to reflect an agitated back-and-forth in the thought processes of the (human) speaker in the poem as they experience guilt and regret. In this way, the processing initiated by the poem's construal can be described as a form of experiential iconicity, via 'psychological sequencing', where 'textual order reflects the order in which impressions occur in the mind' (Leech and Short 2007: 190).

However, readers of this poem often interpret it as reflecting more than just one individual's experience, interpreting it as an allegory, applicable to a range of moral situations in society. The following responses, taken from an online blog post and sample essay, illustrate some of the varied and rich interpretations of this poem in these terms:

> The poisoned mouse is a representation of a person, race, or someone from the lower status of society who is ostracized and experiencing diminution. I may then infer that the mouse in the poem is a somewhat illiterate person who couldn't express himself literally due to limitations imposed on him by lack of education.
> (Alforte 2008)

> The inner struggle within the narrator has already been explained. […] Not only is the mouse confused as to what it has done so wrong that the narrator himself would not do, but the mouse could also be beginning a pattern of blaming this on himself and developing self-esteem issues that have been building up as a result of continued prejudice against the "mouse", or whoever this mouse may be representing
> (Culp 2009)

In such interpretations, the poem's iconicity and the emotions it invites us to enact belong to more than just the poetic speaker and the specific situation presented, instead representing broader, more abstract acts of moral judgement.

Building on these responses, this analysis proposes that the poem's impact arises from its iconic representation of moral judgement itself. The role of moral judgements during reading and our wider ethical interpretation of texts have been approached in a number of ways in stylistics and narratology. Work in rhetorical narratology by Phelan (2005: 23, 2007) described ethical interpretation as involving a 'dynamic interaction' between the 'positions' adopted by a reader in relation to the different author, narrator and character perspectives construed within a narrative. Building on this earlier work in cognitive stylistic terms, Stockwell (2009: 149) and Whiteley (2014: 400) have used Text World Theory to model ethical responses to texts in terms of 'projections' or deictic shifts by readers into the perspectives of different textual 'enactors' (see also Nuttall 2017). Common to these approaches is a sense of the multiple perspectives which must be recognized and responded to in the formation of an overall ethical response.

This understanding of ethical interpretation fits with recent work on morality in the cognitive sciences. A growing number of empirical studies have revealed a close relationship between our attribution of minds and specific mental states to others, and our moral judgement of them as individuals. Perception of an individual as possessing certain mental capacities (e.g. intentions, thoughts and beliefs) correlates with judgements of their actions as morally right or wrong (e.g. Gray et al. 2007; Killen et al. 2011). On the other hand, research into moral disengagement shows that people often fail to ascribe mental states to victims in order to justify acts of wrongdoing towards them, or to reduce associated feelings of guilt (e.g. Osofsky et al. 2005; Castano et al. 2006; Esses et al. 2008). Based on these and other findings, Gray et al. (2012) propose the existence of a basic cognitive template for judging moral situations:

> We suggest that the human mind acts as Picasso did, abstracting out the key elements from various moral transgressions to create a cognitive template. These key elements are intention and pain (i.e. intentional harm) and the essence of moral judgement is the perception of two complementary minds – a dyad of an intentional *moral agent* and a suffering *moral patient*.
>
> (2012: 101, original emphasis)

Fundamentally comprising a conceptualization of two minds in relation to one another (that of an agent and a patient), this basic structure or 'cognitive model' (Johnson-Laird 1983) can be understood as a schema which we draw upon as a 'working model for understanding the moral world' (Gray et al. 2012: 103).

Applied to this poem, the top-down application of such a template, and the mind-modelling of both speaker and mouse invited, could help to explain the rich moral judgements that this text evokes in readers. Furthermore, an analysis using Cognitive Grammar has offered an account of how readers process these two perspectives in parallel during reading, or the multiple acts of 'positioning' (Phelan 2005) or 'projection' (Whiteley 2014) invited by the poem, in terms of the online allocation of attention to its participants. Specifically, this analysis has proposed that the poem's competition for prominence between speaker and mouse in a symmetrical viewing arrangement neatly encapsulates the basic human experience of moral judgement: a 'dyad' of minds.

6. Conclusion

Cognitive Grammar's contribution to stylistics lies in its ability to explain what happens when we read. Crucially, these explanations are posited to be 'psychologically plausible', or based on a principled application of concepts which are widely supported – and, wherever possible, empirically validated – in other cognitive disciplines (Langacker 2008: 14). This chapter hopes to have demonstrated how analysis of a short poem in terms of attention, schemas, scanning and simulation can help us to understand the emergence of its iconic interpretation and the rich emotional and ethical significance that we attach to it as readers. Rooted in research in psychology and neuroscience, the specific claims made here about these processes and their contribution to interpretation can be retrieved, tested and falsified. For example, claims regarding the conflict between the downwards scanning and upwards backtracking invited by the poem could be tested using psycholinguistic methods (e.g. eye-tracking) like those of Richardson and Matlock (2007). For now, the deeper understanding of the poem's meaning that this analysis offers – recognizing the iconic symmetry in its processing alongside its form – enriches its stylistic analysis beyond that possible through other means.

The interpretation of this poem offered here has drawn on other compatible psychological research into mind-modelling and moral judgement. The way in which moral/ethical interpretations of texts arise during reading is an area which is still relatively under-explored in (cognitive) stylistics, despite the growing wealth of research into moral reasoning in the cognitive sciences. By offering a means of drawing together detailed analysis of the linguistic features encountered 'bottom-up' during reading with the cognitive structures and processes which guide this 'top-down', Cognitive Grammar offers a principled basis for applying new lines of psychological research in order to explain how interpretation works.

Notes

1   Short (2005) analyses 'a text based on a poem by the American poet, e. e. cummings, called "me up at does"'. His version of the poem (and his re-write of it) omits the word 'does' at the end of the first line.
2   Support for observations concerning 'conventionality' and 'well-formedness' in cognitive grammar can be obtained through corpus analysis and participant testing, respectively. While none of the examples given here occur appear frequently enough in currently available corpora to serve as evidence of relative conventionality, students given these pairs of sentences will invariably identify sentences (a) to (d) as the more 'normal' sounding.

References

Alforte, A. (2008), Blog post: 3 February, 'An Analysis of the Poem "ME UP AT DOES?"'. Available online: http://aalforte.blogspot.com/2008/02/analysis-of-poem-me-up-at-does.html, (accessed 31 March 2019).

Baron-Cohen, S., A.M. Leslie and U.T.A. Frith (1985), 'Does the Autistic Child Have a "Theory of Mind"?', *Cognition*, 21: 37–46.

Barsalou, L.W. (1999), 'Perceptual Symbol Systems', *Behavioral and Brain Sciences*, 22: 577–609.

Barsalou, L.W. (2009), 'Simulation, Situated Conceptualization, and Prediction', *Philosophical Transactions of the Royal Society of London, Series B: Biological Sciences*, 364 (1521): 1281–9.

Burke, M. (2001), 'Iconicity and Literary Emotion', *European Journal of English Studies*, 5 (1): 31–46.

Burke, M. (2007), '"Progress Is a Comfortable Disease": Cognition in a Stylistic Analysis of E.E. Cummings', in M. Lambrou and P. Stockwell (eds.), *Contemporary Stylistics*, 144–55, London: Bloomsbury.

Castano, E. and R. Giner-Sorolla (2006), 'Not Quite Human: Infrahumanization in Response to Collective Responsibility for Inter-Group Killing', *Journal of Personality and Social Psychology*, 90: 804–18.

Culp, L. (2009), 'Me Up at Does – The Alternative Perspective'. Available online: https://www.bartleby.com/essay/Me-Up-at-Does-Alternate-Perspective-F348QC2LK6ZYA, (accessed 31 March 2019).
Cummings, E.E. (2016), *E.E. Cummings: Complete Poems 1904–1962*, New York: Liveright.
Cureton, R. (1979), 'E.E. Cummings: A Study of the Poetic Use of Deviant Morphology', *Poetics Today*, 1 (1/2): 213–44.
Cureton, R. (1981), 'E.E. Cummings: A Case Study of Iconic Syntax', *Language and Style*, 14 (182): 215.
Enkvist, N.E. (1981), 'Experiential Iconicism in Text Strategy', *Text*, 1 (1): 77–111.
Esses, V.M., S. Veenvliet, G. Hodson and L. Mihic (2008), 'Justice, Morality, and the Dehumanization of Refugees', *Social Justice Research*, 21: 4–25.
Evans, V. and M. Green (2006), *Cognitive Linguistics: An Introduction*, Edinburgh: Edinburgh University Press.
Fairley, I.R. (1975), *E.E. Cummings and Ungrammar: A Study of Syntactic Deviation in His Poems*, New York: Watermill Publishers.
Fischer, O. (2014), 'Iconicity', in P. Stockwell and S. Whiteley (eds), *The Cambridge Handbook of Stylistics*, 379–94, Cambridge: Cambridge University Press.
Fischer, M.H. and R.A. Zwaan (2006), 'Embodied Language: A Review of the Role of the Motor System in Language Comprehension', *Quarterly Journal of Experimental Psychology*, 61 (6): 825–50.
Freeman, M.H. (2009), 'Minding: Feeling, Form, and Meaning in the Creation of Poetic Iconicity', in G. Brone and J. Vandaele (eds), *Cognitive Poetics: Goals, Gains and Gaps*, 169–96, Berlin: De Gruyter.
Giovanelli, M. and C. Harrison (2018), *Cognitive Grammar in Stylistics: A Practical Guide*, London: Bloomsbury.
Glenberg, A. and M. Kaschak (2002), 'Grounding Language in Action', *Psychonomic Bulletin and Review*, 9: 558–65.
Gómez-Jiménez, E.M. (2017), 'Unconventional Patterns in the Experimental Poetry of E.E. Cummings: A Stylistic Approach to Punctuation Marks', *Language and Literature*, 26 (3): 191–212.
Gray, H.M., K. Gray and M.D. Wegner (2007), 'Dimensions of Mind Perception', *Science*, 315: 619.
Gray, K., L. Young and A. Waytz (2012), 'Mind Perception Is the Essence of Morality', *Psychological Inquiry*, 23 (2): 101–24.
Harrison, C. (2017), *Cognitive Grammar in Contemporary Fiction*, Amsterdam: John Benjamins.
Harrison, C., L. Nuttall, P. Stockwell and W. Yuan (eds) (2014), *Cognitive Grammar in Literature*, Amsterdam: John Benjamins.
Hauk, O., I. Johnsrude and F. Pulvermüller (2004), 'Somatotopic Representation of Action Words in Human Motor and Premotor Cortex', *Neuron*, 41 (2): 301–7.
Jeffries, L. (2010), '"The Unprofessionals": Syntactic Iconicity and Reader Interpretation in Contemporary Poems', in D. McIntyre and B. Busse (eds), *Language and Style*, 95–115, Basingstoke: Palgrave McMillan.
Jeffries, L. and D. McIntyre (2010), *Stylistics*, Cambridge: Cambridge University Press.
Johnson, M. (1987), *The Body in the Mind: The Bodily Basis of Meaning, Imagination, and Reason*, Chicago: University of Chicago Press.
Johnson-Laird, P. (1983), *Mental Models*, Cambridge: Cambridge University Press.
Kahneman, D. (1973), *Attention and Effort*, Englewood Cliffs: Prentice Hall.
Killen, M., K. Lynn Mulvey, C. Richardson, N. Jampol and A. Woodward (2011), 'The Accidental Transgressor: Morally-Relevant Theory of Mind', *Cognition*, 119: 197–215.

Lakoff, G. and M. Johnson (1980), *Metaphors We Live By*, Chicago: Chicago University Press.
Langacker, R.W. (1987), *Foundations of Cognitive Grammar: Theoretical Prerequisites*, Stanford, CA: Stanford University Press.
Langacker, R.W. (1991), *Foundations of Cognitive Grammar: Descriptive Application*, Stanford, CA: Stanford University Press.
Langacker, R.W. (2008), *Cognitive Grammar: A Basic Introduction*, New York: Oxford University Press.
Langacker, R.W. (2009), *Investigations in Cognitive Grammar*, Berlin: Mouton de Gruyter.
Leech, G. (1969), *A Linguistic Guide to English Poetry*, Harlow: Longman.
Leech, G. (1985), 'Stylistics', in T.A. Van Dijk (ed.), *Discourse and Literature*, 39–57, Amsterdam: Benjamins.
Leech, G. and M. Short (2007), *Style in Fiction: A Linguistic Introduction to English Fictional Prose*, 2nd edn, Harlow: Pearson Longman.
Lo Justin (2004), 'Me Up at Does: Comments from the Archive', *All Poetry*. Available online: https://allpoetry.com/(Me-up-at-does) (accessed 31 March 2019).
Malle, B.F. and S.D. Hodges (eds) (2005), *Other Minds: How Humans Bridge the Divide between Self and Other*, New York: Guilford Press.
Matlock, T. (2004), 'Fictive Motion as Cognitive Simulation', *Memory & Cognition*, 32 (8): 1389–400.
McIntyre, D. and L. Jeffries (2017), 'Teaching Stylistics: Foregrounding in E.E. Cummings', in B. Knights (ed.), *Teaching Literature Text and Dialogue in the English Classroom*, 155–72, London: Palgrave.
Müller, W.G. (1999), 'The Iconic Use of Syntax in British and American Fiction', in M. Nänny and O. Fischer (eds), *Form Miming Meaning: Iconicity in Language and Literature*, 393–408, Philadelphia: John Benjamins.
Nänny, M. and O. Fischer (eds) (1999), *Form Miming Meaning: Iconicity in Language and Literature*, Amsterdam: John Benjamins.
Navon, D. and D. Gopher (1979), 'On the Economy of the Human Processing System', *Psychological Review*, 56: 214–55.
Nuttall, L. (2017), 'Online Readers between the Camps: A Text World Theory Analysis of Ethical Positioning', *We Need to Talk about Kevin*, *Language and Literature*, 26 (2): 153–71.
Nuttall, L. (2018), *Mind Style and Cognitive Grammar: Language and Worldview in Speculative Fiction*, London: Bloomsbury.
Osofsky, M.J., A. Bandura and P.G. Zimbardo (2005), 'The Role of Moral Disengagement in the Execution Process', *Law and Human Behavior*, 29: 371–93.
Phelan, J. (2005), *Living to Tell about It: A Rhetoric and Ethics of Character Narration*, Ithaca: Cornell University Press.
Phelan, J. (2007), 'Rhetoric/Ethics', in D. Herman (ed.), *Cambridge Companion to Narrative*, 203–16, Cambridge: Cambridge University Press.
Richardson, D.C. and T. Matlock (2007), 'The Integration of Figurative Language and Static Depictions: An Eye Movement Study of Fictive Motion', *Cognition*, 102: 129–38.
Runcie, C. (2013), 'The Master of the Puzzle Poem: Charlotte Runcie Celebrates the Linguistic Riddles of EE Cummings', *The Daily Telegraph*, 9 November. Available online: https://www.telegraph.co.uk/culture/books/10435569/EE-Cummings-Complete-Poems-edited-by-George-James-Firmage-review.html, (accessed 1 March 2019).
Schank, R.C. and R.P. Abelson (1977), *Scripts, Plans, Goals and Understanding*, Hillsdale: Lawrence Erlbaum Associates.

Short, M. (1996), *Exploring the Language of Poems, Plays and Prose*, Harlow: Pearson Education.

Short, M. (2005), 'SPOCA Review: The Grammar of Simple Sentences and Clauses: Task C', *Ling 131 – Language & Style*. Available online: http://www.lancaster.ac.uk/fass/projects/stylistics/topic7/9spocreview3.html, (accessed 1 March 2019).

Simpson, P. (2004), *Stylistics: A Resource Book for Students*, London: Routledge.

Stockwell, P. (2002), *Cognitive Poetics: An Introduction*, London: Routledge.

Stockwell, P. (2009), *Texture: A Cognitive Aesthetics of Reading*, Edinburgh: Edinburgh University Press.

Stockwell, P. and M. Mahlberg (2015), 'Mind-Modelling with Corpus Stylistics in *David Copperfield*', *Language and Literature*, 24 (2): 129–47.

Styles, F.A. (2006), *The Psychology of Attention*, Sussex: Psychology Press.

Tabakowska, E. (1999), 'Linguistic Expression of Perceptual Relationships: Iconicity as a Principle of Text Organization (A Case Study)', in M. Nänny and O. Fischer (eds), *Form Miming Meaning: Iconicity in Language and Literature*, 409–22, Amsterdam: John Benjamins.

Talmy, L. (2000), *Towards a Cognitive Semantics: Vol. 1: Concept Structuring Systems*, Cambridge: MIT Press.

Van Peer, W. (1987), 'Top-Down and Bottom-Up: Interpretative Strategies in Reading E.E. Cummings', *New Literary History*, 18 (3): 597–609.

Wagemans, J., J.H. Elder, M. Kubovy, S.E. Palmer, M.A. Peterson and M. Singh (2012), 'A Century of Gestalt Psychology in Visual Perception: I. Perceptual Grouping and Figure-ground Organization', *Psychological Bulletin*, 138 (6): 1172–217.

Whiteley, S. (2014), 'Ethics', in P. Stockwell and S. Whiteley (eds), *The Cambridge Handbook of Stylistics*, 395–409, Cambridge: Cambridge University Press.

Part Two

Cognitive Grammar in non-literary contexts

6

'28 Palestinians die': A Cognitive Grammar analysis of mystification in press coverage of state violence on the Gaza border

Christopher Hart

1. Introduction

Although developed originally to account for 'traditional' rank levels of linguistic structure (phonological, lexical, morphosyntactic), Cognitive Grammar (Langacker 1987, 1991, 2002, 2008) has proved to be a particularly congenial framework to work with in various forms of text and discourse analysis. There is now a rapidly growing body of work applying Cognitive Grammar in both stylistics and critical discourse analysis (Stockwell 2009; Harrison et al. 2014; Hart 2014, 2019; Harrison 2017; Giovanelli and Harrison 2018; Nuttall 2018). Where, in this nascent area of applied cognitive linguistics, Cognitive Grammar has been especially successful is in explicating, in psychologically plausible terms, the cognitive meaning-making processes that might account for a range of experiences subjectively felt in our encounters with texts. Cognitive Grammar, in other words, offers a credible model for the way that 'texture' is achieved in our readings of texts (Stockwell 2009). In stylistics, the more elusive, subjectively experienced textural qualities that Cognitive Grammar has so far been able to elucidate include senses of poignancy (Hamilton 2003); of atmosphere and ambience (Stockwell 2014, 2019); and of fear, disorientation and claustrophobia (Harrison 2019) (see Harrison et al. 2014 for further examples). Such epiphenomenal effects are accounted for by various conceptual processes defined within the architecture of Cognitive Grammar as giving meaning to linguistic forms, including schematization or action-chaining, dominion-chaining, specification, profiling and various other attentional and perspectival phenomena. In critical discourse analysis, Cognitive Grammar has been applied to account for ideological effects arising from patterns of linguistic representation in political texts. For example, in the context of news reports of violence at political protests, Hart (2015) showed how contrasts in image-schematic representation and viewpoint specification encoded by transitive versus reciprocal verbs give rise to differences in the social perception of protests and of the actors involved. These ideological effects were confirmed in a follow-up experimental study of audience response (Hart 2018). In this chapter, I apply a Cognitive Grammar lens to an ideological effect much studied in critical discourse analysis, namely mystification. I take as data for a case study a convenience sample of media responses to two recent (2018) instances of state violence and mass fatality on the Gaza-Israel border in which a number of Palestinian protesters were killed.

In Section 2, I introduce the notion of mystification as it has been discussed in critical linguistics and critical discourse analysis. In Section 3, I briefly introduce relevant aspects of Cognitive Grammar and the rationale for applying it to the issue of mystification. In Section 4, I present a case study of mystification in news coverage of state violence, highlighting some of the linguistic and conceptual parameters along which mystification may be enacted in discourse. In Section 5, I offer some conclusions and reflections.

2. Mystification

Mystification is the effect that arises from the ability a clause has to downplay or avoid reference altogether to the roles or intentions of social actors in actions and processes. In other words, mystification is characterized by an obtuse sense of responsibility for actions and their consequences. It is achieved in texts through various patterns of exclusion and vagueness realized linguistically in, e.g. metaphors and metonymyies, referential ambiguities, nominalizations, (agentless) passive constructions and the use of intransitive verbs (Merkl-Davies and Koller 2012). Identifying instances of mystification, and inventorying the linguistic resources involved, is a primary concern of critical linguistics (Fowler et al. 1979; Fowler 1991; Hodge and Kress 1993) and has continued to be an important aspect of critical discourse analysis (CDA) more generally (Fairclough 1989, 1995, 2006; van Leeuwen 1996; Reisigl and Wodak 2001; Marín Arrese 2002; Richardson 2007; Koller and Davidson 2008; Hart 2011, 2014; Merkl-Davies and Koller 2012). From a critical perspective, exclusion or vagueness, with the objective of mystification, may be 'strategically employed to conceal persons responsible for discriminatory activities' (Reisigl and Wodak 2001: 47). They may, equally, be employed to mask the effects that discriminatory activities have on vulnerable people (Reisigl and Wodak 2001). In this sense, mystification may be either agent-based or patient-based.

Mystification occurs in contexts where there is a need to reconcile real-world events with prevailing normative backgrounds, assumptions and expectations which those events are in contravention of. This includes direct physical acts of inter- and intra-state violence, such as military attacks on other nations (Merkl-Davies and Koller 2012), police violence including killing of civilians (Trew 1979; Hart 2013, 2014), and restrictions on the rights and movements of migrants (Reisigl and Wodak 2001; Hart 2011), as well as other indirect forms of state and corporate violence, such as the exploitation of labour (Fairclough 2000). A classic and much-considered example comes from Trew (1979) (see also Toolan 1991; Lee 1992; Montgomery 1995; O'Halloran 2003). Trew analysed news reports of events in what was Rhodesia, on 2 June 1975, in which riot police shot and killed eleven African demonstrators.

He found a marked contrast in voice between articles published in *The Guardian* compared to *The Times*. While *The Guardian* reported events in the active voice ('Riot police shot and killed 11 African demonstrators and wounded 15 others'), the same events were reported in *The Times* using the passive voice ('Eleven Africans were shot dead and 15 wounded when Rhodesian police opened fire on a rioting crowd of about 2000'). In the example from *The Times,* agency is only identified by inference through the temporal conjunctive 'when' in 'when Rhodesian police opened fire' (1979: 98). In grammatical terms, the agentless passive in the main clause results in a separation of agent and action (ibid). This separation, Trew showed, was the first step in a process that went further the next day when there was no longer any reference at all to the police as agents of the action ('After Sunday's riots in which 13 Africans were killed and 28 injured'). The mystification of agency is further reinforced by the verb 'kill' (rather than 'shot dead') which does not specify the manner of death. As Montgomery (1995: 240) notes, 'were shot' would at least have implied a human agent. Instead, the text gives the impression that the riots themselves, rather than armed policemen, were the cause of the deaths (ibid). For Trew (1979: 95), what we are witnessing, over time, is a recontextualization of events whereby the original story becomes 'quite transformed and the event appears something quite different from how it started'. The motivation behind such recontextualization is explained by Toolan (1991: 228):

> Newspapers typically espouse some variant or other of the dominant ideology of the community of potential readers, and have to engage in this espousal (or articulation or legitimation) even in the course of reporting events that are 'awkward' for that ideology. Somehow awkward facts which are a threat to the journal's long-held view of the world have to be dealt with so that the newspaper's 'background' narrative of how the world is prevails over any local incongruities.

In a more recent study, Hart (2014) analysed *BBC News Online's* response to the metropolitan police shooting and killing an innocent civilian, Jean Charles de Menezes, outside Stockwell tube station on 22 July 2005, after officers had mistakenly identified him as a suicide bomber. Hart analysed the opening paragraphs of articles, which appeared in bold font, and found that the story followed a similar trajectory. In the first article, published immediately after the incident, the active voice was used ('Police have said they shot a man dead at Stockwell tube station'). The following day, when it had become clear that de Menezes was not a suicide bomber, the clause was reorganized and the passive voice was used instead ('A man shot dead by police hunting the bombers behind Thursday's London attacks was a Brazilian electrician unconnected to the incidents'). By 25 July the story was reported using an agentless passive construction ('The man mistaken for a suicide bomber by police was shot eight times, an inquest into his death has heard'). Here, the police are identified as agents only in the process of mistaking de Menezes for a suicide bomber and not in the action of shooting him. A year after the incident, and following the result of a Crown Prosecution Services review, the action was no longer represented by a transitive clause but had become nominalized ('No police officers are to be prosecuted over the fatal shooting of Jean Charles de Menezes'). Nominalizations, like agentless passives, permit habits of concealment (Fowler 1991: 80; Fairclough 2003: 144). Compared to a fully spelt-out proposition like 'X shot and killed Y', nominalizations are informationally impoverished. As Fowler (1991: 80) points out, missing in a derived nominal form are the participants (who did what to whom?) as well as indications of time – since there is no verb to be tensed – and modality. In the case of nominalizations, in contrast to agentless passives, mystification works by reification. Nominalizations 'create a universe of things, bounded, stable and determinate' (Halliday 1998: 228). Agent recovery then requires more than completing the representation by 'filling in' the slot left empty by an agentless passive; it involves a significant degree of information 'unpacking'. In line with Toolan and Trew, Hart (2014) suggests that what we are observing in these examples is:

> a highly controversial action, inconsistent with the dominant discourse of police as protectors but which the press must nevertheless report, being brought over time into line with that discourse. In other words, [these examples] constitute a natural restoration of legitimacy managed through the mystificatory facilities of linguistic representation.
>
> (p. 33)

The function of linguistic exclusion is not necessarily, in every context, mystification. For example, linguistic exclusion may be a consequence of normal discourse principles (e.g. brevity) or genre constraints. Some critics have therefore argued that CDA may be guilty of over-interpreting its mystificatory effects. For example, Widdowson (2004: 22) points out that people process texts 'in normal pragmatic ways, inferring meanings which have not been explicitly spelled out by reference to what they have already read and what they know of the world'. From a cognitive perspective, this has led researchers like O'Halloran (2003: 234) to ask whether absence at the text level necessarily means there will be absence, and thus mystification, at the discourse level. Hart (2013) refers to this as the 'problem of cognitive equivalence' in CDA. O'Halloran argues that in many cases, processing for relevance (Sperber and Wilson 1995) means that social actors need not be explicitly referenced in the text in order for readers to acknowledge their role in the mental picture where it can be inferred instead from the context, including any situational and background knowledge which has been derived intra- and inter-textually. O'Halloran also recognizes, however, that not all readers will have the requisite knowledge or be willing to invest the extra cognitive effort required to recover implicit information. Similarly, from a cognitive perspective, Billig (2008: 790) questions whether speakers/writers, and so by extension, hearers/readers, engage in nominalization as a psychological process when they use and encounter nominalized forms.

In response to questions such as these, it is worth noting that the presence or absence of social actors in the mental representation is not absolute. From a Cognitive Grammar perspective, as we shall see, it is a matter of degree of attention. Van Leeuwen (1996) identifies two different types of linguistic exclusion: 'suppression' and 'backgrounding'. Suppression involves a radical exclusion so that there is no trace within the text of the excluded information. Backgrounding is less radical; the information is available elsewhere and thus is 'not so much excluded as de-emphasised, pushed into the background' (p. 39). Mystification then relates to the felt sense or impression of responsibility (or lack of it) for normatively incongruous actions that is built cumulatively through the text as well as across texts that make up a particular discourse. Despite potential issues with claims concerning mystification, then, researchers in CDA hold on to the idea that linguistic exclusion can lead to mystification. As Marín-Arrese (2002: 7) states:

> Though the factor of relevance is undoubtedly crucial in the omission of the agent, we may also surmise that the varied use of [impersonalisation] strategies cognitively contributes to construct, in van Dijk's (1998) words, 'preferred models' of a situation, and, socio-politically, to hide institutional or elite group responsibility.

Based on a model of linguistic description that is founded on, and therefore fits with, general cognitive principles, what a Cognitive Grammar analysis may be able to offer is a psychologically plausible account of how linguistic exclusion, in its various forms, might result in mystification as a cognitively real experience felt in reading news and other 'political' texts. That is, Cognitive Grammar has the potential to shed light on the issue of mystification by theorizing the cognitive mechanisms by which it might occur. It may also have the capacity to help identify further instances of mystification, realized by means other than linguistic exclusion, which might otherwise go undetected.

3. Cognitive Grammar

Since this whole book is about Cognitive Grammar and its applications, I shall only very briefly introduce here two aspects of Cognitive Grammar that are most pertinent to the analysis that follows and which serve to illustrate some of the basic principles of Cognitive Grammar. These are the *action chain model* and construal phenomena relating to *prominence*. Cognitive Grammar offers a model of linguistic description dually grounded in cognition and social interaction (Langacker 2008: vii). It is predicated on the claims that (i) grammatical constructions are themselves inherently meaningful and (ii) that grammatical constructions depend for their meanings on more general cognitive principles and processes in terms of which those meanings can thus be characterized. Cognitive Grammar makes no distinction between grammar and the lexicon and instead views all linguistic units as paired with meanings, at different levels of abstraction, inside a system of symbolic assemblies. At the core of the model is the notion of *construal*, which refers to our manifest ability to 'conceive and portray the same situation in alternate ways' (Langacker 1991: 295). Langacker (1991: 294) argues that every linguistic structure 'embodies conventional images and thus imposes a certain construal on the situation it codes'. Indeed, from a functional perspective, he argues that it is 'precisely because of their conceptual import – the contrasting images they impose – that alternate grammatical devices are commonly available to code the same situation' (1991). A key claim of Cognitive Grammar, then, is that meaning is a matter not just of the conceptual content evoked by a linguistic expression but also of the particular construal which every symbolic structure encodes as part of its conventional semantic value (2008: 55). The various works in Cognitive Grammar have been concerned to outline the different dimensions of construal which, applying to conceptions in any domain (like memory, perception, imagination), also provide meaning to linguistic forms.

At the level of clause structure, the conceptual content evoked by different clause types consists in various *archetypal conceptions*, which take the form of *image schemas* representing fundamental aspects of experience (Langacker 2008: 355). In this sense, clause structure is motivated by experience with certain types of clause being suited to coding certain types of occurrence, which stand as their prototype. One such archetypal conception, representing a pattern of energetic interaction particularly common to our experience, is the *action chain*. The action chain is a force schema representing a transfer of energy from one participant, the energy source, 'downstream' to another until it arrives at an energy 'sink' (Langacker 2002: 215–17). Action chains can be of different lengths. However, the *canonical* action chain, arguably representing the most typical pattern of interaction, is a two-participant chain in which an agent (A) acts upon a patient (P) to effect in them a change in state. This schema is modelled in Figure 6.1 (following Langacker, transmission of energy between participants is represented by a double arrow).

This type of interaction, known as the *canonical event model*, is encoded in the structure of a transitive clause, which offers the most natural way of describing it. The transitive clause, in other words, represents the *default coding* for situations conceived as instantiating this canonical event model. This is not to say, however, that other linguistic structures are not also available to code situations taken to instantiate the model which, for discourse purposes, construe it in a different fashion (Langacker 2008: 358). As Langacker (2002: 214) states, 'the objective properties of a situation do not mechanically determine the grammatical organization of a sentence or finite clause describing it'. For example, one dimension of construal relates to *prominence*. In apprehending any scene, there are inherent constraints on distribution of attention. A complex scene cannot be taken in in a global or wholly neutral fashion. We cannot attend to every facet of a complex scene equally and simultaneously. Instead, as a limited cognitive resource, attention must be allocated and, of course, it can be allocated differently depending on circumstance. Two levels at which this focussing of attention shows up in language are: *profile/base* relations and *trajector/landmark* alignments (Langacker 2008).

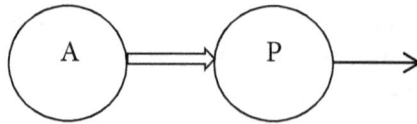

Figure 6.1 Canonical event model: Two-participant action chain.

A linguistic expression selects for attention a certain body of conceptual content, which Langacker calls its *base*. This represents the general locus of attention that is identified by a linguistic expression. By virtue of receiving linguistic representation, particular attention is directed over all or certain portions of the base. The substructure or region given particular attention constitutes the *profile* of a linguistic expression. For example, the base of a transitive clause is provided by the action chain model. Full transitive clauses (in contrast, for example, to agentless passive constructions or nominalizations) profile the whole action chain. However, participants within a profiled relationship are subject to further attentional variance as they are construed with different degrees of prominence relative to one another. In conceiving any scene, one element necessarily stands out with respect to another. Langacker refers to these elements as *trajector* (tr) and *landmark* (lm), respectively.[1] In language, the trajector is the entity construed as being located, evaluated or described and which is characterized as having focal prominence within the profiled structure (Langacker 2008: 70). Linguistic expressions may therefore have the same content, and profile the same structure, but differ in meaning as a consequence of how they assign trajector and landmark (Langacker 2008). One area of language where this fundamental feature of cognition is manifested is in subject-object relations. A subject is a nominal that encodes a trajector in a profiled structure while an object is one that encodes a landmark. At this secondary level of attentional distribution, then, differences in voice (active vs. passive) are associated with contrasting trajector/landmark alignments. In a transitive active clause the agent is the trajector and the participant of primary focus, while in a passive clause the patient is the trajector and the participant of primary focus. Crucially, however, 'trajector status is always imposed: a matter of construal, it is never inherent in the situation described' (Langacker 2008: 368). The alternative construals imposed by active and passive transitive clauses are modelled in Figure 6.2.

Prominence is just one dimension of construal. In Langacker (2008), four broad classes of construal phenomena are identified: *specificity, focusing, prominence* and *perspective*. Analogous with visual perception, these reflect the fact that 'in viewing a scene, what we actually see depends on how closely we examine it, what we choose to look at, which elements we pay most attention to, and where we view it from' (Langacker 2008: 55). In the analysis that follows, I show how action chaining, profiling and other facets of construal might account for mystification in readings of news texts.

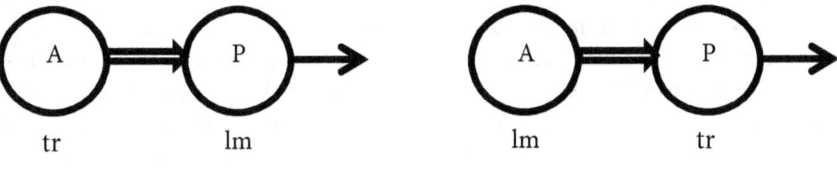

(a) Active transitive   (b) Passive

Figure 6.2 Active transitive versus passive construction.

4. Data

Illustrative data is taken from press coverage of two events that took place on the Gaza-Israel border in 2018 in which large numbers of Palestinian civilians were killed or wounded while demonstrating as part of a six-week protest known as the 'Great March of Return'. On 31 March 2018, sixteen Palestinian demonstrators were shot and killed by Israel Defence Forces. On 14 May 2018, the day the United States opened its embassy in Jerusalem, Israel Defence Forces shot and killed fifty-two Palestinian demonstrators and severely injured thousands more. The data is a convenience sample taken from the online coverage of UK and US news outlets, including *BBC News Online*, *The Guardian*, *New York Times*, *Wall Street Journal* and *NBC*. A total of seven articles were included (see appendix).

5. Analysis

Arguably, a fully profiled two-participant action chain (or conceivably a three-participant chain involving an *instrument* as an additional archetypal role – see below) presents the most natural way of conceptualizing an event in which one (group of) participant(s) shoots and kills another. Any departure from this *default model* can be considered to reflect some discourse purpose, including, potentially, ideological purposes.[2] From a critical perspective, in this chapter, I am therefore concerned with the dimensions along which conceptualizations, evoked by attested language practices, can differ from this default model and how alternative conceptualizations might contribute to mystification. Two types of mystification can be identified: agent-based and patient-based. In agent-based mystification the role and identity of the agent are obfuscated. In patient-based mystification, the agent is identified but the force of the action in which they are agentive is modulated downward and/or the impact of the action on the patient is ambiguated.

5.1 Agent-based mystification

One way in which conceptualizations can depart from the default model is in terms of the image schema evoked as the conceptual base. The distinction between conceptual content and construal is not a sharp one (Langacker 2008: 43). The conceptual content evoked by a linguistic expression does not correspond truth-conditionally with objectively given circumstances. Rather, schematization is already an act of construal, for the same event can be schematized in different ways depending on discourse needs and purposes. While the canonical action chain offers one way of schematizing interactional events, other types of action chain model are also available, which may serve to mystify agency. In particular, as Langacker (2002: 244) points out, there are several ways of construing events with respect to the input of energy.

In the data, this is most apparent in the use of transitive versus intransitive verbs in reference to the Palestinian fatalities. For example, *NBC* used the transitive verb 'kill', evoking a two-participant action chain as the conceptual base and profiling the full structure in 'Israeli forces have killed more than 100 demonstrators' in (1) and 'At least 58 Palestinians were killed by Israeli forces' in (4):

(1) **Scores dead in Gaza fence protest as U.S. moves embassy to Jerusalem**
<u>Israeli forces have killed more than 100 demonstrators</u> and wounded around 12,300 more since protests began on March 30, Gaza's Health Ministry says.[3]

Similarly, *The Guardian* used transitive verbs in 'shoot' and 'kill', again profiling the full two-participant action chain:

(2) Gaza has had its bloodiest day in years on Monday after <u>Israeli forces shot and killed 58 Palestinians</u> and wounded at least 1,200 as tens of thousands protested along the frontier against the opening of the US embassy in Jerusalem.

The conceptualization evoked by examples (1) and (2), then, is that modelled in Figure 6.2a. By contrast, the *New York Times* used the intransitive verb 'die' as in (3).

(3) **At Least 28 Palestinians Die in Protests as U.S. Prepares to Open Jerusalem Embassy**
The relocation of the embassy from Tel Aviv was timed for the 70th anniversary of the formation of Israel – a move that many Israelis have celebrated but that has enraged Palestinians.
<u>Palestinian officials say at least 28 people have died</u> in the latest round of protests.

The action chain evoked by an intransitive verb consists of only one participant (who is thus profiled by default). In Langacker's terms, the conceptualizations evoked by (1) and (2) realize an *agent-oriented* strategy in *trajector alignment* whereby the participant selected as trajector is the agent. This represents the *canonical alignment* for English (Langacker 2008: 367). The conceptualization evoked by (3), alternatively, realizes a *theme-oriented* strategy.[4] Theme-orientation encompasses the passive voice as in (4) (*NBC*) where the patient is selected as trajector but the thematic process is still construed as having been brought about by the exertion of force from an agent.

(4) <u>At least 58 Palestinians were killed by Israeli forces</u> and more than 2,700 others were wounded Monday after thousands of protesters converged on the razor-wire fence between the Gaza Strip and Israel as the U.S. Embassy opened in Jerusalem.

In the case of intransitives, however, the thematic process is construed in an *absolute* fashion, 'without reference to the force or agent that induces it' (Langacker 2008: 385). The intransitive verb 'die' in (3) thus construes the deaths as autonomous events abstracted away from the energy input that drove them. The deaths, in other words, are construed as happening of their own accord, independent of cause or agency. The conceptualization evoked by the use of 'die' in (3) is modelled in Figure 6.3 where any causal input remains outside the *scope of attention* (Langacker 2008: 370–1).

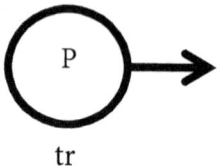

Figure 6.3 Absolute intransitive.

If one way that conceptualizations can depart from the default model is in the conceptual content evoked by a linguistic expression, another is in how that content is construed. The default model involves a fully profiled two-participant action chain. However, the same conceptual content can be construed in an alternative fashion whereby only part of the evoked schema is profiled. When the profiled portion of the action chain moves downstream in the flow of energy represented by the schema, profiling produces agent-based mystification. When the profiled portion moves upstream, it produces patient-based mystification.

One grammatical form that profiles a sub-structure downstream in the action chain is the agentless passive construction. For Langacker (1991: 336), the main function of the passive is to de-focus the agent. In the data at hand, agentless passive constructions are found in prominent regions of the texts, including in the headlines of both the *Wall Street Journal* (5) and *BBC News Online* (6):

(5)   Scores Killed as Palestinians Protest U.S. Embassy Opening in Jerusalem
(6)   Gaza clashes: 52 Palestinians killed on deadliest day since 2014

In contrast to 'die' discussed in relation to (3) above, 'kill' in (5) and (6) acknowledges the presence of an agent in a force-interactive process and thus evokes the canonical two-participant action chain as its conceptual base. The agent therefore exists within the scope of attention. However, in contrast to the use of 'kill' in (1), (2) and (4), the agentless passive forms used in both (5) and (6) leave the agent unspecified and thus profile only the relationship between the patient, who is selected as trajector, and the process, leaving the role and identity of the agent conceptually out of focus.[5] The conceptualization evoked by (5) and (6) is modelled in Figure 6.4.

Another way in which conceptualizations can depart from the default model is in their mode of apprehension. In examples like (1) and (2) above, according to Langacker, the verb invites a *sequential scanning* of the conceptual content. Verbs profile the series of contiguous (in time) relationships that hold between participants to constitute an event so that the 'various phases of an evolving situation are examined serially, in noncumulative fashion' (2002: 78–9). By contrast, when the same content is encoded by an expression belonging to another grammatical category (e.g. a noun), it is construed in summary fashion. *Summary scanning* is thus the mode of apprehension associated with nominalizations (Langacker 2008). The two modes of scanning are modelled in Figure 6.5 (the arrow (t) represents time with the bar along the time arrow representing the particular time-frame in which the construed event takes place).

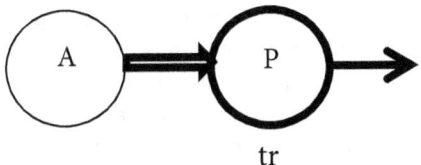

Figure 6.4 Agentless passive construction.

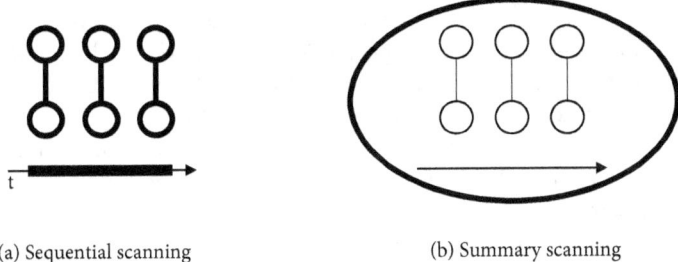

(a) Sequential scanning   (b) Summary scanning

Figure 6.5 Scanning.

In the data we find several instances of nominalization in the form of 'clashes'. For example, in the *Wall Street Journal* this nominalization is used in both the title of a video, which appears prominently at the top of the webpage, and in the lead paragraph:

(7) Clashes Over New U.S. Embassy in Jerusalem Leave Dozens Dead
(8) The U.S. cemented its ties to Israel by opening a new embassy in Jerusalem, as clashes between Palestinian protesters and Israel's military left dozens dead and added to the Trump administration's challenges in the Middle East.

Similar examples are found, involving the same nominalized form, in the headline of the *BBC News Online* article relating to the 31 March events and, involving the nominal form 'mass protests' in reference to the March events, in the *New York Times*:

(9) Gaza-Israel border: Clashes 'leave 16 Palestinians dead and hundreds injured'
(10) At least 1,000 Palestinian demonstrators were also wounded along the border fence with Gaza, the Health Ministry reported, as the mass protests that began on March 30 and that had already left dozens dead erupted again.

'Clashes' is particularly egregious in this context partly because it invokes a by-directional action chain (as opposed to the canonical unidirectional action chain) and thus characterizes a brutal show of state power, in which it was only Palestinians who were killed or injured, as a two-sided event (see Hart 2013 on bi-directional action schemas), but also because, like 'mass protests' in (10), it invites a summary scanning of the event which occludes attention to agency. In verb form, 'clash' profiles a series of relationships between two participants such that each exerts some force on the other. In summary scanning, however, the various facets of the event are examined cumulatively so that the whole complex comes to cohere as a single gestalt. In other words, the event is seen instead as an object or a thing and since things do not pertain to time, we do not scan their internal component states and the processual aspect of the event is lost (Radden and Dirven 2007: 80). Internal event-structure, including agent-patient relations, is therefore conceptually backgrounded. We do not learn from these examples who was the agent responsible for the deaths. Instead, the newly reified thing, encoded by the nominal form, features as an actor in the process designated by another verb so that it is the event itself, rather than another participant in it, that 'leaves' people dead. In other words, the nominalization enters into an EVENT FOR PARTICIPANT metonymy. The Cognitive Grammar analysis thus lends psychological weight to the claims in CDA that nominalizations can 'obfuscate agency, and therefore responsibility' (Fairclough 2003: 144) and that metonymies can, similarly, 'conjure away' responsible actors or 'keep them in the semantic background' (Reisigl and Wodak 2001: 58). From a Cognitive Grammar perspective, however, nominalizations and metonymies are linguistic processes. The cognitive processes activated by them are based in the system of attention with both nominalizations and certain, e.g. generalizing, metonymies accounted for in terms of summary scanning.[6]

From the nominal(ized) forms in (7), (8) and (10), in combination with the impersonal 'dozens', neither do we learn who was the patient. This leads to a second form of mystification in patient-based mystification.

5.2 Patient-based mystification

In patient-based mystification, the identity of the patient rather than the agent is ambiguated and/or the forceful impact of the action on the patient is somehow mitigated. In the case of the latter, patient-based mystification is close to euphemism. Examples (7), (8) and (10) realize a patient-based mystification strategy due to the referential vagueness of 'dozens', which does not explicitly identify Palestinians as the sole victims of the violence, leaving open the possibility that Israeli soldiers were also among the fatalities. Other examples have to do with schematization and profiling.

Recall the default model for an event in which one group of participants shoots and kills another is a two-participant action chain. Another archetypal conception that also applies quite naturally to such an occurrence, and which thus offers an alternative possibility for schematization, is a three-participant action chain involving a further archetypal role in the form of an *instrument*. Within the action chain model, an instrument is neither an energy source nor an energy sink and is instead defined as an intermediary in the transfer of force between an agent and a patient (Langacker 2008: 356). An instrument is something, prototypically an inanimate object, that is used by an agent to effect a change in state in a patient. Different nouns prototypically express particular archetypal roles. Words like 'guns', 'tanks', 'bombs' and 'missiles' express instruments while 'soldiers', 'snipers' etc. prototypically express agents as in (11) found in the *New York Times*:

(11) Israeli soldiers and snipers were using barrages of tear gas as well as live gunfire to keep protesters from entering Israeli territory.

(11) is already somewhat euphemistic as the action in which tear gas and live gunfire feature as an instrument is one of impeding motion and hence affecting the location of Palestinian protesters rather than effecting any change to their internal state (see Hart 2014 for discussion of FORCE versus ACTION schemas). This kind of euphemism goes further in examples like (12) and (13), from *BBC News Online* articles reporting the March and May events respectively, where there is an *instrumentalization of agents*.

(12) Israel deployed tanks and snipers.
(13) Palestinians hurled stones and incendiary devices while the Israeli military used snipers.

In both (12) and (13), 'snipers', which canonically encodes an agent, features as an instrument. Moreover, since neither example includes an infinitival clause there is no reference to the type of action a sniper would, in reality, be engaged in, namely shooting at human targets with an intention to kill or harm. Thus, the profiled portion of the action chain is the relationship between the agent, Israel, and the instrument, snipers. The relationship between 'snipers' and the patient, Palestinian protesters, although accessible as a function of frame-based knowledge, remains conceptually backgrounded. The conceptualization evoked by examples (12) and (13) is modelled in Figure 6.6. (13) is further interesting because of the temporal equivalence established by the *connector* 'while'. The events represented by the two clauses in (13) are construed as happening contemporaneously. This goes some way to mitigating the actions of the Israeli military by presenting the violent interaction as two-sided. This process goes further in examples like (14) from *BBC News Online* in which a temporal sequence is established such that one event is conceived as happening in the wake of another.

(14) The Israeli military said soldiers had opened fire after rioting.

(14) is mystifying for avoiding reference to the impact of the action on the patient. Contrast it with (15) from *NBC*.

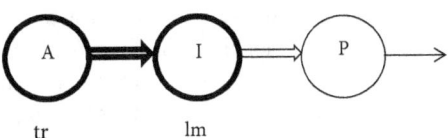

Figure 6.6 Agent-instrument profile.

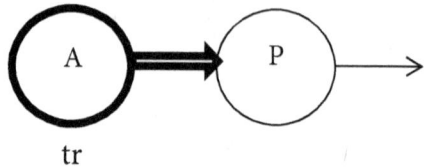

Figure 6.7 Patientless active construction.

(15) The Israeli Defense Forces opened fire on protesters.

In (15), the full action chain is profiled. In (14), alternatively, only the relationship between the agent and the process is profiled. The terminus of the action chain, where the impact of the energy transfer is felt, is evoked as part of the base but remains conceptually out of focus. The conceptualization instantiated by the subordinate clause of (14) is modelled in Figure 6.7.[7]

(14) is also interesting, though, because of the attached adverbial phrase 'after rioting'. 'Rioting' is, of course, a nominalization and so the adverbial phrase can be analysed in much the same way as an adverbial clause, except that the event is viewed summarily. The global organization of this sentence can therefore be modelled as in Figure 6.8. The connector 'after' establishes an explicit temporal relationship between the two events such that one is conceived as succeeding the other. Since trajector-landmark alignments occur across clauses as well as within them, one of the two events is singled out for focal prominence relative to the other. In (14), it is the act of opening fire that is qualified – temporally located – with respect to rioting and therefore has conferred upon it the status of trajector. Implicitly, the connector 'after' establishes a causal relationship between the two events so that the second event is seen as a response to the first. Ideologically, this has the effect that, in the causal chain of interactions evoked, Israeli soldiers are no longer construed as *initiators* but as *reactors* or *respondents* in an action that is restorative rather than gratuitous.

A similar construal is evoked by (16) from the *New York Times* as a function of the verb 'respond', which entails some prior legitimizing event. In (16), the Israeli action of 'responding with rifle fire', which again is euphemistic, is not construed as part of the violence but as a reaction to it.

(16) A mass attempt by Palestinians to cross the border fence separating Israel from Gaza quickly turned violent, as Israeli soldiers <u>responded</u> with rifle fire.

One final form of patient-based mystification worth observing in the data is in the choice of preposition accompanying the verb 'fire'. In the active voice, the verb 'fire', in the sense of shooting, takes a prepositional landmark. In the case of 'fire', in contrast to 'open fire', this is obligatory. There are options, however, in the preposition that can be selected. Much has been written in Cognitive Grammar and cognitive linguistics more broadly about prepositions (Herskovits 1986; Vandeloise 1994; Talmy 2000; Tyler and Evans 2003; Coventry and Garrod 2004; Langacker 2010). From a Cognitive Grammar

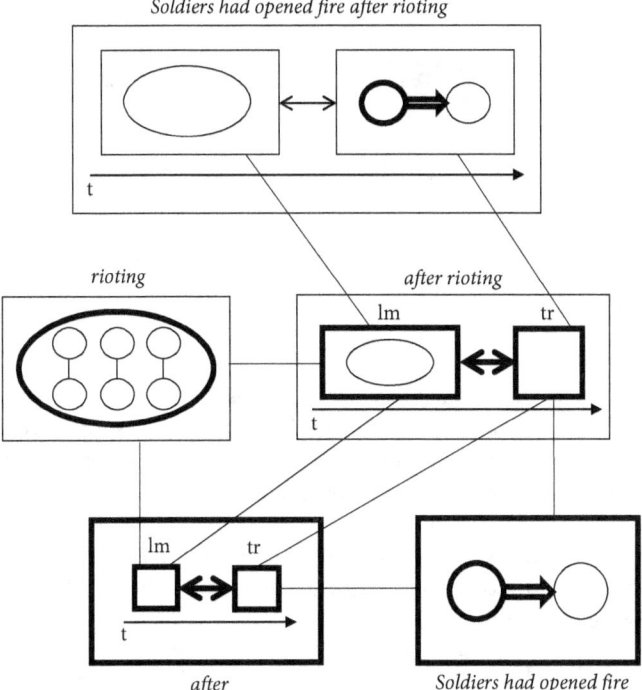

Figure 6.8 'Soldiers had opened fire after rioting'.

perspective, directional prepositions express the *path* an entity takes in relation to the landmark. Such an entity can be an agent or a *mover*. A mover is an entity, prototypically an inanimate object, that undergoes a change of position thus occupying a series of locations through time (Langacker 2008: 370). It is capable of both receiving energy, thus effecting its motion, and exerting energy to bring about some effect in another entity. A mover, like an instrument, can therefore play an intermediary role between agent and patient in a three-participant action chain. Mystification comes in as the path expressed by a preposition can be more or less precise with respect to the landmark. That is, the *goal*, as the place where the mover 'lands', can be the *point* or points in space occupied by the landmark or it can be a *region* of space around the landmark. Consider the contrast between (17) and (18) from *BBC News Online*:

(17) Tomorrow, the Palestinians will bury their dead and head back to the border with Israel to throw stones <u>at</u> the soldiers
(18) The IDF said troops were "firing [bullets] <u>towards</u> the main instigators".

In (17), 'at' construes the goal as a point in space co-locational and co-extensive with the landmark (patient) and thus clearly identifies soldiers as the intended target of the action of throwing stones. By contrast, in (18), 'towards' construes the goal only as a

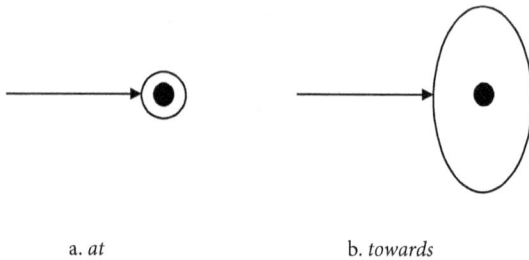

a. *at*   b. *towards*

Figure 6.9 Directional prepositions.

region surrounding the landmark (patient). That is, an area greater in expanse than that occupied by the landmark. The meaning of 'towards', in this context, can therefore be glossed as 'in the general direction of' and is vague as to whether the mover (bullets in this case) hit or was intended to hit the protesters. While 'at' in (17), then, suggests contact between the mover and the patient, 'towards' in (18) leaves this only as a possibility. In this sense, (18) may be said to instantiate a patient-based mystification strategy. The alternative construals associated with 'at' and 'towards' in (17) and (18) respectively are represented in Figure 6.9.

5.3 Multimodal mystification

Given the links between linguistic structure and visual experience posited in Cognitive Grammar, it should not be surprising to find analogous processes in visual semiotization (Hart 2016). Moreover, in multimodal texts, we might expect to find the imagery invoked by specific language usages to be structurally consistent with co-textually present images. That is, we might expect to find language and image in a multimodal text exhibiting what Lui and O'Halloran (2009) call 'intersemiotic parallelism' (cf. 'intersemiotic repetition' in Royce 2007). Intersemiotic parallelism is defined as a cohesive relation that is established between language and image when the two semiotic components share a similar form and which functions to create coherence or textual convergence (Lui and O'Halloran 2009).

In Lui and O'Halloran (2009), intersemiotic parallelism is identified on the basis of shared transitivity structures working within a systemic functional linguistics framework. Cognitive linguistics, however, and Cognitive Grammar in particular, suggests potential new sites or parameters for intermodal convergence based in attentional configurations. Crucially, from a cognitive linguistic perspective, images in a text do not cohere with linguistic structures *per se* but with the mental images evoked by linguistic structures. By way of example, consider the image in Figure 6.10 and its accompanying caption in (19), taken from the *Wall Street Journal*:

(19) Palestinian protesters look up at <u>falling tear gas canisters</u> near the border with Israel in the southern Gaza Strip on Tuesday.

Figure 6.10 Image taken from the *Wall Street Journal*. © Said Khatib/Agence France-Presse/Getty Images.

The relevant *event-frame* here is made up of three phases (cf. 'windowing of attention' in Talmy 2000). An agent (Israeli soldiers) imparts a mover (tear gas canisters) with energy causing it to be propelled through the air, following a path so shaped as to form an arch, before it reaches a patient (Palestinian protesters) where it effects in them a change in state. These three phases correspond to the three elements that make up the *source-path-goal* schema. In (19), however, the nominalization 'falling tear gas canisters' profiles only the path phase of this event-frame, and specifically the second part of that phase, leaving both the agent in the events and its impact on the patient conceptually backgrounded.[8] This is modelled in Figure 6.11 where the single arrow represents the mover's trajectory through space.

If we compare the conceptualization evoked by the caption with the image it accompanies, we find striking similarities. An image presents a snapshot of a moment in time. It therefore necessarily captures only part of reality, focussing our attention on that particular aspect. In the image in Figure 6.10, the gas canisters appear to be falling through the sky like rain without cause or agency. As viewers, we are not shown from where they originate or their impact on the ground. In other words, the image captures the path phase of the event but not the source or goal phases and therefore, like the caption, realizes both agent-based and patient-based mystification. In mystifying the impact of the event on the patient, the image, in Chouliaraki's (2006) terms, represents an anaesthetization of suffering.

Compare this with the image in Figure 6.12 and its accompanying caption in (20), taken from *The Guardian*.

(20) Palestinians killed as US opens embassy in Jerusalem – video report

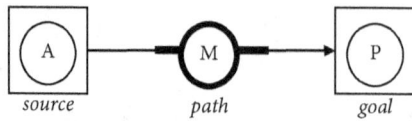

Figure 6.11 Path profiling.

Figure 6.12 Video still from *The Guardian*. © Guardian News & Media Ltd.

The image in Figure 6.12 appeared as the front still from a video located prominently at the top of the article page. It is the image the reader is confronted with when landing on the webpage. In contrast to the image in Figure 6.10, the viewer's attention is focussed on the goal phase of the event as the devastating effects of the tear gas canisters are made clearly visible. This is reinforced in the caption through the transitive verb 'kill'.

At the schematic level, then, in both cases we find intersemiotic parallelisms in attentional focus. The image in the *Wall Street Journal* and its accompanying caption both focus attention on the medial path phase of the event while the image and its accompanying caption in *The Guardian* both focus attention on the final goal phase. Rhetorically, in news photographs and their captions, intersemiotic parallelism functions to tell the same story from the same perspective, with the representation in each semiotic mode serving to corroborate the version of events presented in the other. A Cognitive Grammar analysis shows that the image-caption combinations in *Wall Street Journal* and *The Guardian* are each internally consistent but present quite different narratives to one another.

6. Conclusion

In this chapter, I have used Cognitive Grammar to shed light on the mystificatory qualities of representations in news texts covering specific instances of state violence.

I have shown that Cognitive Grammar is a rich and powerful tool for researchers in stylistics and critical discourse analysis (CDA). Specifically, as has been shown in this chapter, Cognitive Grammar enables potential sites and actualized instances of linguistic exclusion or vagueness to be identified and their mystificatory effects to be theorized in cognitively plausible terms. Cognitive Grammar illuminates the conceptual processes which, evoked by linguistic representations in text, can account for mystification. Specifically, in its notions of trajector/landmark alignment and profiling, Cognitive Grammar adds psychological weight to the concept of the semantic background frequently appealed to in CDA.

CDA is sometimes criticized for not properly theorizing the reader (Fowler 1996: 7). Cognitive Grammar thus offers an account of meaning in texts that is more readerly. This is not to say that readers cannot challenge, enrich or reject the conceptualizations encoded by linguistic forms. Readers are perfectly capable of resistant or oppositional reading (Browse 2019). Indeed, to give an example from the present case study, the *New York Times* posted a tweet pointing to their main news article covering the 14 May events on the Gaza border. The tweet contained the update in (21):

(21) Dozens of Palestinians have died in protests as the US prepares to open its Jerusalem Embassy

Responses to the tweet were revealing and included the following:

(22) WERE KILLED. They didn't all get sudden heart attacks.
(23) "Dozens of Palestinians were shot to death by Israeli soldiers while protesting the US opening of the Jerusalem Embassy" ... There, I fixed it for you.
(24) Here, I fixed it for you: Dozens of unarmed Palestinians have been murdered by Israeli forces in protests as the US prepares to open its Jerusalem Embassy.
(25) You mean Israeli snipers have killed dozens of Palestinians.

What these reformulations have in common is a preference for a transitive verb. From a Cognitive Grammar perspective, they are examples of what Browse (2019) calls *reconstrual* (see also Harrison 2017; Giovanelli 2019). Specifically, (22)–(24) involve a *rescoping of attention* so that an alternative schematization to the one originally proffered is proposed which recognizes the role of an agent in the causal chain of events. What Cognitive Grammar offers, then, is a theoretical account of the conceptual processes to which readers are disposed, by virtue of representational choices in the text, in order to constitute their experience, i.e. their mental apprehension, of the referential event.

As a textual effect, mystification resides in the overall impression readers take from a text or series of texts. It is cumulative, resulting from persistent and varied strategies permeating a text or discourse. In the data that formed the basis for this case study, mystification was found to be enacted through multiple features spanning semiotic modes. Repeated patterns of mystification were upheld particularly in texts produced by the *Wall Street Journal*, the *New York Times* and *BBC News Online*. There is sufficient semiotic evidence in these texts to suggest that their readers might be left with a diminished sense of the violence inflicted and of agency amongst those responsible for it.

Notes

1. Other authors, like Talmy (2000), refer to them as Figure and Ground.
2. Of course, adhering to the default model is also, itself, an ideological discourse move. In this sense, no representation is free from the impart of ideology (Fowler 1991: 66).
3. Throughout, bold is preserved from the original texts. Underlining is mine for emphasis.
4. For Langacker, the term *theme* subsumes a number of 'passive' semantic roles, including patient (2008: 366).
5. Notice also that the circumstantial clause in (5) and adverbial phrase in (6) do nothing to resolve the underspecification.
6. Not all types of metonymy are accounted for by summary scanning. For example, INSTRUMENT FOR AGENT metonymies are a matter of profiling.
7. For present purposes the analysis ignores the fact that the main event in (14) occurs embedded in reported speech.
8. The unnominalized form in *fall* is an intransitive verb which, in a construction like *tear gas canisters fell through the air*, would profile the same sub-structure of the source-path-goal schema.

References

Billig, M. (2008), 'The Language of Critical Discourse Analysis: The Case of Nominalization', *Discourse & Society*, 19 (6): 783–800.

Browse, S. (2019), '"That's Just What We Hear on Telly All the Time, Isn't It?": Political Discourse and the Cognitive Linguistic Ethnography of Critical Reception', in C. Hart (ed.), *Cognitive Linguistic Approaches to Text and Discourse: From Poetics to Politics*, 157–80, Edinburgh: Edinburgh University Press.

Chouliaraki, L. (2006), 'The Aestheticization of Suffering on Television', *Visual Communication*, 5 (3): 261–85.

Coventry, K. and S. Garrod (2004), *Saying, Seeing and Acting: The Psychological Semantics of Spatial Prepositions*, Hove: Psychology Press.

Fairclough, N. (1989), *Language and Power*, London: Longman.

Fairclough, N. (1995), *Critical Discourse Analysis: The Critical Study of Language*, London: Longman.

Fairclough, N. (2000), *New Labour, New Language*, London: Routledge.

Fairclough, N. (2003), *Analysing Discourse: Textual Analysis for Social Research*, London: Routledge.

Fairclough, N. (2006), *Language and Globalization*, London: Routledge.

Fillmore, C. (1982), 'Frame Semantics', in Linguistics Society of Korea (eds.), *Linguistics in the Morning Calm*, 111–37, Seoul: Hanshin Publishing Co.

Fillmore, C. (1985), 'Frames and the Semantics of Understanding', *Quaderni di Semantica*, 6: 222–54.

Fowler, R. (1991), *Language in the News: Discourse and Ideology in the Press*, London: Routledge.

Fowler, R. (1996), 'On Critical Linguistics', in C.R. Caldas-Coulthard and M. Coulthard (eds), *Texts and Practices: Readings in Critical Discourse Analysis*, 3–14, London: Routledge.

Fowler, R., R. Hodge, G. Kress and T. Trew (1979), *Language and Control*, London: Routledge and Keegan Paul.

Giovanelli, M. (2019), 'Construing and Reconstruing the Horrors of the Trench: Siegfried Sassoon, Creativity and Context', *Journal of Literary Semantics*, 48 (1): 85–104.

Giovanelli, M. and C. Harrison (2018), *Cognitive Grammar in Stylistics: A Practical Guide*, London: Bloomsbury.

Halliday, M.A.K. (1998), 'Things and Relations: Regrammaticizing Experience as Technical Knowledge', in J. Martin and R. Veel (eds), *Reading Science: Critical and Functional Perspectives on Discourses of Science*, 185–235, London: Routledge.

Hamilton, C. (2003), 'A Cognitive Grammar of "Hospital Barge" by Wilfred Owen', in J. Gavins and G. Steen (eds), *Cognitive Poetics in Practice*, 55–65, London: Routledge.

Hart, C. (2011), 'Moving beyond Metaphor in the Cognitive Linguistic Approach to CDA: Construal Operations in Immigration Discourse', in C. Hart (ed.), *Critical Discourse Studies in Context and Cognition*, 171–92, Amsterdam: John Benjamins.

Hart, C. (2013), 'Event-construal in Press Reports of Violence in Political Protests: A Cognitive Linguistic Approach to CDA', *Journal of Language and Politics*, 12 (3): 400–23.

Hart, C. (2014), *Discourse, Grammar and Ideology: Functional and Cognitive Perspectives*, London: Bloomsbury.

Hart, C. (2015), 'Viewpoint in Linguistic Discourse: Space and Evaluation in News Reports of Political Protests', *Critical Discourse Studies*, 12 (3): 238–60.

Hart, C. (2016), 'The Visual Basis of Linguistic Meaning and Its Implications for CDS: Integrating Cognitive Linguistic and Multimodal Methods', *Discourse & Society*, 27 (3): 335–50.

Hart, C. (2018), 'Event-frames Affect Blame Assignment and Perception of Aggression: An Experimental Case Study in CDA', *Applied Linguistics*, 39 (3): 400–21.

Hart, C. (2019), 'Spatial Properties of ACTION Verb Semantics: Experimental Evidence for Image Schema Orientation in Transitive versus Reciprocal Verbs and Its Implications for Ideology', in C. Hart (ed.), *Cognitive Linguistics Approaches to Text and Discourse: From Poetics to Politics*, 181–204, Edinburgh: Edinburgh University Press.

Harrison, C. (2017), *Cognitive Grammar in Contemporary Fiction*, Amsterdam: John Benjamins.

Harrison, C. (2019), 'A "Half-remembered Quality": Experiencing Disorientation and Claustrophobia in *The Goldfinch*', In C. Hart (ed.), *Cognitive Linguistic Approaches to Text and Discourse: From Poetics to Politics*, 37–53, Edinburgh: Edinburgh University Press.

Harrison, C., L. Nuttall, P. Stockwell and W. Yuan (eds) (2014), *Cognitive Grammar in Literature*, New Amsterdam: John Benjamins.

Herskovits, A. (1986), *Language and Spatial Cognition: An Interdisciplinary Study of the Prepositions in English*, Cambridge: Cambridge University Press.

Hodge, R. and G. Kress (1993). *Language as Ideology*, 2nd edn, London: Routledge.

Koller, V. and P. Davidson (2008), 'Social Exclusion as Conceptual and Grammatical Metaphor: A Cross-genre Study of British Policy-making', *Discourse & Society*, 19 (3): 307–31.

Lakoff, G. and M. Johnson (1980), *Metaphors We Live by*, Chicago: University of Chicago Press.

Lakoff, G. and M. Johnson (1999), *Philosophy in the Flesh: The Embodied Mind and Its Challenge to Western Thought*, New York: Basic Book.

Langacker, R. W. (1987), *Foundations of Cognitive Grammar, Vol. I: Theoretical Prerequisites*, Stanford: Stanford University Press.
Langacker, R. W. (1991), *Foundations of Cognitive Grammar, Vol. II: Descriptive Application*, Stanford: Stanford University Press.
Langacker, R. W. (2002), *Concept, Image, Symbol: The Cognitive Basis of Grammar*, Berlin: Mouton de Gruyter.
Langacker, R. W. (2008), *Cognitive Grammar: A Basic Introduction*, Oxford: Oxford University Press.
Langacker, R. W. (2010), 'Reflections on the Functional Characterization of Spatial Prepositions', *Corela*, HS-7. Available online: http://journals.openedition.org/corela/999; DOI: https://doi.org/10.4000/corela.999, accessed (23 June 2020).
Langacker, R. W. (2013), *Essentials of Cognitive Grammar*, Oxford: Oxford University Press.
Lee, D. (1992), *Competing Discourses: Perspectives and Ideology in Language*, London: Longman.
Lui, Y. and K. O'Halloran (2009), 'Intersemiotic Texture: Analyzing Cohesive Devices between Language and Images', *Social Semiotics*, 19 (4): 367–88.
Marín-Arrese, J. I. (2002), 'Introduction', in J. I. Marín-Arrese (ed.), *Conceptualization of Events in Newspaper Discourse: Mystification of Agency and Degree of Implication in News Reports*, 1–8, Madrid: Universidad Complutense de Madrid.
Merkl-Davies, D. and V. Koller (2012), '"Metaphoring" People Out of This World: A Critical Discourse Analysis of a Chairman's Statement of a UK Defence Firm', *Accounting Forum*, 36 (3): 178–93.
Montgomery, M. (1995), *An Introduction to Language and Society*, 2nd edn, London: Routledge.
Nuttall, L. (2018), *Mind Style and Cognitive Grammar: Language and Worldview in Speculative Fiction*, London: Bloomsbury.
Nuyts, J. (2007), 'Cognitive Linguistics and Functional Linguistics', in D. Geeraerts and H. Cuyckens (eds), *The Oxford Handbook of Cognitive Linguistics*, 543–65, Oxford: Oxford University Press.
O'Halloran, K. (2003), *Critical Discourse Analysis and Language Cognition*, Edinburgh: Edinburgh University Press.
Radden, G. and R. Dirven (2007), *Cognitive English Grammar*, Amsterdam: John Benjamins.
Reisigl, M. and R. Wodak (2001), *Discourse and Discrimination: Rhetorics of Racism and Anti-Semitism*, London: Routledge.
Richardson, J. E. (2007), *Analysing Newspapers: An Approach from Critical Discourse Analysis*, Basingstoke: Palgrave.
Royce, T. (2007), 'Intersemiotic Complementarity: A Framework for Multimodal Discourse Analysis', in R. Royce and W. Bowcher (eds), *New Directions in the Analysis of Multimodal Discourse*, 63–109, New York: Lawrence Erlbaum & Assoc.
Sperber, D. and D. Wilson (1995), *Relevance: Communication and Cognition*, 2nd edn, Oxford: Blackwell.
Stockwell, P. (2002), *Cognitive Poetics: An Introduction*, London: Routledge.
Stockwell, P. (2009), *Texture: A Cognitive Aesthetics of Reading*, Edinburgh: Edinburgh University Press.
Stockwell, P. (2014), 'Atmosphere and Tone', in P. Stockwell and S. Whiteley (eds), *The Handbook of Stylistics*, 360–74, Cambridge: Cambridge University Press.

Stockwell, P. (2019), 'Shelly's Dominion: Subliminal and Ambient Tonal Effects across a Literary Work', in C. Hart (ed.), *Cognitive Linguistic Approaches to Text and Discourse: From Poetics to Politics*, 20–36, Edinburgh: Edinburgh University Press.
Talmy, L. (2000), *Toward a Cognitive Semantics, Volume I: Concept Structuring Systems*, Cambridge MA: MIT Press.
Toolan, M. (1991), *Narrative: A Critical Linguistic Introduction*, London: Routledge.
Trew, T. (1979), 'Theory and Ideology at Work', in R. Fowler, R. Hodge, G. Kress and T. Trew (eds), *Language and Control*, 94–116, London: Routledge and Keegan Paul.
Tyler, A. and V. Evans (2003), *The Semantics of English Prepositions: Spatial Scenes, Embodied Meaning and Cognition*, Cambridge: Cambridge University Press.
Van Dijk, T. A. (1998), *Ideology: A Multidisciplinary Approach*, London: Sage.
Van Leeuwen, T. (1996), 'The Representation of Social Actors', in C.R. Caldas Coulthard and M. Coulthard (eds), *Text and Practices: Readings in Critical Discourse Analysis*, 32–70, London: Routledge.
Vandeloise, C. (1994), 'Methodology and Analyses of the Preposition', *Cognitive Linguistics*, 5 (2): 157–84.
Widdowson, H.G. (2004), *Text, Context, Pretext: Critical Issues in Discourse Analysis*, Oxford: Blackwell.

Appendix: Data Sources

https://twitter.com/nytimesworld/status/996009245853265920
https://www.wsj.com/articles/at-least-16-palestinian-protesters-killed-as-u-s-opens-embassy-in-jerusalem-1526298531; https://www.wsj.com/video/clashes-over-new-us-embassy-in-jerusalem-leave-dozens-dead/803AEB54-131C-4108-8943-CB34A7F13F13.html
https://www.bbc.co.uk/news/world-middle-east-44104599
https://www.bbc.co.uk/news/world-middle-east-43593594
https://www.nbcnews.com/news/world/palestinians-prepare-major-move-gaza-israel-fence-n873706; https://www.theguardian.com/world/2018/may/14/israel-tells-palestinians-they-are-risking-lives-in-us-embassy-protests; https://www.nytimes.com/2018/05/14/world/middleeast/palestinian-protests-gaza-us-embassy.html?smid=tw-nytimesworld&smtyp=cur

'Hmmm yes, but where's the beef?' Cognitive Grammar and the active audience in political discourse

Sam Browse

1. Introduction

In a critique of critical discourse analysis (CDA), Henry Widdowson (1995: 165) pithily remarks that 'it is your discourse you read into my text'. In the article, he suggests that discourse analysts have suffered from a conceptual confusion over the difference between text and discourse. For him, a text is a stretch of language use identified on the basis that it has some form of 'social intent' (Widdowson 1995: 164) – it is language which we perceive is intended to mean something. Conversely, a discourse is the 'acting of context on code [...] the pragmatic process of meaning negotiation' (Widdowson 1995: 164). This process of meaning negotiation is one that implicates language users' conceived notion of reality – their apprehension of the context of interaction. Such a view of discourse explains the existence of a plurality of textual interpretations because discourse participants have different understandings of the contexts in which they engage with texts. Widdowson's (1995) problem with CDA is that it fails to account for this plurality. Instead, the analyst's commitment to a particular ideological perspective means that they privilege their own discursive context at the expense of considering other interpretations; 'there is usually the implication that the single interpretation offered is uniquely validated by the textual facts' (Widdowson 1995: 169).

Although Widdowson (1995) presents a cogent argument for conceptual clarity in discourse analysis – and helpfully defines two complex terms – his criticisms of CDA are unfair. As Fairclough (1996: 51) notes, his (1992) book is 'committed to, and dependent upon, the assumption of diversity of interpretations of texts [...] and such investigations are perfectly compatible with the theory'. Indeed, it is easy to conceive of 'a CDA of reception in which it is interpretative acts, in addition to proffered meanings, that are the subject of criticism' (Browse 2018a: 208). However, while CDA theory supports such a research agenda, Fairclough (1996: 51) admits that it has 'not carried through into investigations of interpretative diversity'. With some exceptions (e.g. Gavins and Simpson 2015; Hart 2016; Browse 2018a, 2018b, 2019), work in CDA has tended to focus on the production – rather than the reception-side of discourse (Jeffries 2010: 11).

This chapter seeks to address this gap in the research by combining theories of the 'active audience' (Hall 1980; Brunsdon and Morley 1999) with Text World Theory (Gavins 2007; Werth 1999) and Cognitive Grammar (Langacker 1987, 1991, 2008) to account for the socially conditioned ways audiences receive political texts. To do so, I analyse 'think aloud' reader responses to speeches by the then British Conservative Prime Minister, Theresa May, and the leader of the Labour Party, Jeremy Corbyn. The participants were all members of the Labour Party and supportive of the Labour leader – a shibboleth issue in the internal politics of the opposition at the time. In Section 2, I draw on 'active audience' theory (Hall 1980; Brunsdon and Morley 1999) and Text World Theory (Werth 1999; Gavins 2007) to outline a theoretical perspective for analysing audience responses. Section 3 provides more information about the participants and data collection. Section 4 introduces the interpretative framework through which the data is analysed, namely the construal categories of Cognitive Grammar (Langacker 1987, 1991, 2008), and also introduces the concept of 'reconstrual' (Browse 2018a, 2018c, 2019). Finally, in Sections 5 and 6, I use Cognitive Grammar to describe the conceptual processes involved in the participants 'reading their discourse into May and Corbyn's texts' (to paraphrase Widdowson 1995: 165). The chapter, then, offers a version of CDA which empirically addresses interpretation and at the same time suggests a set of conceptual tools – based on categories from Cognitive Grammar – for describing the interpretative practices of active audiences.

2. Cognition, active audiences and the heteronomy of meaning

While CDA has tended not to focus on readers or audiences, their interpretative processes have long been the focus of researchers in cultural and media studies, beginning with Hall's (1980) pioneering theoretical work on the reception of television news. Hall (1980) outlines an encoding-decoding model of television consumption, whereby, through ideological practices of news production, television producers encode a message in the text, which is then decoded by audiences. This decoding is not a neutral process, however, and Hall (1980) outlines three positions that audiences might take up in their consumption of television. The first, the 'dominant-hegemonic' position, involves the viewer accepting 'full and straight' (Hall 1980: 125) the message proffered by the news producers; that is, they decode the semiotic assembly of image, text and voiceover as it was intended by the producers in accordance with the prevailing ideology of the news station. The second form of reception is a 'negotiated position'. This involves the audience member accepting the 'global' ideological framework in which the news story is packaged, but objecting to 'local' elements of it. For example, in their response to a news story which casts trade unions in a bad light and that negatively portrays their own industrial action, they might agree that trade unions generally play a negative role in society (the global framework), but that their own industrial action is warranted (the local element). Finally, the oppositional position totally rejects the encoding of the topic or situation proffered by the television show, and recodes it in accordance with the audience member's own preferred ideological perspective.

Hall's (1980) work is concerned with the moments in the production and reception of television discourse in which producers and viewers encode or decode meanings in ways that may or may not have been intended. His approach to media discourse, then, stands in contrast to 'transmission' theories of media which see the creation, distribution and consumption of news as circulating in frictionless fashion around a closed loop of communication. Whilst Hall (1980) describes the 'relative autonomy' of these moments, he also insists that decoding is not a rule-free system, but is highly structured and proceeds with respect to a 'dominant or preferred meaning' (p. 124):

> We say 'dominant' because there exists a pattern of 'preferred readings'; and these both have the institutional/political/ideological order imprinted in them and have themselves become institutionalized. The domains of 'preferred meanings' have the whole social order embedded in them as a set of meanings, practices and beliefs: the everyday knowledge of social structures, of 'how things work for all practical purposes in this culture', the rank order of power and interest and the structure of legitimations, limits and sanctions.
>
> (Hall 1980: 124)

Decoders who receive television news from the perspective of the dominant hegemonic position align themselves with the dominant ideological viewpoint of the media institution, and the broader social, economic and political structures in which that institution is situated. Hall's (1980) approach thus contextualizes interpretative procedures in a similar manner to the way in which Fairclough (2002 [1989]) contextualizes practices of discourse production; in both, individual cases of interaction dialectically relate to the social practices, wider institutional context and broader (capitalist) social formation in which they are nested. Just as Fairclough (1989) provides a productive framework for linking the linguistic behaviour of discourse participants to wider institutional and social ideological formations, so too does Hall (1980) offer a framework for connecting the interpretative activity of audiences to broader social structures.

Indeed, Hall's (1980) encoding-decoding model provided the theoretical basis for Brunsdon and Morley's (1999) influential empirical study of the *Nationwide* audience (*Nationwide* was a television news programme running from 1969 to 1983). Using focus groups, they examined the regularities and differences in the way various social groups – from blue- and white-collar workers, to trade unionists, to black college students – interpreted news items on the show. The goal of the study was to trace the stratification of interpretative processes according to different demographics and sub-cultures and thus demonstrate the 'structured polysemy' of television news. Hall (1980) and Brunsdon and Morley's (1999) ideas were highly influential in the development of 'active audience' studies – a perspective on media consumption that emphasized the importance of audiences in the active decoding of television discourse (even if the freedom to interpret was at times overstated, see Morley 1993 – for further discussion, see Curran 1990; Seaman 1992; Cobley 1994; Philo 2001).

Hall's (1980) socially contextualized model provides a good starting point for critical analysis of interpretative practices. That television discourse possesses a structured polysemy seems intuitive and is validated by Brunsdon and Morley's (1999) subsequent empirical work. However, within the literature cited above, the linguistic and conceptual processes involved in decoding are left under-specified. For these analysts of television discourse, it suffices to say that different groups decode in structured and variegated ways to produce a particular interpretative output, but *how* they get from a dominant hegemonic to a negotiated or oppositional 'code' does not fall significantly within the scope of the discussion.

Cognitive linguistic approaches to text and discourse provide the best way to theorize these processes because they focus on the knowledge structures discourse participants 'bring' to the communicative event, and their interaction with the linguistic forms encountered there. This chapter uses Text World Theory (see Werth 1999; Gavins 2007) to account for the active audience's construction of meaning. Text World Theory is a cognitive discourse grammar (Werth 1999) that describes the mental representations – 'text-worlds' – that language users create in interaction. According to the theory, discourse participants communicate in the 'discourse world' – their mental representation of the immediate context, plus the relevant background knowledge required to understand the discourse. What counts as relevant is 'text driven'; the text itself determines which aspects of discourse participants' knowledge are required to process the discourse (Gavins 2007: 29)[1]. In Text World Theory, 'knowledge' is operationalized in terms of frames: 'experiential models of (part of) human life which direct and influence human understanding of aspects of the world, as mediated through human perceptions and cultural knowledge' (Werth 1999: 107; for further elaboration, see Fillmore 1982). Thus, as participants interact with a text, they access their frame knowledge in order to construct text-world representations of the events and situations depicted by the discourse.

From this perspective, textual meaning is 'heteronomous' (see Stockwell 2002a, following Ingarden 1973) in that it has no independent existence apart from the cognitive activity of a discourse participant. This heteronomy is important because it means that discourse participant knowledge is always implicated in the act of communicating. To return to Hall (1980), this does not mean to say that interpretatively 'anything goes'. As Fairclough (2001: 9) points out, the cognitive 'resources' we bring to a text are 'socially determined and ideologically shaped'. Indeed, much work in cognitive CDA has outlined the ideological conceptual models (e.g. van Dijk 1998; Chilton 2004; Cap 2013; Hart 2014) and metaphors (e.g. Lakoff 2002; Charteris-Black 2004; Koller 2005; Goatly 2007; Musolff 2016) that presuppose processes of discourse production. These cognitive structures should not be seen as arbitrarily held by individuals, but rather socially situated – models of reality shared and propagated by social, cultural and political groups and actors. Insofar as they are shared, they constitute not only resources for producing discourse, but also heuristics for interpreting texts. In what follows, then, I analyse the processes by which participants construct meaning from texts with respect to socially shared frames, linking these processes to the discourse structures respondents highlight as important to their own interpretations.

3. An active audience thinking out loud

The seven participants in the study – John, Tom, Richard, Harry, James, Charles and Karen (all pseudonyms) – are all political activists and members of the Labour Party in a large city in the north of England. To varying degrees, they all know one another and therefore comprise a loose but multiplex network (Milroy 1987). Politically, they represent the left-wing of the Labour Party and all supported – and were variously involved in organizing local aspects of – the 2015 and 2016 party leadership campaigns of the current Labour leader, Jeremy Corbyn (which is important to note, given contemporaneous and highly publicized ideological divisions at the top of the party between Corbyn and members of his shadow cabinet). As such, they form a community of practice (Wenger 1998) who share in what Wodak (2009) has called the 'frontstage' (party meetings, campaigning and policy debates, etc.) and 'backstage' activities of the party (strategizing and organizing to win internal elections, attempting to win the party to a particular policy agenda, etc.). One might expect, then, the participants to share a repertoire of conceptual-ideological frames (and, indeed, as will be demonstrated in Section 5, this turns out to be true).

Participants in the study were asked to perform two online 'think aloud' activities (see Norledge 2016: 66–8; Short and van Peer 1989). In the first, they read a section of the then British Conservative Prime Minister, Theresa May's, speech to her 2017 Party conference. They were shown one paragraph of the speech at a time. After they had read the paragraph, they were asked to provide any feedback they might have in a comment box below. After they had commented, they would click the 'next' button which would take them to the next paragraph, to repeat the process. There were twelve paragraphs providing a corpus of eighty-four comments. Having completed this task, they were then asked to do the same with Jeremy Corbyn's 2017 Labour Party conference address. This second speech was eight paragraphs long, providing a corpus of fifty-six comments. Both speech sections were selected on the basis of their shared topic, the economy (hence the disparities in their relative length).

4. From text to interpretation

The central aim of this chapter is to advance a framework that describes the conceptual processes involved in the active audience's construction of meaning, and specifically to link these processes to structures in the text. Cognitive Grammar (see Langacker 1987, 1991, 2008) provides a means of achieving this. In Cognitive Grammar, all linguistic forms evoke conceptual structure (such as a frame) at the same time as they *construe* it in some manner:

> The full conceptual or semantic value of a conceived situation is a function of not only its content [...], but also how we structure this content with respect to such matters as attention, selection, figure/ground organisation, viewpoint and level of schematicity.
>
> (Langacker 1987: 138)

Stylistic choices thus place different construals on an underlying conceptual frame (Langacker (1987: Ch.4) calls the conceptual substrate of any mental representation evoked by a linguistic form a *domain*, but for the sake of terminological uniformity with Text World Theory, I will continue to refer to these structures as frames). Construal works along four dimensions: *specificity, focus, prominence* and *perspective* (Langacker 2008: 55). The first of these, specificity, relates to the granularity of detail encoded by a linguistic structure. The noun, 'thing', provides a highly schematic construal; the noun phrase, 'a desk ornament', is relatively more detailed; whereas 'the lucky wooden statue of Buddha given to me by my sister that sits on my office desk in front of my computer' construes the ornament in a comparatively elaborate fashion. On a clausal level, grammatical constructions such as, say, the ditransitive, can be said to be schematic construals of their instantiations, such as 'Jo gave Sam the Buddha statue'.

Frames are complex assemblies of knowledge. While linguistic forms evoke frames, not all frame structure is selected for inclusion in the conceptualization prompted by them. The second dimension of construal, focusing, is concerned with what is in the *immediate scope* of any conceptualization (Langacker 2008: 63). All frames can be said to have a *maximal scope* (Langacker 2008: 63). We expect to find desks in offices, which might themselves be part of larger institutions and institutional contexts, such as businesses, civic buildings and, indeed, universities. In a noun phrase like 'desk ornament' these wider contexts are backgrounded. While they feature in our encyclopaedic knowledge of where we are likely to find desks and thus the maximal scope of the frame, they need not feature in the immediate scope of our mental representation of the desk ornament, the likely scope of which is outlined in Figure 7.1 and includes only the ornament and the space around it.

Focusing can be manipulated with respect to grammatical relations in the clause. For example, the clause 'Jo gave the desk ornament to Sam' can be diagrammatically represented as an *action chain* – or 'billiard-ball' model of energy transference – as in Figure 7.2a (see Langacker 1991: 283). However, one might change the scope

Figure 7.1 The immediate scope of 'desk ornament'.

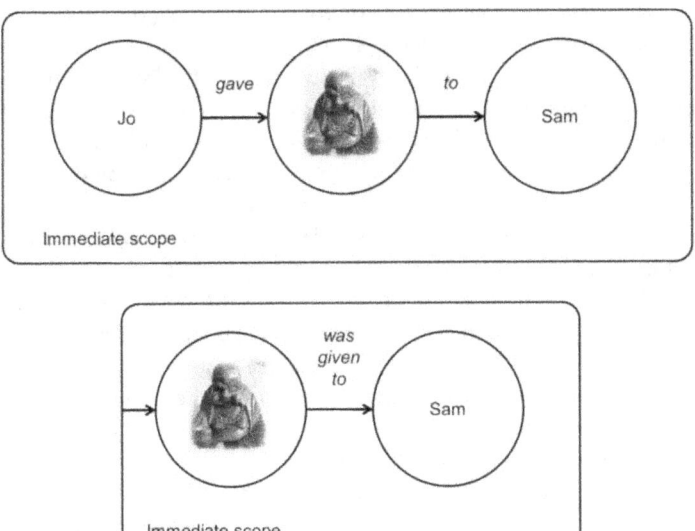

Figure 7.2 Focusing in the clause.

of predication by deleting the agent – 'Sam was given a desk ornament' – and the immediate scope of construal would change as indicated in Figure 7.2. Here, Jo vanishes from the 'onstage' portion of conceptual structure.

If focusing relates to the spotlighted aspects of frame structure, prominence is the attention given to elements of conceptual structure within this region. In the nominal, 'the desk ornament', it is the ornament – not the desk – that is the subject of our attention and is thus *profiled* (Langacker 2008: 66). The profile of a clause is prototypically the main agent (Stockwell 2002b: 61). For example, in 'Jo gave Sam the ornament', Jo is profiled in the action chain. However, one might use a marked linguistic form, such as the passive voice, to change this aspect of construal to profile 'Sam' ('Sam was given the ornament by Jo') or even the ornament ('the ornament was given to Sam by Jo').

The final dimension of construal is perspective. This is a complex category, but it will suffice for the purposes of the analysis below to detail two related concepts that fall within it: *subjective* and *objective construal* (Langacker 2008: 77). All conceptualizations presuppose someone who is conceptualizing and something that is being conceptualized. To return to the visual metaphor, we might call the former the viewer (the subject) and the latter what is viewed (the object). Subjective and objective construal concerns the salience of the subject and object in the conceptualization. For instance, 'the ornament is on the desk' provides an objective construal of the ornament because it 'is the focused object of attention: the entity [the] expression puts onstage and profiles' (Langacker 2008: 77). Conversely, the viewer is construed with maximal subjectivity because it is 'a tacit conceptualizing presence that is not itself conceived' (Langacker 2008: 77). An expression like 'I think the ornament is on the desk' switches this perspective. Instead, the viewer is construed with maximal objectivity – the 'I' conceiving the scene is profiled – and what they view is construed with maximal subjectivity. Subjective and objective construal are not absolute values, but exist on a cline. For example, the evaluative premodifier, 'strange', in 'the strange ornament is on the desk' more objectively construes the viewer and subjectively construes the object than does 'the ornament is on the desk', but it is not as explicit in profiling the conceiver as the expression, 'I think the ornament is on the desk'.

Cognitive Grammar's categories of construal are useful because they provide a vocabulary for describing the 'reconstrual' processes active audiences might employ as they take part in a discourse (Browse 2018a, 2018c, 2019). The language participants encounter in texts places a construal on the frames they themselves bring to the communicative event in order to construct meaning. As per the discussion of heteronomy in Section 3, this means that the meanings constructed by discourse participants are always construals of their own frames for the given topic of discussion. However, the construal proffered by the text is not necessarily the construal preferred by the reader. Indeed, as the body of cognitive CDA cited in Section 3 reminds us, the frames participants bring to the discourse are already structured according to their ideological predispositions. The negotiation of meaning that Hall (1980) describes can thus be recast as the interrelation the discourse participant perceives between their own already established construal and that proffered by the text; that is, to negotiate the meaning of a text is to reconstrue it in accordance with one's own construal preferences for the frame. This underlying frame knowledge acts as the pivot between the text and discourse participant's own – critical, in the case of oppositional and negotiated readings – interpretation (see Browse 2018c). Cognitive Grammar thus provides a way of linking participant responses to structures in the text. In the next section I explore these responses, starting with the comments on Theresa May's speech.

5. The case of the 'wealth creators'

Of the seven participants in the study, six remarked upon Theresa May's use of the term 'wealth creators'. This is the noun phrase as it appears in the context of her conference speech:

> Let this party celebrate the wealth creators, the risk takers, the innovators and entrepreneurs – the businesses large and small – who generate jobs and prosperity for our country, and make British business the envy of the world. Because we understand that it is the wealth creators whose taxes fuel our public services. It is their success that funds the things we want to do.

The six responses to this paragraph were as follows:

1. aaaaahgh ... (Karen)
2. I hate the term 'wealth creators'. (John)

3. Wealth creators are celebrated and very well rewarded. Not so much teachers and doctors. We wouldn't get far with a workforce composed of people with rickets, tuberculosis, measles or one that couldn't read. Isn't making people productive creating wealth? (Tom)
4. Wealth creators stuff a bit dated. (Richard)
5. She's used the term 'wealth creators' twice in this short paragraph. I'm not actually sure it's a term that resonates with people. People see that public services are being cut and that their own economic prospects are poor. I don't think that they'll be too grateful to supposedly benevolent 'wealth creators' who in actuality go to extraordinary means to avoid paying tax. (James)
6. Don't talk to me about the rich and taxes. The population paid for the system and services to allow the 'wealth creators' to leverage profit and influence. (Charles)

In (1), Karen clearly demonstrates her dissatisfaction with the paragraph, exclaiming only 'aaaaahgh ...'. Similarly, in (2) John expresses his hatred of the term 'wealth creators'. Comments (4) and (5) represent meta-level judgements of the effectiveness of May's use of the phrase. Richard remarks that it is 'a bit dated' whereas James provides a commentary on how the term does not 'resonate' with people. Richard's comments constitute a form of 'mind-modelling' (Stockwell 2009: 140) of the general audience – a strategy which is often used by discourse participants in oppositional forms of reading where a hypothesized audience's response is used as a surrogate for their own (see Browse 2018a and forthcoming). Of the six comments, (3) and (6) most clearly represent forms of reconstrual. They can, respectively, be described in terms of re-focusing and re-specifying.

5.1 Refocusing 'wealth creators'

Langacker (2008) defines focusing as follows:

> Through linguistic expressions, we access particular portions of our conceptual universe. The dimension of construal referred to here as focusing includes the **selection** of conceptual content for linguistic presentation, as well as its arrangement into what can broadly be described (metaphorically) as **foreground** vs. **background**.
>
> (Langacker 2008: 57, emphasis in original)

A key part of focusing is related to how we compose symbolically complex conceptual structures (Langacker 2008: 60–2). The nominal 'wealth creators' brings together two words ('wealth' and 'creator') which select two areas of frame knowledge – the reader's conceptualization of WEALTH, and also what it means to CREATE something – which are backgrounded by the noun phrase. The *compositional pathway* (Langacker 2008: 61) by which these knowledge structures are combined has been represented as in Figure 7.3.

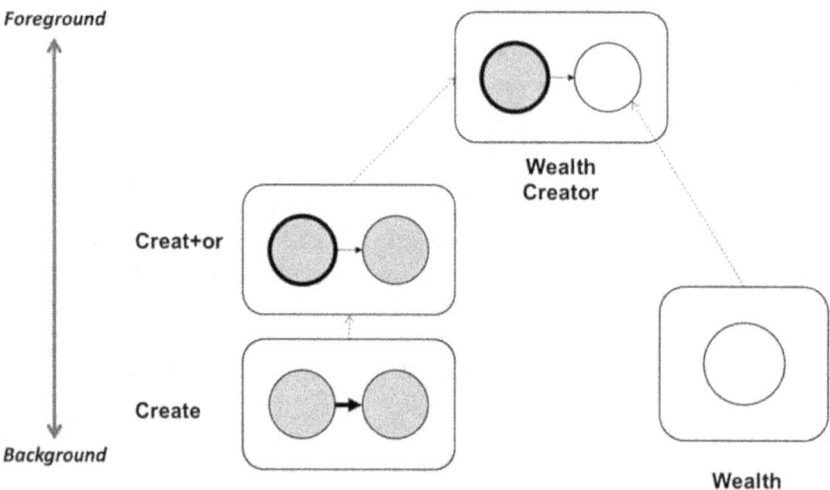

Figure 7.3 The composition of 'wealth creator'.

The underlying conceptual substrate of the word 'create' is represented in the bottom left box. 'To create' entails an entity or thing that creates another entity or thing. The entities and things involved are not specified by the verb and are therefore yet to be determined 'slots' (Cook 1994: 81; Stockwell 2002b: 78) in the frame, represented by the grey circles. Create is a verb, and consequently profiles the process in the frame, represented by an emboldened arrow on the diagram. Adding the suffix '-or' to 'create' has the effect of instead profiling the (unspecified) agent, rather than the process. Again, this is represented by the thick line around the circle on the left in the 'creator' box. Finally, in bringing together the two words 'wealth' and 'creator', the patient 'slot' in the creator frame is filled by 'wealth'. The final construction, then, profiles the unfilled slot – the 'creator'.

Theresa May fills the 'creator' slot with 'the risk takers, the innovators and the entrepreneurs – the businesses large and small' on the basis of how she defines wealth as 'jobs and prosperity'. In comment (3), Tom constructs an oppositional position to this rhetorical move by decomposing the noun phrase, refocusing to its conceptual constituents and redefining 'wealth'. Rather than 'jobs and prosperity' he asks, 'Isn't making people productive creating wealth?' This allows him to recompose the constituent conceptual structures of the noun phrase to render 'teachers and doctors' as wealth creators, too. The oppositional position thus arises as a result of Tom's alternative frame for 'wealth', which he accesses via refocusing the noun phrase.

5.2 Respecifying and refocusing 'wealth creators'

While Charles's comments in (6) also rely on refocusing (which I describe in more detail below), they employ an additional process of respecifying the 'wealth creators'. In his commentary, he suggests that the only reason the wealth creators are able to generate 'jobs and prosperity' is because they have 'profit and influence' to use as 'leverage'. Here, Charles introduces an extra component into the action chain May describes – 'profit and influence'. This has been represented in Figure 7.4. I have designated this insertion a form of respecification because it adds an extra level of granularity into the chain of cause and effect predicated by the prime minister's original contribution. This form of respecification is the inverse of what Turner (2006) has called 'compression', the process by which we transform 'diffuse and distended conceptual structures that are less congenial to human understanding so that they become more congenial to human understanding, better suited to our human-scale ways of thinking' (Turner 2006: 1). Compression often involves abbreviating causality – a kind of 'scaling [that] can consist in shortening the causal chain from many steps to few or only one' (Fauconnier and Turner 2002: 313). In his comment, Charles instead decompresses the Conservative politician's short chain of cause and effect (wealth creators → generate → jobs/prosperity) by adding an extra step, respecifying the proffered representation by supplementing it with his own frame knowledge.

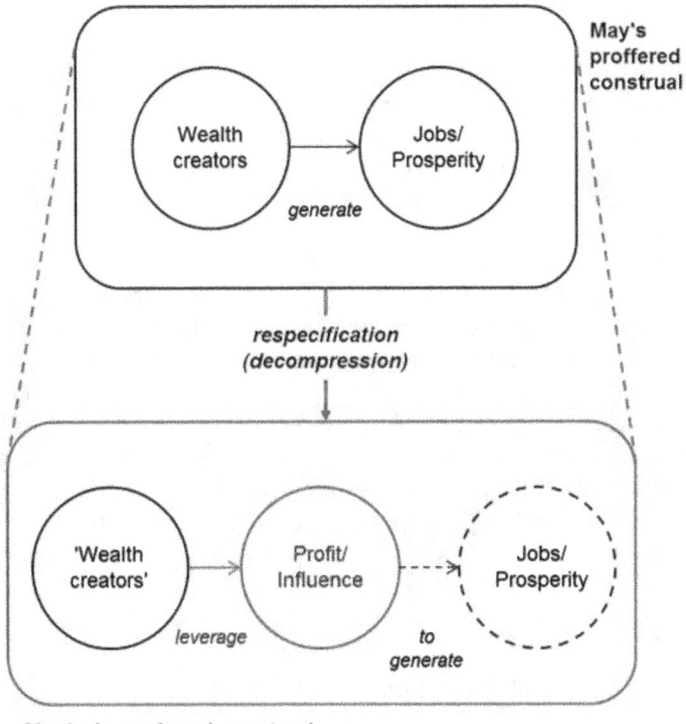

Figure 7.4 Respecifying the 'wealth creators'.

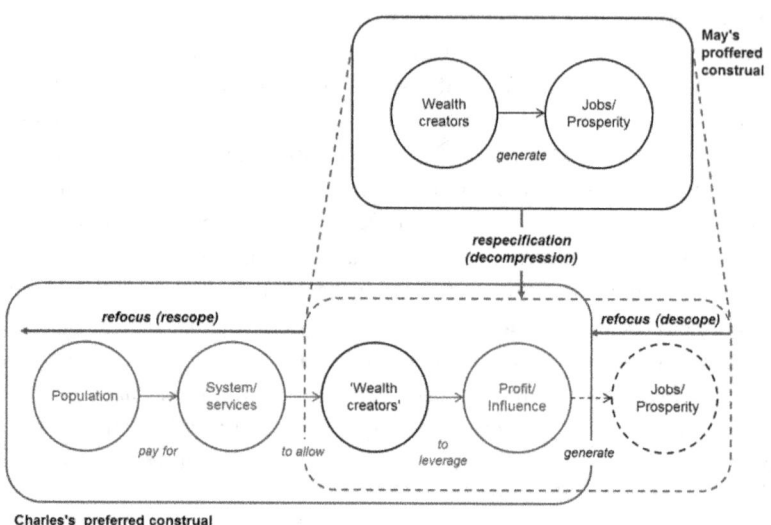

Figure 7.5 Multi-process reconstrual of 'wealth creators'.

Charles's respecification is accompanied by a further process of refocusing. Not only does his comment insert a new object between 'wealth creators' and 'jobs and prosperity', it also deletes the latter (represented in Figure 7.4 by a dashed circle) and adds a series of actors 'upstream' in the action chain – 'the population' and 'systems and services'. This has been diagrammed in Figure 7.5.

The construal mechanism, here, is one of re- and defocusing. On the one hand, the representation is defocused in comment (6) because 'jobs and prosperity' are removed from the immediate scope of predication. On the other hand, Charles rescopes in order to include 'the population who pay for the systems and services that allow the "wealth creators" to leverage profit and influence'. The wider scope of the action chain is consequently made to include what, according to Charles's pre-existing frame of economic activity, are the agents and objects that enable the activity of May's 'risk takers', 'innovators' and 'entrepreneurs'. This more holistic conception of economic relations shares with Tom's frame an emphasis on the structures that make wealth creation possible, evidencing a shared ideological perspective which stands in distinction to the prime minister's.

6. Hmmm yes, but where's the beef?

These responses to a Conservative politician are what one might imagine from members of the Labour Party and vocal supporters of the opposition front benches. Conversely, one might expect responses to Corbyn's speech to be encouraging and sympathetic. Certainly they are in most cases, for example:

7) Yeah just great (Harry)
8) Sounds good (James)
9) Spot on - how can anyone disagree (Charles)
10) Yes (Karen)

All four of these comments were made in response to the following paragraph from the Labour leader's conference address:

> Now is the time that government took a more active role in restructuring our economy. Now is the time that corporate boardrooms were held accountable for their actions. Now is the time that we developed a new model of economic management to replace the failed dogmas of neo-liberalism. That is why Labour is looking not just to repair the damage done by austerity but to transform our economy with a new and dynamic role for the public sector particularly where the private sector has evidently failed.

However, three participants, Richard, Tom and John, expressed frustration with this particular passage:

11) Again change narrative but do people no neo liberalism. Bit political speak (Richard)
12) A bit universal for me. I'd need more evidence of which kind of corporate boardrooms (John)
13) Hmmm yes, but where's the beef? This is just words (Tom)

Like his comment in (4) and James's in (5), Richard addresses his response to the effectiveness of this section from the speech. In comment (11), he mind-models Corbyn's potential audience, asking if people '[know] neo liberalism', and suggests that the socialist politician's use of the term is 'political speak'. While containing a negative appraisal, this form of assessment is potentially sympathetic insofar as it orients to the likelihood of the rhetorical success of the speech. It could therefore be posed as a 'constructive' criticism - presumably Richard's concern is that he wants Corbyn to be persuasive, and fears that he is not. This is supported by Richard's initial mention of a positive feature of the speech (that the Labour leader is 'chang[ing the] narrative') and that the comment is syntactically structured as a question - despite not possessing a question mark - which suggests a level of hedging to mitigate the potential face-threatening act (Brown and Levinson 1987) of offering criticism.

In (12), John's criticism is directed at the lack of evidence and detail in this section of speech. Like, Richard, though, he also employs hedging in the form of epistemic 'modal shading' (see Simpson 1993: 58). He writes 'a bit universal for me', where the final 'for me' locates his negative assessment in a personal - rather than universal - benchmark of what counts as a satisfactory argument. Similarly, in the subsequent sentence, the evidential requirements for making reliable claims about corporate boardrooms are qualified with respect to John's own idiosyncratic needs - he says '*I'd need* more evidence' (my emphasis) - rather than any general standard of admissibility. The effect of this epistemic shading is to foreground John and construe him with greater objectivity, thereby providing a subjective reconstrual of the text-world proffered by Corbyn; that is, in foregrounding his own higher standard of evidence, he also highlights the subjectivity of the opposition leader's representation of events. Strangely, with the exception of an initial reluctant agreement (signalled by 'hmmm'), this hedging is almost entirely absent in (13). 'The beef' in Tom's comment is a metaphorical allusion to the (lack of) detail, or 'meat', in this passage. Tom's remark that 'this is just words' resonates with Richard's comment that the paragraph is a 'bit political speak'. Again the force of the criticism is directed at the imprecision and the absent details in the speech.

Of the seven participants, John and Tom demonstrate the most scepticism towards Corbyn's speech. Where they express dissatisfaction, it usually takes the form of demanding more information or more detail. For example, Tom's comment on this passage from Corbyn's speech follows a similar pattern:

> The Tory approach to the economy isn't entrepreneurial; it's extractive. They've not focused on long-term investment and wealth creation. When you look at what they do rather than what they say it's all about driving down wages, services and standards to make as much money as quickly as possible with government not as the servant of the people but of global corporations. And their disregard for rampant inequality the hollowing out of our public services, the disdain for the powerless and the poor have made our society more brutal and less caring. We are going to ask big business to pay a bit more tax.

His response goes as follows:

14) Excellent critique of what the Tory strategy is. But what's Labour going to do to change it. I'm far from clear (Tom)

Like Richard in (11), Tom leads with a positive comment ('excellent critique of what the Tory strategy is') but subsequently requests more detail from Corbyn on how Labour will address the issue. Similarly, where the Labour leader says 'When I've met business groups I've been frank: we will invest in the education and skills of the workforce', John replies:

15) Depends what kind of education and where. Training an army of plumbers will not solve the problem because you can't predict where demand will be in job market (John)

Here, the respondent is querying the level of detail inhering in the noun 'education'. He adds more detail to the noun by respecifying it as 'training an army of plumbers' and dismissing this form of 'education' as inadequate. Interestingly, there is no respecification of what would be a satisfactory form of education. All examples (12–15) demonstrate a form of thwarted respecification, then, in which the proffered representation is not deemed to be detailed enough, but no alternative frame knowledge is advanced to 'fill the gap', so to speak. This is a qualitatively different form of critique than the oppositional positioning in response to May's conference speech. In examples (1-6), participant's existing frame knowledge supplemented and clashed with the construal proffered by May. Conversely, the critical responses to Corbyn all involve the absence of an existing frame of reference. For this reason, I would hesitate to call them 'oppositional' or 'negotiated' (Hall 1980) because they do not involve any kind of recoding – the critique is oriented to a lack in *both* the proffered representation and the reader's frame knowledge, rather than reconstruing with respect to a pre-existing frame. However, while these participants are more broadly sympathetic to Corbyn's political perspective, neither do their comments fall within the remit of a 'full and straight' (Hall 1980: 125) acceptance of the socialist politician's rhetorical performance. In tracing the conceptual processes involved in the active audience's reception of the discourse, then, Cognitive Grammar can add a finer level of analytical granularity to Hall's (1980) tripartite mode.

7. Conclusion

This chapter began with a discussion of Widdowson's (1995) argument that any interpretation of a text is always a product of bringing the reader or audience's discourse to the communicative event. I have explored this perspective using Text World Theory (Werth 1999; Gavins 2007) and Cognitive Grammar (Langacker 1987, 1991, 2008), supplementing with both a socially and politically oriented perspective from Hall's (1980) encoding-decoding model. The outcome of this synthesis is (the beginning outline of) a CDA of reception which situates the interpretative practices of discourse participants with respect to their social context. In this example, that context was provided by Corbyn-supporting members of the Labour Party and the conceptual frames – the models of reality – they brought to bear in their responses to the conference speeches of Conservative and Labour Party leaders. The particular emphasis of this chapter was to analyse the interaction of linguistic forms in the texts – such as the noun phrase 'wealth creators' – with the readers' pre-existing frame knowledge. Cognitive approaches allow such a pivot between text and frame because of their emphasis on the heteronomy of meaning in discourse (Stockwell 2002a); there is no meaning without the cognitive activity of discourse participants. As such, the proffered meaning of any discourse is always a construal of the discourse participants' own pre-existing knowledge frames – a representation that readers may reject if it clashes with their preferred construal of that conceptual domain. However, the focus on language not only acted as augmentation of Hall (1980) and Brunsdon and Morley's (1999) work. Responses to Corbyn's speech also problematized the cline of readerly positions they outline (oppositional → negotiated → dominant hegemonic). Participants played an active role in the discourse in the sense that they provided partial critique of the conference address, but there was no easy fit between their comments and Hall's (1980) tripartite model of reader positions. This speaks to the importance of not only creating a typology of reader responses, but also a descriptive framework for linking them concretely to discourse structures, that is, specifying the cognitive-ideological relationship between text and frame knowledge. Cognitive Grammar provides a starting point in developing that descriptive framework.

Note

1. To anticipate later discussion, while accounts of meaning in Cognitive Grammar hinge on the relationship between linguistic form, background knowledge and conceptualization, the readerly emphasis in Text World Theory on the text-driven process of meaning-making provides a stronger foundation for investigating critical reception.

References

Brown, P., and S. Levinson (1987), *Politeness: Some Universals in Language Use*. Cambridge: Cambridge University Press.

Browse, S. (2018a), *Cognitive Rhetoric: The Cognitive Poetics of Political Discourse*, Amsterdam: John Benjamins.

Browse, S. (2018b), 'Reading Political Minds: "Backstage" Politics in Audience Reception', in M. Kranert and G. Horan (eds), *'Doing Politics': Discursivity, Performativity and Mediation in Political Discourse*, 333–59, Amsterdam: John Benjamins.

Browse, S. (2018c), 'From Functional to Cognitive Grammar in Stylistic Analysis of Golding's *The Inheritors*', *Journal of Literary Semantics*, 47 (2): 121–46.

Browse, S. (2019), '"That's Just What We Hear on Telly All the Time, Isn't It?" Political Discourse and the Cognitive Linguistic Ethnography of Critical Reception', in C. Hart (ed.), *Cognitive Linguistic Approaches to Text and Discourse: From Politics to Poetics*, 157–80, Edinburgh: Edinburgh University Press.

Browse, S. (forthcoming), 'Towards an Empirical Stylistics of Critical Reception: The Oppositional Reader in Political Discourse', in A. Bell, S. Browse, A. Gibbons and D. Peplow (eds), *Style and Response: Minds, Media, Methods*, Amsterdam: John Benjamins.

Brunsdon, C. and D. Morley (1999), *The Nationwide Television Studies*, London: Routledge.

Cap, P. (2013), *Proximization: The Pragmatics of Symbolic Distance Crossing*, Amsterdam: John Benjamins.

Charteris-Black, J. (2004), *Corpus Approaches to Critical Metaphor Analysis*, Basingstoke: Palgrave.

Chilton, P. (2004), *Analysing Political Discourse: Theory and Practice*, Abingdon: Routledge.

Cobley, P. (1994), 'Throwing Out the Baby: Populism and Active Audience Theory', *Media, Culture and Society*, 16 (4): 677–87.

Cook, G. (1994), *Discourse and Literature*, Oxford: Oxford University Press.

Curran, J. (1990), 'The New Revisionism in Mass Communication Research: A Reappraisal', *European Journal of Communication*, 5 (2): 135–64.

van Dijk, T. (1998), *Ideology: A Multidisciplinary Approach*, Thousand Oaks, CA: Sage.

Fairclough, N. (1992), *Discourse and Social Change*, Cambridge: Polity Press.

Fairclough, N. (1996), 'A Reply to Henry Widdowson's "Discourse Analysis: a Critical View"', *Language and Literature*, 5 (1): 49–56.

Fairclough, N. (2001), *Language and Power*, 2nd edn, Harlow: Longman.

Fauconnier, G. and M. Turner (2002), *The Way We Think: Conceptual Blending and the Mind's Hidden Complexities*, New York: Basic Books.

Fillmore, C. (1982), 'Frame Semantics', in Linguistics Society of Korea (eds), *Linguistics in the Morning Calm*, 111–37, Seoul: Hanshin Publishing Company.

Gavins, J. (2007), *Text World Theory: An Introduction*, Edinburgh: Edinburgh University Press.

Gavins, J. and P. Simpson (2015), 'Regina v John Terry: The Discursive Construction of an Alleged Racist Event', *Discourse and Society*, 26 (6): 712–32.

Goatly, A. (2007), *Washing the Brain: Metaphor and Hidden Ideology*, Amsterdam: John Benjamins.

Hall, S. (1980), 'Encoding/Decoding', in S. Hall, D. Hobson, A. Lowe and P. Willis (eds), *Culture, Media, Language*, 128–38, New York: Routledge.

Hart, C. (2014), *Discourse, Grammar and Ideology: Functional and Cognitive Perspectives*, London: Bloomsbury.

Hart, C. (2016), 'Event Frames Affect Blame Assignment and Perception of Aggression in Discourse on Political Protest: An Experimental Case Study in Critical Discourse Analysis', *Applied Linguistics*, 39 (3): 400–21.

Ingarden, R. (1973), *The Cognition of the Literary Work of Art*, Evanston: Northwestern University Press.

Jeffries, L. (2010), *Critical Stylistics: The Power of English*, Basingstoke: Palgrave.

Koller, V. (2005), 'Critical Discourse Analysis and Social Cognition: Evidence from Business Media Discourse', *Discourse and Society*, 16 (2): 199–224.

Lakoff, G. (2002), *Moral Politics*, Chicago: Chicago University Press.

Langacker, R.W. (1987), *Foundations of Cognitive Grammar, Vol. I: Theoretical Prerequisites*, Stanford: Stanford University Press.

Langacker, R.W. (1991), *Foundations of Cognitive Grammar, Vol. II: Descriptive Application*, Stanford: Stanford University Press.

Langacker, R.W. (2008), *Cognitive Grammar: A Basic Introduction*, Oxford: Oxford University Press.

Milroy, L. (1987), *Language and Social Networks*, Oxford: Blackwell.

Morley, D. (1993), 'Active Audience Theory: Pendulums and Pitfalls', *Journal of Communication*, 43 (4): 13–19.

Musolff, A. (2016), *Political Metaphor Analysis: Discourse and Scenarios*, London: Bloomsbury.

Norledge, J. (2016), 'Reading the Dystopian Short Story', Unpublished PhD thesis, University of Sheffield.

Philo, G. (2001), 'Media Effects and the Active Audience', *Sociology Review*, 10 (3): 26–9.

Seaman, W. (1992), 'Active Audience Theory: Pointless Populism', *Media, Culture and Society*, 14 (2): 301–11.

Short, M. and W. van Peer (1989), 'Accident! Stylisticians Evaluate: Aims and Methods in Stylistic Analysis', in M. Short (ed.), *Reading, Analysing and Teaching Literature*, 22–71, London: Longman.

Simpson, P. (1993), *Language, Ideology and Point of View*, London: Routledge.

Stockwell, P. (2002a), 'A Stylistics Manifesto', in S. Csabi and J. Zerkowitz (eds), *Textual Secrets: The Message of the Medium*, 65–75, Budapest: Eotvos Lorand University.

Stockwell, P. (2002b), *Cognitive Poetics: An Introduction*, London: Routledge.

Turner, M. (2006), 'Compression and Representation', *Language and Literature*, 15 (1): 17–27.

Wenger, E. (1998), *Communities of Practice: Learning, Meaning and Identity*, Cambridge: Cambridge University Press.

Werth, P. (1999), *Text Worlds: Representing Conceptual Space in Discourse*, London: Longman.
Widdowson, H. (1995), 'Discourse Analysis: A Critical View', *Language and Literature*, 4 (3): 157–72.
Wodak, R. (2009), *The Discourse of Politics in Action: Politics as Usual*, Basingstoke: Palgrave.

8

Modelling intentionality in Cognitive Grammar

Matthew Voice

1. Introduction

Reflecting on the applicability of Cognitive Grammar to stylistic analysis, Pincombe (2014: 174) outlines a key limitation in its functionality, writing that 'one of the reasons grammarians – of any school – tend not to stray beyond the sentence, surely, is that close grammatical analysis takes up so much time to complete and so much space on the page'. Discussing Langacker's efforts to conceptualize language at the discourse level (Langacker 2008: 488–9), Pincombe reflects that 'it would be wonderful to have a whole short-story diagrammed this way. But who would do it? And who would read it?' (Pincombe 2014). Owing to the limitations of space in any given research paper, Cognitive Grammar's detail-oriented modelling is more readily suited to sentence-level analysis. Reviewing recent work in cognitive approaches to stylistics, however, Harrison (2017: 25–7) concludes that a scalable application of Cognitive Grammar to the analysis of discourse-grammar is possible, although the interaction between micro- and macro-scale discourse analysis remains problematic (cf. Dancyier 2008). Understanding how Cognitive Grammar can scale its analysis of language to the level of discourse while maintaining the precision of its clause-level modelling, then, is an ongoing project.

This chapter contributes to this research by highlighting the perceived intentionality of actions as an overlooked conceptual element of language comprehension, which connects sentence-level construal with the overarching interpretation of discourse. While Cognitive Grammar's model of verb processes deals in detail with explicit directions of force and the causal relationship between grammatical participants as part of a 'highly selective' (Langacker 2014: xiv) and fine-grained clausal analysis, it does not include a representation of the linguistic function – and therefore the conceptual effect – of an agent's intentionality. Yet contextualizing individual actions within a broader understanding of the actor's character is essential to the process of understanding characters and their identities across a discourse. As a result, the present process of analysing individual events in language can sometimes appear distant from the context provided by the discourse in which it appears. This chapter therefore proposes a framework for the modelling of intentionality in the analysis of events in language.

After introducing the conceptual distinction between intentional and unintentional actions through constructed example sentences, the primary theoretical discussion developed in this chapter is applied to extracts from military memoirs in which the authors describe performing act of violence during conflict, originally collected and discussed in Voice (2018), where differentiating between intentional and unintentional actions was an essential element of a critical linguistic analysis. By focusing on texts in which the ability to explain how actions and intentions are construed is connected to an evaluation of a morally complex or taboo action, the nuances in the construal and perception of intentions are set out as clearly as possible. As these examples move from sentence to discourse-level analysis, the chapter concludes by reflecting on potential future applications to further critical and literary research.

2. Intentionality in language and cognition

Bandura (2006) lists intentionality – defined as the capacity to 'form intentions that include action plans and strategies for realising them' (164) – as one of the core properties of human agency, allowing us to rationally explain our own actions and those of others in relation to ongoing goals, beliefs and desires (cf. Dowty 1991: 601–2). Likewise, the capacity to infer intentions from the actions of others has been described as 'a hallmark of the human cognitive apparatus' (Behrend and Scofield 2006: 291), whereby interaction with other individuals assumes that their perceptions and decision-making processes are comparable to our own, or at least recognizable, and thus they can act based upon the same kinds of private motivations that might drive our own actions. This situates the study of intentionality within the context of 'mind-modelling' (Stockwell 2009; Stockwell and Mahlberg 2015) as an active process of simulating the mental lives of others (cf. Tomasello 1999: 66–70), which can be applied to the perception of both real and fictional actors. The process of approximating the mental lives of others in both language and perception is therefore one which requires some ability to predictively infer the reasons, or minimally the capacity for reasoning, which account for rational, volitional actions.

While intentionality is not an exclusively linguistic concept, it is the construal of events and their perspectivization in language which inform judgements regarding whether a described action was performed for a reason, and consequently whether or not the agent of the actor should be considered responsible for it. In Systemic Functional Linguistics, as per Figure 8.1, the subdivision of material process verbs readily distinguishes between the kinds of activity that have the capacity to be performed intentionally (intention processes), those which can only be carried out unintentionally (supervention processes), and clauses which position inanimate objects as agents (event processes).

Figure 8.1 shows the functional difference between intentional and superventional acts, although Simpson remarks that 'these subdivisions should be regarded more as

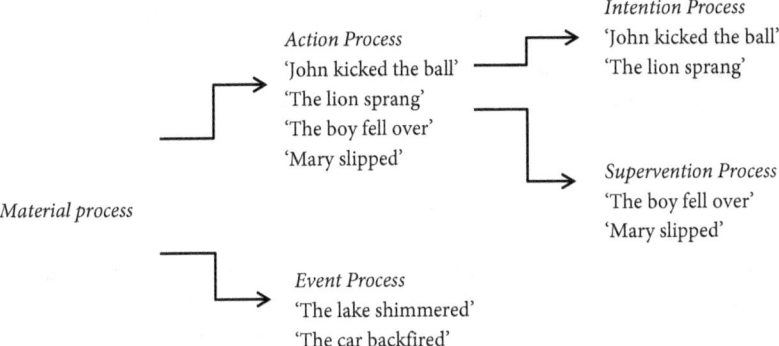

Figure 8.1 Modelling intentional and superventional processes in SFL (adapted from Simpson 1993: 89).

handy approximations than as strictly delineated categories' (90). Nonetheless, the process of actively differentiating between intentional and superventional actions in Systemic Functional Linguistics demonstrates the value of distinguishing between actions which connote intentionality, and those which do not. A stylistic analysis which separates the frequency with which a character is construed as an intentional and superventional actor, for instance, will come to far more nuanced conclusions with regard to the agency exerted by the character through their grammatical positioning within the discourse. Although these subdivisions help to distinguish between the kinds of material process being construed semantically, the process of identifying and distinguishing between intentional and superventional processes relies exclusively on the interpretation of the reader. In the sentence 'John kicked the ball', for example, John might not have meant to kick the ball, as the act of kicking is not always intentional. As a result, the categorization of processes reveals little about the process through which intentionality is perceived in language, only that it *is* perceived.

While Cognitive Grammar's model of verb processes deals in detail with explicit directions of force and the causal relationship between grammatical participants as part of a highly selective and fine-grained clausal analysis, it does not include a comparable representation of the linguistic function – and therefore the conceptual effect – of an agent's intentionality. There is no explicit distinction in the *canonical event model* (Langacker 2008: 357) between actions performed intentionally and those events performed by agents without underlying goals, desires or motivation (cf. Popova 2014: 2). Rather, Cognitive Grammar takes volitional action as prototypical to the *agent role* (Langacker 1991: 210), suggesting that grammatical agents are prototypically actors with the capacity to intend. Mental activity is not exclusively implied by the agent category, however, as Langacker explicitly acknowledges the 'actor-like' status of *experiencers* (2008: 392), the subjects of perceptual processes such as seeing and hearing. While this is an adequate account for the majority of processes performed by participants with the capacity for intentional action, the present model of canonical events does not demonstrate how acts performed unintentionally might differ conceptually, or how readers might determine intentionality in ambiguous instances. Given the potentially wide-ranging social implications behind the distinction between intentional and unintentional actions, it is important to understand how these forms of action can be distinguished and represented distinctly.

3. Intentional actions in Cognitive Grammar

Cognitive Grammar provides an intricate means of discussing and investigating the conceptual structure of language. Langacker (1987) defines Cognitive Grammar as a model of language in which 'grammatical structures do not constitute an autonomous formal system or level of representation: they are claimed instead to be inherently symbolic, providing structuring and conventional symbolization of conceptual content' (1–2). For the purposes of this chapter, the discussion will simply focus on what this means for the conceptualization of events. Key concepts such as the canonical event model and action chains will first be introduced and reviewed, before exploring how intentions can be represented within this conceptual framework.

3.1 Canonical events

In Cognitive Grammar, the canonical event model represents the prototypical conceptual structure of a transitive clause. In the most straightforward iteration of a sentence composed of an agent, theme and force viewed from a third-person perspective (e.g. 'The boy hit the ball'), all elements within the action's immediate scope are present within the discourse, as the reader is told explicitly what kind of action takes place, who performs it and who or what it was performed upon. In instances where these relationships are less explicit, such as a passivized sentence ('The ball was hit by the boy') the agent role can be framed less prominently or even omitted entirely ('The ball was hit'). Regardless of variety in the construal of the process, the force dynamic emphasis of the canonical event model foregrounds the physicality of material interaction as either the literal or metaphorical frame of understanding for the interaction between participants in an event. Building outward from individual clauses, the notion of *action chains* (Langacker 2008: 355) reflects the causal connection between a series of events ('The boy hit the ball, which knocked over the vase, which scared the cat'), demonstrating how readers might infer responsibility for the indirect consequences of an action, even at some distance from the source of the original act.

While this model of event representation succeeds in conceptualizing the relationship between participants in terms of the transfer of force and perceived causality, it does not distinguish between acts performed purposefully, and those with no guiding intentions. Consider the following example sentences:

a) The wind knocked down the tree.
b) The lumberjack knocked down the tree.
c) The lumberjack accidentally knocked down the tree.

With regard to the canonical event model, each sentence can be modelled almost identically. Each has an agent and a patient, as well as a clear transfer of force from one to the other, viewed by the reader from a third-person perspective. However, it would be inaccurate to describe all three as conceptually identical: in the case of (a) and (c), it makes no sense to ask *why* such events occurred, as they cannot have been intentional: understanding of 'the wind' renders the inference of any intention meaningless, and the adverb 'accidentally' precludes any question of reason behind the lumberjack's action. While sentence (b) could describe the same event as sentence (c), the lack of adverbs or prepositions to further define the context of the act makes it unclear whether it is performed intentionally or not. However, with schematic knowledge of a lumberjack as a human actor who regularly and deliberately knocks down trees, sentence (b) may prototypically be interpreted as an intentional action. For events in which acts of violence occur, such as those in the text analysed later in this chapter, the identification of and distinction between intentional/superventional actors can drastically alter the construal of a scene:

d) The heart attack killed John.
e) The burglar killed John.

Both (d) and (e) can be modelled identically as canonical events within the CG model, where an agent acts on or towards a patient, and force is transferred or motion enacted regardless of the agent's intentions. Were these two sentences to reflect two possible rulings in a legal case, however, then the construal of an intentional or superventional agent in relation to John's death would have profound consequences. Determining the relevance of different intentions in relation to actions and events can therefore be seen as an important dimension in the conceptualization of event structure, for both interpretative and social reasons.

Langacker describes the archetypal agent as 'a person who *volitionally* carries out physical activity' (1991: 210, my emphasis), in which case only (b) and (e) of the above examples could be properly considered a canonical event. But Langacker gives no account of what conceptual change occurs if expectations of intentionality are subverted: the canonical event model's representation of an action remains unchanged regardless of whether the action in question is performed by an agent with the capacity to act intentionally or not. Given the social and conceptual significance often associated with the evaluation of an agent and their actions as intentional, this chapter is concerned with the development of the framework of Cognitive Grammar to clearly distinguish between volitional and non-volitional acts, and its subsequent ability to examine the role of such construals in discourse.

Although intentionality itself is not associated with a single grammatical feature, there are demonstrable instances in which isolated grammatical variations appear to influence readers' perceptions of agentive intentionality. As well as the association between transitivity and intentionality discussed so far (cf. Nuttall 2018; 2019), Astington (1999) notes that adjectives and adverbs can readily be used to describe accidental or skilful actions, as in (c) above, while Halliday (1970) demonstrates that prepositions (e.g. 'the window was broken *by a storm*') can provide additional context to affirm or deny the interpretation of an event as intentional. More recently, Strickland et al. (2014) have shown that under speeded conditions, readers are more likely to perceive grammatical subjects than grammatical objects as intentional, but that order of mention within a shared subject position (e.g. 'John and Susan exchanged books') did not affect judgements of intentionality. Interestingly, however, Hart (2018: 414) demonstrates that with reciprocal verb constructions ('protestors clashed with police', or 'police clashed with protestors'), the agent positioned first in the sentence order is more frequently blamed for the event, or marked as aggressive. Furthermore, Nakamura (2018) suggests that intentionality of action in relation to harmful versus helpful behaviour is related to probabilistic inference. Essentially, the perception of intentionality appears to rely on the interplay between a variety of grammatical and semantic features of discourse. The model of intentionality advanced in this chapter, then, is not the analysis of a single linguistic feature, but the conceptualization of an impression construed through many different elements and contexts, often in concordance with one another.

As van Leeuwen (1997) observes of social agency, 'there is no neat fit between sociological and linguistic categories' (32), as not all aspects of understanding evoked in relation to a given word or phrase can be located at a specific point in the text itself. Cognitive Grammar is well equipped to account for the role of background knowledge and previous language use in the act of interpretation. Indeed, the *conceptual substrate* (Langacker 2008: 42) outlines the role of previous language usage and physical, social and cultural context in the understanding of an utterance's meaning. In the case of intentionality, the recognition of particular kinds of actors and actions provides readers with prototypical scripts through which to assess the probability that an action was performed intentionally, and if so the kinds of goals that might be associated with the actor in question.

In order to demonstrate the relationship between intentions and the description of actions more directly, Figure 8.2 represents a clause from Stainton (n.d.), an extract from the memoir of a British soldier who served in the First World War, in which the narrator describes killing an enemy sniper. The area consisting of solid lines represents the conceptualization of the clause which appears in the source text ('I squeezed the trigger'), while the dotted boxes represent hypothesized intentions for the initial action. As 'I' represents a first-person adult human narrator, they can reasonably be considered an actor with the capacity to intend. Taken in isolation, it may not be clear in many cases what the intention behind an act might be. In these cases, while the exact intentions which cause the agent to perform the act remain unknown or uncertain, agents are prototypically perceived as having the *capacity* to act volitionally by virtue of their actor-like qualities (2008: 392). This tendency to ascribe or infer intentions where none are explicit is a part of everyday perceptual processes. Indeed, the 'intentionality bias' (Rosset 2008; Strickland et al. 2014) indicates that in speeded conditions, adult readers will describe ambiguously construed actions as intentional, even if the action in question is typically performed unintentionally. Hence, modelling the capacity for an intentional action does not require the identification of a specific intention *per se*.

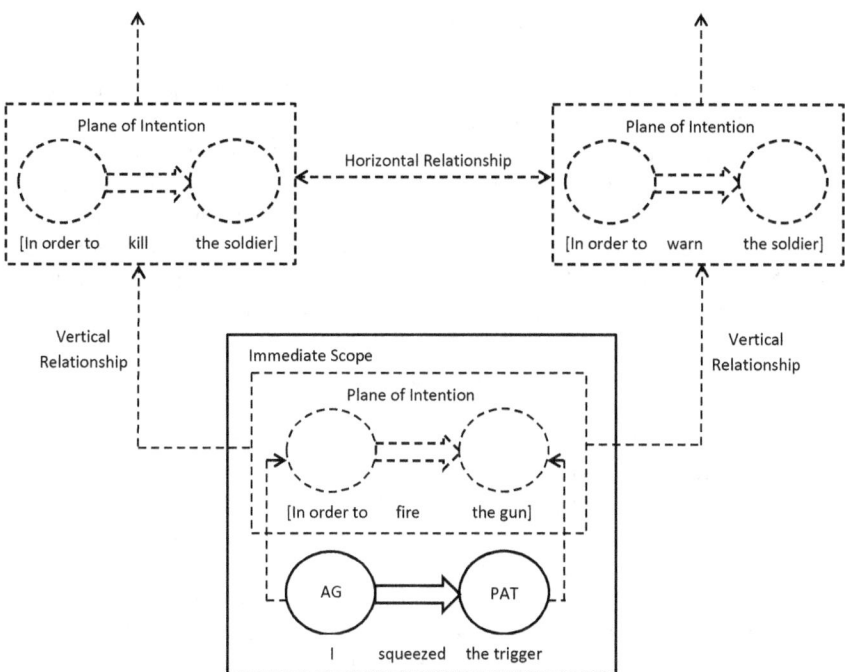

Figure 8.2 Planes of intention in relation to an example canonical event.

In the case of the sentence 'I squeezed the trigger', contextual knowledge of the scripts associated with the act identifies it as a granular aspect of the process of firing a gun. Hence, the dashed box and arrow extending from the initial construal in Figure 8.2 represents the fact that both the identification of the narrator as a human agent and the act of squeezing probabilistically construe an intention. Likewise, the patient 'trigger' and further foregrounding of Stainton's rifle within the surrounding discourse frame the act of squeezing as directly associated with the operation of the weapon. Hence, the initial intention of squeezing the trigger in order to fire the gun is positioned within the immediate scope of construal, as understanding the relationship between the action and this intention is important to the immediate interpretation of the text. I use the term 'plane of intention' here to show that while this particular relationship is not construed explicitly, its structure represents how a perceived goal associated with the initial action might itself be construed. Given that this is a direct and instantaneous consequence of pulling the trigger, no other alternative intentions at this level are offered. Beyond the immediate scope, however, is the further question of *why* the narrator intended to fire the gun at all.

Crucially, the plane of intention as modelled here is distinct from the mental space label 'belief' in Langacker (2008: 480), first because intentions refer to a comparable but more typically goal-oriented category of mental activity than active belief, and second because Langacker's label marks an explicit proposition of belief within the discourse.

Whether or not they are described directly, the perceived intentions associated with rational actions affect the perceptions of events in discourse. As van Dijk (1975) puts it, actions take place 'under the "scope" of a global intention and purpose controlling the local intentions and purposes' (281), meaning that intentions and goals themselves can be construed as part of an ongoing, larger network of intentions which may account for a series of actions. Similarly, Plaks and Robinson (2015) distinguish between 'proximal' and 'distal' intentions, referring to the proximity of the goal to the granularity of the event performed. Moving further 'up' the series of intentions in Figure 8.2, represented by the 'vertical relationship' label, indicates a more distal and abstract intent which may persist over a greater deal of time or number of activities. These can in turn be extended further: the narrator may intend to kill the enemy sniper in order to win the battle, in order to win the war, in order to return home. As the intentions related to an action become further abstracted along this vertical plane, they refer to longer-term goals, and may serve as a unifying intention to explain a series of actions across a narrative. Equally, however, they become harder to verify as reasonable representations of the intentions associated with the initial action without further supporting evidence, in the form of either additional actions which support the interpretation, or an explicit statement of intent within the discourse.

In contrast to the vertical relationship between intentions of greater or lesser abstraction, possible explanations for an action may have a 'horizontal relationship', as represented in Figure 8.2 by the dual suggestions that the narrator of the initial clause intends to fire his gun to either kill or warn the enemy sniper. Horizontally related intentions can be supported or challenged independently of one another, and in some cases co-occur: the narrator may wish to simultaneously warn the enemy sniper to leave the location and alert his allies to his location, for instance. Without broader context to support one intention over another, or prior knowledge on behalf of the reader to produce a script of expected activity, any number of horizontally related intentions could be considered a plausible explanation for an agent's actions. Furthermore, just as the structure of events around Langacker's canonical event model can deviate from the straightforward transfer of energy from one participant to another, it is also possible for the conceptual structure of intentions to deviate from the archetypal form. As well as prototypical transfers of force from agent to patient, intentions may equally be movements to or from a location, internal changes of state or any other possible variation within the event category. Unlike an action chain (Langacker 2008: 355–6), there may be no direct causative connection between an action and the intentions which drive it, as an action may fail to cause the intended consequences. I might pick up a glass in order to drink from it with the intention of quenching my thirst, but realize on closer inspection that my glass is already empty. In these cases, even though the desired state of the intention is unrealized, the attempt to produce the effect can nonetheless be inferred from the sequence of activity as an explanation for the actions which occurred.

Although there are a near-infinite number of possible reasons for performing any given act, making sense of an action does not require considering the reasons for its performance from all angles. Indeed, as Anscombe (1957: 80) observes, to suggest that each action we perform and observe is actively considered in terms of each constituent reason for the act would be 'quite absurd'. The majority of possible explanations for an action are often instead eliminated quickly with reference to the context in which the act takes place, 'thus usefully constraining our interpretative domain and enabling us to start considering endlessly nuanced choices *within that domain*' (Zunshine 2006: 14, original emphasis). Similarly to the principle of minimal departure (Ryan 1980), schematized knowledge may lead the reader to a path of least resistance in interpreting action: an intention or cause most readily inferred from broader knowledge of its context. This interpretation of an actor's intentions may later be revealed to be false, but these cognitive shortcuts allow the reader to form explanatory models of activity which remain open to revision in the course of reading. In the context of literary texts, Stockwell (2020: 141) has argued that ambiguity in literature provides grounds for readers to map their own feelings and experiences to the events and characters described. The ability to interpret the actions of literary characters without the prescription of a single, definitive intention behind the act allows for much literary discussion, both academically and informally. In both cases, readers are shown not only to have the capacity to extend their understanding of a text beyond the features presented to them explicitly in its language, but that doing so is part of the everyday process of engaging with literature, and narratives more generally.

That readers' knowledge of the intentions which govern action can develop according to the information present demonstrates the versatility of an analysis of intentionality: actions across a text can be grouped thematically through their association with a given order of intention. Accordingly, readers may contextualize actions in relation to either proximal or distal perceived intentions, depending upon how readily each intention makes sense of the act, as well as the intentions of the explanation itself. Similarly, profiling the expression or inference of agents' intentions can serve as the foundation for a unified understanding of their character across a series of events and scenarios. As this chapter goes on to argue, intentions may also function as reference points (Langacker 2008: 83–8, 504–5) in the dynamic evolution of the reader's understanding of a character and their contexts. The purpose of modelling intentions in Cognitive Grammar, then, is to model the possible interactions between the context afforded by a particular linguistic construal, and the schematic knowledge and interpretative practices of individual readers.

3.2 Intentions across clauses

The discussion so far has outlined the role of perceived intentions related to an action in relative isolation from further narrative context. However, the process of engaging with discourse is not merely the sequential process of interpreting one sentence at a time. As the following example demonstrates, as more information is revealed to the reader in the course of reading, possible interpretations of character intentions narrow down, and patterns of activity can be recognized. Beginning with an individual clause, the discussion of this text will gradually expand to include additional context laid out within the discourse, to demonstrate how different features of levels of discursive structure contribute to the perception of the intentions associated with this initial clause. In describing his experiences during the First World War, A.C. Warsop (1965) writes, similarly to Stainton, that:

f) [I] very carefully squeezed the trigger

(15)

First of all, the adverb 'carefully' construes an intentional action without specifying a particular intention. Although it could be the case that Warsop misses his shot or wounds the wrong person, thereby producing unintended consequences, the act of squeezing the trigger itself is intended. Despite the absence of a specific intention, the default perception of the first-person narrator, particularly outside of literary fiction, is of an autonomous human agent mind-modelled as capable of volition. Thus, even though the reader cannot know precisely *why* the narrator acts from the information provided in this sentence alone, it remains possible – even prototypical – to consider the agent in this instance as performing a goal-directed activity.

Once the analysis moves beyond the clause, however, it becomes clear that the broader discourse provides context which affects the scope of probable intentions. Immediately prior to the clause above, Warsop describes how 'I thought I saw two men behind some bushes twenty five yards in front. By now I was thoroughly frightened but I did draw my rifle, check my sights to twenty five yards' (Warsop 1965), before carefully pulling the trigger. Taken as part of a script of activity, these actions support an interpretation of Warsop's actions as granular components of a larger goal of deliberately hitting the enemy soldiers with bullets fired from his rifle. An interpretation of his intentions which suggests that he squeezes the trigger in order to hit these men is also supported by the prepositional phrase which immediately follows clause (f), where Warsop describes how he squeezed the trigger 'at the first one then the other indistinct figures'. In other words, narrative context and grammatical structure limit the reasonable interpretation of the narrator's intentions: while we cannot say for sure why Warsop fired at the figures (intending either to kill, to wound, to warn them), there is a direct causal connection between them which Warsop describes as deliberate, via an act prototypically assumed to have been performed for some reason. As discussion in Section 4 will show, further context from elsewhere in the narrative can be used to narrow down the number of probable intentions associated with a given action.

While the discussion above has inferred the goals associated with the actions described by Warsop, some writing explicitly construes actors' intentions. For instance, Heavens (1916), in describing a re-capture of a trench, explains that 'the first line of our infantry jumped in [to the trench] *with the intention of capturing it, retiring and leaving it empty*' (my emphasis). Even though the narrator provides the reader with a direct presentation of goals relating to the initial action of jumping into the trench, a resistant reader (Browse 2018) may be inclined to infer further intentions vertically related to those construed by Heavens, and otherwise rendered absent. Instead, a resistant reader may substitute their own construal, foregrounding different intentions or rejecting the construal of the action as volitional altogether, such as an intention to harm enemy soldiers in the process of 'leaving [the trench] empty'. Explicit construals of intentions within discourse thus serve to *profile* (Langacker 2008: 68) a particular perspective on a character's goals and motivations, foregrounding a particular plane of intention related to a specific goal and narrowing the perception of possible motives associated with the action (cf. Palmer 2004: 119; Nuttall 2018: 123).

Although narrators rarely state the intentions behind actions explicitly as Heavens does, evaluative comments can also be used to justify the perception of particular intentions. In the case of Warsop, before describing firing his gun, he describes how he believed 'there was only one thing to do – if we stayed in our trench, we should have been shot from above like rats in a trap' (1965: 15). These disnarrated clauses (Prince 1988, 2003) construe his actions in relation to an unrealized alternative series of events, allowing Warsop to establish a propositional logic which the reader can follow to infer and justify the 'one thing to do' without stating it explicitly, while simultaneously reminding the reader of the risk of harm to Warsop should he choose not to act. A reasonable series of intentions inferred from this passage, then, could be that Warsop squeezes the trigger in order to fire his gun, in order to disable the enemy sniper, in order not to be harmed. These intentions exist in a vertical relationship with the more immediate goal of squeezing the trigger to hit the men, construed here as an activity which allows Warsop to not be harmed.

In addition, the negative shading (Simpson 1993) which precedes the act of firing the gun ('*I thought* I saw two men ...') foregrounds Warsop's intention to fire at two individuals, while simultaneously casting a degree of doubt on their presence. Likewise, although Warsop suggests that the events which took place require accepting that his assessment of events is accurate, in order to explain their outcome ('how I escaped I shall never know *unless* I got them first' (16, my emphasis), he continually foregrounds his perceptual processes, providing the opportunity to reconstrue the scene in a way which avoids positioning himself as a violent actor altogether. Again, it may not be the case that the reader of the narrative in which this sentence appears acknowledges all of these inferred intentions as the reason for squeezing the trigger. The text itself may foreground a particular intention, while the reader may draw upon cultural knowledge to parse probable scripts of activity and associated goals. The role of intentionality set out here is a network of *possible explanations* readers might infer in accounting for action, and making sense of the decisions and actions made by characters during the course of a narrative. Abbott (2015: 104) describes narrative as the 'perceptible tracks on the surface of a universe of possibility', meaning much of the knowledge we infer about the world of a text is not explicitly stated. Instead, readers employ probabilistic knowledge to fill these gaps. In the majority of cases, the direct intentions behind a character's actions are not marked explicitly within the text. Recognizing that characters have the capacity to act intentionally, and using this knowledge to begin theorizing as to what those intentions may be, means that readers employ the kinds of Theory of Mind processing which take place throughout reading to conceptualize the goals, beliefs and motivations which might precede the performance of a given act.

3.3. Intentionality as gradation

Although the discussion so far has been primarily concerned with identifying the capacity for intentional action and its significance in interpretation, it is clear that our conceptualization of agents with the potential to act volitionally does not preclude the same agents from performing unintentional acts. In the example sentences (b) and (c) at the beginning of this chapter, the same agent (a lumberjack) was shown to produce the same outcome (knocking down a tree) both intentionally and unintentionally. While this example affords a straightforward movement between both construals, not all agents are equally likely to elicit an assessment of their actions as intentional in otherwise identical clauses. For instance, consider the following examples:

g) The soldier killed the man.
h) The child killed the man.

Here, both agents have the capacity to act volitionally, as per the canonical event model. Although readers may attribute the potential for intentionality to the agents of both sentences, it would be unusual to ascribe equal potential to both, assuming that the reader has cultural scripts whereby soldiers are likely to perform acts which lead to the death of another, but a child (though capable of acting volitionally) will more rarely be capable of deliberately causing lethal harm. Simply because an agent *can* be associated with intentional actions does not necessarily mean that they will *always* be perceived as acting intentionally, as additional context in discourse can lead to the violation of prototypical expectations.

Judgements of intentionality are thus influenced by socio-cognitive factors, including prior knowledge and scripts unique to individual readers. However, these judgements are also dynamic, capable of being revised in an ongoing assessment of actors and actions as the discourse continues. As with the concept of 'world repair' in Text World Theory (Gavins 2007: 141), and the role of re-reading in cognitive stylistics more broadly (Harrison and Nuttall 2018), a revised or expanded account of an actor's intentions can cause a reader to revisit their schematic understanding of an event, or indeed an entire text. The following examples gradually introduce an extract of an autobiographical account from the First World War (Hill 1915), examining how the introduction of new information requires the reassessment of probable goals and intentions. Hill describes how, after a battle, German soldiers 'ran towards us with their hands above their heads crying, "Mercy, Kamarad"'. Following this, he narrates how:

i) We gave them mercy

In isolation, 'giving mercy' prototypically refers to an act of kindness, here given from a first-person plural group of actors to an unknown number of individuals. However, the sentence then provides additional context, affecting the immediate scope in which the reader's frame of reference for scripts of mercy can be applied:

j) We gave them mercy, the same mercy they would have given us.

Here, Hill employs the modal verb 'would' to elicit the construal of a disnarrated reciprocal action by the enemy soldiers. Similarly to Warsop, Hill's disnarration justifies his own actions in relation to other, anticipated actions. Accordingly, while the specifics of 'giving mercy' are undefined, Hill's volitional decision to act in this way is presented to the reader as a pre-emptive response to other possible agents, and the possible reasons for acting are now foregrounded. As a result, by the point at which Hill makes explicit the metaphorical nature of his construal of his own actions thus far, the reader has already been presented with his reasoning for intentionally performing an act of violence:

k) We gave them mercy, the same mercy they would have given us. It sounds impossible to shoot a man in cold blood but in an affair like this, morality seems changed.

With these additional clauses, the meaning of the previous sentence is finally made explicit: 'mercy' is no longer a straightforward description of the acts which took place, but a sarcastic reconstrual of events. Hill's metaphor of killing as mercy delays the perception of his actions as violence. Such foregrounding of the rationalization behind his action affords Hill the opportunity to remark that the killing was 'in cold blood', a detail which, if presented earlier, may affect the reader's perception of the justification for killing. Likewise, the potential surprise in revealing the specific details of his actions supports his observation that 'morality seems changed'. In this short passage, Hill's stylistic choices serve to prime readers with a perceived justification for an act he acknowledges as morally ambiguous, perhaps leading to a less critical interpretation than alternative construals in which the killing 'in cold blood' is presented first, to be justified after the initial description.

In paying close attention to the attribution of intention, this approach can begin to make sense of a novel dimension of a text's stylistic function. By foregrounding or backgrounding contextual information, the narrator draws attention towards particular inferences. In cases where the reader has no personal experience of the events described, or any further evidence from which to infer the causes of the events or the intentions of the actors described, the possibility of a resistant reconstrual of events as they occurred is diminished. Given that examples (i) through (k) have no further context, the aim of this reading cannot be to uncover any 'original' or 'authentic' intention behind a given action. As the reader has no access to additional evidence to support the validity of either construal, each claim remains equally valid. Instead, it serves to demonstrate how the linguistic frame provided by an event's description affects not only the construal of a single event, but potentially their schematic understanding of the narrator more generally. Modelling the relationship between event structure, cognition and our understanding of intentional activity allows a critical analysis to comment on the ways in which readers are compelled to make sense of actions and characters within the narrative.

4. Connecting intentions across discourse

According to Langacker, 'grammar is shaped by discourse' (2008: 457), and the final chapters of *Cognitive Grammar: A Basic Introduction* perform preliminary work in considering the challenges in moving beyond clause-level analysis. More recently, however, Langacker has acknowledged that 'there are limits to what [Cognitive Grammar] can offer literature' (2014: xiv) at present. Langacker's own comments on the relationship between the different 'levels' of analysis provide an indication as to why connecting sentence and narrative-level analyses might be seen as a challenge for Cognitive Grammar:

> Structures at a given [linguistic] level have to be characterized in relation to constitutive elements of the *proper sort*. There is no point describing a chapter directly in terms of phrases, or a complex sentence in terms of words. It is not just that skipping levels yields an incomplete description – it actually makes the descriptive task far more difficult.
>
> (Langacker 2008: 480, my emphasis)

Langacker is keen to establish that grammar is affected and influenced by the discursive context in which a given utterance is situated, but the analytical processes often demonstrated through Cognitive Grammar require such a fine-grained approach that larger units of narrative may feel unwieldy. Indeed, in his chapter on the transition towards the analysis of discourse, even the modelling of a single clause (2008: 489) requires extensive diagramming. Moreover, while he suggests that the transition to discursive analysis should employ the 'proper sort' of 'levels' of attention, it is not made clear exactly what these levels are. 'Skipping' directly from a discussion of individual events to large-scale narrative, as we have seen, cannot account for much of the nuance of identity development. Mink (1978: 146–7) has observed a similar disparity, arguing that:

> there is something incompatible about our concept of "event" and our concept of "narrative", which might be put as follows: the concept of event is primarily linked to the conceptual structure of science ... but in this conceptual structure it is purged of all narrative connections, and refers to something that can be identified and described without any necessary reference to its location in some process of development – a process which only narrative can represent. Therefore, to speak of a "narrative of events" is almost a contradiction in terms.

Mink's observation is based upon the belief that an analysis of events can be meaningfully isolated from their 'narrative connections'. As I have shown repeatedly throughout this chapter, however, efforts to model the cognitive connections which govern the perceptions of causality and intentionality associated with a given action or event eventually require the consideration of the clause within a broader spectrum of activity.

As constitutive elements of linguistic structure, moving from the analysis of individual sentences to overarching discursive structure represents a fine balancing act of scalability in stylistic analysis. However, the need to contextualize the perception of intentionality beyond the clausal level is highly intuitive. Van Dijk (1975: 282) examines the role of action in structuring narrative, and suggests that in categorizing whether or not events are performed intentionally, 'the notion of an "action sentence" is not strictly decidable without the specification of the context of the whole *action discourse*. In action discourses we may be able to interpret or infer that a given action was intentional' (original emphasis). An action discourse, as opposed to the discourse of the text more generally, refers to the descriptive passages which contextualize and present or imply the rationale for an act, or group of actions. Following this approach to the identification and analysis of discursive elements between the sentence and full-discourse level, this section examines how a cognitive approach might similarly select, describe and analyse such features.

In Cognitive Grammar, the notion of 'reference points' (Langacker 2008: 83–8, 504–5; Harrison 2017: 20–2, 49–69) provides an account of how individual events within narrative can be conceptualized in relation to ongoing observations across a text. Essentially, as the discourse develops, salient information is construed which modifies the reader's conceptualization of target objects or events. For example, prepositional phrases such as 'over there', 'towards the path' and 'behind the shelf' guide the reader's attention, and can be built upon with further reference points to provide a more salient and granular construal of an object's relative spatial position. Given that references connect construals and propositions from across discourse, van Vliet (2009) proposes that the Reference Point Model can be employed to trace the information associated with actors across a text, including background information about characters' lives and beliefs (455–6), and moreover that 'global reference points' (442) can hold across large spans of discourse. Given that a single distal intention may govern many of an actor's decisions, the intentions perceived by readers can function as macro-scale reference points, which affect and are contextualized by the reader's ongoing understanding of the actor as a character across the discourse.

While reference points are typically discussed in terms of explicit construals within the text, the model of intentionality advanced in this chapter suggests that readers' inferences can function as reference points, salient moments against which the perception of characters develops across the full breadth of the discourse. Making intentionality the focus of a sustained analysis gives grounds for connecting clausal analysis with narrative structure without requiring the extensive modelling of each clause within the discourse. Instead, the process requires a thematic selection, based on the kind of agent(s) being investigated. Returning to Warsop's narrative, it is possible to map each of the actions the narrator performs leading up to and including the firing of his rifle (shown in bold) according to an intention (italicized).

Mapped in this way, Figure 8.3 shows the contextual relationship between Warsop's act of violence and earlier actions performed with the explicit aim of ensuring his safety. Following the disnarrated clause in which he describes the danger of not acting ('we should have been shot …'), the highly granular description of the acts which constitute the firing of his gun is subsumed within an overall concern with personal safety, justifying the act of killing as part of an ongoing process of self-defence. In other words, the descriptions of these earlier activities produce intentions which function as reference points when evaluating the decision-making associated with the act of killing. Moreover, this extract simply represents the intentions and associated actions of the narrator over the span of a short paragraph, and it remains possible to continue to

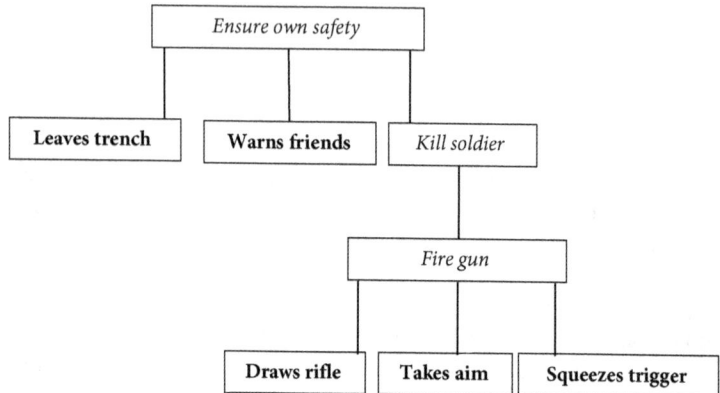

Figure 8.3 Connecting intentions hierarchically across discourse.

extend the network of intentions associated with the actions and construals of Warsop's narrative across broader sections of the text. Shortly after this scene, for instance, he describes how 'there was a flash in the sky. I realised with a shock I had been badly hit. My right arm jumped up on its own and flopped down. It felt as though my left arm and part of my chest had been blown away' (16), before passing out and waking in hospital several days later. Although Warsop is primarily divorced from the agentive role throughout this passage, and does not perform any actions that could be inferred to be intentional, there is a clear thematic relationship with his earlier foregrounded overarching goal of ensuring his own safety, which serves as the overarching explicit intention behind each of his earlier actions.

The point is, as Pincombe (2014) has observed, that drawing upon all aspects of a Cognitive Grammar analysis in approaching units of discourse beyond several clauses quickly becomes unwieldy. Moreover, examining event structure exclusively in relation to individual clauses risks misrepresenting the relationship between event-level construal and the structure of discourse. As Herman (2002) explains, actions in narrative should be treated as 'construction materials that have to be fashioned – custom-fit – in a manner directed by the kind of narrative being told' (73). Using perceived intentions as reference points across discourse, however, provides a means to discuss individual actions and events in relation to these overarching character and discourse goals. In turn, characters' actions can be tracked across the narrative, as they work towards achieving – or perhaps wrestle with competing – goals, beliefs, desires and motivations inferred from the narrative context. In the critical analysis performed in this chapter, this allowed for an account of the motivations presented across a passage of discourse, leading to the justification of the narrator performing an otherwise taboo act. In a literary analysis, the tracking of a character's intentions across the span of a novel could be used as the starting point for contextualizing a stylistic analysis of the ways in which they act (e.g. transitivity) at specific points within the text.

5. Conclusions and future directions

This chapter has outlined a novel approach to modelling the role of intentionality in Cognitive Grammar for the purposes of both critical and literary linguistic analyses. Building up from clause to sentence to discourse-level discussion, it has examined how the cognitive process of mind-modelling the capacity for intentionality in actors can affect and be affected by the construal of events in language. The use of intentions to selectively analyse the relationship between thematically connected passages across a text challenges Langacker's assertion (2008: 457) that the next 'level' after complex sentences is 'discourse', or rather that discourse can be thought of as a single homogenous category. Categories such as van Dijk's (1975) notion of 'action discourse' demonstrate how elements of discourse above the sentence level can be productively grouped together, providing analytical focus around key discursive features. From a cognitive perspective, van Vliet's (2009) global reference points acknowledge that single clauses work to contextualize perceptions across discourse, and the analysis of intentionality aims to follow this precedent by treating individual actions within discourse as a site of interaction between existing and emerging perceptions of a character's intentions and identity. Accordingly, the identification and modelling of intentions and their interrelations offer a way of producing selective commentary on longer passages of text through its focus on specific, salient discursive features. The next stage of this process will be to further explore how and when these events are deemed significant enough by the reader to function as reference points in character development.

To fully develop this model of linguistic analysis requires ongoing application of the framework to a wide variety of literary and non-fiction genres. The examples above have shown how the perception of intentions can be central to a critical analysis, but a steadfast theory of language should be applicable to all genres of discourse. One of the strengths of literary linguistic research is its capacity for bi-directional commentary: not only do innovations in linguistics inform the analysis of texts, but the analysis of texts can itself be used to interrogate and challenge preconceptions about language, linguistics and style. While this chapter proposes a provisional framework for the study of intentionality through Cognitive Grammar, its future application to texts and modes as yet unconsidered will doubtless yield further insights into the mechanics of discourse and its analysis.

References

Abbott, H.P. (2015), 'How Do We Read What Isn't There to Be Read? Shadow Stories and Permanent Gaps', in L. Zunshine (ed.), *The Oxford Handbook of Cognitive Literary Studies*, 104–19, Oxford: Oxford University Press.

Anscombe, G.E.M. (1957), *Intention*, Oxford: Basil Blackwell.

Astington, J. (1999), 'The Language of Intention: Three Ways of Doing It', in P. Zelazo, J. Astington and D. Olson (eds), *Developing Theories of Intention: Social Understanding and Self-Control*, 295–316, London: Psychology Press.

Bandura, A. (2006), 'Towards a Psychology of Human Agency', *Perspectives on Psychological Science*, 1 (2): 164–80.

Behrend, D. and J. Scofield (2006), 'Verbs, Actions, and Intentions', in L. Hirsh-Pasek and R. Golinkoff (eds), *Early Verb Learning: Action Meets Words*, 286–307, Oxford: Oxford University Press.

Browse, S. (2018), *Cognitive Rhetoric: The Cognitive Poetics of Political Discourse*, Amsterdam: John Benjamins.

Dancygier, B. (2008), 'The Text and the Story: Levels of Blending in Fictional Narratives', in T. Oakley and A. Hougaard (eds), 51–78, *Mental Spaces in Discourse and Interaction*. Amsterdam: John Benjamins.

Dowty, D. (1991), 'Thematic Proto-roles and Argument Selection', *Language*, 67 (3): 547–619.

Gavins, J. (2007), *Text World Theory: An Introduction*, Edinburgh: Edinburgh University Press.

Halliday, M.A.K. (1970), 'Language Structure and Language Function', in J. Lyons (ed.), *New Horizons in Linguistics*, 140–65, Harmondsworth: Penguin.

Harrison, C. (2017), *Cognitive Grammar in Contemporary Fiction*, Amsterdam: John Benjamins.

Harrison, C. and L. Nuttall (2018), 'Re-reading in Stylistics', *Language and Literature*, 27 (3): 176–95.

Hart, C. (2018), 'Event-frames Affect Blame Assignment and Perception of Aggression in Discourse on Political Protests: an Experimental Case Study in Critical Discourse Analysis', *Applied Linguistics*, 39 (3): 400–21.

Heavens, W. (1916), *Private Papers of W. Heavens*, IWM Documents.17485.

Herman, D. (2002), *Story Logic: Problems and Possibilities of Narrative*, London: University of Nebraska Press.

Hill, S.E. (1915), *Private Papers of S.E. Hill*, IWM Documents.15126.

Langacker, R.W. (1987), *Foundations of Cognitive Grammar, Vol. 1: Theoretical Prerequisites*, Stanford: Stanford University Press.

Langacker, R.W. (1991), *Foundations of Cognitive Grammar, Vol. 2: Descriptive Application*, Stanford: Stanford University Press.

Langacker, R.W. (2008), *Cognitive Grammar: A Basic Introduction*, Oxford: Oxford University Press.

Langacker, R.W. (2014), 'Foreword', in C. Harrison, L. Nuttall, P. Stockwell and W. Yuan (eds), *Cognitive Grammar in Literature*, xiii–xiv, Amsterdam: John Benjamins.

Mink, L. (1978), 'Narrative Form as a Cognitive Instrument', in R.H. Canary and H.Kozicki (eds), *The Writing of History: Literary Form and Historical Understanding*, 129–49, Madison: University of Wisconsin Press.

Nakamura, K. (2018), 'Harming Is More Intentional Than Helping Because It Is More Probable: TheUnderlying Influence of Probability on the Knobe Effect', *Journal of Cognitive Psychology*, 30 (2): 129–37.

Nuttall, L. (2018), *Mind Style and Cognitive Grammar: Language and Worldview in Speculative Fiction*, London: Bloomsbury.

Nuttall, L. (2019), 'Transitivity, Agency, Mind Style: What's the Lowest Common Denominator?' *Language and Literature*, 28 (2): 159–79.

Palmer, A. (2004), *Fictional Minds*, Lincoln: University of Nebraska Press.

Pincombe, M. (2014), 'Most and Now: Tense and Aspect in Bálint Balassi's 'Áldott Szép Pünkösdnek', in C. Harrison, L. Nuttall, P. Stockwell and W. Yuan (eds), *Cognitive Grammar in Literature*, 161–76, Amsterdam: John Benjamins.

Plaks, J. and J. Robinson (2015), 'Construal Level and Free Will Beliefs Shape Perceptions of Actors' Proximal and Distal Intent', *Frontiers in Psychology*, 6. Available online: https://doi.org/10.3389/fpsyg.2015.00777.

Popova, Y. (2014), 'Narrativity and Enaction: The Social Nature of Literary Narrative Understanding', *Frontiers in Psychology*, 5. Available online: https://doi.org/10.3389/fpsyg.2014.00895.

Prince, G. (1988), 'The Disnarrated', *Style*, 22 (1): 1–8.

Prince, G. (2003), *The Dictionary of Narratology*, Lincoln, NE and London: University of Nebraska Press.

Rosset, E. (2008), 'It's No Accident: Our Bias for Intentional Explanations', *Cognition*, 108 (3): 771–80.

Ryan, M. (1980), 'Factuals, Non-Factuals, and the Principle of Minimal Departure', *Poetics*, 9 (4): 403–22.

Simpson, P. (1993), *Language, Ideology, and Point of View*, London: Routledge.

Stainton, H.H. (n.d.), *Private Papers of H.H. Stainton*, IWM Documents.6763.

Strickland, B., M. Fisher F. Keil and J. Knobe (2014), 'Syntax and Intentionality: An Automatic Link between Language and Theory-of-Mind', *Cognition*, 133 (1): 249–61.

Stockwell, P. (2009), *Texture: A Cognitive Aesthetics of Reading*, Edinburgh: Edinburgh University Press.

Stockwell, P. (2020), *Cognitive Poetics: An Introduction*, 2nd edition, London: Routledge.

Stockwell, P. and M. Mahlberg (2015), 'Mind-Modelling with Corpus Stylistics in David Copperfield', *Language and Literature*, 24 (2): 129–47.

Tomasello, M. (1999), 'Having Intentions, Understanding Intentions, and Understanding Communicative Intentions', in P. Zelazo, J. Astington and D. Olson (eds), *Developing Theories of Intention: Social Understanding and Self-Control*, 63–76, London: Psychology Press.

Van Dijk, T. (1975), 'Action, Action Description, and Narrative', *New Literary History*, 6 (2): 273–94.

van Leeuwen, T. (1997), 'The Representation of Social Actors', in C. Caldas-Coulthard and M. Coulthard (eds), *Texts and Practices: Readings in Critical Discourse Analysis*, 32–70, London: Routledge.

Van Vliet, S. (2009), 'Reference Points and Dominions in Narrative: A Discourse Level Exploration of the Reference Point Model of Anaphora', in V. Evans and S. Pourcel (eds), *Human Cognitive Processing, Vol 24: New Directions in Cognitive Linguistics*, 441–64, Amsterdam: John Benjamins.

Voice, M. (2018), 'Writing Fighting: Critical Cognitive Approaches to the Language of Killing in War', PhD thesis, University of Sheffield.

Warsop, A.C. (1965), *Private Papers of A.C. Warsop*, IWM Documents.1876.

Zunshine, L. (2006), *Why We Read Fiction: Theory of Mind and the Novel*, Columbus: Ohio University Press.

Part Three

Cognitive Grammar in multimodal contexts

9

'Subject and object and the nature of reality' in *Are You My Mother?*

Richard Finn

1. Introduction

In their analysis of Bechdel's *Fun Home*, Pleyer and Schneider (2014) show how the textual-pictorial multimodality of comics can prompt distinct *viewing arrangements* in text and pictures relating to the same situation. These lead to multiple *construals* of the same objective scene, both of which frame potential reader conceptualization. Langacker (2008: 73, 1995) describes 'viewing arrangement' as 'the overall relationship between the "viewers" and the situation being "viewed"'. A 'construal' is a particular conceptual framing of a situation that in the context of comics can refer to either reader or author conceptualization (Langacker 2008: 43–6). Through these concepts, Pleyer and Schneider (2014) illustrate how different modalities can represent the same referent situation.

They identify how two particular viewing arrangements impose different types of perspectival construal on visually depicted and textually narrated situations. Their analysis of Figure 9.1 shows how adjacent narrative and depictive construals relating to the same topic in the text and image of this panel provide different viewpoints on the same basic proposition of Bechdel's dad's love of Fitzgerald's writing. The textual narration is temporally and socially oriented through tense ('was', 'had') and social deixis (Dad). They also point out the 'unreliability' of the overall portrayal of her father reading, which results from the clash of the textual and pictorial viewing arrangements, i.e. how the example is multiply grounded. While the text is grounded in Alison's subjective experience as narrator, the picture is from outside of her 'subjective grasp' (Pleyer and Schneider 2014: 49).

Pleyer and Schneider (2014: 47) also describe how 'Bechdel's view usually includes herself both as narrator and as subject', exploring the dual roles identified with her through narration and depiction. They present an example of a depictive *egocentric viewing arrangement* (Figure 9.2), which Langacker (1987: 488–9) describes as a configuration where 'the objective scene is expanded beyond the region of perceptual optimality to include the observer (or analogously, the conceptualizer) and [their]

Figure 9.1 Optimal viewing arrangement in *Fun Home* (Bechdel 2006, quoted in Pleyer and Schneider 2014: 49).

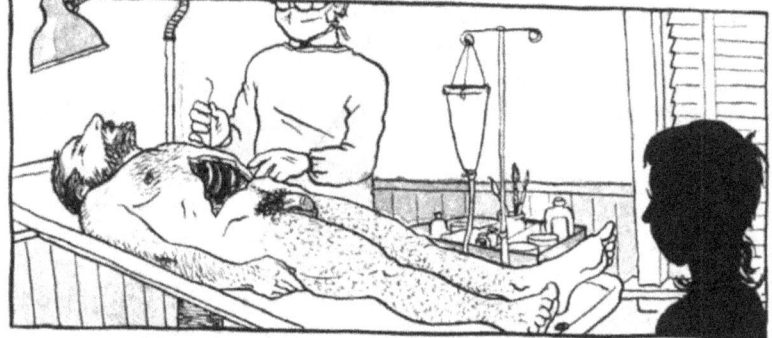

Figure 9.2 Egocentric viewing arrangement in *Fun Home* (Bechdel 2006: 44, quoted in Pleyer and Schneider 2014: 47).

immediate surroundings'. In this instance, the egocentric viewing arrangement relates to the *vantage point* of the depicted character of Alison who is silhouetted in the foreground (Langacker 2008: 76–8).

The idea of egocentricity in relation to viewing arrangements and vantage points is complicated here by the fact that it involves placing a *conceptualizer* – any entity to which subjectivity can be ascribed (Langacker 2008: 431–52) – 'onstage' as part of an objective scene in such a way that they can be either *subjectified* or *objectified* depending on how the depicted scene is focally construed by a reader. Subjectification describes conceptually shifting an entity towards the discursive *ground* (discourse participants' understanding of the discourse situation), making it more implicit. Objectification describes conceptually shifting an entity away from the discursive ground, making it more explicit and (conceptually) observable. While the depictive vantage point of a single comics panel like in Figure 9.2 is fixed, the conceptual viewing arrangement is not fixed. So, while this example is egocentric in relation to the depicted Alison's conceptualization, there are other ways in which this image can be construed. The image in Figure 9.2 can be read as focusing the relationship between Alison's father and the corpse against the setting of the room, focusing more specifically on his hand pulling on a thread or even on the physical details of the corpse. These focal construals objectify the listed entities, while subjectifying Alison in the manner described above. Here, she is the conceptualizing subject of a depicted act of conceptualization, i.e. the person doing the experiencing. However, at another level the image can also be focally construed with Alison onstage as part of the depicted scene, *profiling* – i.e. making prominent (Langacker 2008: 66–73) – the act of her looking at the other depicted entities. This configuration is grounded through an implicit subjectivity that has selected and organized entities for depiction without drawing explicit attention to these processes. The implicit subjectivity is Alison Bechdel the author and, more broadly, the author-complex of editors, publishers, printers and so on.

Pleyer and Scheider also point to the importance of considering the *current discourse space* – a mental space in which interlocutors track and update their understanding of discourse content and context, including understanding of the circumstances of the *usage event* – i.e. actual, contextualized production of discourse (Langacker 2008: 17). How discourse is understood to relate to the usage event is a matter of *grounding*. Grounding is how discourse relates to the experiences, perspectives and contexts of discourse participants. As a basis for analysis, this is useful because it forces consideration of how discourse relates to discourse participants and how the subjective and objective focus within participants' conceptualizations can shift between different attentional configurations and different levels of discourse. Since *Fun Home* is an autobiographical comic, the various discursive Alisons described above are more likely to be identified with Bechdel the discourse participant.

Through this focus on grounding, I will examine how following the dynamic progression of conceptualization *within* a single comics panel can yield multiple possible construals in relation to discourse participants and conceptualized experiencing entities. I will begin by examining different dimensions of subjectivity and objectivity posited by Cognitive Grammar and other cognitive linguistic approaches to discourse. This will lead into an application of these ideas specifically to the usage event of reading comics, in which I suggest that depiction (drawing) and narration (writing) are construed differently by readers. Finally, I will apply these proposals to an analysis of the depiction and narration of subjectivity in an example taken from Bechdel's (2012) autobiographical comic *Are You My Mother?*

2. Subjectivity and objectivity

Cognitive Grammar lends itself well to the analysis of subjectivity and objectivity because, like Bechdel's comic, and the above extracts in particular, it engages with the concepts of subject and object in relation to human experience of engaging with the world, both generally, and specifically how we engage with others' subjectivity through discourse (Langacker 2008; Nuttall 2014). However, the intuitive nature of Cognitive Grammar also leads to a proliferation of terminology with necessarily overlapping conceptual foundations, which can be easily confused with related terminology in other fields. For example, Langacker's (1991: 554) working definition of *subject* is 'a nominal that elaborates the trajector of a process profiled at the clausal level of organization. Its profile is thus the primary clausal figure'. Although schematically related to experiential subjectivity and the subject as described in psychoanalysis, this is specifically relevant to clausal predication.

As a dimension of construal, Giovanelli and Harrison explain how subjectivity and objectivity are mutually dependent and asymmetrically weighted:

> we can think about levels of subjectivity/objectivity working in inverse tandem, depending on how prominent the speaker or conceptualizer is in relation to the scene being described. In other words, when the conceptualizer becomes more prominent and viewed more objectively, the scene that is being conceptualized becomes more subjective.
>
> (Giovanelli and Harrison 2019: 52)

This captures Langacker's (1987: 128) assertion of the importance of 'the dual role of ground elements in a deictic expression: they serve both as the source of the predication, and as participants within the predication'.

The experiential subjects in a canonical speech event are referred to as conceptualizers (e.g. Langacker 2008: 431). Their subjectivity may or may not be placed 'onstage' or objectified as part of the objective scene through grounding elements such as modality and deixis. The objectification of a conceptualizer within discourse is described in Text World Theory as an 'enactor' (Werth 1999: 82; Gavins 2007: 42). This describes how an instance of a character projected spatiotemporally, modally or hypothetically away from an original instance can be understood differentially. In Figure 9.2, for example, there are implicit narrating and depicting enactors of Alison posited by the text and picture, an explicitly depicted Alison, and an Alison projected as a character within the narration of the text. As an input space within the current discourse space, these disparate enactors are conceptually integrated to form Alison's dynamic and developing identity, akin to what Palmer (2003: 325, 2004: 15) describes as a 'continuing consciousness frame'.

The inverse of objectification is described by Langacker (1991: 554) as subjectification, which is 'a semantic extension in which an entity originally construed objectively comes to receive a more subjective construal'. Attributing consciousness to discursive entities in this way is a part of 'mind-modelling', which Stockwell and Mahlberg (2015: 132) describe as:

the capacity that humans evidently have for imagining and maintaining a working model of the characteristics, outlook, beliefs, motivations and consequent behaviours of others. It is this fundamental cognitive capacity that allow us to understand that other people are people, and that they are in some ways similar to us and in some ways different.

Where active minds are implied or reported, these conceptualizers are construed as part of the *surrogate ground*, which Langacker (1991: 554) defines as 'the circumstances of a speech event being described (as opposed to the actual speech event)'. Through subjectification, reported conceptualizers can effectively become part of the ground when focus is placed on the objective content of their thought, speech or experience. This is not to say that subjectified conceptualizers from the imagined world of the discourse are invited into the real world of the usage event. Rather, this shows the extent to which the ground is a conceptual component of the current discourse space in which conceptualizing activity is brought into and out of focus as and when it is relevant to discourse.

The conceptualizers in relation to whom the ground is focused and structured can change as discourse progresses. In speech or writing, this can happen as a result of shifting focus from predication to predication; in a picture this can happen as a result of shifting focus around the depicted scene. That is, not just looking from object to object, but shifting the relative focus, grouping and subjectification of objects while viewing an image. Because of this, subjective construal should be understood as construal of an entity in relation to *a* conceptualizer and not just *the* speaking/authoring/listening/reading conceptualizer. This conceptualizer may be a discursive manifestation of a conceptualizer who is a real discourse participant in the usage event or a subjectified conceptualizer who was previously an entity in the objective scene, but whose conceptualization is real and has been made fundamental in the imagined world of the discourse. This marks a shift from being a *reported* conceptualizer (surrogate ground) to a *reporting* conceptualizer (ground). Discursively the conditions of this are exactly the same; the difference lies in the *attenuation* of subjective experience of conceptualization itself (Langacker 2008: 536–7; Stockwell 2014: 30). I propose that, when considered alongside progressive usage event grounding and surrogate grounding, the example in Figure 9.2 can be construed as involving such a shift.

More significant still to the case of autobiographical comics is the related idea of *cross-world identification* which 'involves a correspondence established between a ground element G and some entity G' in a distinct "world," such as the world of a picture, movie, or novel' (Langacker 1987: 132; cf. Fauconnier 1994). Langacker (1987: 132) offers the following example:

(ii) *That's me in the top row.* [said when examining a photograph]

Although G' in this instance is fully objective, Langacker describes the deictically asserted correspondence to G (first person object pronoun) as a type of subjectification marked by 'the use of a first-person form to describe the objective entity' (Langacker 1987: 130–1). The idea that entities in distinct 'worlds' or realities can be identified like this helps to understand the multiply grounded worlds presented in an autobiographical comic. In the following section, I will present some of the explanations offered by Cognitive Grammar for these focal relationships and shifts between enactors.

3. Usage event grounding, subjectification and surrogation in comics

In its simplest form, the ground can be outlined as in Figure 9.3, where ground is understood as author and reader conceptualizing objective content through the medium of a comic book. With comics, the usage events tend not to be shared by discourse participants as in face-to-face conversation. As with most instances of drawing, writing and reading, the discourse situations of comics' production and reading are spatiotemporally separated (see, for example, Gavins 2007: 37). In a canonical conversation, the ground comprises non-discursive apprehension and conceptualization of the usage event. It is a dynamic mental simulation of the conditions of the usage event that provides a contextualizing resource in the current discourse space. Author and reader are real-world participants whose conceptualization of the usage event and its immediate context constitute the ground of the discursive interaction. The processes of authoring comics and reading comics, though spatiotemporally distal, are analogous to the more proximal processes of speaking and hearing in a canonical speaker–hearer interaction. I read a comic from the maximally subjective viewpoint of my own experience (primarily vision and cognitive processes relevant to reading text and looking at images). Because grounding preliminarily takes place in relation to disparate usage events and discourse participants, the lack of an immediately shared conversational context causes the focus to fall on the conceptualizing subjectivities within the text-world. As well as providing a basis for shifting viewing arrangements and developing or distinct contexts in relation to the usage event, the focus of the ground can also shift into the discourse while further subjectifying the usage event. This is evident in Pleyer and Schneider's (2014: 47)

Figure 9.3 Usage event grounding in comic books.

description of egocentricity in Figure 9.2. Their analysis shows how the subjective basis of the proposition is Alison's conceptualization of the scene in front of her, which is a fictive ground within the discourse through which readers can appraise the rest of the depicted scene. Objectification of the depicted Alison occurs when text or image points back to a distinct subjectivity at a higher level of discourse, such as the unspecified vantage point of the image or the temporally distinct vantage point of the narration. Although the ground always implicitly incorporates the actual usage event, part of the experience of reading is focusing attention away from these aspects of experience to occupy the imaginary vantage points posited by narration or depiction. This amounts to a clear delineation between discourse participants (offstage, real conceptualizers) and discourse *per se* (onstage objective scene, symbolization, conceptualization) that is itself applied to the world conceptualized through discourse. Where usage event grounding is highly subjective (offstage, backgrounded), passive and distal, the surrogated and subjectified grounding from the world of the discourse is more likely to be prominent, differing only in the non-immediacy and discursive nature of referent situations, entities and relationships.

This example also suggests that text and image prompt conceptualization of grounds that contextualize the conceptualizing activities of narration and depiction. Within the world presented by the discourse, narration and depiction posit distinct intermediary conceptualizers on the basis of the type of conceptualizing activity that they approximate. For example, presenting and reading text in narration primarily approximates the acts of speaking and hearing. Reading text visually approximates sound perception and linguistic comprehension of conversation. Similarly, composing and viewing pictures through depiction primarily approximates the acts of showing and seeing. Narrative and depictive viewing arrangements and their relation to usage event grounding are outlined in Figure 9.4.

According to this description, both narrative and depictive construal involve author (A) and reader (R) as grounded discourse participant roles with separated grounds on the basis of the distal usage events (G). Within the discourse, grounded conceptualizing roles of narrator (Nr) narratee (Ne) form the basis of narrative grounding, while depictor (D) and viewer (V) form the basis of depictive grounding in more conventionally shared (fictive) discourse contexts (G'). In Cognitive Grammar notation, G' is often used to denote the surrogate ground, which offers a possible means of understanding of how subjectification, objectification and conceptualizing activity are presented in discourse. In relation to clausal predication, 'surrogate ground' is used to refer to instances where report of conceptualizing activity results in fictive grounding that is construed as part of the objective scene. A common example of this is reported speech or thought, as in (iii) and (iv).

(iii) *He says he understands*
(iv) *He thinks he understands*

By reporting a speech event in actual discourse, a discourse participant posits a ground as the basis of the discursively simulated usage event (Langacker 1991: 258; see also Taylor 2002; Davidse and Vandelanotte 2011). As discourse progresses, this fictive

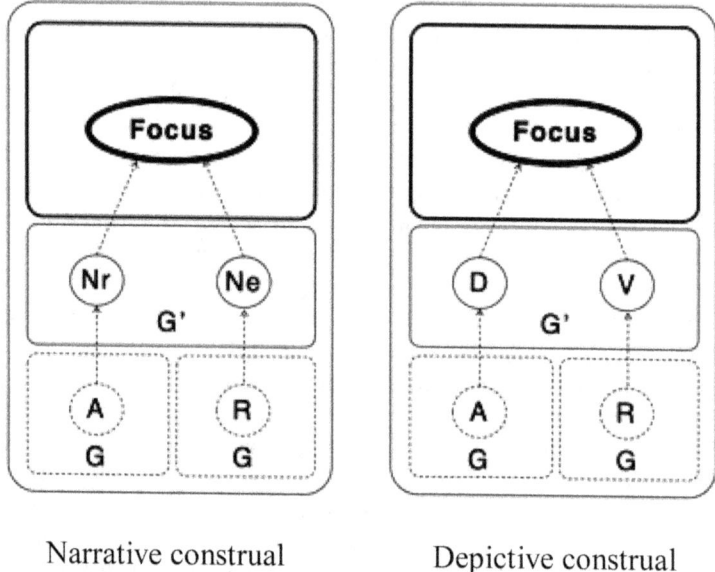

Figure 9.4 Narrative and depictive viewing arrangements.

grounding can in turn become the basis of another surrogate ground (i.e. subjectified) and so on in a theoretically indefinite manner. Because surrogate grounding involves a conceptualizer (either real or discursive) describing conceptualization, each instance amounts to an act of mind-modelling relative to the level of discourse in which it is embedded.

Although not real in the sense of a discourse participant, the narrating enactor of Alison (Nr) in Figure 9.4 is actual within the situation prompted by the discourse, and more likely to primarily ground the conceptualization of the text-world experienced by readers than her real-world counterpart. This is illustrated in Figure 9.4 by the separation and dotted outline of G. The grounding here is available to participants as part of the reading experience, but more likely to be backgrounded in the immediacy of reading. It is the grounding of G' that provides the subjective base for focusing on objective content. Part of this, as suggested by the dotted arrows in Figure 9.4, involves cross-world identification with conceptualizing roles that have actual access to the reality posited by the discourse.

Even without asserting identity across worlds, identification of author with narrator and reader with narratee arises from the schematic similarity of these roles (e.g. relative activity and passivity of participants), and the relative inaccessibility of the author to the reader. In the case of autobiography, this can be reinforced through first-person deictic reference in narration. Regardless of the type of usage event, G' is always part of grounding that asserts the distinction between discursive conceptualizers (e.g. 'I', 'you') and conceptualizers *per se* (i.e. real thinking, talking, writing and drawing discourse participants). The surrogate ground in relation to this is best understood as being part of the objective focus.

Returning to Figure 9.2, this is one reason why I describe the depiction as offering multiple perspectival construals. The egocentric construal that Pleyer and Schneider (2014) describe is one where the prominently grounded depictive conceptualizer is the foregrounded silhouette of Alison. In this construal, her conceptualization is the focus of overall conceptualization in relation to the ground, even though she is not a 'real' discourse participant. Figure 9.2 can also be considered egocentric through cross-world identification of conceptualizers at different levels and in different modes of discourse. The textually narrating Alison, the narrated Alison and Alison the author are all differently grounded, but are all identified in different ways with the same idea of *Alison Bechdel*. This relies to some extent on reader experience and expectations of authorial intention in biography, where first-person narration prompts strong identification between discursive and usage event conceptualizers (Lejeune 1989; Gibbons 2019). On this basis, there is a *natural path* of identification (Langacker 2008: 490) between the depicted foreground conceptualizer and a discourse participant – in this case, Bechdel the author. This identification is reinforced throughout the two comics by the similar path of identification between the recurring 'I' of the textual narration and the author. The frequent co-occurrence of this first-person narration with objective depiction reifies Alison's identity across these modes and instances. The depictive vantage point (i.e. the notional subjective origo of the depiction) is subjectified to the same extent as the narrative vantage point (i.e. the notional subjective origo of the narration). Visually, Alison is relatively subjectified as a depicted entity because her vantage point intercedes the depictive vantage point, which in turn intercedes readers' vantage point as fixed by the depiction. Therefore, within the same panel, the act of Alison looking can be construed as part of the objective scene. As readers, we can either construe her as part of the objective scene, or subjectify her as part of the ground; we can both look at her looking and look with her. A shift in attention to the onstage focus of *her* conceptualization causes a shift in perspective that subjectifies her, but neither perspective is fixed by either the depiction or narration. This suggests that where conceptualizers are presented as part of the objective content, they can be either surrogated or subjectified depending on construal. As part of the surrogate ground, their subjectivity is placed onstage as part of the objective content through objectification of conceptualizing activity. As outlined above, this conceptualizing activity can then be subjectified as construal shifts, causing this subjectivity to be incorporated into the ground as the subjective base of ongoing objective conceptualization.

To build on Pleyer and Schneider's (2014) exploration of construal in *Fun Home*, it feels fitting to look to Bechdel's sequel, *Are You My Mother?*, which, appropriately, engages significantly with a theoretical discussion of subjectivity and objectivity. In the following section I will provide an outline of the comic and introduce the section I will use to exemplify developing subjective complexity in Bechdel's storytelling.

4. Are You My Mother?

In *Are You My Mother?* Bechdel (2012: 255) quotes a passage from *To the Lighthouse* where Andrew explains to Lily that his father's books are about 'subject and object and the nature of reality'. By pointing out that 'the joke is that this vast and pompous-sounding topic is also what To the Lighthouse is about', Bechdel (2012: 255), in turn, draws attention to the fact that this is also what *Are You My Mother?* is about. Just as the primary topic of *Fun Home* is Bechdel's father's biography, *Are You My Mother?* is presented as a biography of Bechdel's mother. However, it tells the story not just of events from Bechdel's mother's life, but also the story of Bechdel's experience of authoring the book, including writing, researching, documenting and analysing her relationship with her mother. Bechdel engages with the idea that writing involves objectification of experience to such an extent that it interrupts actual experience: 'You can't live and write at the same time' (Bechdel 2012: 7). This is further exemplified in one-sided phone conversations with her mother, in which she documents her mother's speech extensively without fully attending to the content of what either of them is saying.

She also engages with the development of a sense of self both as a facet of general human development and through the lens of her own experience of growing up. The comic deals extensively with psychoanalysis both as a practical means of understanding experience and as a theoretical means of engaging with the concepts of subject and object as facets of the human psyche. Bechdel engages specifically with the work of Winnicott as a means of investigating both her sense of self and how this has been shaped by her relationship with her mother. Many panels in the comic are depictions of highlighted extracts from Winnicott's books or Bechdel's interpretation of his work. For example, Alison (as narrator) appraises his core theory through a text-only panel:

> Here's the vital core of Winnicott's theory:
> The subject must destroy the object.
> And the object must survive this destruction.
>
> (Bechdel 2012: 267)

In the context of her relationship with her mother, the objective 'destruction' and 'survival' amount to a schematic version of Freud's Oedipus complex which can be more generically applied to parent-child relationships and the subject's understanding of their identity.

The section I will look at in my analysis is taken from the sixth and penultimate chapter of the comic, titled 'Mirror'. The chapter contains extensive narration and depiction of Bechdel's research on, and understanding and application of, the Lacanian notion of the 'mirror stage' (Lacan 2007) and Winnicott's (1967) related notion of the 'mirror role'. These refer to a developmental phase in which an infant develops a sense of subjectivity:

> The mirror stage is a drama whose internal pressure pushes precipitously from insufficiency to anticipation – and, for the subject caught up in the lure of spatial identification, turns out fantasies that proceed from a fragmented image

of the body to what I will call an "orthopedic" form of its totality – and to the finally donned armor of an alienating identity that will mark his entire mental development with its rigid structure.

(Lacan 2007: 97)

As Bechdel (2012: 232) observes, Winnicott's development of this idea suggests that 'the self is not alien and illusory. It's coherent and authentic ... and, if all goes well, feels "real"'. He posits that subjective mirroring first occurs through family (especially a mother) mirroring an infant's facial expressions and emotions. An infant engages with reality through perception of, apperception of and interaction with objects. Family establish a sense of subjectivity by being objects that can mirror the infant's subjective experiences. Because of this, subjectivity is experienced through the 'mirror' of the subjectivity of others. The second phase is the recognition of the self as an objective entity that reflects its own subjectivity in a literal mirror. This results in a unitary (yet always divided) identity between the bounded experiencing self and the reflected image of the self as a cohesive object of apperception:

The reflection in the mirror is you ... but not exactly. It's backwards, for one thing. And it's all of a piece, unlike the diffuse way you've experienced reality until this moment.

(Bechdel 2012: 231)

In this chapter, Bechdel (2012: 218) observes that 'my heavy investment in my own mind is also a kind of narcissistic cathexis'. In her words, narcissistic cathexis, a concept that she picks up from Miller (1981), is where 'you invest more energy into your ideas about another person than in the actual, objective, external person' (Bechdel 2012: 217). Through the development of her relationship with her mother, Bechdel suggests that this is how she relates both to herself and to her mother.

The panel I will focus on (Figure 9.7) is part of a somewhat discontinuous sequence of panels and pages throughout this chapter that relate a revelatory telephone conversation between Alison and her mother (Figures 9.5–9.7). They present a resolution of Bechdel's internalized conflict, perhaps ironically, through the 'heavy investment in [her] own mind' involved in authoring the comic. In the depiction, this is achieved through presenting multiple construals of similar objective scenes relating to this event and to the process of communicating it in comics form.

First, as shown in Figure 9.5, Bechdel depicts the culmination of this conversation, while contextualizing and evaluating it in the narration. After further discussion of the mirror phase, Bechdel then narrates a continuation of the events of the phone conversation, while depicting herself posing, then photographing herself in the same position (Figure 9.6). This is a performance of the self-as-object as a function of self-examination. It presents the vantage point of the panels from Figure 9.5 as being digitally and deliberately framed through staged photography. As well as a culmination of Bechdel's examination of her sense of self through her relationship with her mother, this disjointed sequence across non-consecutive pages also presents an examination of the nature of subjectivity and objectivity in comics depiction.

Figure 9.5 Depiction and narration of telephone call (Bechdel 2012: 229).

Figure 9.6 Depiction and of re-enacting telephone call (Bechdel 2012: 233).

Figure 9.7 Multiple depictive and narrative perspectives (Bechdel 2012: 234).

The narration in Figure 9.7 synthesizes and differentiates Bechdel's understanding of her mother's life and her own life, before asserting awareness of her mother's disapproval of her writing the book. In basic terms, the depiction shows Bechdel looking at the screen of the camera previously foregrounded in the previous panel (i.e. the second panel of Figure 9.6), which is reflected in a mirror behind her. I will use this panel to examine how multiple conceptualizers are presented in the depiction and narration, and how these are grounded in relation to the usage events of authoring and reading the comic.

4.1 Textual grounding

To better explore the potential complexity of enactors of Alison at different levels of discourse, for the rest of this analysis I will refer to enactors where possible with prefixes taken from the conceptualizing roles set out in Figure 9.4 ($_{Nr}$Alison for Alison as narrator, $_{A}$Alison for Alison as author and so on). I will use $_{C}$Alison to refer to enactors of Alison that function as characters in her storytelling.

Aside from paratextual and onomatopoeic functions, text mostly occurs in comics in three forms: speech balloons, thought bubbles and narrative captions. Speech balloons and thought bubbles function as speech or thought simulation *within* a depicted situation. Through tails pointing to characters, word balloons and thought bubbles tend to clearly indicate the depicted discourse participant who is speaking or thinking (Forceville et al. 2010). The lack of such indexical features in narrative captions symbolizes the fact that they are grounded *outside of* depicted situations. In comics narration, first-person textual reference points back to a grounded situation that is distinct from the grounding of any conceptualizers in the depicted situation.

Separating portions of text out into boxes prompts conceptual grouping and segmentation beyond clausal and sentential organization. It permits an additional layer of structure similar in function to prosody and intonation in spoken discourse management (Langacker 2008: 461–6). On this basis, there are three basic narrative predications separately captioned in the panel in Figure 9.7:

i) we're not so different
ii) I'm playing myself
iii) [I'm] writing this book about her

The predications most prominently focus on a comparison between Alison and her mother that draws on her mother's previously narrated acting career (anaphorically summarized in Figure 9.6 through the nominal 'Mom's acting career') as being analogous with Alison's sense of self. This captures the overall project of the comic in microcosm: Bechdel explores her own identity and subjective experience by telling the story of authoring a biography about her mother. The complex domain of DRAMA introduced in the first caption extends into Alison's metaphoric self-description in the second caption: 'It's just that instead of playing a character I'm playing myself'.

The use of the progressive 'playing' suggests that this is an ongoing feature of Alison's experience. 'I'm playing myself' can also have the sense of *I'm undermining myself*, which further resonates with the sense of subjective reflexivity and self-sabotage that Bechdel highlights in these initial conclusions. Because the 'I' in these instances is relatively generic (rather than referring to a specific instantiation of Alison), it points more generally to a broader sense of Alison's identity, asserting this as a feature of her experience that extends beyond the immediacy of the fictive narrative usage event, the fictive realizations (i.e. 'When I think about Mom's acting career') and the depicted situation. These fictive realizations are further genericized by being distributed along a timeline by the adverb 'When' with the sense of 'on occasions that'.

As these fictive projections and generalizations suggest, the grounded conceptualizer referred to by 'I' in these captions is $_{Nr}$Alison while the objective referent instantiated by the discourse is $_C$Alison. By extension of contextual awareness of the autobiographical nature of the comic, this also indirectly refers to $_A$Alison as a real-world author. On the basis of the current discourse space and grounding outlined in the previous section, the first-person reference of these predications can be identified with Alison at all levels of discourse as author ($_A$Alison), narrator ($_{Nr}$Alison) and a fictive co-referent character who is the object of narration ($_C$Alison). The co-referential nature of 'I' means that it refers to both subject ($_{Nr}$Alison) and object ($_C$Alison) of conceptualization as discursively grounded in G', while the autobiographical nature means that it also refers indirectly to $_A$Alison as the implicit author of the comic. All of these levels of grounding and objectification of conceptualizers invoke embedded subjectivities that mark progressive *modal projection* away from G' (and implicitly, from G). Modal projection describes conceptual divergence to a projected reality from a baseline *conception of reality*, which Langacker (2008: 297) describes as 'the history of what has occurred up through the present moment'. The phrase 'I know she wishes I weren't writing this book about her' involves modal projection in the form of the assertion 'I know', which foregrounds $_C$Alison's reality conception, then 'she wishes' which projects her mother's reality conception and related desire, and finally a fictive Alison, posited through a negative subjunctive, who is not 'writing this book'. Zunshine (2006: 28) describes this sort of local embedding of subjectivity as 'levels of intentional reference', which she suggests become harder to track as more levels of subjectivity are locally embedded. Unlike instances of surrogation that serve only to focus subjectivities across worlds, the embedding structure here can also be construed as a profile rather than the shift in perspective guiding the construal.

Setting aside these projections and modulations, a basic construal of the above proposition would be 'I am writing this book about her'. However, through the complex modal predication and embedding, this reality, actual to the grounded $_{Nr}$Alison, is distanced from the objective scene as set out in Figure 9.8. Focus on this predication is mitigated by the modal projections at P1 and P2. P3 adds further notional distance through subjunctive mood and tense shift. Rather than a temporal shift, tense is used here as another means of distancing this proposition from the ground in the domain of definiteness.

The distancing of the modal projections and the subjunctive mood draws readers further away from the narrative ground via $_N$Alison's thoughts about her mother's inclination about what should be happening. This submersion of $_N$Alison's subjectivity

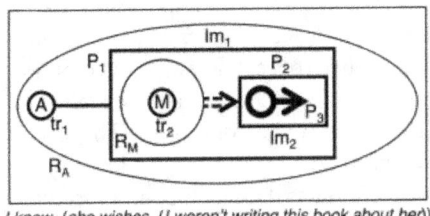

Figure 9.8 Complex modal predication and basic implicit predication.

reflects the same outcome within the comic as a whole. On the basis of the cumulative topic focus on Alison's subjectivity through her relationship with her mother, another implicit construal of the situation 'I'm writing this book about myself' is folded into the narration in a manner that is analogous to the comic as a whole. This dimension of the comic is made more explicit in the depiction in this panel, which I will look at in the following section.

4.2 Pictorial grounding

I have separated my analysis of narrative and depictive grounding on the basis that reading a comic does not involve simultaneous construal of narration and depiction. As suggested above, depictive grounding is distinct from narrative grounding because it approximates a different conceptualizing experience. The transience of printed pictures in comics differs from the transience of textual or spoken sounds, words, phrases and so on. Although adept readers scan sequentially from panel to panel according to comics' reading conventions and situational prompts within the depicted scene (Cohn 2013; Cohn and Campbell 2015), the pictures in comics do not constitute unitary focal construals to the same extent as linguistic predications. Textual predication construes a situation in a particular way by fixing the conditions of engagement with the simulated proposition. Readerly construal, as influenced by the context of reading, differs on a case-by-case basis to such an extent that the same person can read a predicated proposition on different occasions and understand it in a different way. Contrastingly, the resources afforded by authorial construal do not change and serve to constrain readerly construal (see Harrison 2017: 72).

The same is true of pictures in that the vantage point on the objective scene is fixed through the act of depiction. The conditions and potentialities of viewing are delimited by the author of the picture though processes such as selection (choice of entities for inclusion), granularity (level of detail) and perspectivization (choice of vantage point on the depicted scene). However, whereas linguistic predication posits focal construal of entities through clausal predication and sequential presentation (e.g. Nuttall 2014), a complex image presenting multiple entities in multiple possible relationships permits multiple potential focal configurations. This can include perspectival shifts that go against the spatial logic of foregrounding and prominence vis-à-vis the depictive vantage point. Like with vision in general, this permits multiple attentional fixations, scans and focal arrangements in a single image. Unlike viewing a real scene, individual pictures remain fixed in terms of movement, vantage point and objective content (i.e. things available to be looked at in relation to other things). In comics, these conditions are altered and progressed through the conventionalized presentation of pictures in a sequence. This suggests that seriality of depictive conceptualization in comics occurs initially through scanning a picture, then tracking changes between pictures and appraising depicted events on the basis of content and context (see Foulsham et al. 2016; Cohn et al. 2017; Cohn and Paczynski 2019).

Whereas a textual narrator is deictically referred to through grounding features such as modals and deixis, the analogous conceptualizing entity in relation to which a picture is grounded is mostly only implicit in the act of depiction itself. The actual identity of the conceptualizer associated with a depictive vantage point is rarely important unless the context or co-text places it onstage. This affects the meaning through limitations on perspectival construal, rather than through the identity of the depicter or viewer. Like narrators, depictors are not grounded in the actuality of the objectively depicted scene, though as with narration, an objectively depicted conceptualizer can be subjectified within the depiction if the focus of their conceptualization becomes the focus of a reader. Because of this, choice of vantage point frames an *actual* depictive viewing arrangement without precluding additional fictive viewing arrangements. In this example, the choice of vantage point prompts consideration of what $_c$Alison can and cannot see as different construals of the same scene, which includes fictive simulation of her vantage point from the locally fixed depictive vantage point.

On this basis, there are two conceptualizing viewpoints that can figure as the subjective basis of construal of the depicted objective scene:

1. Unspecified depictor/viewer occupying the vantage point on the scene as a whole
2. Vantage point of the depicted Alison

In the first instance, diagrammed in Figure 9.9, $_c$Alison's conceptualizing activity is objectively construed. Because of the pictorial vantage point (framed by the depictor),

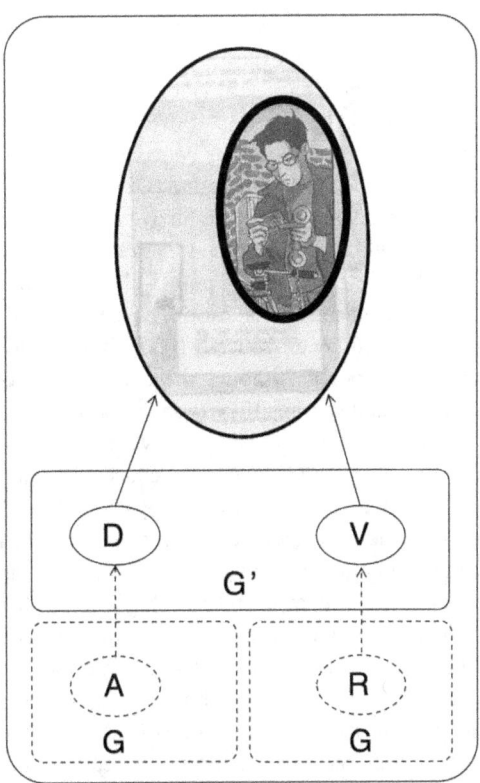

Figure 9.9 Depictive grounding focusing on $_c$Alison's conceptualizing activity.

it is the process of $_C$Alison looking at herself in the camera that is profiled in this construal rather than the content of what she's looking at and thinking. Where the objective focus is on $_C$Alison, entities such as door, wall, mirror, chimney breast and tripod are generally subsumed as part of the setting. The focus on Alison also incorporates relationships that are more or less likely to be focal according to how readers mind-model $_C$Alison in this scene. For example, the camera, the telephone receiver and how she interacts with them. Mind-modelling her conceptualizing activity draws on readers' awareness of the content of depiction in previous panels which showed the parallels between experiencing the phone call with her mother (Figure 9.8) and staging/photographing that scene as a prompt for illustration (Figure 9.9). Because of this, focus is more likely to fall on her conceptualizing activity of 'looking at (herself in) the camera'. The fact that she is holding the phone is more likely to be a secondary focal consideration within this focal arrangement, but it helps to establish continuity with the act of staging. The significance of the phone diminishes across these three panels from an instrument $_C$Alison uses to disconnect herself from her mother, to a prop used to objectify this meaning, to an object that only points back to this sense and is now of secondary consequence in the objective scene.

Because readers do not share the vantage point of $_C$Alison, what she is looking at is not specified in this panel. However, as suggested above, it can be inferred from previous panels that establish an event structure of what she is doing with the camera. On the basis of this inference and previous characterization, there is the potential to construe Alison's viewpoint subjectively. A previous profile can become the base of a subsequent construal. Where that base is a conceptualizer, that conceptualizer becomes discursively grounded.

Within in the construal seen in Figure 9.10, her conceptualizing activity shifts from being depicted objectively in the surrogate ground (i.e. objectively construed) to being a subjective basis of mind-modelling in the discursive ground (subjectively construed as part of G'). Here, the profile and base of the focus of depictive construal align with the force dynamics of the depicted vantage point, where $_C$Alison is subject and the camera is the object of depicted conceptualization. For readers, the observable camera from the depictive vantage point metonymically profiles the content of its screen as the object of $_C$Alison's conceptualization. Although the content of this conceptualization is not specified in this instance, it can be inferred on the basis of the previous panels as likely being a photograph of her. $_C$Alison's subjectivity can be understood in the context of the repeated topic focus on Alison's identity, the concepts of subject and object, and the 'mirror phase' as a psychoanalytic notion.

The difference between these two construals is one of degrees of attenuation and the nature of the mind-modelling that takes place. The construal in Figure 9.9 focuses on $_C$Alison as an objective entity in processual relationship with another entity. Figure 9.10 represents construal of her as a conceptualizer and on the camera as the object of her conceptualization. Figure 9.11 illustrates the extent to which access to conceptualizing experience is attenuated by the depiction. Although we can infer and engage with $_C$Alison's subjectivity, it is less likely to be immediately prominent to a reader. In the depiction, we have more access to the reality conception presented through the depiction. $_C$Alison's reality conception is attenuated by the fact that it can only be

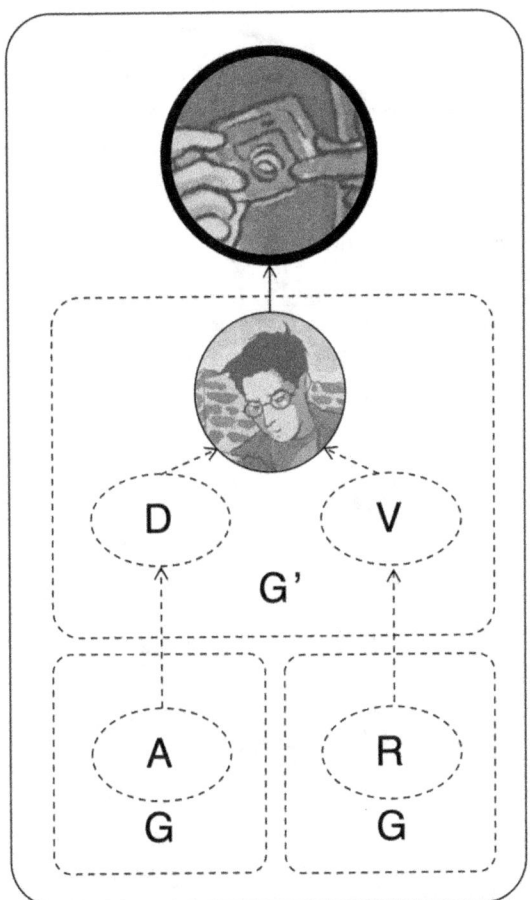

Figure 9.10 $_C$Alison as discursively grounded conceptualizer.

fictively simulated through metonymy and contextual inference. This exemplifies Langacker's (1999: 78) observation that 'both implicature and metonymy are extremely prevalent and contribute greatly to the indirectness of the relation between linguistic expressions and the situations of concern'.

The relative reality conceptions of the depictor (R_D) and the depicted Alison (R_A) diagrammed in Figure 9.11 are also relevant to the final construal of this depiction that I want to discuss. An important thematic component of the depiction here is what cannot be seen from vantage points. Readers cannot see the specific content of the screen and can only engage with $_C$Alison's subjectivity in an attenuated manner. Similarly, the reflection of $_C$Alison in the mirror is only part of R_D and falls outside of in the depicted situation R_A.

In this construal (Figure 9.12), the foregrounding involved in focusing on $_C$Alison's reflection in the mirror is the inverse of the imagined physical logic of foregrounding in the objective scene. This exemplifies how smaller, further away entities can be figural

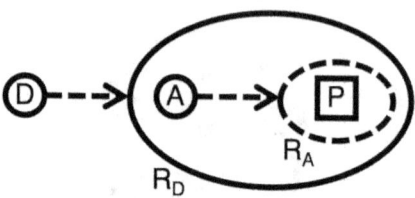

Figure 9.11 Relative reality conceptions.

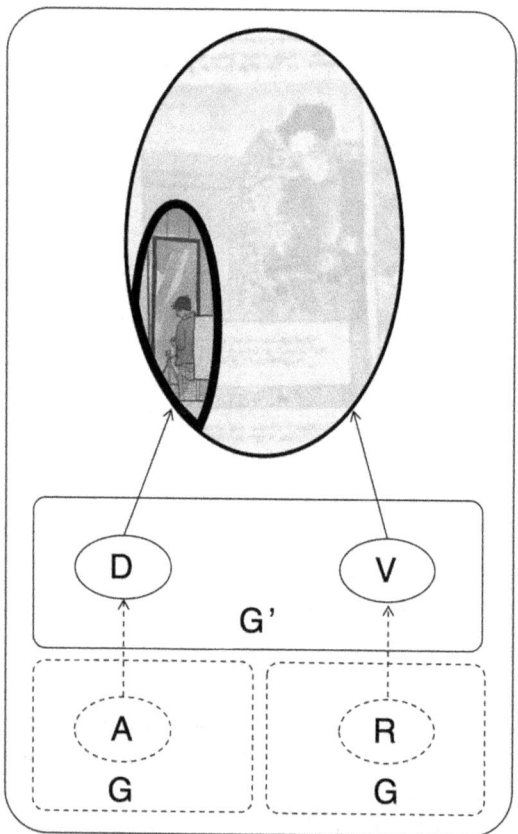

Figure 9.12 Focusing on $_C$Alison's reflection.

in relation to a nearer, larger ground. Again, this construal is prompted by the topic focus at the ongoing discourse level relating to the mirror phase and self-awareness. $_C$Alison is not paying attention to this feature of her immediate situation. In light of the mind-modelling of $_C$Alison's conceptualization of the situation, the readerly pictorial construal that focuses on the mirror – and within this, $_C$Alison's reflection – includes as part of its matrix the idea that $_C$Alison is not aware of this aspect of the situation, and in an extended sense, cannot be aware of it. In other words, the reflection of $_C$Alison is not part of her reality conception, but it is part of the reality conception of $_D$Alison, $_A$Alison and of readers' reality conception of the depicted situation. The process of authoring is made thematically prominent here, which has the potential to snap focus onto the usage event ground. The irony of this construal is that this vantage point is framed by $_D$Alison, and, at the original point of authoring, $_A$Alison as something that is unavailable to $_C$Alison at this particular moment.

5. Conclusion

Building on Pleyer and Schneider's (2014) explanation of construal in *Fun Home* (Bechdel, 2006) this study has examined the shifting focus on focal subjectivity in an example taken from *Are You My Mother?* (Bechdel 2012). This reaffirms Herman's (2009) assertion that Cognitive Grammar can offer fine-grained ways of engaging with the concept of focalization in storytelling. Through this, I have examined how mind-modelling discursive conceptualizers in comics can take place at multiple levels across both depiction and narration. As Langacker (2008: 446) notes, 'each conceptualizer is invoked for certain purposes'. These can be enactors of the same conceptualizer subjectified and objectified across discursive worlds, with different conceptions of reality, different degrees of prominence and different (conceptual) perspectives. Examining this lensing of subjectivity yields a more multifaceted notion of conceptualization in discourse. Through mind-modelling and integrating conceptualizers as discourse progresses, readers are able to imagine complex subjectivities with reference points in different times, spaces and worlds.

This way of framing subjectivity also offers a Cognitive Grammar-specific means of investigating Deictic Shift Theory in storytelling (Duchan et al. 1995). By understanding deictic shifts in terms of surrogation of subjectivity starting from usage event grounding, matters of projection and identification can be understood as the extent to which a reader is invited, or able, to focus on the conceptualizing activity of an enactor as part of grounding, surrogate grounding and subjectification within discourse. The idea of losing the self in reading might be understood in these terms as a result of lensing of subjectivity. Surrogation of discursive subjectivities shifts a reader away from the actuality of their own subjectivity and their awareness of the usage event:

> In discourse the interlocutors advance, negotiate, and adjust their conceptions of reality. Though never identical, usually their reality conceptions have enough in common to allow successful interaction. Their overlap centers on the immediate reality of the ground itself – the here-and-now of the speech situation.
> (Langacker 2008: 297)

The lack of a shared here-and-now in the grounding of reading as a usage event accounts for the extent to which readers engage with the surrogated text-world grounds presented by authors through fictive conceptualizers:

Because it [reality] encompasses the mental, reality has many levels and dimensions. One thing we accept as real is the existence of other conceptualizers whose conceptions of reality differ from our own. Moreover, because we conceptualize the content of other conceptualizations, layers of conception – each representing the content of the next – must also be acknowledged as real.

(Langacker 2008: 297)

Through its examination of her own subjectivity in relation to both her mother and her past selves, Bechdel's (2012) *Are You My Mother?* provides an excellent test-bed for these ideas. Although this thematic focus makes these features more prominent in Bechdel's comic, these ideas are equally applicable to other forms of storytelling, including other significantly multimodal media. As with the separation of depiction and narration in my own analysis, examining how conceptualizers, or enactors, are introduced in different modes may help in understanding subjectivity in multimodal media more generally.

References

Bechdel, A. (2006), *Fun Home: A Family Tragicomic*, Boston: Houghton Mifflin Harcourt.
Bechdel, A. (2012), *Are You My Mother? A Comic Drama*, Boston: Houghton Mifflin Harcourt.
Cohn, N. (2013), 'Navigating Comics: An Empirical and Theoretical Approach to Strategies of Reading Comic Page Layouts', *Frontiers in Cognitive Science*, 4.
Cohn, N. and H. Campbell (2015), 'Navigating Comics II: Constraints on the Reading Order of Page Layouts', *Applied Cognitive Psychology*, 29.
Cohn, N. and M. Paczynski (2019), 'The Neurophysiology of Event Processing in Language and Visual Events', in R. Truswell (ed.), *The Oxford Handbook of Event Structure*, 623–37, Oxford: Oxford University Press.
Cohn, N., M. Paczynski and M. Kutasa (2017), 'Not So Secret Agents: Event-related Potentials to Semantic Roles in Visual Event Comprehension', *Brain and Cognition*, 119.
Davidse, K. and L. Vandelanotte (2011), 'Tense Use in Direct and Indirect Speech in English', *Journal of Pragmatics*, 43 (1): 236–50.
Duchan, J.F., G.A. Bruder and L.E. Hewitt (1995), *Deixis in Narrative: A Cognitive Science Perspective*, Hillsdale: Lawrence Erlbaum.
Fauconnier, G. (1994), *Mental Spaces: Aspects of Meaning Construction in Natural Language*, New York: Cambridge University Press.
Forceville, C., T. Veale and K. Feyaerts (2010), 'Balloonics: The Visuals of Balloons in Comics', in J. Goggin and D. Hassler-Forest (eds), *The Rise and Reason of Comics and Graphic Literature: Critical Essays on the Form*, 56–73, Jefferson: McFarland & Company.
Foulsham, T., D. Wybrow and N. Cohn (2016), 'Reading without Words: Eye Movements in the Comprehension of Comic Strips', *Applied Cognitive Psychology*, 30.
Gavins, J. (2007), *Text World Theory: An Introduction*, Edinburgh: Edinburgh University Press.
Gibbons, A. (2019), 'The "Dissolving Margins" of Elena Ferrante and the Neapolitan Novels: A Cognitive Approach to Fictionality, Authorial Intentionality, and Autofictional Reading Strategies', *Narrative Inquiry*, 29 (2): 391–417.

Giovanelli, M. and C. Harrison (2019), *Cognitive Grammar in Stylistics: A Practical Guide*, London: Bloomsbury.

Harrison, C. (2017), *Cognitive Grammar in Contemporary Fiction*, Amsterdam: John Benjamins.

Harrison, C., L. Nuttall, P. Stockwell and W. Yuan (eds) (2014), *Cognitive Grammar in Literature*, Amsterdam: John Benjamins.

Herman, D. (2009), 'Beyond Voice and Vision: Cognitive Grammar and Focalization Theory', in P. Hühn, W. Schmid and J. Schönert (eds), *Narratology: Point of View, Perspective, and Focalization: Modeling Mediation in Narrative*, 119–42, Berlin: Mouton de Gruyter.

Lacan, J. (2007), *Ecrits*, trans. B. Fink, London: W. W. Norton.

Langacker, R.W. (1987), *Foundations of Cognitive Grammar Vol. 1: Theoretical Prerequisites*, Stanford: Stanford University Press.

Langacker, R.W. (1991), *Foundations of Cognitive Grammar, vol. II: Descriptive Application*, Stanford: Stanford University Press.

Langacker, R.W. (1995), 'Viewing in Cognition and Grammar', in P.W. Davis (ed.), *Alternative Linguistics: Descriptive and Theoretical Modes*, 153–212, Amsterdam: John Benjamins.

Langacker, R.W. (1999), 'Virtual Reality', *Studies in the Linguistic Sciences*, 29 (2): 77–103.

Langacker, R.W. (2002), *Concept, Image and Symbol: The Cognitive Basis of Grammar*, 2nd edn, Berlin: Mouton de Gruyter.

Langacker, R.W. (2008), *Cognitive Grammar: A Basic Introduction*, Oxford: Oxford University Press.

Lejeune, P. (1989), *On Autobiography*, trans. K. Leary, Minneapolis: University of Minnesota Press.

Miller, A. (1981), *The Drama of the Gifted Child*, New York: Basic Books.

Nuttall, L. (2014), 'Constructing a Text World for *The Handmaid's Tale*', in C. Harrison, L. Nuttall, P. Stockwell and W. Yuan. (eds), *Cognitive Grammar in Literature*, 83–100, Amsterdam: John Benjamins.

Palmer, A. (2003), 'The Mind beyond the Skin', in D. Herman (ed.), *Narrative Theory and the Cognitive Sciences*, 322–48, Stanford: CSLI Publications.

Palmer, A. (2004), *Fictional Minds*, Lincoln: University of Nebraska Press.

Pleyer, M. and C. Schneider (2014), 'Construal, Cognition, and Comics: Analysing the Multimodal Construction of a Gothic Autobiography in Alison Bechdel's *Fun Home*', in C. Harrison, L. Nuttall, P. Stockwell and W. Yuan. (eds), *Cognitive Grammar in Literature*, 35–52, Amsterdam: John Benjamins.

Stockwell, P. (2014), 'War, Worlds and Cognitive Grammar', in C. Harrison, L. Nuttall, P. Stockwell and W. Yuan. (eds.), *Cognitive Grammar in Literature*, 19–34, Amsterdam: John Benjamins.

Stockwell, P. and M. Mahlberg (2015), 'Mind-modelling with Corpus Stylistics in *David Copperfield*', *Language and Literature*, 24 (2): 129–47.

Taylor, J. (2002), *Cognitive Grammar*, Oxford: Oxford University Press.

Werth, Paul (1999), *Text Worlds: Representing Conceptual Space in Discourse*, Harlow: Longman.

Winnicott, D. (1967), 'Mirror-role of Mother and Family in Child Development', in P. Lomas (ed.), *The Predicament of the Family: A Psychoanalytical Symposium*, 26–33, London: Hogarth.

Zunshine, L. (2006), *Why We Read Fiction: Theory of Mind and the Novel*, Columbus: Ohio State University Press.

10

'All the figures I used to see': Using Cognitive Grammar to grapple with rhythmic and intertextual meaning-making in Radiohead's 'Pyramid Song'

Clara Neary

1. Introduction

The first single released from their fifth studio album, *Amnesiac* (2001), Radiohead's 'Pyramid Song' is noteworthy for the extent to which it is foregrounded by its musical, rhythmic and lyrical arrangements, constituting a deviation both from the internal norms established by Radiohead's oeuvre up to that point and from comparative external norms of the industry. In terms of external deviation, the song is seen as an exemplar clearly demonstrating how, 'as time progresses [Radiohead] appear to be attempting ever harder to confound every expectation an audience might have of a mainstream band' (Hainge 2007: 63). Lansky, for example, remarks upon the song's 'inventive use of rhythmic levels'; its 'sophisticated and unusual' relation to harmony; and 'the more abstract harmonic and formal nature of its language' (2007: 174–5).

As both *Amnesiac* and its 'twin' album release *Kid A* (2000) contain numerous lyric-less songs (e.g. 'Treefingers' on *Kid A*; 'Hunting Bears' on *Amnesiac*), these albums may be seen as at least partially constituting an internal deviation from the band's previous output, all of which contains lyrics. While 'Pyramid Song' does contain lyrics, their importance has been problematized by Yorke's contention that he 'will never allow the lyrics to be printed and that listeners are expressly not meant to focus on them' (quoted in Reynolds 2001: 26). (As detailed more fully below, I have accessed the printed lyrics via the song's official sheet music and cross-checked them against the lyrics as heard in the song). The lyrics are also riddled with ambiguity, and, as noted by Hesselink: 'With no direct references to Egypt or the pyramids [...] the larger [musical] community has been tireless in its efforts to nail down the meaning and inspiration behind the otherworldly images evoked' (2014: 80). The song has also been subjected to studio modifications and vocal distortions that 'often render it difficult to understand individual words or phrases' (Hainge 2007: 62), with the latter at least partially achieved by playing the vocals through the palm speaker of Greenwood's ondes martenot (Rose 2011: 82). Finally, the song has an atypical lyrical structure that largely does not follow the 'verse/chorus/verse/chorus' pattern typical of their previous output.[1]

Its rhythmic structure is seen as particularly unusual due to a time signature perceived as creating complex rhythms 'that are out of joint with those of our ordinary experience' (Thompson 2009: 221). This, Thompson continues, is what makes the song so 'compelling' (2009: 221): 'Its timing, rhythm, and beat are literally out of sync with the way we ordinarily experience the world' (2009: 222). This deviant rhythmic structure has prompted some very interesting audience response. Thompson, for example, points out that 'After hearing "Pyramid Song" from *Amnesia*, most people say, "Something's not quite right with that song" [...] Yet neither the vocals nor Yorke's delivery seems to account for the arresting qualities [...] It is, rather, the mood of the song that seems to grab and keep your attention. And that mood has everything to do with the song's rhythm' (2009: 62). Listeners may assume that lyrics and harmony bear the heaviest semantic load in terms of musical meaning-making, but rhythm, particularly when used in an unusual way, can also play a crucial role in this regard; as Hesselink notes, rhythm has proven to be 'a fundamental aspect of music and its appreciation' (2013). Indeed, the rhythmic form of 'Pyramid Song' makes the listener pay attention to issues of time, with temporality a key theme in the song: here, Radiohead use time and rhythm to illustrate 'how time affects our experiences and perceptions and points us toward the relationships between the rhythms of our lives and the events and interconnections within them' (Thompson 2009: 223). Indeed, one of the few clarifications Yorke has made regarding the song's meaning is his concession that it is about 'time and the idea that time is completely cyclical' (*MTV* interview 2001).

The band, however, has not made any attempt to clarify the rhythm debate, with Yorke claiming the song does not have a definite time signature, that 'it is simply felt as the song is played' (cited in Thompson 2009: 223). As Thompson remarks, Yorke's comment highlights the 'subjectivity of perception' (2009: 223) particularly in the realm of aesthetic experience, and subjective experiences of the song are encouraged by its ambiguity, an ambiguity which the band further reinforces through both its lyrical and musical structure, and their refusal to clarify either. Indeed, 'deliberate ambiguity' is something of a 'hallmark' of Radiohead's work (Letts 2005: vi; cited in Hesselink 2013), and the subject of much research conducted on the '[i]ntentional vagueness and/or multiplicity of meanings' found in much of their output (see Hesselink 2013: 4). As Hesselink notes, ambiguity is not only central to the experience of music due to 'its lack of one-to-one correspondence to language, emotions, and tangible objects of human experience' but provides a vital means of 'feed[ing] our imaginative and interpretive engagement' (2013: 2). This is particularly the case within popular music, in which, 'lack of concrete references – visual, lyrical, musical – allows a fertile space for active listeners to personalize the experience in ways that are deeply and completely emotional, intellectual and spiritual' (2013: 2). Ambiguity foregrounds the subjectivity of human perception, particularly in the realm of the aesthetic, and one of the main focuses of this analysis of 'Pyramid Song' will be on highlighting the ways in which this ambiguity is both musically and lyrically constructed.

While popular music as a genre has finally begun to garner scholarly attention, until very recently this attention was focused on either its linguistic or its musical semiotic structure but rarely both (see Morini 2013). Recent exceptions to this include research by Morini (2013), Neary (2019) and Whiteley and Voice (2019), all of which endeavours to bridge the gap between these differing semiotic modes by utilizing analytical frameworks for language and music which have common principles of cognitive scientific thinking at their core. The focus here, given the discussion above, will be on representations of time and temporality throughout the text, as well as on the construction of ambiguity, both of which are key aspects of the text's meaning-making processes. To this end, the cognitively-derived frameworks of Langacker's (1987, 1991) Cognitive Grammar and Zbikowski's theory of Musical Grammar (2002, 2012, 2017) are utilized here. In the next section, relevant aspects of Langacker's framework will be introduced in brief alongside its application to 'Pyramid Song'; this will be followed by introduction of Zbikowski's theory of Musical Grammar and its subsequent application. The chapter will conclude with an attempt to merge these findings.

2. A Cognitive Grammar analysis of 'Pyramid Song'

Langacker states that '[t]he basic tenet of Cognitive Grammar is that nothing beyond symbolic structures need be invoked for the proper characterization of complex expressions and the patterns they instantiate' (2008: 5). By this, he means that grammar itself is inherently 'meaningful' (Langacker 2008: 4) in that there is a direct symbolic link between linguistic form (which he terms *phonological structure*) and semantic structure. As such, Cognitive Grammar forges a strong connection between what we say and how we say it; and, relying heavily on the notion of perceptual *construal*, it asserts that, given 'our manifest ability to conceive and portray the same situation in alternate ways' (Langacker 2008: 32), a prototypical linguistic representation of an event, for example, must demonstrate a prototypical conceptualization of that event. In a construal operation, the linguistic content of the utterance is likened to a scene, which is perceived or construed by potential *conceptualizers*, typically the text producer and the text recipient. The way in which we conceptualize events or situations is determined by our embodied – both physical and social – experience of the world; in particular, it relies upon activation of an appropriate image schema, an 'abstract representation that results from our everyday interactions with the world' (Littlemore and Taylor 2014: 11). *Image schemas* can be thought of as 'schematized patterns of activity abstracted from everyday bodily experience, especially pertaining to vision, space, motion, and force' which 'function as components of more elaborate conceptual configurations' (Langacker 2013: 32, 33).[2] Our reliance on image schemas is not limited to making sense of linguistic structures, but is integral to our attempts to decode meaning in all aspects of the world around us, including musical structures. Because of the song's temporal concerns, my focus here will be on the construal of time, as represented by the *relational profiles* – i.e. predication processes – constructed in 'Pyramid Song'.

2.1 Action chains and construal

Key to the structuring of the conceived situation and its component parts is the notion of an *action chain*. In the case of relational profiles – i.e. when the entity being profiled is a verb – the figure/ground distinction is relabelled as *trajector/landmark*. Trajector/landmark alignment is useful to consider as differing versions of a linguistic utterance can profile the same relationship between two entities, but represent each of these entities in a different way, such that one or the other is given more prominence. Cognitive Grammar conceptualizes the events depicted at clause level in terms of an energy transfer metaphor (Langacker 1991: 283), such that each of the entities in the clause (usually designated by a noun phrase) is perceived as playing a particular semantic role determined by the relational profile of the clause; these roles are based upon *cognitive archetypes* (see Langacker 2008: 356). Prototypically, according to what Langacker terms a *canonical event model* (2008: 357), there will be at least one participant in a clause acting as *agent* of an action. The *patient* is the entity on the receiving end who is typically altered in some way by the action, and is also known as an *energy sink* (Langacker 2008: 356). If an agent utilizes another participant in the clause in any way, this participant is labelled the *instrument*. A prototypical utterance will profile an action chain in which the predicative 'energy' flows from agent to patient via an instrument, if one is present; hierarchically, the agent is perceived as highest on this dynamic chain, the patient being second highest and the instrument coming last. If the relational profile represents a cognitive process, the actor is renamed an *experiencer*[3], while if the profile represents a process of spatial relocation, the actor is relabelled a *mover*. In English, the agent, experiencer and mover roles are prototypically represented by the grammatical subject; as such they are perceived as having control over the represented predication. However, clausal elements do not always participate in the predication process: in the example 'the baby is in the pram', the baby is considered a *zero participant* as it exists without performing an action, while the pram does not participate at all, merely being part of the background *setting*. The zero position is the default role for all participants in a clause as 'all participants begin fundamentally with existence and attributes' (Stockwell 2002: 64).

The opening line of 'Pyramid Song' – 'Jumped in the river and what did I see?' – contains two relational profiles, i.e. two instances in which the profiled entity is a verb. In the first, a physical process is profiled, in which the speaker (though there is ellipsis of 'I') is perceived as a mover who in jumping into the river physically relocates to a different space. 'Jumped' acts as an intransitive verb here, so there is no energy sink. In the second relational profile, the speaker asks a rhetorical question relating to his process of perception – seeing – and so becomes an experiencer. In both cases, the conceptualization is grammatically prototypical, with subject acting as mover/experiencer. The remainder of the verse comprises an answer to the question – 'what did I see?' – via listing of the various stimuli seen. As such, the first line has a sort of dominion over the seven lines that follow.

Within the listed stimuli, there are further relational profiles. The construction of Line 2 – 'Black-eyed angels swam with me' – is interesting. Upon first glance, this line seems to answer the question posed in Line 1, and contains the first stimulus 'seen' by the speaker – 'black-eyed angels' – with the relational profile 'I saw' assumed to have been ellipted from the opening of the clause. As such, the speaker is again the experiencer, and the angels are the stimulus. However, this perception is problematized by the further construction of the angels as movers swimming with the speaker; the assumed construction '[I saw] black-eyed angels swam with me' no longer makes sense, not least because of the verb tenses, and the participant role of the angels therefore becomes ambiguous. In effect, the angels' other-worldly status is emphasized by depicting them as capable of simultaneously inhabiting the roles of both active mover and passive stimulus, an effect further heightened by the song's strange atemporality as indicated through its conflicting use of verb tenses ('saw' and 'swam' are both in the simple past tense but the correct tense for 'swam' in this construction is the present). The oddity of this linguistic construction is further highlighted by the simultaneous representation of the speaker as both the grammatical subject 'I' and 'me', the latter a relegation to grammatical object status. Perhaps entrance into another realm has enabled the speaker to simultaneously occupy both positions. In any case, the angels become the trajector here, while the speaker is backgrounded to landmark.

The ambiguity of Line 2 is not resolved in Line 3, which is missing a relational profile and therefore demands insertion of the ellipted process 'I saw' that was so problematic in the preceding line. The proposition '[I saw] a moon full of stars and astral cars' makes sense as a prototypical utterance, with speaker 'I' again acting as experiencer and the 'moon' acting as stimulus. However, the use of co-reference again creates ambiguity: should the sentence actually read '[I saw] a moon full of stars and [I saw] astral cars'? Or was the moon full of both 'stars' and 'astral cars'? If 'astral' here is taken as referring, not simply to the stars, but to its second meaning as a non-physical plain of existence [upon which 'various psychic and paranormal phenomena' occur and 'in which the physical human body is said to have counterpart' (*OED*)], then 'astral cars' could be understood as vehicles moving across this other-worldly plain in which it is perhaps possible to have a moon containing stars. In this case, the 'black-eyed angels' are perhaps manifestations of the swimming speaker's counterpart. Line 4 also seems to activate insertion of the ellipted relational profile 'I saw', although the result – 'And [I saw] all the figures I used to see' – is also cognitively challenging. Temporality is again an issue here: 'used to' conveys a past tense event which is no longer occurring but this is undermined by the fact that the speaker/experiencer is now seeing again things he used to see; none of this is clarified by the fact that the whole clause already operates in the simple past tense ('saw'). This ambiguity is further propounded by the vagueness of the nominal profile 'figures' (see section on specificity).

Line 5 continues 'All my lovers were there with me'; here, these 'lovers' are zero participants, merely existing while nonetheless being the trajector, while the speaker is again relegated to grammatical object position and therefore landmark status. However, once again it is possible that we are meant to understand this line as beginning 'I saw that', in which case the speaker is experiencer and the 'lovers' are the stimulus. As Line 6 lacks a relational profile, again we are encouraged to search for the ellipted process: this could make the utterance '[I saw] all my past and futures' or 'All my past and futures [were there with me]'. Given the abstract nature of the nominal profiles 'past' and 'futures', it is difficult to make a case for them acting as either co-stimuli or zero participant as they can neither be seen nor are they physically present. Line 7 – 'And we all went to heaven in a little row boat' – comprises the movers 'we', the instrument 'a little row boat' and the destination 'heaven', which can be considered the final recipient of the energy in this dynamic action chain (i.e. the energy sink). The final line is fraught with ambiguity. In 'There was nothing to fear and nothing to doubt', 'there' acts as a dummy subject while the participant in this existential process is 'nothing' (what SFL would label an 'existent'); the result is a semantically empty proposition involving a form of negation which creates further ambiguity in the text.

Overall then, the speaker's only 'movement' is his jumping into the river; from then on, it is his role as experiencer that is foregrounded, with references to him swimming alongside the entities he meets being symbolically backgrounded by placing him in grammatical object ('me') position. His passage into another realm is also highlighted in Line 2 by his appearing to occupy the roles of experiencer/trajector and mover/landmark simultaneously, although for the rest of the song he largely remains in landmark position. The only exception to this is in Line 7, when the speaker belongs to the movers 'we' in the 'little row boat'; however, this return to focal prominence is somewhat undermined as his subjectivity is subsumed by that of the group of which he now forms part. It could also be argued that the repeatedly ellipted 'I saw' functions to further background the speaker, with the 'seen' stimuli gaining successively greater prominence. Time begins behaving oddly from Line 2, in which 'saw' and 'swam' conflict with one another, while Lines 3 and 4 are both missing a relational profile and temporal confusion reaches its climax in Line 6 with the notion that past and future can co-exist simultaneously.

Relational profiles are further sub-divided in Cognitive Grammar into *perfective* versus *imperfective*. Perfective verbs are those that are 'bounded in time', and 'profile a particular occurrence of an event, and ones that indicate a change through time', while imperfect verbs describe an 'ongoing situation' (Giovanelli and Harrison 2018: 66). The relational profiles in 'Pyramid Song' – 'jumped', 'see', 'swam', 'were', 'went', 'was' – are all perfective, describing events which occurred in (various levels of) the past. The relationships themselves can also be seen to become increasingly static, from 'jumped' to the simple existential 'was'. This increasing lack of movement could be construed as conceptualizing timelessness, which could accord with Yorke's assertion that time is cyclical.

Cognitive Grammar also provides us with a means of investigating how conceptualizers mentally track the unfolding of events over time. While 'a *summary scan* occurs when the scene viewed is static, [...] a *sequence scan* occurs if the scene depicts movement of some kind' (Harrison 2017: 21, italics added; see also Langacker 1987: 248, 2013: 111). The events in 'Pyramid Song' are scanned sequentially as a series of events through time – from the moment the speaker jumps into the water to his final heaven-bound journey – via the construction of a *scanning chain*, comprising a sequence of reference points (such as 'river', 'angels', 'moon' etc.) which function to direct the conceptualizer's attention from one textual figure to the next. However, this is not to say that we are unable to simultaneously view the events as a summary. Langacker argues that '[s]equential and summary scanning should not be thought of as mutually exclusive but as two facets of the normal observation of events [...]

We thus have the option of conceptualizing an event by focusing selectively on either mode of scanning. Depending on which mode predominates, we can either highlight its inherent sequentiality or impose a holistic construal' (2013: 111–12). He proceeds to state that sequential scanning is 'implied by categorization of a verb' (2013: 112), which highlights the possibilities when a verb is implied but absent. It is my contention that the repeated ellipsis of relational profiles in 'Pyramid Song' encourages the conceptualizer to construe each of the events depicted as individual snapshots superimposed upon the ongoing process of sequential scanning. The result is a kind of playing with time, caused by simultaneous continuity and discontinuity, which reinforces the text's concern with time as a cyclical, rather than a linear, construct.

The varying degrees of *specificity* with which these reference points are sketched also succeed in highlighting the relational profiles that bind them rather than the nominal profiles which define them. Specificity is a dimension of construal which refers to 'the degree of precision with which we express ourselves […] from quite schematic to very specific' (Bennett 2014: 33). At the outset, the use of definite reference tells us the speaker does not jump into just any river, but into 'the river'. There is also elaboration upon what the speaker sees: the angels are described as 'black-eyed' while the moon is 'full of stars and astral cars'; the speaker sees not just some but 'all the figures' he used to see, and 'all' his lovers and 'all' his 'past and futures'. In Line 7 – 'And we all went to heaven in a little row boat' – the entities 'we' and 'little row boat' along with their destination are all specified, while in Line 8 we are told there was 'nothing' to fear or doubt. And yet, this supposed specificity is simultaneously undermined by a lack of specificity when we consider the following: which river did the speaker jump in? What kind of 'figures' did he see and why, when or how did he 'used to see' them? Why does he no longer see them? We are told that 'all my lovers' were there, but who are they and what are their names? And how can one's 'past and futures' be present when these are abstract, non-countable entities? Finally, is there such a place as 'heaven'? Can one go there? Can one go there in a 'little row boat'? How? The final line of the song is repeated four times, its repetition attempting to convey certainty by reinforcing the fact stated within; and yet, this certainty is completely undermined by the semantic emptiness of the word 'nothing'. As stated above, in the absence of specific information on the text's reference points, it is their relationships with one another that are foregrounded, with the temporality of such relationships occupying the spotlight.

Finally, the *perspective* of the conceptualized events in the song – i.e. the 'overall relationship between the "viewers" and the situation being "viewed"' (Langacker 2013: 73) – is *covertly*, rather than *overtly*, constructed in that it is 'explicitly attached to the speaking platform' (Harrison 2017: 16). In 'Pyramid Song', the subject of conceptualization, i.e. the entity who is, often quite literally, viewing the scene, is the first-person narrator, as evidenced in 'I jumped in … and what did I see?'; 'were there with me'; 'my lovers'; 'my past and future'; and 'we all went to heaven'. The objects of conceptualization are the 'black-eyed angels'; 'a moon full of stars' etc. As Giovanelli and Harrison note, when the subject of conceptualization is placed onstage in this way through the explicit use of the first-person pronoun 'I', the content being conceptualized is construed more subjectively, while at the same time the conceptualizer is construed objectively, or phrased another way, 'when the conceptualizer becomes more prominent and viewed more objectively, the scene that is being conceptualized becomes more subjective' (2018: 52). This accords well with the emphasis placed by Yorke on the subjectivity of perception in the context of the band's refusal to clarify the ongoing debate regarding perceptions of the song's rhythmic structure. Essentially, the fact of the viewer being foregrounded here potentially acts to highlight that the events being represented are the subjective construal of one entity, and hence reinforces the importance of individual perception. Why reveal to fans the 'official' rhythmic structure of 'Pyramid Song' when each listener experiences the rhythm subjectively? Why clarify its rhythmic structure when rhythmic ambiguity creates a multiplicity of potential meanings which could only be curbed by such a revelation?

Having considered how the lyrical composition of the song constructs its central themes of ambiguity and temporality, the next section considers the ways in which its musical composition reinforces these thematic concerns.

3. Zbikowski's theory of Musical Grammar

As Zbikowski notes, his theory of Musical Grammar 'takes as its basic model the grammars developed by cognitive linguists over the past thirty years' (2017: 16), particularly those of Langacker (1987, 1991) and Croft (2001). The compatibility of Zbikowski's theory of Musical Grammar with Cognitive Grammar therefore lies in their mutual recognition that all aspects of form, regardless of size or type, can be considered form-function pairings; that is, all form, whether linguistic or non-linguistic, has meaning potential. However, Zbikowski's focus is musical form and he considers language solely in terms of how it is affected by musical structure so that his approach should not be considered an application of the cognitive grammars of Langacker and Croft, but rather as having been informed by them.

Zbikowski's (2017) theory of Musical Grammar uses analogous thinking to understand 'how sequences of patterned sound can, independent of language, create meaning' (2017: 55). He asserts that music functions as a semiotic resource by encouraging listeners to construct analogous relationships – in the form of 'sonic analogues' – between musical form and meaning. Brower's (2000) cognitive theory of musical meaning informs on how these sonic analogues are constructed. She draws upon Margolis's (1987) concept of 'pattern-matching' and Johnson's (1987) theory of embodied meaning to demonstrate that listeners compare incoming musical information to three types of stored schematic knowledge. First, we identify a musical text's 'intra-opus patterns', i.e. similarities and differences within the musical text itself. Secondly, listeners compare the musical text to their stored knowledge of musical conventions, of which all musical listeners, expert or otherwise, have some experience. These first two types of schematic knowledge involve the comparison of music with music, and hence give rise to what Brower terms '*intra-domain*' mappings (2000: 324; italics in original). These sets of knowledge can overlap, enabling the listener to simultaneously identify patterns in a piece of music, such as a repeated musical phrase or refrain, and how they correspond to musical conventions more generally, as such, facilitating identification of both internal and external musical foregrounding through processes of parallelism and deviation. The third type of stored knowledge is especially relevant given the simultaneous application of Cognitive Grammar carried out in this analysis: it concerns image schemas, which enable the construction of 'metaphorical, or *cross-domain*' mappings (2000: 324; italics in original), which in this case enable comparison of musical information with non-musical, typically embodied, patterns of experience. According to Brower, the image schemas used in music comprehension are those predominantly used in everyday life: CONTAINER, CYCLE, VERTICALITY, BALANCE, CENTRE-PERIPHERY and SOURCE-PATH-GOAL schemas (2000: 326). As such they reflect our common embodied experience of space, time, force and movement, such as our propensity to conceptualize as a bounded unit; time as being composed of cycles; our bodies as centred entities ideally characterized by their stability; and, finally, our tendency to perceive motion as a route towards a goal. Our image schemas tend to overlap – for example, the body is frequently perceived as both CENTRE and CONTAINER – causing us to combine them in the process of interpretation. Those image schemas recognized by Brower as most persistent in musical communication are united, as Zbikowski notes, by their 'appeal to causality' (2017: 92); that is, they are all goal-directed dynamic processes. A state of instability, for example, typically triggers the search for a way to regain stability, while a departure typically activates the goal either of return or of reaching an intended destination.

Zbikowski's theory of Musical Grammar comprises four distinct analytical stages. The first involves identification of the musical text's 'syntactic processes', i.e. the musical features that contribute to meaning, namely rhythm and harmony, which Zbikowski labels the text's temporal (rhythm) and tonal (pitch) frameworks. Examples of such syntactic processes include repetition, sequencing and grouping: a sequence of ascending or descending pitch, for example, or use of rhythmic patterns can communicate meaning. The second stage involves identification of the sonic analogues constructed by the temporal and tonal frameworks by linking them to the most appropriate image schema(s). Fixed pitch is a particularly meaningful semiotic resource here: it refers to how an arrangement of harmonic pitches can be construed as 'anchored' by one specific pitch, often the tonic or dominant of the key being played (see glossary of musical terms). Fixed pitch hence activates Brower's (2000: 326) CYCLE and SOURCE-PATH-GOAL schemas, creating a sonic analog of departure and return (from and to the anchoring pitch) (see Zbikowski 2017: 126). In the third stage, any sonic analogues resulting from interactions between the rhythmic and harmonic layers are considered, while the focus of the final stage is the coordination between the text's musical structure and its lyrical composition.

3.1 Analysis of the musical structure of 'Pyramid Song'

As Radiohead did not publish the song lyrics from *Amnesiac* on the album sleeve, both the lyrics and music analysed here are largely those found in the official sheet music[4]; however, there are some disparities between the latter and the music and lyrics as sung in the album version of the song. These occur because sheet music tends to value standardization and exact repetition over representation of the more idiosyncratic musical and lyrical behaviour of a song such as 'Pyramid Song' (e.g. 'I' is inserted before 'jumped' in the first line of the sheet music, and the differences in musical structure between the first and second verses are not noted). In cases where the content of the sheet-music has not matched my listening experience, either musically or lyrically, I have prioritized the latter in the knowledge that, while it potentially problematizes my attempts at total objectivity, in these instances my listening experience is closer to other listeners' experiences of the song as actually recorded by Radiohead (as opposed to as noted in the sheet music); these disparities are flagged up in this analysis where appropriate.

The song comprises two distinct verses, with the second being an almost-complete lyrical and musical repetition of the first, with some minor exceptions. In terms of the lyrics, there are only two differences. The first stanza's opening line 'Jumped in the river and what did I see?' is shortened in the second stanza to 'Jumped in to the river', with the word 'river' being held over a significantly longer vocal duration to duplicate the harmony of the first stanza's opening musical phrase. Also, the final line of the second stanza is repeated three times, with the harmony remaining the same in each instance. In terms of its musical structure, each eight-line verse can be sub-divided into two, with the musical composition of the first four lines being repeated in that of Lines 5–8. As such, the whole song effectively comprises the same musical pattern repeated four times, twice within each verse.

As such, in the consideration of the song's musical grammar that follows, I will analyse only the musical structure of the first four lines. However, I will also point out any musical disparities between verses, and, when considering the interaction of music with lyrics, I will obviously comment on how the meaning of the lyrics of Lines 5–8 is affected by their interaction with its musical structure.

3.1.1 Rhythmic processes in 'Pyramid Song'

While, as outlined above, analysis of the song's harmonic processes and the interaction of music with words constitute distinct stages in Zbikowski's methodology, it makes sense in this context to amalgamate them, on a line-by-line basis. This allows detailed consideration of the musical structure of each line to be immediately followed by analysis of how this interacts with lyrical structure, as well as avoiding unnecessary repetition. The third stage – coordination of rhythmic and harmonic layers – will be omitted here because, as will be seen, the song's rhythmic and harmonic process invoke almost exactly the same sonic analogues, thereby making their interaction a simple process of reinforcement.

As previously discussed, the rhythmic structure of 'Pyramid Song' has long been the focus of considerable debate and dissent largely because, as Thompson notes, the rhythm of the song 'seems skewed'; the notes appear to be 'played a split-second too late' (2009: 221). Hesselink (2013) notes that the rhythmic ambiguity in the song is categorized as 'underdetermination', which is defined by Butler as occurring 'when one or more layers of motion needed to make a decisive metrical interpretation are absent' (2006: 129–30). Thompson presents three predominant perceptions of the song's rhythmic structure: first, that the time signature is 4/4 'but with syncopated stress points'; secondly, that the signature is 8/8 but with a grouping of notes into pairs and trios; and, finally, the 'oddest theory' is that 'the timing itself alters periodically throughout the song' (2009: 222). Hesselink (2013) has studied five years' worth of online debate on the song's rhythmic structure and concludes that there are no fewer than nine different interpretations, centring upon whether or not the song contains a single regular metre and, if so, what that is. The majority of fans perceive the metre as regular throughout, while the rhythm is predominantly interpreted as being in 4/4 time, meaning there are four beats to a bar, although interpretations varied as to whether this was 'simple' or 'compound time', the latter referring to the perception of each beat as further composed of three equal parts. Thompson's (2009: 223) assertion that listeners who 'tend to see life as a sequence of small clusters of events with strange emphases' will recognize a simple time signature is difficult to substantiate, but Hesselink notes that research by music theorists and cognitive scientists has shown that Western listeners are more likely to perceive an unknown rhythm as simple time due to the 'predominance of binary meters in Western music (especially popular genres)' (2013). The predominant interpretation of 4/4 simple time also accords with that provided in the official sheet music.

While it is important to remain keenly aware of the ambiguity that characterizes responses to the rhythmic structure of 'Pyramid Song', the fact that consensus was reached by the majority of Hesselink's respondents does enable tentative identification of the sonic analogue constructed by its temporal framework. The regularity characteristic of 4/4 simple time invokes the CYCLE image schema,[5] and it appears to be this invocation of cyclicity that Hesselink has in mind when he supports the 4/4 interpretation on the basis of Yorke's assertion of the song's preoccupation with the cyclical nature of time, which Hesselink construes as 'a reference to a regular meter' (2013).

3.1.2 Harmonic processes in 'Pyramid Song'

The song is in the key of F♯ minor (natural) which has three sharps (F, G and C); its tonic (main) note is F♯; dominant note is C♯ (the fifth note in the scale); and subdominant is B (the fourth note in the scale). Following an eight-bar musical

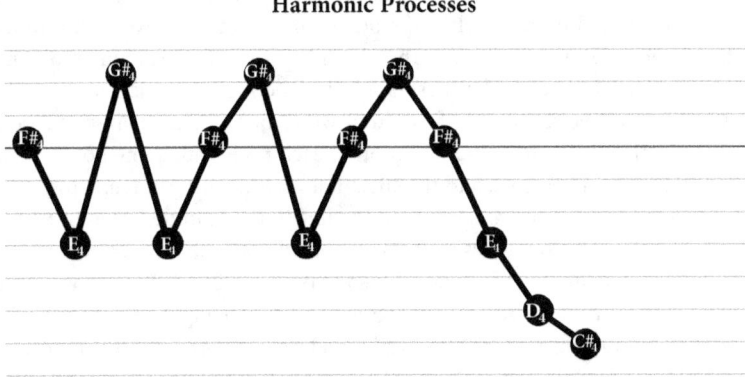

Figure 10.1 *Oooh, ooh, ooh.*

introduction, the vocal line commences with three plaintively rendered 'Oooh's; the first is held across four notes (F♯$_4$, E$_4$, G♯$_4$, E$_4$) and released on the return to F♯$_4$; the second is held over a repeated sequence of G♯$_4$-E$_4$-F♯$_4$ and again released on the return to F♯$_4$; the third commences on G♯$_4$ and descends across F♯$_4$ -E$_4$-D$_4$ to rest on C♯$_4$, some three notes below the originating pitch. The most frequently used notes are the key's tonic F♯$_4$ – from which the phrase commences and to which it returns three times – and E$_4$, which features four times. As evidenced in the visual representation of the musical structure in Figure 10.1, this thrice-repeated return to the originating pitch, the key's tonic, initially creates a sonic analogue of DEPARTURE/RETURN, as well as conveying the completion of various CYCLE image schemas. However, the final two notes in the phrase successively descend to rest two pitches below the tonic note, suggesting the commencement of a new journey/cycle, but one left unfinished. The fact that this is the first time in the musical phrase that the harmony has descended below E$_4$ suggests a certain negativity, or certainly an ominous tone, which is further foregrounded by this first use of the key's dominant pitch C♯$_4$, on which to rest.

In terms of the interaction between music and words, the lyrics enter with what seems to be three repetitions of 'Oooh', following eight bars of musical introduction. The first 'Oooh' is held over five notes, totalling 3.5 bars or fifteen beats in total. As Figure 10.1 demonstrates, its pitch first falls then rises to a note above the originating pitch, before falling to the same point and then returning to its starting point of F♯$_4$. The completion of this harmonic cycle is accentuated by the fact that it corresponds with the complete articulation of the first 'Oooh'; as such, the harmonic and linguistic structure perfectly mirror one another, thereby accentuating both. The second 'ooh' is held for five beats over three notes which first descend by 2.5 pitches then ascend by 1.5, not returning to its origin; the last note is held for a full four counts. Once again, this complete three-pitch cycle corresponds with the full articulation of the second 'ooh', again foregrounding both. The final 'ooh' is held over five notes which steadily descend to rest four pitches below their starting point; the first four notes are a single beat each while the final note is held for two beats. This schematic departure from the two previous 'oohs', marked by a steady descension in pitch, forms a kind of internal deviation which also acts to foreground its harmonic structure; coming to rest on C♯$_4$, the key's dominant also stands out as a plaintive note, being only half a pitch below its preceding note, while the others in the sequence were a minimum of one pitch or more apart. Also, the fact that the G♯$_4$-E$_4$-F♯$_4$ phrase is sung more quickly each time functions to somewhat destabilize its repetition, so it is heard anew each time. Add to the above repetition of this 'non-word' 'ooh', the constant rise and fall of pitch, and the alternating temporal duration of each note, with some notes held for a disproportionately longer time, and the effect is a very haunting opening to the song.

The lyrics proper then commence with the line 'Jumped in the river and what did I see?'. There are only two pitches in this ten-note phrase: the key's dominant C♯ and subdominant B. The first word 'jumped' is sung on B$_3$ while each of the words in the phrase 'in the river and' is sung on a repetition of C♯$_4$ (see Figure 10.2). The 'what' in 'what did I see' is sung on a return to B$_3$ while 'did I see' is sung on a thrice-repeated C♯$_4$. The return to B$_3$ suggests a completion of that cycle of seven notes, while the following

Harmonic Processes

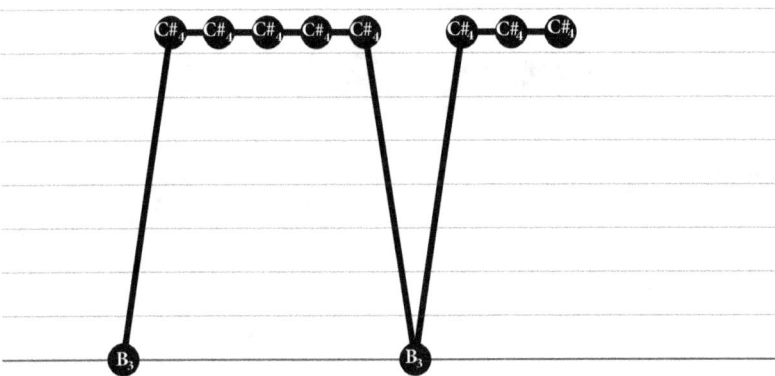

Figure 10.2 Line 1: *Jumped in the river and what did I see?* and Line 5: *All my lovers were there with me.*

return to $C\sharp_4$ suggests another cycle has been embarked upon, but not completed. Once again, the sonic analogue constructed relates to the DEPARTURE/RETURN and CYCLE image schemas, with one journey/cycle completed and another embarked upon.

With the exception of the first word 'jumped', which is a disyllabic word sung on a single crotchet, the music interacts with the lyrics so that all other words in this phrase are sung on a single note–single syllable pattern, with the only other disyllabic word 'river' broken into two syllables, each of which is sung on a repeated $C\sharp_4$. The fact that both 'jumped' and 'what' are sung on B_3 means they stand out against the pattern of repeated $C\sharp_4$ that forms the background, while being simultaneously linked to one another by being sung on the same note. This is further accentuated by the fact that both words are held over one single beat (a crotchet in the first instance and a tied quaver in the second), whilst the other words in the phrase are only held for half that duration (i.e. a quaver).

The second line in Verse 1 – 'Black-eyed angels swam with me' – contains eleven notes, but only four pitches. It starts on A_3, a note subsequently repeated four times and over which the noun phrase 'black-eyed an-gels' is sung as four distinct but musically corresponding units. The harmony then ascends one note to the sub-dominant B_3, which is sung three times to correspond with the three syllables in 'swam with me' with the final phoneme in 'me' being sung across four falling/rising/falling notes – $A\sharp_3$, B_3, $A\sharp_4$, $F\sharp_3$. Interestingly, the sheet music represents both of these A_3 as natural; however, it is clear when listening that their disarming effect is entirely based on the fact that the A here, and only here in the whole piece, is actually A sharp. As Figure 10.3 shows, the parallelism in the repetition of the opening two notes suggests a stability that is subsequently undermined by the unstable falling/rising/falling pattern, whose dominance is evidenced in its resting on $F\sharp_3$, 1.5 pitches below its starting point. Here, a sonic analogue of instability is conveyed, with the final fall in pitch to the 'anchoring' tonic note suggesting a lack of control.

Harmonic Processes

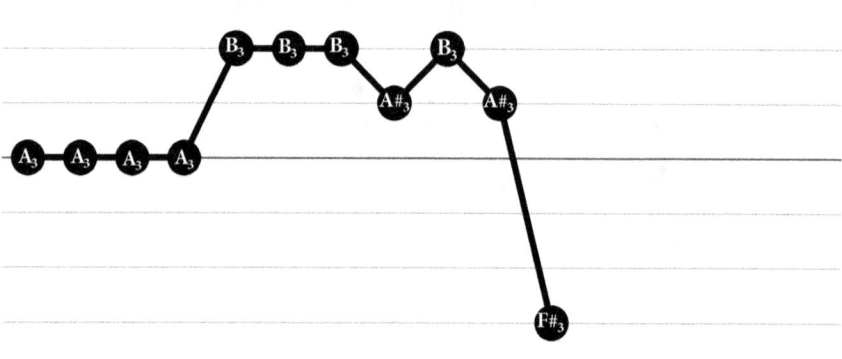

Figure 10.3 Line 2: *Black-eyed angels swam with me* and Line 6: *All my past and futures.*

This second line is also sung almost completely on a one-syllable–one-note pattern, with the exception of the final word 'me', as mentioned above. One could argue that the repetition of the two pitches A_3 and B_3 lends a monotony to the event being depicted, which surely belies its exotic and unexpected subject matter. Interestingly, the musical emphasis here falls not on the spectacle of swimming with angels, but rather on the egocentric speaker's 'me', as it is sung over five notes which is almost half of the phrase. This foregrounding corresponds with that of the Cognitive Grammar analysis above, in which the oddity of the speaker occupying the role of patient rather than agent was noted. 'Me' is the main participant here, the entity with which the angels swim. It is as though the speaker is autonomously swimming, and is joined by angels: the angels are accommodating the speaker rather than the other way around.

Musically, Line 3 is a complete repetition of Line 1, with only one exception: there is an extra note as the opening word 'A' is sung on $F\#_3$ before the ascension to B_3, from which there is the same pattern of repetitions of $C\#_4$ and return first to B_3 and then to a twice-repeated $C\#_4$. But, as Figure 10.4 attests, the extra opening note and the pitch on which it is sung result in a very different visual representation, with the phrase now having a much wider musical scope (ranging from $F\#_3$ to $C\#_4$). The sonic analogue of DEPARTURE-RETURN created by the harmony of Line 1 has been transformed by this extra opening note: it now resembles a journey commenced (on $F\#_3$) with strong (upward) strides, but which runs into difficulty and is ultimately uncompleted.

Again, in terms of music/lyric coordination, this line follows the same pattern of singing each syllable on a single note. The only disyllabic word 'astral' is emphasized by being sung over two different notes – B_3 and $C\#_4$ – with the drop to B_3 constituting an internal deviation against a monotonous background of six repetitions of the dominant $C\#_4$. As in Line 1, the words 'moon' and 'astral' could be seen as linked as they are the only words sung on a different note, the same B_3, although the connection is not as strong because only the first syllable of 'astral' is on B_3, while the addition of the opening $F\#_3$ somewhat undermines what was a stronger harmonic pattern.

Harmonic Processes

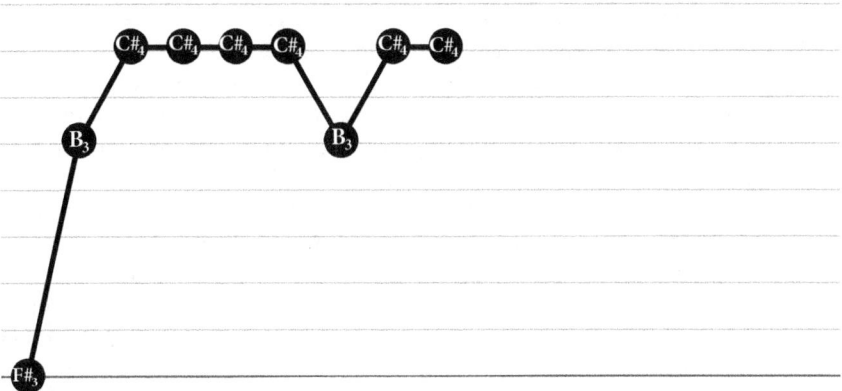

Figure 10.4 Line 3: *A moon full of stars and astral cars* and Line 7: *And we all went to heaven in a little row-boat.*

Harmonic Processes

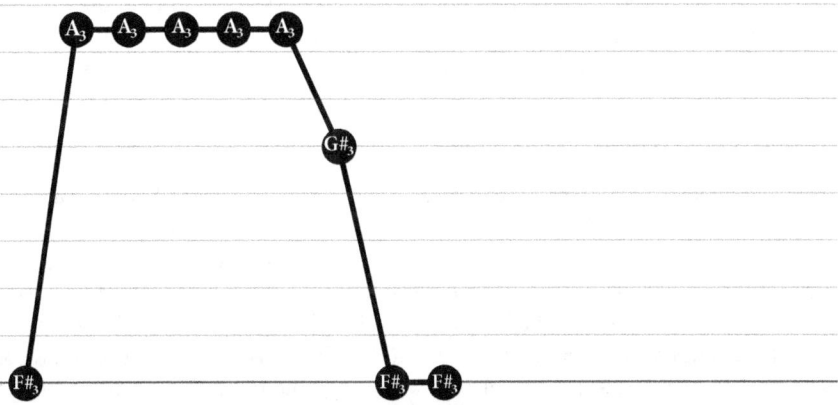

Figure 10.5 Line 4: *And all the figures I used to see* and Line 8: *There was nothing to fear, nothing to doubt.*

The final line of the first verse – 'And all the figures I used to see' – commences on the same opening note $F\sharp_3$ as the preceding line, with the first word 'And'. This is followed by repetition of A_3 five times to coincide with each syllable of the words 'all the fig-ures I' before descending to $G\sharp_3$ on 'used' and again to a twice-repeated $F\sharp_3$ on which 'to see' is sung. Figure 10.5 shows another completed cycle/journey, with the repetition of the final anchoring tonic note $F\sharp_3$ serving to reinforce this return.

The fact that 'all the figures I' is sung over a five-note repetition of the same pitch – A_3 – initially foregrounds the phrase but the effect is then overshadowed by the emphasis placed on the word 'used' by being sung on $G\sharp_3$, a pitch not yet used (although G♯$_4$ was used in the opening 'ooh' sequence). The emphasis here, then, is on temporality: the speaker 'used' to see these figures, but does so no more. This, of course, highlights the incongruity of his 'seeing' these figures now.

Lines 5–8 follow the same harmonic structure as Lines 1–4, with a few minor exceptions that may be considered to affect the interaction between music and words. First, Line 5 contains two fewer syllables than Line 1, so the phrase 'my lovers were' is sung over four repetitions of C♯$_4$, rather than the initial five in Line 1, while 'there with me' is sung on B$_3$-C♯$_4$-C♯$_4$, i.e. one fewer C♯$_4$. Similarly, there is one fewer syllable in Line 6 than Line 2, resulting in one fewer B$_3$. Line 7 comprises an attempt to integrate a full and very specific intertextual lyrical reference into what is a very different musical structure. The line 'and we all went to heaven in a little row boat' originates from the (rather too catchy!) refrain of the 1965 Shirley Ellis hit 'The Clapping Song', although it subsequently appears as a single lyric in the 1985 Tom Waits' song 'Clap Hands'. To accommodate the intertextual reference, the line commences with an extra syllable, with 'and we' sung on a repetition of F♯$_3$, while the phrase itself is somewhat crammed in, resulting in a total of three extra C♯$_4$ such that the musical phrase (with the extra notes underlined) becomes: F♯$_3$-F♯$_3$-B$_3$-C♯$_4$-C♯$_4$-C♯$_4$-C♯$_4$-C♯$_4$-C♯$_4$-B$_3$-C♯$_4$-C♯$_4$-C♯$_4$. To the ear, this sounds like what it is: a rather clunky attempt to shoehorn a pre-existing linguistic structure into a quite different pre-existing musical structure, which of course foregrounds the phrase and its intertextuality$_6$. Line 8 commences with an extra F♯$_3$ on 'there was' but otherwise is a perfect replication of Line 4.

Verse II

The only difference between Verse I and II is in the opening line: in Verse II 'Jumped in the river and what did I see?' is shortened to 'Jumped in to the river'. The musical structure of the line remains approximately the same (and indeed the sheet music erroneously records it as an exact replication), but there are some alterations, with the ten notes in the original being reduced to six: B$_3$-C$_4$-C$_4$-C$_4$-B$_3$-C$_4$. The duration of each note has been extended to accommodate fewer lyrics and, as a result, there is some deviation in terms of where the words fall. The most notable distinction is that of the word 'river', which was sung on the third and fourth repetitions of C♯$_4$ in Line 1 and is now sung over only two notes, beginning on the more deviant B$_3$ before moving to C♯$_4$. However, most obvious is the fact that the word seems to be held for almost two complete bars, with the second syllable sustained for over ten beats (again, this is not evident in the sheet music). This of course draws more attention to both the line as a whole and the river in particular. Finally, the last line in Verse II – 'There was nothing to fear, nothing to doubt' – is sung three times. Musically, there is no alteration in the melody of these repetitions, but they are followed by a 55-second orchestral arrangement, in which strings effectively replace voice in creating the musical top line.

As noted above, the entire song is made up of the same musical pattern repeated four times, twice within each verse. Such replication of the song's musical structure would of course be evident to the listener, constituting recognition of what Brower (2000) terms its *intra-opus patterns*. This pattern recognition then forms a background against which the above-mentioned deviations become foregrounded. Such deviation surely serves to defamiliarize, unsettling the listener by preventing them from experiencing the anticipated comfort of familiarity. This acts to reinforce the lyrical content of the song, in particular the construction of an alternative realm which defies the rules of our world.

4. Conclusion

While multimodality, as Pleyer and Schneider note, 'complicates traditional literary and linguistic approaches' (2014: 35), Cognitive Grammar, and indeed cognitive approaches more generally, recognises 'that the construction of meaning is intrinsically multimodal in nature' (2014: 39). The cognitive focus at the heart of the two analytical frameworks applied here makes them more amenable to contiguous application to the same text, with their emphasis on image schemas as a primary mode of meaning-construction enabling parallels to be drawn across semiotic modes, most notably in how the musical and lyrical composition of the text reinforce one another in their simultaneous and complementary constructions of the song's central concerns. Both the text's rhythmic and harmonic layers repeatedly draw upon the DEPARTURE/RETURN and CYCLE image schemas in the construction of the sonic analogues that convert form to meaning, reinforcing the text's linguistic composition and thereby foregrounding the multimodal manner in which 'Pyramid Song' constructs its contention that time is essentially cyclical in nature. As time itself is a subjectively experienced phenomenon, this links neatly with the song's other emphasis on the importance of interpretive ambiguity. The defamiliarization of the song's content may unsettle the reader at a fundamental level, setting them adrift from the comforts of the known and forcing them to come face-to-face with the subjective nature of perception, and aesthetic interpretation in particular. This is further reinforced by the song's structure, in particular its lack of a refrain, whose predictability usually provides the listener with 'a sense of recognition that creates a homely space' (Hainge 2007: 63). Structurally, musically and lyrically, 'Pyramid Song' emphasizes 'our need for ambiguity' in the interpretive process and highlights the crucial space that ambiguity carves out for the experience of 'our feelings and personal stories' (Hesselink 2013).

Glossary

♮ = natural version of note
♯ = sharp version of note
♭ = flat version of note
numbers in subscript denote the octave, e.g. 'middle C' is C_4
crotchet = a quarter
quaver = an eighth
tonic = main note in any key, e.g. tonic of C major is C
dominant = fifth note in any key, e.g. dominant of C major is G
subdominant = fourth note in any key, e.g. subdominant of C major is F

Notes

1. As noted by Hainge, 'Radiohead's first two albums, *Pablo Honey* and *The Bends*, are made up entirely of songs structured according to a verse/chorus/verse/chorus pattern' (2007: 63).
2. Langacker, however, points out the 'vagueness' in identifying, defining and categorizing image schemas, preferring instead to distinguish certain image schemas from others on the basis of what he refers to as 'fundamental notions': as such, he reclassifies the CONTAINER image schema as a conceptual archetype (2013: 33).
3. However, as Taylor notes (2002: 422), cognitive processes do not lend themselves as well to the energy-transfer metaphor encoded in action chains, which profile dynamic processes.
4. Radiohead produced both *Kid A* and *Amnesiac* while signed to EMI Records. The official sheet music is published by Alfred Music who bought Warner Bros Publications in 2005, thereby obtaining the rights to EMI's back-catalogue (see https://www.alfred.com/history/).
5. In previous work (Neary 2019), I have asserted that rhythmic regularity can convey progression along a SOURCE-PATH-GOAL schema but have recently been persuaded otherwise (personal correspondence with M. Antovic 2019).
6. While regrettably beyond the scope of this paper, it should be noted that 'Pyramid Song' is rife with intertextuality, of which this is but the most obvious example. While Rose notes that 'every Radiohead album since *OK Computer* illustrates a characteristic intertextuality' (2011: 78), 'Pyramid Song' contains intertextuality which tantalizingly operates across semiotic modes. For example, thematically, the lyrics are thought to have been influenced by Dante's *Divine Comedy*, the Tibetan and Egyptian *Books of the Dead* and Hermann Hesse's *Siddhartha* (1922) (see c.f. Thompson 2009: 221) while there are also lyrical similarities to the American negro-spiritual song 'Swing Low, Sweet Chariot', as evidenced in a comparison of both songs' opening lines. Thompson suggests further potential lyrical intertextuality with reference to Talking Head's 'In a Lifetime' (1981), pointing out that '[b]oth Byrne and Yorke depict time as flowing water that sustains life silently and without drawing attention to itself' (2009: 228). The song also contains specific musical intertextuality, with Rose noting that the rhythmic structures of 'Freedom' by Charles Mingus provided Yorke's musical model for 'Pyramid Song' (2011: p. 83n2).

References

Alfred Music, 'Our History'. Available online: https://www.alfred.com/history/, accessed (25 June 2019).

Bennett, P. (2014), 'Langacker's Cognitive Grammar', in J. Littlemore and J.R. Taylor (eds), *The Bloomsbury Companion to Cognitive Linguistics*, 29–48, London: Bloomsbury.

Brower, C. (2000), 'A Cognitive Theory of Musical Meaning', *Journal of Music Theory*, 44 (2): (Fall): 323–79.

Butler, M. (2006), *Unlocking the Groove: Rhythm, Meter, and Musical Design in Electronic Dance Music*, Bloomington: Indiana University Press.

Croft, W. (2001), *Radical Construction Grammar: Syntactic Theory in Typological Perspective*, Oxford: Oxford University Press.
Fanning, D. (2000), 'Here's Looking at You, Kid', *Hot Press*, 29 (19): 28.
Giovanelli, M. and C. Harrison (2018), *Cognitive Grammar in Stylistics*, London: Bloomsbury.
Hainge, G. (2007), 'To(rt)uring the Minotaur: Radiohead, Pop, Unnatural Couplings and Mainstream Subversion', in J. Tate (ed.), *The Music and Art of Radiohead*, 62–84, Aldershot: Ashgate.
Harrison, C. (2017), *Cognitive Grammar in Contemporary Fiction*, Amsterdam: Philadelphia: John Benjamins.
Hesselink, N. (2013), 'Radiohead's "Pyramid Song": Ambiguity, Rhythm, and Participation', *Music Theory Online*, 19 (1). Available online: http://mtosmt.org/issues/mto.13.19.1/mto.13.19.1.hesselink.html, accessed (29 March 2019).
Hesselink, N. (2014), 'Rhythmic Play, Compositional Intent and Communication in Rock Music', *Popular Music*, 33 (1): 69–90.
Johnson, M. (1987), *The Body in the Mind: The Bodily Basis of Meaning, Imagination, and Reason*, Chicago: University of Chicago Press.
Langacker, R. W. (1987), *Foundations of Cognitive Grammar Vol. 1: Theoretical Prerequisites*, Stanford: Stanford University Press.
Langacker, R. W. (1991), *Foundations of Cognitive Grammar Vol. 2: Descriptive Application*, Stanford: Stanford University Press.
Langacker, R. W. (2002), *Concept, Image and Symbol: The Cognitive Basis of Grammar*, 2nd edn, Berlin: Mouton de Gruyter.
Langacker, R. W. (2008), *Cognitive Grammar: A Basic Introduction*, Oxford: Oxford University Press.
Langacker, R. W. (2013), *Essentials of Cognitive Grammar*, Oxford: Oxford University Press.
Letts, M. T. (2005), '"How to Disappear Completely": Radiohead and the Resistant Concept Album', unpublished Ph.D. dissertation, University of Texas-Austin.
Littlemore, J. and J.R. Taylor (2014), 'Introduction', in J. Littlemore and J.R. Taylor (eds), *The Bloomsbury Companion to Cognitive Linguistics*, London: Bloomsbury.
Margolis, H. (1987), *Patterns, Thinking, and Cognition: A Theory of Judgment*, Chicago: University of Chicago Press.
Morini, M. (2013), 'Towards a Musical Stylistics: Movement in Kate Bush's "Running Up That Hill"', *Language and Literature*, 22 (4): 283–97.
Neary, C. (2019), '"Please Could You Stop the Noise": The Grammar of Multi-modal Meaning Making in Radiohead's "Paranoid Android"', *Language and Literature*, 28 (1): 41–60.
Pleyer, M. and C. Schneider (2014), 'Construal, Cognition and Comics: Analysing the Multimodal Construction of a Gothic Autobiography in Alison Bechdel's *Fun Home*', in C. Harrison, L. Nuttall, P. Stockwell and W. Yuan (eds.), *Cognitive Grammar in Literature*, 35–52, Amsterdam: John Benjamins.
Reynolds, S. (2001), 'Dissent into the Mainstream', *The Wire*, 209 (July 2001): 25–33.
Rose, P. (2011), 'Radiohead and the Media: Fallout of *OK Computer*', *Explorations in Media Ecology*, 10 (1 & 2): 75–90.
Stockwell, P. (2002), *Cognitive Poetics: An Introduction*, London: Routledge.
Taylor, J.R. (2002), *Cognitive Grammar*, New York: Oxford University Press.
Thompson, M. (2009), 'The Signature of Time in "Pyramid Song"', in B.W. Forbes and G.A. Reisch (eds), *Radiohead and Philosophy: Fitter Happier More Deductive*, 221–8, Chicago & La Salle: Open Court.

Whiteley, S. and M. Voice (2019), '"Y'all Don't Wanna Hear Me, You Just Wanna Dance": A Cognitive Approach to Listener Attention in Outkast's 'Hey Ya!', *Language and Literature*, 28 (1): 7–22.

Zbikowski, L. (2002), *Conceptualizing Music: Cognitive Structure, Theory, and Analysis*, New York: Oxford University Press.

Zbikowski, L. (2012), 'Music, Language, and What Falls in Between', *Ethnomusicology*, 56 (1): 125–31.

Zbikowski, L. (2017), *Foundations of Musical Grammar*, New York: Oxford University Press.

11

Allocating meaning across the senses: Cognitive Grammar as a tool for the creation of multimodal texts

Alison Bown

1. Introduction

In this chapter I explore the ways that Cognitive Grammar can be used to conceptualize and design multimodal interactive texts. Specifically, this chapter is informed by research that draws on my experience as a sound designer and writer, and so focuses on texts that combine reading with listening. Cognitive Grammar will be discussed in terms of how it offers writers an insight into the ways that readers interact with texts and process their contents. The precision of this insight, as defined by Langacker, allows for a way of thinking that can be meaningfully applied to the management of non-linguistic textual elements. I will also explore the fact that reading and operating audio-heavy texts require writers to consider the impact of listening on attention. To do this, I will make reference to studies of digital fiction and theories of immersion within digital media. In this way, the chapter can be used as a point of reference for writers moving into interactive narrative design, where a conceptualization of the user's experience is key to collaborative and multimodal practice.

In order to outline how Cognitive Grammar can be applied to the design of multimodal texts, the chapter opens with an overview of some key terms used by Langacker. Where useful connections can be made between Cognitive Grammar and theories of immersion, I will make reference to critical works in the field of digital media. The multimodal nature of mental simulation is then explored through Barsalou's (1999) framework for describing how such simulations draw upon our prior experiences. Following this, Zbikowski's (2017) work on the grammar of music is set out in order to demonstrate how sound and music are perceived differently to written language. This is complemented by an overview of Chion's (1994) theories of listening within the context of cinema. Once these key terms and ideas have been set out, I apply them to a reading of a prose-only text rich in sensory data so as to discuss and exemplify the ways that language simulates sound and contributes to a sense of 'being there' in a scene. I then present a reading of a multimodal text that effectively combines sound with writing before ending with some recommendations for writers who wish to draw on ideas from Cognitive Grammar and related frameworks within their own practice.

2. Construal

In order to begin to discuss how writers might usefully apply Cognitive Grammar to multimodal text creation, a good place to start is Langacker's conceptualization of *construal,* described as our 'ability to perceive and portray the same situation in alternate ways' (Langacker 2008: 43). This definition positions writing as an act of making decisions, for example from which point of view to tell a story, and which elements of a situation to highlight within this point of view. To draw out this idea, Langacker further defines the construal relationship as 'the relationship between a speaker (or hearer) and a situation that he [*sic*] conceptualises and portrays, involving focal adjustments and imagery' (Langacker 1987: 487–8). In this definition, the construal relationship involves an individual speaker or hearer on the one hand, and a conceived situation on the other (Verhagen 2012: 59). Nuttall (2018: 37) suggests that 'construal applies to all encounters with language, including that of a writer, who makes choices in coding his or her conceptualization, and a reader, who conceives this meaning based on these linguistic cues'. This definition is key within the context of this chapter as it not only reiterates that the writer must first conceptualize – or mentally simulate – a situation before turning to the task of coding it within their work, but also foregrounds the idea that writing involves the design of a mental simulation that will be decoded by readers drawing upon their own experiences.

2.1. Construal as visual field

The particular methodology proposed in this chapter combines ideas from Cognitive Grammar with theories of listening to cinematic sound design in order to develop an approach to incorporating audio into digital fiction. The link with cinematic sound is possible due to Langacker's explanations of construal phenomena frequently employing visual metaphors, such as *focus* (Langacker 2008: 57) and *perspective* (Langacker 2008: 73), and the way that he presents conceptualizations as scenes and construal as a particular way of viewing the scene.

Langacker's concepts of *vantage point* (Langacker 2008: 75) and *viewing arrangement* (Langacker 2008: 73) can help illustrate this idea further. Vantage point, which can be thought of as the viewing position taken in a scene, is a central aspect of construal involving the focus, or foregrounded content of an expression, and the *specificity* with which it is conceptualized (Langacker 2008: 55). When an expression brings into focus a relationship (rather than a thing), the participants in the relationship are profiled by the reader and degrees of prominence are afforded to each, with the most prominent participant termed a *trajector* (Langacker 2008: 70–3). Other participants in the relationship – those given secondary focus – are called *landmarks* (Langacker 2008: 70–3). When using the preposition 'above', the trajector is conceived as higher than the landmark, while the opposite is true of 'below' (Langacker 2008: 71). Langacker says: 'One component of the viewing arrangement is a presupposed vantage point […] Many expressions undeniably invoke a vantage point as part of their meaning (arguably, all expressions do). In one of their basic uses, for example, 'in front of' and 'behind' rely on vantage point to specify the trajector's location' (Langacker 2008: 75–6). Talmy (1983: 232) refers to Langacker's concepts of trajector and landmark as being directly comparable to the idea of 'figure' and 'ground'. This reference to Gestalt psychology helps describe how a moveable or moving object is perceived in a scene against a static, less attended to background. This enables a way of thinking about the way that attention is paid to movement within a scene and the way that newly emerging elements, including sonic or graphic elements within multimodal scenes, become objects of focus.

In Cognitive Grammar, conceptualization is *dynamic* (Langacker 2008: 31) and unfolds through processing time along a *compositional path* (Langacker 2008: 61). This process involves *mental scanning* (Langacker 2008: 82) of symbolic components until the *composite* construction foregrounds particular elements over time (Langacker 2008: 60–5). In terms of how the dynamic scanning processes involved in conceptualization affect the composite construction, Langacker sets out how 'the specific course of development is a significant aspect of our mental experience' (Langacker 2008: 32). Choosing which word to use alters the view of two identical spatial relationships and influences the way that movement in an image is simulated in the mind of the reader. Langacker offers the following as an example: 'The hill gently rises from the bank of the river', as contrasted with 'The hill gently falls to the bank of the river', where the direction of mental scanning is directed upwards ('rises') or downwards ('falls') (2008: 82). In Langacker's example, the hill does not move, but motion of the vantage point is simulated: the mental scanning processes involved in reconfiguring a mental space as new elements are encountered alter the view of the scene. The particular phenomenon exemplified here is known as 'fictive motion' (Talmy 1983: 232), where motion is simulated through the figure in a scene being a moving or conceptually moveable object against the ground. Fictive motion occurs specifically when the object in the scene is not capable of movement itself. Matlock (2004) examines the way that fictive motion manifests itself in the mind of readers. Using an experimental design, she concludes that sentences containing fictive motion, such as 'the fence runs along the coast', result in readers building a spatial model and simulating movement of the vantage point as they dynamically construe a text (Matlock 2004: 1391).

The concept of the reader being physically involved in a simulated scene as it is construed is underpinned by the cognitive linguistic notion of an *image schema*. Langacker (2008: 32) describes image schemas as:

> Schematized patterns of activity abstracted from everyday bodily experience, especially pertaining to vision, space, motion, and force. Image schemas are seen

as basic, 'preconceptual' structures that give rise to more elaborate and more abstract conceptions (or at least provide their skeletal projection).

An illustrative example given by Langacker is ENTER. The image schema for ENTER is based on the physical experience of moving towards a source along a path and then reaching a goal (Langacker 2008: 33). Other examples of image schemas are CONTAINER, ITERATION, ATTRACTION, NEAR-FAR, MERGING, CONTACT and COMPULSION (see Johnson 1987).

The idea of the bodily basis of image schemas, combined with the idea of a moving vantage point as construal progresses, can help writers seeking to create a strong sense of 'being there' physically in a scene. Langacker refers to the sense of being 'on scene' in terms of deixis (Langacker 2009: 110). Deixis is a psycholinguistic term that is language universal and is associated with self-world orientation and was originally developed by Karl Bühler (1934), who disconnected the symbol of words such as 'here – now – I' from the deictic (pointing) field and called the orientational axis 'origo' (Galbraith 1995: 21). Orientation and navigation of a mentally simulated world are linked to recall of embodied experiences of positioning in the real world and of spatial relationship to other objects. Prepositions such as 'across' and 'beyond' can be used by writers to orientate the reader's embodied position within the world of the story.

Overall, these concepts help us understand how it is possible to produce a text so that the reader simulates physicality when construing a scene. This is important because it enables writers to anchor the reader in space. In this way, Cognitive Grammar can be seen to offer descriptive concepts that can be usefully applied during the process of conceptualizing and encoding a construal that embeds physical presence. Cognitive Grammar can further be used as a tool with which to steer a clear vantage point and deictic position within a scene. From this point, it becomes possible to begin to conceptualize how a multimodal scene might incorporate audio. I will continue to develop this idea throughout the rest of this chapter.

2.2. Cognitive Grammar and interaction

When working with digital multimodal material, writers can face the challenge that some interactive digital texts require non-trivial effort to read (Aarseth 1997). Walker Rettberg (2001: 36–7) likens being asked to interact with a text in order to progress through it as being asked to take a turn as the narrator (as opposed to being the narratee). Cognitive Grammar provides a framework that can be used to analyse the elements of digital multimodal texts that succeed in immersing readers as they operate (Aarseth 1997: 21) the text.

To begin to develop this idea, this section sets out Langacker's concept of viewing arrangement in more detail. During construal, the viewing arrangement is the overall relationship between the 'viewers' and the situation being 'viewed' (Langacker 2008: 74). Langacker further defines the *viewer* and the *viewed* as the *subject* and the *object* of perception (Langacker 2008: 77). In visual terms, the perceiving subject is the viewer, who lacks self-awareness of the mentally constructed perspective from which they look out at the object. They are instead totally involved in apprehending the object, which is clearly delineated (Langacker 2008: 261). Langacker sets out subjective construal of the self as being characteristic of the subject's role as 'an offstage locus of perceptual experience that is not itself perceived' within the object of conceptualization (Langacker 2008: 77). This is useful because definitions of viewing arrangements in Cognitive Grammar provide a way to think about the shift of consciousness along an axis of subjectivity and objectivity. This is particularly useful when conceptualizing the impact on the reader of being asked to interact with a text through second-person address, a device commonly used in hypertext work (Bell and Ensslin 2011). Walker Rettberg (2001: 41) argues that the use of the second-person address in digital texts 'can make you feel included; you feel seen by the text'. Cognitive Grammar allows for this to be described in terms of the impact on the reader's position and arrangement with the scene: grammatical choices can explicitly position the conceptualizer to be construed more objectively. The extreme is to put them on-stage as the focus of attention by use of first- and second-person pronouns ('I', 'you', 'we' and their variants); the use of which means that the speaker and hearer are profiled, explicitly mentioned and *objectively construed* within the object of conceptualization (Langacker 2008: 78). This concept is helpful in analysing the challenges of writing for a format that deliberately draws attention towards the reader: if the text asks the reader to interact, it is essentially 'viewing' the reader and placing them on-stage, shifting the viewing arrangement away from subjective immersion.

I will now develop this idea through a discussion of the way that sound can contribute to the reader feeling 'involved in a scene' (Giovanelli and Harrison 2018: 51). For example, if a reader perceives a sound that they must consciously process while reading – perhaps because they cannot identify the source until it is described – then this can be used to positive effect: they become absorbed in identifying and assessing the qualities of a sound as they construe and operate the multimodal work. This can help readers stay within the scene as they read and interact with the text. A fuller discussion of this idea follows.

3. Sensory input: Listening

While the perceptual processes involved in listening are complex, and full discussion of the nature of auditory attention is beyond the scope of this chapter, Chion (1994) provides a framework that enables a conceptualization of the processes involved in listening to sounds synchronized with image. While Chion's work is centred on cinematic sound, the way that construal in Cognitive Grammar is framed as a visual experience enables a synthesis of Chion's framework with Langacker's ideas.

Chion (1994: 40) uses the term 'acousmatic' to describe off-screen sound sources that are not seen within the viewing frame of a film. Chion sets out that viewers perceiving something unseen employ a mode of listening he calls 'reduced listening' (Chion 1994: 29–33; Schaeffer 2012). Reduced listening is the type of perceptual state involved in listening to sound detached from image, where attention is paid to the traits of a sound itself, rather than its cause or meaning, potentially resulting in perception of its emotional resonance (Chion 1994: 31). Two other modes of listening as categorized by Chion will be discussed: 'coded' (or 'semantic') listening and 'causal' listening (Chion 1994: 25–35).

Causal listening occurs when the cause of a sound is visible in the on-stage scene and sound provides supplementary information about the object. Consider, for example, being told or shown that a door is being closed: the sound of it closing would convey additional information as to the weight of the door, the material it is made of and the force with which it was closed. Spatial information about the scene would also be conveyed through causal listening if reverberation is added to this sound, setting out the wider context of the room that the door is in. The final mode of listening categorized by Chion is called coded (or 'semantic') listening. This mode is engaged most commonly when instrumental music or speech occurs, as there is a need to turn attention to decoding the semantic elements of structure or meaning.

By categorizing these modes of listening, Chion makes it possible to understand that altering the relationship between audio and vision causes shifts in the perceptive and cognitive processes engaged by the listener. Some of these processes pertain to semantic perception and some refer to spatial perception. To explore how these ideas can be further understood by writers wishing to use sound to create spatio-temporal immersion (Ryan 2001: 130) in digital multimodal work, I will now set out Zbikowski's (2017) formulation of the grammar of music.

4. Musical grammar

Before discussing musical grammar, I will first define music as it is understood in this chapter. Because the methodology proposed here refers to cinematic sound design (rather than film score composition), music in this chapter predominantly refers to a form of electroacoustic music known as musique concrète. Musique concrète is a type of soundscape composed from recorded sound and is created through techniques such as editing, looping, time-stretch/compression and layering (Schaeffer 2012). Its influence in the field of film sound design is widely discussed (e.g. Murch 2017).

Zbikowski (2017) adopts Langacker's work on Cognitive Grammar to the structure and meaning of music. Music, and by extension musique concrète, is explored for its ability to represent dynamic phenomena through its structure, in contrast to the grammatical functions employed in language to direct attention (Zbikowski 2017: 6). Zbikowski suggests that music has an analogous, rather than symbolic, function and uses the term 'sonic analog' to define this. Sonic analogs are based on form-function pairs representing emotions, gestures and dance (Zbikowski 2017: 1). As an example of what he means by the term 'sonic analog', Zbikowski describes a motif (or 'token') that involves two notes, the first higher than the second and with no accent on the second, commonly used in music to refer to a sigh. This is an example of a sonic analog, with the analogical reference being made to the dropping of shoulders involved in the physical act of sighing. Zbikowski further argues that music provides sonic analogs for dynamic processes, such as weather or movement (Zbikowski 2017: 9–10). One sound can stand in for another, and the capacity of humans for such analogous interpretation 'makes possible a form of reference quite different from that employed by language, one that is uniquely explored by music' (Zbikowski 2017: 4). Zbikowski (2017: 10) thus sets out how musical grammar differs from the grammar of verbal language:

> Symbolic tokens are very useful for picking out objects and events, and characterizing relationships between them. Analogical tokens are less useful in this regard but very good at representing complex spatial relationships and summoning dynamic processes that unfold over time.

Zbikowski further asserts that precisely because music – and by extension sound design – makes fewer demands on interpretation whilst symbolizing dynamic processes, it has an ability to serve as a sonic analog for the dynamic of our emotions (Zbikowski 2017: 11). To relate back to Langacker's concept of viewing arrangement, and the position of a reader in relation to an interactive text, it can be said that sound can bring the experience of the text closer to the locus of consciousness and encode a more subjective construal.

Langacker's (2008: 55) assertion that the construal phenomena of specificity, focusing, prominence and perspective apply to conceptions 'in any domain' is key to the flexibility of the framework. This flexibility is beneficial to the writer, who may begin to consider the way in which some domains are not as accessible through language as they are through sound. It could also be useful to the writer to understand the ways in which sensory data contained within domains (such as the domain of auditory experience) can be cued by language and included in the mental simulation of a scene. To explore this idea in more detail, I now provide an overview of the work of Barsalou (1999) on the way that multiple sensory domains are called upon during mental simulation.

5. Multi-sensory simulation

Frames (or domains in Cognitive Grammar) are seen by Barsalou (1999) as integrated systems of perceptual symbols that are used to construct specific simulations of a category (Barsalou 1999: 583–4). Perceptual symbols are defined by Barsalou as records of the neural states that underlie perception, rather than mental images: the brain activates configurations of neurons to represent the properties of perceived events and entities (Barsalou 1999: 582). These associated patterns of neurons are stored records of aspects of experience and are multimodal, operating on any aspect of a perceived experience, from touch to visual to auditory (Barsalou 1999: 585). These patterns of neurons can be reactivated in a wide variety of ways from various bottom-up sources, and are organized in a simulator.

> Simulation is the re-enactment of perceptual, motor, and introspective states acquired during experience with the world, body, and mind. As an experience occurs (e.g., easing into a chair), the brain captures states across the modalities and integrates them with a multimodal representation stored in memory (e.g., how a chair looks and feels, the action of sitting, introspections of comfort and relaxation). Later, when knowledge is needed to represent a category (e.g., chair), multimodal representations captured during experiences [...] are reactivated to simulate how the brain represented perception, action, and introspection associated with it.
> (Barsalou 2008: 618–19)

Barsalou's formulation of mental simulation echoes Zwaan and Madden's definition of construal, where construal is seen as a mental simulation conveyed by an attentional frame, with words and grammar cueing, activating and combining traces of experience (Zwaan and Madden 2005: 236–8). These articulations of the multimodal nature of simulation and construal are important to writers seeking to understand how and when to use language to evoke sound and when to use music or sound as a sensory input. The writerly techniques that can be used to simulate sound can therefore be usefully learned and applied. To examine these techniques, the following section presents a reading of a literary text that renders an environment through sound and centres a protagonist's response to this sound.

6. A reading of *Annihilation* by Jeff VanderMeer

Annihilation is the first of a trilogy that explores Area X, an area of green and strange space that has encroached on a coastal area of America and has become the subject of numerous scientific missions conducted in order to try to understand it. Those who attempt the missions either do not return or die in the months after returning. This passage is taken from a part of the story where a biologist, who is struggling to make sense of Area X, perceives a presence there that makes her fear for her life. The passage has been chosen because it is set in an alien environment, necessitating the writer to construct a simulation without reference to stored experiences of that place; VanderMeer cannot simply write 'the sound of Area X' to provoke a simulation. Furthermore, the environment is rendered largely through reference to auditory experiences. As it opens, we find the protagonist listening to something she believes is pursuing her through the reeds on her journey back to base.

> The dragging sounds had intensified, almost equal to the moaning. A thick musk clung to the air [...] Now the darkness was so complete I could only see a few feet ahead of me, the flashlight revealing little or nothing. I felt as if I were moving through an encircling tunnel. The moaning still grew louder, but I could not determine its direction [...] There came the moaning again, as close as I'd ever heard it, but now mixed with a loud thrashing sound. I stopped and stood on tiptoe to shine my flashlight over the reeds to my left in time to see a great disrupting wave of motion ahead at a right angle to the trail, and closing fast. A dislocation of reeds, a fast smashing that made them fall as if machine-thrashed. The thing was trying to outflank me [...] I could feel the thudding vibration of its passage, the rasping clack of the reeds beneath its tread, and there was a kind of expectant tone to its moaning now that sickened me with the urgency of its seeking.
>
> (VanderMeer 2014: 141–2)

This passage establishes the deictic position of the protagonist, who is placed on-stage as the conceptualizer of the scene, within the landscape by referring to visual experience, specifically the experience of trying to see through fog at night with a torch. This is done through the construction 'Now the darkness was so complete I could only see a few feet ahead of me, the flashlight revealing little or nothing'. The use of the preposition 'ahead' draws on a SOURCE-PATH-GOAL image schema and demonstrates how physical experience can be conceptualized to create a vantage point within a scene. This vantage point is further directed by the phrases 'over the reeds to my left' and 'at a right angle to the trail', where the position of objects in the simulated scene is set out in terms of their spatial relationship to the deictic centre of the protagonist.

In contrast to the on-stage conceptualizer, the source of the 'dragging sounds' is off-stage for the extract. The identity and origin of the sound remain uncertain and changeable. The schematic language used to describe the sound means that the 'dragging' and 'moaning' sounds are not construed with any specificity and remain out of focus within the perceived situation. This contributes to the sense that the protagonist in the piece is fearful because she cannot identify or see the sound source (see Giovanelli and Harrison 2018: 36–7). Because the 'moaning' and 'dragging' cannot be profiled or identified, the experience of attempting to identify sounds in the dark is simulated, along with the introspective state associated with this (Barsalou 2008: 616–17). By writing 'I could feel the thudding vibration of its passage, the rasping clack of the reeds beneath its tread', VanderMeer references the sense of being touched to embody an external force and begins to build a mental image of the size of the source ('a thudding machine') of the sound. He codes a construal that involves dynamic reprofiling of the proximity of the sound by opening with the schematic, off-stage 'thudding vibration' before consonant-charged words ('rasp' and 'clack') shift focus to the sharpness of the sound, which is scanned last in the sentence as being caused by reeds 'beneath its tread'. In this way, the order of the compositional path can be seen to be instrumental in directing both attention and moving the vantage point and deictic position of the protagonist within a simulation. Consequently, spatial immersion (Ryan 2001: 121) is invited through a series of deictic shifts that occur as the reader reprofiles and scans the text when trying to recentre themselves in the scene (Ryan 2001: 135; Harrison 2019: 42).

The way that the passage cues deictic shifts and creates spatial immersion can be further understood through a closer analysis of the way the vantage point taken on the scene shifts and moves. For example, the construction 'I felt as if I were moving through an encircling tunnel' positions the protagonist as a trajector on a path through a landmark before the word order leads the reader to profile and shift focus towards the moving tunnel. By using the preposition 'through' and then placing 'encircling tunnel' last in the sentence, scanning processes applied during the construal process simulate movement of the vantage point and shift the deictic position to one of being surrounded and contained, looking around and ahead. The scene is further punctuated by the words 'thrashing', 'dislocation', 'disrupting' and 'smashing', all of which are embodied experiences that simulate physical forces and the consequential sound of impact and movement. This codes a construal where elements are rapidly reprofiled in an order that suggests the protagonist is scanning erratically and perceiving only in disjointed glimpses of panic. Furthermore, repeated use of these verb profiles suggests cut-off (e.g. 'disrupting') or ineffective action (e.g. 'thrashing'), and this contributes to the sense of panic felt by the conceptualizer (see Harrison 2019: 42).

Through this reading, it has been demonstrated that the sound of an environment can be rendered through a linguistically cued simulation of dynamic forces. Using language to simulate 'off-stage' schematic sounds has been discussed in terms of spatial immersion and simulation of introspective states and emotions. In this way, it has been possible to understand how the domain of auditory and physical experience is drawn upon and coded into a mental simulation. However, *Annihilation* is a monomodal, non-interactive text, and so this reading and analysis has not yet covered how interaction and sound can be reconciled with spatiotemporal immersion (Ryan 1999, 2001). To address this, and to explore how sound and text can be combined and synchronized in an interactive text, I now present a reading of a digital, multimodal work, *Loss of Grasp*.

7. A reading of *Loss of Grasp* by Serge Bouchardon and Vincent Volckaert

Loss of Grasp (Bouchardon and Volckaert 2010) is a piece of work designed to be read and navigated on a computer screen. In this multimodal piece, sound and text are entwined with interaction design. Ensslin (2014: 74, 80) describes it as a cognitive-ergodic literary game where the reader feels they are being played with by the text. In this reading of the work, I will use Cognitive Grammar and Zbikowski's theories of Musical Grammar to explore how the sound design contributes to this experience of 'being played with by the text'. Furthermore, the way that sound and interaction design creates spatio-temporal immersion, interactional deixis and audio deixis (Bell et al. 2018) will be explored. To do this, I use Cognitive Grammar to break down and analyse particular examples of ways that interactional deixis and audio deixis are managed in the piece.

Chapter 1 of *Loss of Grasp* begins with the display of a single line written in white in the centre of a black screen. The text reads 'All my life I believed I had infinite prospects before me'. Rolling over the text with the mouse causes a series of moving, incomprehensible symbols to animate before stopping to reveal further single lines telling about the protagonist's youthful optimism. This 'ludosemiotic' interface design (Ensslin 2014: 80) contributes to a sense of play by requiring only minimal effort from the reader: simply rolling the mouse animates the graphics. These moving letters and punctuation marks provide feedback to the reader that they have changed the state of the story by interacting with it. Furthermore, Cognitive Grammar allows for an understanding that these moving graphics will be construed and profiled as trajectors, leading to them becoming a focus for attention within the conceptualization. As the graphics eventually cease to roll, they cease to be trajectors and attention is drawn towards the fact that the new line of text ('I control my own destiny') is underlined, indicating that the reader must click (rather than roll) to further progress the story. Clicking causes a short bright sound and produces coloured circles on the screen. More clicking produces more bubbles and bright sounds. As the reader continues to interact, the bright circles become increasingly unruly, their size and position difficult to predict, with the sounds becoming increasingly discordant and erratic, beginning to overlap as the text describes the feeling of a loss of control setting.

The way that this sequence engages the reader in subjective construal can be discussed in terms of which emotions and movements are coded into sonic analogs (Zbikowski 2017). The musical tokens used in the piece have a tone similar to the sounds made by a music box and these evoke, at least in this reader, memories of upward, fleeting and childlike movements. As the sounds begin to become discordant and to overlap, and the text describes losing control, the shape and nature of the sonic analogs can be seen to encode a simulation of faltering or falling over. While the nature of subjective construal will mean that these sounds cue a distinct personal response within each reader, the general ability of sonic analogs to encode emotional and physical cues (Zbikowski 2017: 4) means they can be designed to create particular effects with some degree of accuracy. Taken together, these ideas offer an insight into why the musical elements of this scene are construed with subjectivity and create a feeling that the text is 'playing with the reader' (Ensslin 2014: 80).

In the next chapter of *Loss of Grasp*, the scene opens with the ambient sound of a restaurant or bar. This ambient sound carries the spatial characteristics of a reverberant restaurant full of conversational diners: it communicates the space from which the narrator is telling the story by engaging the reader in auditory perception of the scene. The schematic quality of the ambient sound of the restaurant can be understood in terms of Cognitive Grammar as being likely to be construed in a non-specific way: it creates a general impression and does not seek to bring forward elements (such as the sound of specific voices or crashes of cutlery) that might cause a shift in focus. Furthermore, as the sound is perceived through 'reduced listening' (Chion 1994; Schaeffer 2012), the quality of the sound itself evokes a particular 'mood', and this tone contributes to the reader's overall construal of the perceived situation. In this way, the schematic quality of the sound can be understood to influence the perceptive state of the reader. Furthermore, the schematic nature of the ambient (background) sound allows the reader to maintain attention on the situation being conveyed through the written text as the scene is conceptualized. This text describes how the narrator feels himself to be dumbstruck as he sits and looks at his dinner date. In this case, the text shifts the deictic position and vantage point taken on the scene. As the scene progresses, the ambient restaurant sound stays in the background but continues to contribute to the mood as a list of questions appear on the screen. Rolling over these one by one causes the sound of a man's voice asking questions such as 'Do you want a drink?' to play. The sound of the narrator's voice is construed with more specificity than the ambient sounds, and this shifts the deictic centre of the reader closer to the narrator/speaker. The proximity of the voice codes a construal that conveys the self-consciousness experienced by the narrator as he hears himself speak. Furthermore, the fact that the timing of his voice is controlled by the reader input demonstrates the way that interaction design can be used to place the reader in the protagonist's position. This use of sound to position the reader close to the narrator within the scene is termed audio deixis (Bell et al. 2018: 14). Audio deixis occurs when music and sound create a sense of the spatial landscape of a multimodal scene and successfully position the reader within this (Bell et al. 2018: 14).

After the sound of speaking comes to an end, a large question mark appears on the screen. Clicking on this question mark produces a coloured shape, which is revealed

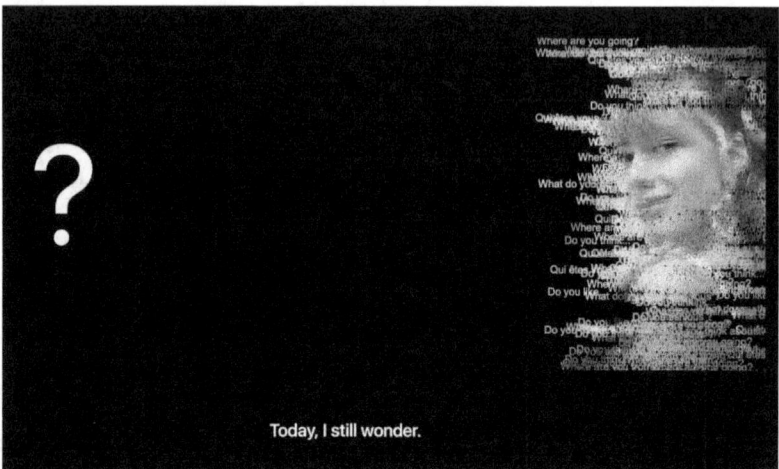

Figure 11.1 Chapter Two of *Loss of Grasp*: Meeting in the Restaurant.

line by line on the right-hand side of the screen. The schematic ambient sound continues. As the reader moves the mouse, a piece of typographic art emerges on the screen, as though the reader (and narrator) is 'painting' the woman sitting on the opposite side of the restaurant table. Eventually, a photographic image of the narrator's wife (comprising lines of coloured, typed questions) emerges out of the dark on the right of the screen, as though from the crowd in the restaurant to which the reader is still listening. It seems as though his questions have led to knowing her, or at least to building an impression.

Figure 11.1 exemplifies how graphic design can be used to influence the construal of a multimodal work. By graphically framing the different temporal and semantic aspects of the conceived situation (the developing relationship of the narrator with his wife) separately on the screen, the piece can be seen to manage construal multimodally. Rather than the events contained in the separate graphic frames being construed as separate and unrelated, a composite meaning emerges when reading across them. The semantic success of the graphic framing can be understood through the concept of *windows* found in Cognitive Grammar (Langacker 2008: 428–9; Giovanelli and Harrison 2018: 42–3), where dynamic construal processes are seen to involve breaking down larger meaning structures into separate windows of attention that remain nevertheless conceptually connected to each other. In Cognitive Grammar, relative clauses 'make successively greater semantic contributions encouraging their apprehension in a separate window of attention' (Langacker 2008: 428). In this example, the separate framing of the question mark, the emerging picture of the woman being questioned and the text displaying the narrator's introspective state can be understood as attentional windows that contain elements scanned, profiled and blended dynamically over time until the composite meaning emerges. Furthermore, the changes that result from interacting with the graphic frames (e.g. clicking the question mark results in an alteration to her image as it produces questions) engage the viewer (subject) in dynamic mental scanning and in making focal adjustments of the perceived situation. In this way, the ludosemiotic properties of the user interaction design (Ensslin 2014: 80) can be seen to further contribute to subjective construal and immersion even when asked to 'take a turn as narrator' (Walker Rettberg 2001: 36-7).

The piece finishes on an almost empty black title screen. A soundscape plays an atmosphere of sparsely distributed birds, music and wind. By way of the spatial information contained in the mix, the sound situates the deictic centre, or vantage point, both of the reader and of the protagonist, whose position is aligned with the narrator. The reverberant quality of the audio, by encoding spatial characteristics of a tunnel, positions the viewing position within the scene as one that is far away from the source of the happy music. This is a good example of how audio deixis can contribute to spatio-temporal immersion (Bell et al. 2018: 14). The temporal aspect of this immersion is enhanced due to the composition of this acousmatic sequence of musique concrète: the sound perceived from the unseen sources is largely schematic, but elements of wind, birds and music move in and out of prominence over time as auditory attention is allocated to reduced listening and subjective construal of the piece. Furthermore, the evolving soundscape contains an emotional resonance when construed within the wider context of the story of *Loss of Grasp*, which ends with the narrator having lost his sense of optimism and direction.

The quality of immersion generated by this final chapter of *Loss of Grasp* can be analysed further through Langacker's concept of viewing arrangement, where subjective construal brings the reader's locus of consciousness closer to the perceived situation and results in the reader being involved to some degree (Giovanelli and Harrison 2018: 51). As the reader listens to the musique concrète composition (employing reduced listening), they engage in subjective construal and perceive the emotional qualities of the sound. Essentially, the design of this multimodal text uses sound to enable the mind and emotions of the reader to stand in for the mind and emotions of the protagonist. A further concept that enables an understanding of this idea is that of empathetic deixis, i.e. indication of how the speaker is 'personally involved with the entity, situation or place to which he is referring or is identifying himself with the attitude or viewpoint of the addressee' (Lyons 1977: 677). If audio deixis situates the reader spatially within the scene, then increased empathetic deixis moves 'origio farther' to 'origio near' (Rühlemann and O'Donnell 2014: 399). This concept mirrors that of subjective construal and of shifting viewing arrangements. In this sense, through analysing how the sound in this sequence encodes a subjective construal, Cognitive Grammar has been used to account for the way a multimodal text situates the reader both spatially and emotionally within a simulation cued across sound and text.

8. Recommendations for practical application

In this final section, I offer some further specific recommendations for the practical application of the concepts described here, building on findings from empirical studies exploring immersion in digital fiction.

Bell et al. (2018) argue that spatio-temporal immersion must take place before any other forms of immersion, and that 'immersion in digital fiction is a fully embodied, multimodal experience' (2018: 16). They further argue that this is brought about through auditory and interactional deixis. As such, techniques for directing the deictic position of the reader are considered in these recommendations to be of central importance.

8.1 Construal

Developing an ability to direct attention and cue shifts in the deictic position of the reader is possible through familiarization and application of concepts of construal. Construal in Langacker's framework includes aspects of scanning, the identification of prominent elements and the profiling of the focus of attention. It also identifies how elements can alter and animate the vantage point taken on a scene. These concepts can be generalized to include the way that non-linguistic symbols or tokens might be incorporated within a scene. Writers can first begin to develop an ability to simulate how readers may construe a multimodal scene by applying Cognitive Grammar to readings of monomodal texts rich in sensory data. Identifying how language draws on sensory data enables the writer to imagine how readers might construe a scene influenced by modalities other than language and allows for multimodal simulations to be conceptualized in terms of their components. I have included the reading of *Annihilation* within this chapter to illustrate this methodology.

Once the components of a multimodal scene have been identified, it becomes necessary to conceptualize the way that non-linguistic elements will be moving and changing in the final text in order that the writer can structure the timing and semantic composition of these elements. In this instance, the writer may choose to create a storyboard to set out the way their written text interrelates with these non-linguistic elements over time, particularly in terms of what is foregrounded or separated into an attentional frame as interactions with the text cause the story to change state. As this storyboard is developed, a consideration of the construal phenomena identified within Cognitive Grammar could be useful: writers could reflect on the profile and specificity of each aspect of the text as readers interact with the work.

The reading of *Loss of Grasp*, where the protagonist first meets his wife in a busy restaurant or bar, illustrates this idea further. The reader can conceptualize this setting, despite the opening screen being black, due to the specific choice made with regards to the sound, which is an unfocussed ambience of a restaurant. The lack of focus and change in the sound foreground the events taking place at the protagonist's location within the restaurant. This deictic position is drawn more specifically when the narrator's voice is heard speaking: it is very close. The way that the timing of the narrator's voice is controlled by the reader input demonstrates the way that interaction design can be used to place the reader in the protagonist's position (closer to the voice), producing the effect of both interactional and audio deictic proximity.

During the development stages of a piece, writers can also use Cognitive Grammar to manage when to introduce movement in graphics and sound. Although not all trajectors in Langacker's framework are movers, the way in which elements gain prominence through movement is an example of a way in which Cognitive Grammar might be used to support design thinking. For example, a trajector could be conceptualized in terms of a blinking icon on an application, a bird suddenly in flight across a still sky or a new sonic element panning across the sound field; all of these moving objects can be designed into a text to direct and frame attention. An example of this working meaningfully can be seen in the reading of the opening of *Loss of Grasp*, where bright bubbles of colour and playful music appear randomly on the screen to convey the youthful optimism written in the text. However, trajectors can also cause a disruption to attention. For example, if the background restaurant sound in the scene where the protagonist asks questions of his wife suddenly foregrounded ear-catching elements – such as clattering plates or smashing glasses or a burst of laughter – attention could potentially be drawn to the reader thinking about the unpleasantness of the sound, altering their conceptualization of the scene. This call to attention would need to be managed at the text design stage, which is why creating a storyboard that addresses the prominence of elements over time can be useful.

8.2 Sound and subjectivity

If engagement in listening encourages an immediate subjective or emotion-led construal, it can be seen that sound could, if designed badly, easily detach the reader from the events conceptualized in the text or create an incoherence in the construal as elements are scanned over time. An example of these ideas in practice can be found in the reading of the final scene of *Loss of Grasp*, where the concepts of empathetic deixis and audio deixis are applied to an analysis of the impact of the sound sequence of birds and music heard from far away. Writers could imagine the impact of the sound being different: perhaps angry or fast sounds would communicate an entirely different introspective state and encode a very different construal. In order to ensure that there is coherence in the construal of the scene, the reader's emotional and allegorical mapping (Ensslin 2014 : 11) need to be considered when sound is being designed. This idea is explored in detail in the reading of the opening section of *Loss of Grasp*.

9. Conclusion

Cognitive Grammar provides a way of analysing how mental simulations are built. The specific formulation of construal processes developed by Langacker enables writers to maintain a focus on the experience of the reader as a conceptualization develops. Read alongside complementary frameworks of multimodal simulation, such as the one developed by Barsalou (1999), it becomes possible to understand how even small amounts of text can cue very rich dynamic scenes in the mind of the reader. This empowers writers to begin to take knowledge from their area of expertise – language – and apply it within the design of multimodal work. By applying Cognitive Grammar to the reading of multimodal texts, writers can understand how graphic and interaction design influences construal and therefore reader experience. When further combined with Zbikowski's (2017) work on the grammar of music and Chion's (1994) analysis of the perceptual processes involved in listening, writers can use Cognitive Grammar to develop an approach to sound design based on their understanding of how sensory input affects the viewing arrangements created by their scenes. In summary, and as I have demonstrated in this chapter, Cognitive Grammar can be used to analyse the ways that spatio-temporal immersion in multimodal texts can be created by maintaining focus on the reader's experience.

References

Aarseth, E. (1997), *CyberText*, Baltimore: Johns Hopkins University Press.

Barsalou, L.W. (1999), 'Perceptual Symbol Systems', *Behavioral and Brain Sciences*, 22: 577–660.

Barsalou, L. (2008), 'Grounded Cognition', *Annual Review of Psychology*, 59: 617–45.

Bell, A. and A. Ensslin (2011), '"I know what it was. You know what it was": Second-Person Narration in Hypertext Fiction', *Narrative*, 19 (3): 311–29.

Bell, A., A. Ensslin, I. van der Bom, and J. Smith (2018), 'Immersion in Digital Fiction: A Cognitive, Empirical Approach', *International Journal of Literary Linguistics*, 7 (1). Open Access.

Bouchardon, S. and V. Volckaert (2010), *Loss of Grasp*. Available online: https://bouchard.pers.utc.fr/deprise/home, (accessed 20 August 2019).

Bühler, Karl (1934), *Sprachtheorie. Die Darstellungsfunktion der Sprache*, Jena: Gustav Fischer.

Chion, M. (1994), *Audio-Vision: Sound on Screen*, New York: Columbia University Press.

Citron, F.M.M. and A.E. Goldberg (2014), 'Metaphorical Sentences Are More Emotionally Engaging than Their Literal Counterparts', *Journal of Cognitive Neuroscience*, 26 (11): 2585–95.

Ensslin, A. (2014), *Literary Gaming*, Cambridge: MIT Press.

Evans, V. and M. Green (2006), *Cognitive Linguistics: An Introduction*, Edinburgh: Edinburgh University Press.

Galbraith, M. (1995), 'Deictic Shift Theory and the Poetics of Involvement in Narrative', in J. F. Duchan, G.A. Bruder and L. Hewit (eds), *Deixis in Narrative: A Cognitive Science Perspective*, 19–59, Hillsdale: Lawrence Erlbaum.

Gavins, J. (2007), *Text World Theory: An Introduction*, Edinburgh: Edinburgh University Press.

Giovanelli, M. and C. Harrison (2018), *Cognitive Grammar in Stylistics: A Practical Guide*, London: Bloomsbury Academic.

Harrison, C. (2019), '"A Half-Remembered Quality": Experiencing Disorientation and Claustrophobia in *The Goldfinch*', in C. Hart (ed.), *Cognitive Linguistic Approaches to Text and Discourse: From Poetics to Politics*, 37–53, Edinburgh: Edinburgh University Press.

Johnson, M. (1987), *The Body in the Mind: The Bodily Basis of Meaning, Imagination, and Reason*, Chicago: University of Chicago Press.

Langacker, R.W. (1987), *Foundations of Cognitive Grammar: Volume I: Theoretical Prerequisites*, Stanford: Stanford University Press.

Langacker, R.W. (2008), *Cognitive Grammar: A Basic Introduction*, Oxford: Oxford University Press.

Langacker, R.W. (2009), *Investigations in Cognitive Grammar*, Berlin: De Gruyter.

Lyons, J. (1977), *Semantics: Vol II*, Cambridge: Cambridge University Press.
Matlock, T. (2004), 'Fictive Motion as Cognitive Simulation', *Memory & Cognition*, 32: 1389–400.
Murch, W. (2017), 'What Is Musique Concrète?' Available online: https://www.youtube.com/watch?v=Lm48OzyLnU8, (accessed 17 August 2019).
Nuttall, L. (2018), *Mind Style and Cognitive Grammar*, London: Bloomsbury.
Rühlemann, C. and M. O'Donnell (2014), 'Deixis', in K. Aijmer and C. Rühlemann (eds), *Corpus Pragmatics: A Handbook*, 331–59, Cambridge, Cambridge University Press.
Ryan, M-L. (1999), 'Immersion vs. Interactivity: Virtual Reality and Literary Theory', *SubStance*, 28 (2): 110–37.
Ryan, M-L. (2001), *Narrative as Virtual Reality. Immersion and Interactivity in Literature and Electronic Media*, Baltimore, MD: Johns Hopkins University Press.
Schaeffer, P. (2012), *In Search of a Concrete Music*, Berkeley: University of California Press.
Talmy, L. (1983), 'How Language Structures Space', in H.L. Pick and L.P. Acredolo (eds), *Spatial Orientation: Theory, Research, and Application*, 225–82, Boston, MA: Springer.
VanderMeer, J. (2014), *Annihilation*, Kindle ed., London: Fourth Estate.
Verhagen, A. (2012), 'Construal and Perspectivization', in D. Geeraerts and H. Cuyckens (eds), *The Oxford Handbook of Cognitive Linguistics*, 48–81, Oxford, Oxford University Press.
Walker Rettberg, J. (2001), 'Do You Think You're Part of This? Digital Texts and the Second Person Address', in M. Eskelinen and R. Koskimaa (eds), *CyberText Yearbook 2000*, 34–51, Jyväskylä, Finland: Research Centre for Contemporary Culture/Publications, University of Jyväskylä.
Zbikowski, L. (2017), *Foundations of Musical Grammar*, New York: Oxford University Press.
Zwaan, R.A. and C.J. Madden (2005), 'Embodied Sentence Comprehension', in D. Pecher and R. Zwaan (eds), *Grounding Cognition: The Role of Perception and Action in Memory, Language, and Thinking*, 224–45, Cambridge: Cambridge University Press.

Part Four

Cognitive Grammar in educational contexts

12

From theoretical to pedagogical grammar: The challenges of writing a textbook on Cognitive Grammar

Marcello Giovanelli and Chloe Harrison

1. Introduction

As the chapters in this book demonstrate, Cognitive Grammar offers an innovative and psychologically plausible model for analysing a range of discourse types. Cognitive Grammar is, however, fundamentally a theoretical grammar and despite receiving considerable interest from applied linguists, there have been few successful attempts to present it in a suitable and accessible pedagogical format to support students undertaking textual analysis in the stylistics classroom. This chapter examines the process of designing, writing and reflecting on our textbook *Cognitive Grammar in Stylistics: A Practical Guide* (Giovanelli and Harrison 2018). Through reflection and analysis of a number of examples, we outline the various decisions we faced and made in reconfiguring key aspects of Cognitive Grammar in order to present and articulate the model for novice learners. In doing so, we examine how the process of writing the book helped our own understanding of the affordances and limitations of Cognitive Grammar and led us to re-evaluate its value in a pedagogical context.

The chapter is organized in the following way. In Section 1 we outline the origins of the book and our motivations for wanting to develop a resource that would be the first book-length treatment of Cognitive Grammar *in stylistics*. In Section 2 we consider some of the challenges that this presented, given that Cognitive Grammar can be perceived as a complex model that has not always been presented in an accessible form. In Section 3 we argue that Cognitive Grammar does, however, have the potential to be an enabling accessible grammar and position the model more broadly within the practice of pedagogical stylistics. Section 4 provides an in-depth discussion and analysis of how we primarily drew on and adapted Ronald Langacker's (1987, 1991, 2008a) model for our textbook. In doing so, we draw on specific decisions we made as part of the planning and writing process, discuss how we used diagrams to support students' learning and provide examples of and justification for some of the teaching activities we designed. Finally, Section 5 positions the textbook within the broader context of module design and considers some implications of our work in the light of the further development of Cognitive Grammar as an integral part of stylistics teaching and as an analytical method for research.

1.1 Origins and motivations

The motivation for the conception of a Cognitive Grammar textbook largely started with our own interests as academic stylisticians in developing applications of Cognitive Grammar in stylistics. In our own research we have drawn on Cognitive Grammar in a number of ways, considering it to be a valuable and enabling tool for the analysis of texts (see for example Giovanelli 2014, 2018a, 2018b, 2019; Harrison 2014, 2017a, 2017b; Harrison and Nuttall 2019). Indeed more generally, Cognitive Grammar has emerged over recent years as a credible and innovative method of analysis for stylisticians with a growing number of researchers now drawing on insights from Cognitive Grammar, either as a singular analytical method or in conjunction with other approaches (see the Introduction to this book for an overview of the growing work in this field). We are also teachers as well as researchers, and consequently view the stylistics classroom as an exciting forum where innovative work often takes place. As McIntyre (2012: 113) warns, however, it is commonplace for novel research paradigms, methodologies and methods to transfer relatively slowly from a theoretical platform to a pedagogical one. This may be due to the fact that pedagogical affordances and implications of a new theory or concept are not always immediately obvious or because, more practically, the introduction of one topic or module usually has to come at the expense of another in what is always a crowded curriculum. We believe that Cognitive Grammar does have a clear place in the classroom since we view it as theoretically sound and practically intuitive. During the course of writing the book, we also found ourselves in the fortunate position of being able to dedicate around half a module's teaching time (five weeks) to Cognitive Grammar through the introduction of a new 'Cognitive Poetics' module into our programme, an aspect that we return to and discuss in Section 4.

As Cognitive Grammar is as much a theory of language as it is a method for stylistic analysis, any book-length coverage that is pedagogically focused requires more than just the simple outlining of its framework. Although undergraduate students can and do make use of research monographs and scholarly articles, a pedagogically oriented entry-level reader needs to explain principles and provide exercises and activities that students can undertake both in seminars and independently. Mindful of this, we wanted to develop a resource that introduced students to the theory of Cognitive Grammar and enabled them to apply that theory in a practical way to support the analysis of texts. Our aim therefore was to recontextualize (Bernstein 1991) Cognitive Grammar from a theoretical model into a pedagogical one. In this respect, we were influenced by publications such as Coffin et al. (2009) and Fontaine (2012) both of which have presented Systemic Functional Grammar to a student audience in a user-friendly and enabling format. Specifically within cognitive stylistics, Gavins' (2007) *Text World Theory: An Introduction* also offered us an example of a book that had both a rigorous and accessible outlining of theory and, with its range of texts, activities and recommendations for further reading, an equally strong pedagogical dimension.

Whereas Text World Theory is now well established within stylistics in terms of research and teaching, Cognitive Grammar remains peripheral and, in our experience and to our knowledge, appears relatively infrequently in undergraduate stylistics modules. This may reflect the fact that, unlike Text World Theory, a textbook exclusively on Cognitive Grammar for the stylistics classroom that students can draw on had not yet appeared. Where textbooks on Cognitive Grammar do exist, these tend to outline the model (e.g. Taylor 2002; Radden and Dirven 2007) and provide short activities rather than introduce students to applying Cognitive Grammar in the service of extended textual analysis. In turn, the stylistics textbooks that do cover Cognitive Grammar (e.g. Gavins and Steen 2003; Stockwell 2009; Gibbons and Whiteley 2017) present Cognitive Grammar as one method among many rather than providing an exclusive or longer treatment. Equally, both of Langacker's most recent distillations of his work, *Cognitive Grammar: A Basic Introduction* (Langacker 2008a) and *Cognitive Grammar: The Essentials* (Langacker 2013), offer an exclusively theoretical overview and, at times, very complex discussion that serves more as a point of linguistic reference rather as a springboard for genuine practical applications.

Overall then, we envisaged producing a book that would address what we perceived to be a critical gap in the pedagogical literature and that we hoped would reflect the growing enthusiasm for Cognitive Grammar among contemporary stylisticians. We hoped that such a book would act as a strong pedagogical resource recontextualizing Cognitive Grammar for a new audience and hopefully support the development of Cognitive Grammar as a genuinely valuable area of study for the stylistics undergraduate. We also hoped that our writing journey would provide us with the opportunity to think critically about Cognitive Grammar within stylistic scholarship more broadly and support the needs of module programme development at our own institution.

2. Perceptions of Cognitive Grammar

Despite the fact that it is largely very intuitive, one of the major barriers to Cognitive Grammar becoming a more mainstream method in stylistics may be down to the feeling that it can appear abstruse. It does not take very long to find examples of students appearing puzzled by Cognitive Grammar's perceived complexities; during our research for this chapter we easily found several examples on social media. Academic linguists have also commented on how Langacker's model, for instance, may appear 'notoriously difficult to read and understand' (Pihlaja 2019: 65), with 'its idiosyncratic notation and terminology that leave some readers cold' (Heath 2014: 276). It is true that the complex ways in which existing Cognitive Grammar literature presents ideas and the impenetrable nature of some of the diagrams can make Cognitive Grammar seem to be a difficult and unwieldy framework. Indeed in our own reading and work we have found Langacker's discussion of some key ideas vague in places and sometimes even self-contradictory. Consequently, we would argue that it might well be difficult to expect students to be able to gain much from the original sources to support their own understanding of Cognitive Grammar or to provide a foundation for their own interaction with and analyses of texts.

We should, however, point out two key points in mitigation of the above. The first, and most important, is that Langacker is a theoretical linguist and although he advocates the potential for more diverse applications of Cognitive Grammar (see Section 3), his work maps out its theoretical and descriptive parameters rather than outlining the ways in which the model might be applied. The second is that Cognitive Grammar has not held a central position as a pedagogical framework and so has lacked the kind of empirical testing through classroom work that has been afforded to other grammars. For example, in both L1 and L2 contexts, applications of systemic functional linguistics (SFL) (Halliday 1985) have been recontextualized and well established over time as pedagogical grammars. The SFL paradigm therefore has a long-standing tradition across numerous sub-fields of education, arising initially from Halliday's groundbreaking work on *Schools Council Programme in Linguistics and English Teaching* that ran in England from 1964 to 1971 which subsequently inspired a range of teaching models and materials in L1 contexts and which, in turn, has more broadly developed into a powerful pedagogical model underpinning different kinds of learning and teaching methods across different phases of education (see for example Williams 1998; Unsworth 2005; Macken-Horarik 2009, 2012; Rose and Martin 2012; Coffin and Donoghue 2014).

Within stylistics, key SFL topics such as transitivity relations have been foregrounded in established textbooks in the field (e.g. Toolan 1998; Simpson 2014). As we have previously indicated, although a few major publications do reach out to embrace the model, it would appear that there is not yet a firm consensus as to whether Cognitive Grammar occupies enough of an important position in the discipline to warrant universal inclusion. Indeed, another leading textbook (Jeffries and McIntyre 2010) devotes space to several cognitive stylistic topics (Text World Theory, deictic shift theory, contextual frame theory, figure and ground, schema theory and cognitive metaphor) but has no coverage at all of Cognitive Grammar.

A significant reason for this may be due to the fact that, as Stockwell (2014) suggests, grammar-oriented analyses in stylistics have been historically rooted in the systemic functional tradition and consequently pedagogical motivations and practices may well follow research ones. As Stockwell (2014: 20) argues:

> Perhaps there is a sense that SFG [Systemic Functional Grammar] works well enough for the job at hand; perhaps it is felt that its ideological reach gives it an advantage; perhaps there is a notion that a common currency of description has been established and so there is no need for radical innovation.

The ways in which Cognitive Grammar might appear to offer such an innovation for the stylistician are now, as we have argued already in this chapter, becoming more established. Current research drawing on Cognitive Grammar has demonstrated both its value as an analytical tool both in conjunction with and in lieu of systemic functional approaches (see Harrison 2017a; Nuttall 2018). Indeed some researchers are now articulating Cognitive Grammar's value beyond SFG. For example, Browse

(2018), in answering Stockwell's caveat that 'the use of Cognitive Grammar in literary stylistics must be at least as good as previous practices' (2014: 20), has demonstrated how Cognitive Grammar can explain the nuances of how readers construct meaning more systematically and effectively than is possible simply by drawing on SFG.

3. Towards a pedagogical Cognitive Grammar for the stylistics classroom

Although his own work largely remains concerned with the theoretical, Langacker does recognize the pedagogical potential of Cognitive Grammar:

> I cannot help thinking, however, that the cognitive linguistic view of language is a matter of universal interest, and that its conceptual descriptions of linguistic phenomena are sufficiently natural and revealing to be widely appreciated. **In some form, I can imagine these ideas being an integral part of general education or first language instruction**. I can further imagine them as being useful in second language learning, especially at more advanced levels.
> (Langacker 2008b: 29, added emphasis)

Students studying stylistics are concerned with learning both a methodological stance and a set of methods or tools that can be used for analysis in order to examine the ways in which different kinds of texts operate. As a theory about language that is concerned with both the cognitive and the social, Cognitive Grammar would appear to be pedagogically sensitive both methodologically and methods-wise. As Langacker (2008a: 8) argues, 'It [Cognitive Grammar] fully acknowledges the grounding of language in social interaction, but insists that even its interactive function is critically dependent on conceptualization'. The emphasis on the symbiotic relationship between cognition and a wider social context means that Cognitive Grammar is fundamentally meaning-centred. Cognitive Grammar's attention to the ways in which conceptualizers conceive, or construe, scenes as both inherently meaningful and goal-driven highlights the importance of examining the actual instances and contexts in which language occurs. Cognitive Grammar thus mirrors the systemic functional focus on language as a social system with an added dimension of foregrounding embodied cognition (Lakoff and Johnson 1999). The model thus aims to take 'seriously the goal of psychological reality in linguistic description' (Langacker 1987: 56).

These fundamental principles have formed attractive rationales for developing experimental pedagogical work, particularly in L2 contexts where ideas from Cognitive Grammar specifically and from cognitive linguistics more generally have been shown to improve student outcomes when teaching modality (Tyler 2012), metaphor (Littlemore and Low 2006), conditionals (Dolgova Jacobsen 2018) and prepositions (Evans and Tyler 2004; Tyler, Mueller and Ho 2010). More general handbooks and edited volumes (e.g. De Knop and De Rycker 2008; Robinson and Ellis 2008; Littlemore 2009) include coverage of topics broadly within the area of Cognitive Grammar. Within L1 contexts, however, this coverage is more minimal, with only a few exceptions that examine the ways, both theoretically and empirically, in which Cognitive Grammar might support language awareness and text analysis (e.g. Giovanelli 2014; Trousdale 2016; and see Cushing in this volume).

The use and development of language-informed methods when they form part of an overall teaching strategy for textual analysis is commonly known as pedagogical stylistics (Short 1989; Weber 1996; Clark and Zyngier 2003; McIntyre 2010, 2012) or 'stylistics in pedagogy' (Hall 2014). As Carter (1996: 3) argues, pedagogical stylistics is 'student-centred, activity based and process-oriented', aiming to provide students with the tools with which to undertake textual analysis so as to develop their skills as independent analytical readers. The emphasis on process as much as product highlights the practical and reflective aspects of a stylistics-informed pedagogy; students develop meta-reflective skills as well as insights about the texts that they study. Hall (2014: 140) offers a number of ways that 'stylistics in pedagogy' may be of use in pedagogical contexts for both teacher and student:

- Stylistics can be used to teach literature, or at least to facilitate the study of literature or the study of linguistic creativity as it is more broadly understood;
- Stylistics can support the study of texts in contexts and discourse more widely, in terms of genre, register, sociolinguistics and variation, as well as the grammar of standard spoken and written language through its fundamentally comparative method;
- Stylistics is of value for foreign language or second language learning programmes, where attention to language use should facilitate language acquisition or where study of language use is valued;
- Stylistics can be used to teach language use, language awareness and language arts as a resource for language users;
- Stylistics is claimed to be of value in creative writing programmes, as well as in professional, academic or technical writing development;
- Stylistics can be used to teach linguistics, an inductive way into a sometimes demanding subject area (involving 'bottom-up' rather than 'top-down' investigation) that teaches as much (or prompts as many questions) about 'language' as it does about 'literature';
- Stylistics may be used to teach empirical research skills, but also transferable intellectual and social skills and rhetoric (evidence-based argument, careful and systematic description and presentation, argumentation);
- Stylistics has recently been used in the study of readers and reading, to investigate questions of social and cognitive psychology and topics in psycholinguistics, particularly the study of cognition in reading, including topics such as 'noticing', attention, value and affect [...];
- Stylistics can be used to introduce and learn corpus stylistics and ICT skills, quantitative and qualitative learning and understanding;
- In more recent multimodal stylistics, it is argued that film, cultural studies, the internet and complex multimodal texts more generally can be explored more precisely and systematically with the aid of stylistics [...]

We would acknowledge our belief in these fundamental principles and characteristics of pedagogical stylistics in several ways. These are developed with some later extended exemplification from our book in Sections 3.2 and 3.3 but are briefly summarized here.

First, we wanted to ensure that the book's design was grounded in ways that were both *language-oriented*, with an emphasis on developing language knowledge, and *task-oriented*, with an emphasis on meaningful and engaging tasks (see Johnson 2000: 301). This balance was important to ensure that our design of content, tasks, exercises and reading suggestions was both informative and readable. Second, we wanted to empower students through engaging them from the start in practical work that allowed them to apply their learning and develop as stylisticians as well as linguists or grammarians, or, as Burke et al. (2012: 2) suggest 'allowing them [students] to learn stylistics through reading and analyzing texts: in short, learning stylistics through doing stylistics'. We wanted the book to encourage practical application so as to emphasise a critical and evaluative and process-oriented approach. Since textbooks are also authoritative material artefacts that codify and promote particular ways of conceiving and conceptualizing knowledge (De Castell et al. 1989), and legitimize particular ways of viewing subject content (Apple 1986, 1992), we wanted the book to stress what we believed were key and important messages about Cognitive Grammar within the discipline of stylistics. In other words, we wanted to emphasize what we thought practising stylisticians would need and want to know about Cognitive Grammar in order to improve their analyses of texts.

Finally, in our own thinking about and enacting the process of recontextualization, we were conscious of the need to put together something coherent that built on but moved beyond the discrete Cognitive Grammar exercises that we had both used in previous teaching. As Atkinson argues:

> Textbook design is, in fact, much more than task design; it involves the development not only of tasks, but of whole units which must fit together seamlessly in order to reflect a coherent end product.
>
> (Atkinson 2008: 2)

We were therefore mindful that the book should be a coherent narrative in its own right, providing the book-length treatment with a strong pedagogical orientation that we felt was a real affordance of Cognitive Grammar, and which would provide a convincing argument more generally for the value of using Cognitive Grammar in stylistic analysis.

4. Designing the textbook: Structure

The design of the textbook was centred on providing, first and foremost, 'a practical guide' for analysis. The idea was that such a textbook would help develop the initial work on Cognitive Grammar applications in literary linguistic research by presenting another 'tool' (see Wales 2014) for stylisticians, but also, synergistically, that it would help to clarify and develop some of the 'fuzzier' concepts within the cognitive grammar model.

As we observe in Section 1.1, despite its theoretical origins, Cognitive Grammar, like other cognitive linguistic models, is a 'usage-based' framework which means that it is 'particularly productive for language learning and teaching as it traces form to underlying meanings'; as such an approach provides 'the best framework for the transfer of grammatical schemata into immediate, everyday language use by the learner' (Roche 2014: 330). To continue with the usage-based ethos, the emphasis with activities in the textbook has therefore been on both the practical application of ideas and consideration of texts that we encounter in our day-to-day lives (such as advertisements, headlines, TV sitcoms and cartoons, as well as literary examples such as multimodal children's texts, poetry, graphic novels, prose fiction and drama). The driving idea here is that these ideas are universally applicable to all instances of language use.

Such a central claim is also one which, we hope, is reassuring and liberating for those who worry about their knowledge of grammar and the correct application of these terms. Linguistic constructions work differently in different contexts, and ideas from Cognitive Grammar help us to think about how these particular choices are functioning within these various contexts. This is a claim that is also true of existing grammars, such as systemic-functional grammar, but while the functionality of the linguistic unit is of paramount importance to the systemic-functional grammarian, the representation of experience is of equal or greater importance in a Cognitive Grammar approach.

At the same time, one of the primary aims of stylistics is to avoid simple intuitive and impressionistic comments about texts which are not driven by textual choices, and so such an approach needed to be balanced alongside literary linguistic rigour and systematicity. Traditionally, (cognitive) stylistics textbooks follow the linguistic rank scale (see, for examples, Stockwell 2009; Jeffries and McIntyre 2010; Simpson 2014), a progression that entails moving from smaller to larger units of language. Such a progression outlines a systematic approach to the analysis of texts, allowing exploration of both micro- and macro- structures of language. This textbook similarly follows this movement from smaller (nouns, verbs, conceptual semantics etc.) to larger concepts of language (grounding, clauses etc.) from within the Cognitive Grammar model, although through necessity there is also some movement between the two throughout. Many of the extended examples at the end of each of the chapter sections applied the central Cognitive Grammar concepts at the 'discourse level' of the text, for example, although a chapter was also devoted to this towards the end of the book, as a logical part of this progression.

Finally, given the scarcity of existing guides for Cognitive Grammar, the book is also fundamentally, and by necessity, research-driven, based on the results of emergent analyses carried out by researchers in the incipient applications of this model for stylistics. Consequently, the textbook makes no claims to be a definitive guide, but rather a representation of the affordances of this new and developing method.

4.1 Adaptation for stylistics

In Section 1 we outlined how, while the aim was to provide a comprehensive overview of the key ideas of the original Cognitive Grammar model, we also wanted to produce a handbook for stylistic analysis, specifically. Pursuant to this, the book focuses primarily on those tenets of the model that are most useful for stylisticians. There are parts of the original theory that we have had to road-test for the first time, as their application in the original work is fairly limited. There is an emphasis on spoken discourse contexts with some of the examples included in the original Langacker texts, for example, which can certainly be more straightforwardly applied to conversations in drama or dialogue in fiction (see, for example, activities in the textbook which examine humour in dialogue in *The Importance of Being Earnest* or discourse cooperation in a scene from the TV series *The Big Bang Theory*), but which in other cases we have recontextualized in reference to prose fiction. The idea of the Current Discourse Space (Langacker 2008a: 59), for example, in the original theory relates to how we manage and conceptualize discourse spaces in ongoing conversations. There are, however, many similarities with this idea and the Text World Theory model, which suggests its potential for more general application beyond spoken discourse examples. Consequently, the textbook applies ideas in ways that have not been outlined in the original model and this has involved some exploratory and, in some cases, incipient analyses.

Another difficulty was consistency of terms. Some labels from Cognitive Grammar overlap with existing ideas, whether everyday ('construal') or more specialist ('ground' and the associated process of 'grounding' in Cognitive Grammar; cf. the concept of discourse 'ground' in Text World Theory (Werth 1999; Gavins 2007)). To help address this and to clarify whether an idea was a Cognitive Grammar term specifically, we italicized first mentions of key ideas, and then provided a glossary of terms at the back of the book. We also openly acknowledged those cases where ideas from Cognitive Grammar intersected with existing stylistic models or ideas. Although these connections were not expanded on in detail, given the scope of the book, the text contained discussion prompts to invite readers to consider these intersections – and the potential for the Cognitive Grammar model to be supplemented by other theories – in the further questions.

In addition to gaps in the original model, there were other elements of Cognitive Grammar that were particularly difficult to translate for stylistic application. This was either because the ideas had not yet been road-tested in particular contexts (the scalability of the model had yet to be properly explicated in the original model, for example, although it is identified by Langacker (2008a) as a potential 'frontier') or because of perceived inconsistency with original explanations. One of the more cumbersome areas to 'translate', for example, was Langacker's overview or differentiation of *subjective* and *objective construal*. Generally speaking, '[s]cenes may be construed objectively when they appear more remote from a conceptualizer's own position, or more subjective when the conceptualizer is more involved to some degree' (Giovanelli and Harrison 2018: 51). The original theory argues that the more a scene is construed subjectively, the more objectively the conceptualizer is construed (because they become more 'on-stage', or more prominent). However, in texts, we know that in order for a conceptualizer to be construed objectively, subjective language needs to be used. It is the fact that Langacker talks about this movement of levels of objectivity in tandem (described by Nuttall, this volume, as 'see-sawing') that makes it complicated to untangle – and in some cases feel somewhat contradictory. In our textbook, we decided to focus our examples and analyses on one facet of this see-sawing action at a time, and simply describe how a scene (or character or object) is either more subjectively or more objectively construed, depending on how prominent, or conversely, backgrounded, a focalizer or narrator is. Part of this explanation entailed the combination of these Cognitive Grammar ideas with existing stylistic concepts, such as modality and 'shading' (Simpson 2014). An absence of modalization suggests that a scene is being construed more objectively, and we consequently pay less attention to the narrator – and vice versa. Of course sometimes texts do toggle between the two states: Harrison (2017a), for example, explores a scene from *Enduring Love* (McEwan 1997) whereby the narrator continually intrudes in on an objective account of a scene, despite the fact that he professes to be recounting it factually and mathematically. Such a style feature is often revealing about the nature of the text in question; in this case, this intrusive voice is part of the self-reflexive style of the text as a whole, which openly questions the idea of reliability throughout the narrative. Despite these difficulties, we wished to include these concepts, as these ideas are actually central, helpful and 'implicitly familiar' to us as readers, and demonstrate how

> breaking down different sentences to investigate the way actions and scenes can be portrayed affects how users interact with texts and how objective and subjective perspectives are taken. These tools then allow students to move beyond impressionistic analysis of texts, thinking vaguely how they feel when reading, to rich descriptions that make sense of those feelings.
>
> (Pihlaja 2019: 66)

In summary, stylisticians are applied linguists, looking to explain how we 'feel when reading' through 'rich descriptions' and systematic accounts of language. Our default standpoint as stylisticians is to interpret theories through an applied lens, first and foremost, and it is this position that allows us to successfully adapt what is fundamentally a theoretical grammar into a working, fit-for-purpose framework.

4.2 Illustrations and diagrams

Another key challenge for translating the original theoretical grammar into a practical, usable guide was the incorporation of pictorial and diagrammatic representations of grammatical constructions. Cognitive Grammar is often talked about in relation to its diagrams, which have a 'trademark cartoon-like' (Heath 2014: 269) style and gained a status of notoriety (Ebensgaard 2013). Langacker (2008a: vii) acknowledges this view in his *Basic Introduction*: he describes how the original 'numerous and unfortunately rather crudely drawn diagrams must have startled and dismayed readers', which he later jocularly describes in a subsection heading as 'Those diagrams' (9). However, the reasons why readers of the grammar are 'dismayed' by diagrams used in Cognitive Grammar still persist.

Arguably, part of the negative reaction to Cognitive Grammar's use of diagrams can be traced to a couple of 'misconceptions' about their functionality, which Langacker (2008a:10) identifies as:

i) that they are offered as precise and rigorous formal representations and
ii) that they are merely ad hoc, informal 'pictures'

Such criticisms or misconceptions can be aligned with the two types of diagrams used in expositions of the theory: there are both 'picture-like sketches' at the same time as others that are 'meticulously assembled from an inventory of specific notations' (Langacker 2008a: 10). It is worth highlighting, however, that Langacker's original diagrams – both the more meticulously crafted and the more picture-like – are not designed to be formal representations of grammatical structures, but are instead, as Langacker (2008a: 10) describes, intended to be 'heuristic', i.e. a hands-on way of representing how we conceptualize units of language.

A reliance on diagrams has also led some critics of Cognitive Grammar

> to the incorrect conclusion that semantic structure is claimed to be entirely visual or spatial in nature. A related misconception is that CG can only deal with visuospatial notions. On the contrary, the essential constructs proposed for semantic description (e.g. various kinds of prominence) are applicable to any cognitive domain and independent of any particular mode of presentation.
> (Langacker 2008a: 10)

To help address this problem area, in our textbook we aimed for simplicity and clarity with the diagrams and illustrations. There are some diagrams which accord with the trademark geometric shapes of the original designs such as Figure 12.1, which represents *types and instances* (Langacker 2008a: 264), but we have also included more metaphorical illustrations of particular Cognitive Grammar phenomena such as Figure 12.2, which outlines a cat's descent from a tree to illustrate how *summary scanning* (Langacker 2008a: 83) works.

Roche and Suner define 'grammatical metaphor' as the adaptation of grammatical ideas to learners' mindsets by recontextualizing ideas in everyday situations (2016: 91; see also Roche and Suner 2015). In these more metaphorical figures and illustrations, such as Figure 12.2, this recontextualization helps 'make the conceptual motivation of grammar more transparent (e.g. using a spotlight metaphor to explain the function of the subject of a sentence)' (Roche and Suner 2016: 90). Cognitive Grammar lends itself well to these kinds of metaphorical interpretations. The concept of *construal* Langacker 2008a: 4), for example, which entails how we select and focus our attention when we use different expressions, can be described using a stage metaphor (Giovanelli and Harrison 2018: 47–8; see also Langacker 1987: 129): where we sit when we watch a play will impact on our construal of how a scene from the play is represented to us.

232   *New Directions in Cognitive Grammar and Style*

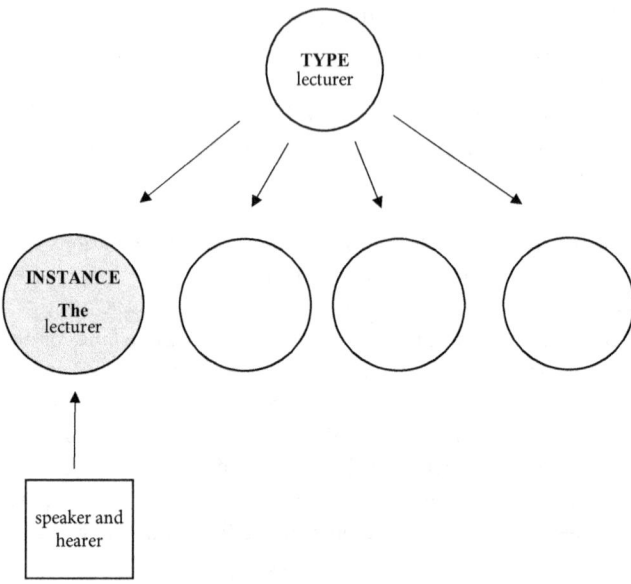

Figure 12.1 A more traditional geometric diagram representing types and instances (from Giovanelli and Harrison 2018: 109).

Figure 12.2 A metaphorical illustration of summary scanning (from Giovanelli and Harrison 2018: 68).

Such a metaphor can be used to explain spatial proximity/distance, as well as the idea of grammatical *vantage points* (Langacker 2008a: 73).

It is hoped that the content of the book is understood without recourse to the diagrams, but, as Langacker (2008a: 10) argues, the diagrams do 'provide a level of precision and explicitness sufficient for most purposes, together with a kind of usability that facilitates discovery'. Simply put, diagrams, illustrations and other visual representations or translations of linguistic concepts – metaphorical or otherwise – help develop our understanding and 'facilitation of discovery' of concepts such as iconicity (Tyler 2012; Giovanelli 2014) and other principles of embodied cognition (see Section 3) that underpin cognitive linguistic models of language. Even more helpfully, they provide more specific affordances that are not offered by text examples alone (see Stenning and Oberlander 1995). By combining the use of such grammatical metaphors with more traditional approaches to illustrating and explaining linguistic phenomena, we also hoped to demonstrate how more analogous pictorial representations can be translated simply and intuitively to the diagrammatic templates associated with the field of cognitive linguistics more generally. As Cushing (2018: 273) argues '[f]or the stylistician, meaning construction takes place within socio-cultural contexts and through a combination of text, author and reader(s), where reading is construed as a highly creative activity'. We wished to extend this 'creativity' inherent in reading to all parts of stylistics – from the explanation and application of ideas, to the interpretative, reader-focused side of the process.

4.3 Activities and extended examples

In addition to being task- and language-oriented, the book also follows a 'repertoire-driven' (Johnson 2000: 307) design, whereby we drew on our existing schemas as lecturers/teachers and our experiences of teaching language and grammar in classroom contexts in order to devise tasks specifically suited for students. In a secondary school context, there exists an anxiety around teaching grammar, with some teachers worrying about 'getting things right' in classroom contexts and applying the 'correct' labels for concepts or responses to questions (Myhill et al. 2012); arguably, such anxiety extends beyond secondary school contexts to teachers and lecturers teaching grammars at university level – and probably to the students of such courses. To support practitioners the textbook both contains a number of close analysis questions to check learning, and provides example answers for these questions. For example, there are a number of activities in the book that ask for a rigorous, fine-grained analysis that rely on the correct identification of particular phenomena, such as the activity below:

Text 4D

a. Trump *swings* the majority
b. May *leads* UK congratulations for the new president elect
c. Trump's conversation with Farage *leaves* Britain leaders red-faced
d. Trump *is* victorious
e. Inside the mind of Theresa May

1. First, identify whether the verbs (in italics) in each headline are perfective or imperfective.
2. Second, consider how this distinction impacts upon how we scan each headline. What is the effect of representing the events in this way?
3. The final headline does not have a verb. How we scan this headline?

(Giovanelli and Harrison 2018: 69)

This example enables readers to pinpoint particular instances of verb use, while also guiding the discussion of our wider interpretative implications ('What is the effect?'). In addition, as a counterbalance to these focused and more highly specified activities, the textbook also includes more macro-activities that ask participants to plan out more extended or self-directed analyses, such as the following example, taken from the further activities section in Chapter 6:

3. Find examples of extracts from both literary and non-literary texts that contain dominant and/or interesting patterns of modality. How can you relate the use of modal forms to narrative point of view, genre, purpose and implied readership?

(Giovanelli and Harrison 2018: 131)

Equally, the final chapter of the textbook provides example answers for students and teachers to cross-reference with their own analyses, as well as extended activities, which are discussion-based and theoretically driven, so that the conversation could continue externally to the ideas presented in the book:

2. The question of embodiment is interesting to analyse in respect of cultural variation. Can you find examples of how different cultures conceive and construe concepts such as 'front' and 'back' and 'time'? What implications do you think that this has for stylistic analysis drawing on cognitive grammar?

(Giovanelli and Harrison 2018: 182)

In addition to these different levels of activities, we also outline an extended analysis of a text extract at the end of each chapter. These examples draw together the various central concepts introduced in each respective chapter for a sustained and systematic application. Chapter 5 on clauses, for example, finishes with an account of the clause patterns in the Red Wedding scene from *A Storm of Swords* (Martin 2000) in the *Song of Ice and Fire* (Game of Thrones) series. Combining ideas about clause types, action chains and building textual cohesion from earlier in the chapter, this analysis specifically explores the build-up of suspense and the representation of action in this scene. It also brings in ideas represented earlier in the book in other chapters, such as domains, reference points and subjective construal to consider why this scene feels so unsettling in the first half, and disorienting in the second. It is these analyses which students of our module identified as finding most helpful about the textbook; it was noted how they help to not only further clarify the ideas, but also demonstrate how they can be used to draw out the more interesting stylistic patterns in a text and explain the significance of these language choices on our interpretation of a particular scene.

In choosing texts for these examples, and others throughout the textbook, it was important that we included a range of texts, from different contexts, to demonstrate how these ideas can be explored across texts of varying degrees of 'literariness' (see Carter and Nash 1990). It was our hope that including such a breadth of everyday texts would invite greater transparency of concepts, enabling students to draw clearer connections between form-meaning pairings as well as encounter language choices of different genres and registers, and the stylistic features of their distinctive communicative environments (Roche 2014: 331).

5. Developing a Cognitive Grammar model: Looking ahead

It is encouraging to see that ideas from Cognitive Grammar are being increasingly used to support stylistic studies. However, in order for Cognitive Grammar to grow and develop as a stylistic tool, then it needs be integrated more fully in stylistics classes and courses. This is a phenomenon that has already been observed in the burgeoning popularity and widespread application of Text World Theory, for example, which is now widely included in stylistics undergraduate modules. At Aston University, where both authors of this chapter teach courses in English language and literature, we have launched a new final year module on cognitive poetics which places Cognitive Grammar as one of the central frameworks (in fact, half of the course is an overview of Cognitive Grammar). As part of the assessment process, students are asked to apply ideas from Cognitive Grammar to analyse reader-response data (generated from either a naturalistic or an experimental study) alongside a text analysis. We hope that such a task enables students to develop their empirical skills (Hall 2014) as independent analytical readers, which consequently accords with the ethos that Carter (1996: 3) identifies as underpinning pedagogical stylistics: maintaining a classroom environment which is 'student-centred, activity based and process-oriented'.

Incorporating Cognitive Grammar in this way in degrees of English is essential for the development of the theory for, as Hall argues, 'stylistics research will often come out of classroom activity, or it will be immediately clear how an analysis or approach can offer productive affordances to teachers and learners' (Hall 2014: 239). Arguably, these affordances are even more necessary for newer than comparatively more established theories; such a collaborative process is critical for developing, refining and fine-tuning the theory. In other words, 'stylistics and pedagogy are effectively inseparable. They feed off each other, and this symbiotic relationship is as strong and healthy today as it has ever been' (Hall 2014: 249). Such a symbiotic relationship between pedagogy and the field of stylistics can also be identified through the potential for the textbook to act as a touchstone for both teaching and research, a potential acknowledged through the fact that researchers have begun to reference the textbook in their analyses (see, for examples, Browse 2018; Neary, this volume).

In conclusion, we hope that this textbook can help empower and encourage future researchers of (Cognitive) Grammar and stylistics to put these ideas into practice, and to carry out original analyses that will both synergistically improve and help develop the model and at the same time enrich the stylistician's tool-kit. Among other challenges, we have noted that a potential limitation for the development of Cognitive Grammar, in particular, has been its reputation for being complex and 'difficult', as well as the absence of accessible overviews. We hope the textbook addresses these problems, and that it can be treated as a primer to demonstrate the usefulness – and, in actual fact, the user-friendliness – of Cognitive Grammar, and its potential for new and exciting analyses at the intersection of interpretation and style.

References

Apple, M. (1986), *Teachers and Texts: A Political Economy of Class and Gender Relations in Education*, New York: Routledge.
Apple, M. (1992), 'The Text and Cultural Politics', *Educational Researcher*, 21 (7): 4–11.
Atkinson, D. (2008), 'Investigating Expertise in Textbook Writing: Insights from a Case Study of an Experienced Materials Writer at Work', in M. Khosravinik and A.Polyzou (eds), *Papers from LAEL PG 2007*, 1–20.
Bernstein, B. (1991), *The Structuring of Pedagogic Discourse, Volume 4: Class, Codes and Control*, London: Routledge.
Browse, S. (2018), 'From Functional to Cognitive Grammar in Stylistic Analysis of Golding's', *The Inheritors. Journal of Literary Semantics*, 47 (2): 121–46.
Burke, M., S. Csab, L. Week and J. Zerkowitz (2012), 'Introduction: Teaching Stylistics', in M. Burke, S. Csab, L. Week and J. Zerkowitz (eds), *Pedagogical Stylistics: Current Trends in Language, Literature and ELT*, 1–10, London: Bloomsbury.
Carter, R. (1996), 'Look Both Ways before Crossing: Developments in the Language and Literature Classroom', in R. Carter and J. McRae (eds), *Language, Literature and the Learner Creative Classroom Practice*, 1–15, Harlow: Longman.
Carter, R. and W. Nash (1990), *Seeing through Language: A Guide to Styles of Writing*, Oxford: Blackwell.
Clark, U. and S. Zyngier (2003), 'Towards a Pedagogical Stylistics', *Language and Literature*, 12 (4): 335–51.
Coffin, C. and J. Donoghue (2014), Language as Social Semiotic-Based Approach to Teaching and Learning in Higher Education, New York: John Wiley.
Coffin, C., J. Donoghue and S. North (2009), *Exploring English Grammar: From Formal to Functional*, London: Routledge.
Cushing, I. (2018), 'Stylistics Goes to School', *Language and Literature*, 27 (4): 271–85.
De Castell, S., A. Luke and C. Luke (eds) (1989), *Language, Authority and Criticism: Readings on the School Textbook*, London: Falmer Press.
De Knop, S. and T. De Rycker (2008), *Cognitive Approaches to Pedagogical Grammar: A Volume in Honour of René Dirven*, Berlin: Mouton de Gruyter.
Dolgova Jacobson, N. (2018), 'The Best of Both Worlds: Combining Cognitive Linguistics and Pedagogic Tasks to Teach English Conditionals', *Applied Linguistics*, 39 (5): 668–93.
Ebensgaard, K. (2013), 'Review of *Essentials of Cognitive* Grammar by Ronald W. Langacker', *Linguist List*, 24 (2533).
Evans, V. and A. Tyler (2004), 'Rethinking English "Prepositions of Movement": The Case of To and Through', *Belgian Journal of Linguistics*, 18 (1): 247–70.
Fontaine, L. (2012), *Analysing English Grammar: A Systemic Functional Introduction*, Cambridge: Cambridge University Press.

Gavins, J. (2007), *Text-World Theory an Introduction*, Edinburgh: Edinburgh University Press.
Gavins, J. and G. Steen (2003), *Cognitive Poetics in Practice*, London: Routledge.
Gibbons, A. and S. Whiteley (2017), *Contemporary Stylistics: Language, Cognition, Interpretation*, Edinburgh: Edinburgh University Press.
Giovanelli, M. (2014), *Teaching Grammar, Structure and Meaning*, London: Routledge.
Giovanelli, M. (2018a), '"Something Happened, Something Bad": Blackouts, Uncertainties and Event Construal in *The Girl on the Train*', *Language and Literature*, 27 (1): 38–51.
Giovanelli, M. (2018b), 'Construing the Child Reader: A Cognitive Stylistic Analysis of the Opening to Neil Gaiman's *The Graveyard Book*', *Children's Literature in Education*, 49 (2): 180–95.
Giovanelli, M. (2019), 'Construing and Reconstruing the Horrors of the Trench: Siegfried Sassoon, Creativity and Context', *Journal of Literary Semantics*, 48 (1): 85–104.
Giovanelli, M. and C. Harrison (2018), *Cognitive Grammar in Stylistics: A Practical Guide*, London: Bloomsbury.
Hall, G. (2014), 'Pedagogical Stylistics', in M. Burke (ed.), *The Routledge Handbook of Stylistics*, 239–52, London: Routledge.
Halliday, M.A.K. (1971), 'Linguistic Function and Literary Style: An Inquiry into the Language of William Golding's *The Inheritors*', in S. Chatman (ed.), *Literary Style: A Symposium*, 330–65, Oxford: Oxford University Press.
Halliday, M.A.K. (1973), *Explorations in the Functions of Language*, London: Edward Arnold.
Halliday, M.A.K. (1985), *An Introduction to Functional Grammar*, London: Edward Arnold.
Harrison, C. (2017a), *Cognitive Grammar in Contemporary Fiction*, Amsterdam: Benjamins.
Harrison, C. (2017b), 'Finding Elizabeth: Construing Memory in *Elizabeth Is Missing* by Emma Healey', *Journal of Semantics*, 46 (2): 131–51.
Harrison, C. and L. Nuttall (2019), 'Cognitive Grammar and Reconstrual: Re-experiencing Margaret Atwood's "The Freeze-Dried Groom"', in B. Neurohr and E. Stewart-Shaw (eds), *Experiencing Fictional Worlds*, 135–54, Amsterdam: Benjamins.
Harrison, C., L. Nuttall, P. Stockwell and W. Yuan (2014), *Cognitive Grammar in Literature*, Amsterdam: John Benjamins.
Hart, C. (2014), *Discourse, Grammar and Ideology: Functional and Cognitive Perspectives*, London: Bloomsbury.
Hart, C. (2016), 'Event-Frames Affect Blame Assignment and Perception of Aggression in Discourse on Political Protests: An Experimental Case Study in Critical Discourse Analysis', *Applied Linguistics*, 39 (3): 400–21.
Heath, J. (2014), 'Review of *Investigations in Cognitive Grammar* by Ronald Langacker', *Language*, 90 (1): 269–76.
Holme, R. (2009), *Cognitive Linguistics and Language Teaching*, London: Palgrave Macmillan.
Jeffries, L. and D. McIntyre (2010), *Stylistics*, Cambridge: Cambridge University Press.
Johnson, K. (2000), 'What Task Designers Do', *Language Teaching Research*, 4 (3): 301–32.
Lakoff, G. and M. Johnson (1999), *Philosophy in the Flesh: The Embodied Mind and Its Challenge to Western Thought*, New York: Basic Books.
Langacker, R.W. (2008a), *Cognitive Grammar: A Basic Introduction*, Oxford: Oxford University Press.

Langacker, R.W. (2008b), 'The Relevance of Cognitive Grammar for Language Pedagogy', in S. De Knop and T. De Rycker (eds), *Cognitive Approaches to Cognitive Grammar*, 7–36, Amsterdam: John Benjamins.

Langacker, R.W. (1987), *Foundations of Cognitive Grammar, Vol I. Theoretical Prerequisites*, Stanford: Stanford University Press.

Langacker, R.W. (1991), *Foundations of Cognitive Grammar, Vol II. Descriptive Application*, Stanford: Stanford University Press.

Langacker, R.W. (2013), *Essentials of Cognitive Grammar*, Oxford: Oxford University Press.

Littlemore, J. (2009), *Applying Cognitive Linguistics to Second Language Teaching and Learning*, London: Palgrave Macmillan.

Littlemore, J. and G. Low (2006), 'Metaphoric Competence, Second Language Learning, and Communicative Language Ability', *Applied Linguistics*, 27 (2): 268–94.

Macken-Horarik, M. (2009), 'Navigational Metalanguages for New Territory in English: The Potential of Grammatics', *English Teaching: Practice and Critique*, 8 (3): 55–69.

Macken-Horarik, M. (2012), 'Why School English Needs a "Good Enough" Grammatics (And Not More Grammar)', *Changing English: Studies in Culture and Education*, 19 (2): 179–94.

Martin, J.R.R. (2000), *Storm of Swords*, New York: Bantam Books.

McEwan, I. (1997), *Enduring Love*, London: Jonathan Cape.

McIntyre, D. (2010), 'The Place of Stylistics in the English Curriculum', in L. Jeffries and D. McIntyre (eds), *Teaching Stylistics*, 9–29, Houndmills: Palgrave Macmillan.

McIntyre, D. (2012), 'Corpus Stylistics in the Classroom', in M. Burke, S. Csabi, L. Week and J. Jerkowitz (eds), *Pedagogical Stylistics: Current Trends in Language, Literature and ELT*, 113–25, London: Continuum.

Myhill, D., S.M. Jones and H. Lines (2012), 'Re-thinking Grammar: The Impact of Embedded Grammar Teaching on Students' Writing and Students' Metalinguistic Understanding', *Research Papers in Education*, 27 (2): 139–66.

Nuttall, L. (2015), 'Attributing Minds to Vampires in Richard Matheson's *I Am Legend*', *Language and Literature*, 24 (1): 23–39.

Nuttall, L. (2017), 'Online Readers between the Camps: A Text World Theory Analysis of Ethical Positioning in *We Need to Talk About Kevin*', *Language and Literature*, 26 (2): 153–71.

Nuttall, L. (2018), *Mind Style and Cognitive Grammar: Language and Worldview in Speculative Fiction*, London: Bloomsbury.

Pihlaja, S. (2019), 'Review of *Cognitive Grammar in Stylistics* by Marcello Giovanelli and Chloe Harrison', *JALT Journal*, 41 (1): 65–7.

Radden, G. and R. Dirven (2007), *Cognitive English Grammar*, Amsterdam: John Benjamins.

Robinson, P. and N.C. Ellis (eds) (2008), *Handbook of Cognitive Linguistics and Second Language Acquisition*, London: Routledge.

Roche, J. (2014), 'Language Acquisition and Language Pedagogy', in J. Littlemore and R. Taylor (eds), *The Bloomsbury Companion to Cognitive Linguistics*, 325–51, London: Bloomsbury.

Roche, J. and F. Suñer (2015), 'Grammatik und Methode', in C. Peschel and K. Runschke (eds), *Sprachvariation und Sprachreflexion in Interkulturellen Kontexten*, 283–304, Frankfurt am Main: Peter Lang.

Roche, J. and F. Suñer (2016), 'Metaphors and Grammar Teaching', *GCLA*, 4: 89–112.

Rose, D. and J. Martin (2012), *Learning to Write, Reading to Learn: Genre, Knowledge and Pedagogy in the Sydney School*, London: Equinox.
Short, M. (1989), *Reading, Analysing and Teaching Literature*, London: Longman.
Simpson, P. (2014), *Stylistics: A Resource Book for Students*, 2nd edn, London: Routledge.
Stenning, K. and J. Oberlander (1995), 'A Cognitive Theory of Graphical and Linguistic Reasoning: Logic and Implementation', *Cognitive Science*, 19 (1): 97–140.
Stockwell, P. (2009), *Texture: A Cognitive Aesthetics of Reading*, Edinburgh: Edinburgh University Press.
Stockwell, P. (2014), 'War, Worlds and Cognitive Grammar', in C. Harrison, L. Nuttall, P. Stockwell and W. Yuan (eds), *Cognitive Grammar in Literature*, 19–34, Amsterdam: John Benjamins.
Taylor, J. (2002), *Cognitive Grammar*, New York: Routledge.
Toolan, M. (1998), *Language in Literature: An Introduction to Stylistics*, London: Edward Arnold.
Trousdale, G. (2016), 'Cognitive Linguistics', in M. Giovanelli and D. Clayton (eds), *Knowing about Language: Linguistics and the Secondary English Classroom*, 114–24, London: Routledge.
Tyler, A. (2012), *Cognitive Linguistics and Second Language Learning: Theoretical Basics and Experimental Evidence*, London: Routledge.
Tyler, A., C. Mueller and V. Ho (2010), 'Applying Cognitive Linguistics to Learning the Semantics of English *to, for* and *at*: An Experimental Investigation', *Vigo International Journal of Applied Linguistics*, 8: 181–206.
Unsworth, L. (ed) (2005), *Researching Language in Schools and Communities: Functional Linguistic Perspectives*, London: Continuum.
Verhagen, A. (2007), 'Construal and Perspectivization', in D. Geeraerts and H. Cuyckens (eds), *The Oxford Handbook of Cognitive Linguistics*, 48–81, Oxford: Oxford University Press.
Wales, K. (2014), 'The Stylistics Tool-Kit: Methods and Sub-Disciplines', in P. Stockwell and S. Whiteley (eds), *The Cambridge Handbook of Stylistics*, 13–31, Cambridge: Cambridge University Press.
Weber, J. (1996), *The Stylistics Reader*, London: Edward Arnold.
Werth, P. (1999), *Text-Worlds: Representing Conceptual Space in Discourse*, London: Longman.
Williams, G. (1998), 'Children Entering Literate Worlds: Perspectives from the Study of Textual Practices', in F. Christie and R. Misson (eds), *Literacy and Schooling: New Challenges, New Possibilities*, 18–46, London: Routledge.

13

Recontextualizing Cognitive Grammar for school teaching

Ian Cushing

1. From rules to meaning

In the following statement, the architect of Cognitive Grammar, Ronald Langacker, problematizes two issues concerning the teaching and learning of grammar:

> Learning grammar does not [...] have to be the soulless internalization of arbitrary restrictions.
>
> (Langacker 2008a: 78)

The 'soulless internalization' of grammar points to a mechanical, decontextualized pedagogy with a focus on the learning and regurgitation of metalinguistic labels and the identification of grammatical constructions, showing little concern for how grammar is used in social contexts. The 'arbitrary restrictions' refers to a conceptualization of grammar based on a series of rules and constraints, rather than a grammar based on meaning. As an alternative model, Langacker goes on to propose the affordances of a language pedagogy informed by Cognitive Grammar, which this chapter takes up and applies as a pedagogical L1 grammar in schools, drawing on wider developments, methods and applications from cognitive stylistics. The grammar presented in this chapter, then, is a 'cognitive pedagogical stylistics', building on related work and principles (e.g. Giovanelli 2017; Cushing 2018a, 2020) which have theorized and applied various aspects of cognitive stylistics to pedagogical contexts. The relative lack of classroom-based research and Cognitive Grammar pedagogy in L1 contexts is taken to be a motivating factor in exploring this further.

2. Research context

English teachers in schools in England are working with National Curriculum 2014 (henceforth NC 2014) (e.g. Department for Education 2013), a body of policy documents which set out the prescribed classroom content for individual subjects. In the last two years of secondary school, English is separated into two distinct qualifications of 'literature' and 'language', although there are an increasing number of contact points between these two subjects, which might be understood as stylistics, even though English teachers might not use this phrase themselves (see Cushing 2018b for an overview of stylistics in schools). One significant aspect of NC 2014 is that it features a much-increased focus on grammatical content, with students required to learn about grammatical form-function and how writers use language to construct meanings and create literary effects (see Harris and Helks 2018). The grammatical content of NC 2014 includes an extensive glossary of grammatical terms (Department for Education 2013: 7–25), based on what might be called 'traditional', clause-level grammar, which has long been the prototypical model used in schools (see Van Rijt et al. 2019 for an overview of L1 linguistic concepts in grammar education). In this sense, 'traditional' grammar terms are largely derived from formal-structural grammars.

Curriculum policy in England is focused on content and includes very little detail on pedagogy. Thus, teachers have a certain amount of autonomy in being able to adapt their teaching styles and methods in whatever way they see fit. However, despite the increased emphasis on grammar content at policy level, English teachers typically have limited linguistic subject knowledge, partly as a result of the majority of English teachers entering the profession from a literature background, often citing a passion for literature as a motivating factor in choosing to enter the profession (e.g. Ellis 2003). Content and pedagogical methods for grammatical and linguistic concepts on teacher training courses are typically low, and many English teachers can come to see grammar as being about rules and regulations (Cushing 2019), and language work as intimidating, difficult and a threat to their own professional identity, especially those who identify as 'literature specialists' (Watson 2015). Recently, a body of work has repeatedly demonstrated that if English teachers are given access to linguistic and pedagogical training that foregrounds a cognitive-functional construal of grammar – rather than a set of formal rules – then this can have a positive, transformative impact on their own conceptualizations of grammar (Watson 2015), their own professional identity (Giovanelli 2015) and their classroom practice (Myhill 2018; Cushing 2019). It follows then that a meaning-orientated grammar such as Cognitive Grammar has huge potential when actualized not only as a stylistic tool (e.g. Harrison et al. 2014), but as a pedagogical tool for engaging in practical, investigative language work in the classroom. Indeed, a growing research movement combined with teacher workshops and outreach work is building a productive and energetic time for pedagogical stylistics in the UK, yet the specific application of Cognitive Grammar as an L1 pedagogical grammar in secondary schools has been virtually non-existent, despite a large research output on cognitive approaches to grammar in L2 settings. I discuss some of these studies and the nature of Cognitive Grammar as a pedagogical grammar in the following section.

3. Cognitive Grammar as a pedagogical grammar

Cognitive Grammar is a grammar built around meaning, which interprets grammatical form in conceptual ways (e.g. THING for noun; PROCESS for verb; ACTION CHAIN for clause). Both lexical and syntactical structures are inherently meaningful, with words polysemous in nature and existing as part of a rich semantic network, working as triggers which call up an individuals' experiences and memories of the world. The focus on meaning presents Cognitive Grammar as a potentially attractive grammar for English teachers who wish to integrate aspects of language work into their teaching, given that the perceived 'rules' and 'technicalities' of grammar are the things that can make grammar appear intimidating (Cushing 2019), amidst a culture of 'suspicion' of the value of linguistic terminology in English teaching (see Harris and Helks 2018). Given that NC 2014 grammar is based on formal-structuralist frameworks, an important part of the 'recontextualization process' (Bernstein 1990) in building a pedagogical Cognitive Grammar is 'mapping on' Cognitive Grammar concepts to NC 2014 terms, without simply giving teachers and students additional metalinguistic terms to handle. In the analysis sections that follow, I demonstrate how Cognitive Grammar terms provide a conceptual and functional interpretation of traditional terms, and so provide an additional 'layer' of grammatical description rather than a replacement.

This chapter began with a quotation from Langacker (2008a) in which he sets out to argue for a pedagogical Cognitive Grammar. Langacker's argument rests on the embodied, 'meaningfulness' of Cognitive Grammar and its conceptual basis, in the sense that it is a description of language which begins with what students already know about the world: vision, spatial orientation, movement and force. He suggests teachers having 'explicit awareness' of Cognitive Grammar may lead to insights about how language works, even if these are simply used to guide pedagogical decisions in the form of material writing, classroom talk and text analysis (Langacker 2008a: 85). Although a useful rationale, Langacker's outline is wholly theoretical in nature and restricted in terms of pedagogical guidance or educational theory, which he does recognize as a limitation and calls for cognitive grammarians to conduct classroom-based research in order to probe the nature of a pedagogical Cognitive Grammar (Langacker 2008a: 84). Numerous other works exploring the scope and potential of cognitive linguistics in education (e.g. Pütz et al. 2001; Achard 2008; De Knop and De Rycker 2008; Robinson and Ellis 2008; Holme 2009; Littlemore 2009; Tyler 2012) argue that a cognitive approach offers a conceptually sound and accessible way into earning and teaching about language, where meaning takes priority and language is framed as a series of conventionalized patterns rather than by/as abstract rules and constraints. Again, although theoretically convincing and foundational, a limitation of such works is the lack of empirical evidence from the classroom. Work that has involved empirical exploration of Cognitive Grammar concepts in the classroom has tended to focus on one specific grammatical construction and is almost completely focused on L2 grammar pedagogy. For example, Verspoor and Huong's (2008) work on the English article system drew on the notion of construal to teach definiteness/indefiniteness; both Bielak and Pawlak (2013) and Niemeier and Reif (2008) explored the semantic function of the perfect/progressive aspect, and Taniguchi (2018) theorizes the notion of action chains to suggest methods for teaching canonical clause structures in English and Japanese.

In terms of L1 applications, the research output is limited, but growing. Giovanelli (2014a) provides a book-length treatment on pedagogical principles and theoretical ideas for the application of cognitive linguistics to the teaching of grammar and meaning, including a section on action chains (Giovanelli 2014a: 78–82), one of the aspects of Cognitive Grammar which this chapter explores. Trousdale (2016) also provides an outline of what cognitive linguistics might offer to teachers, focusing on word meaning, conceptual metaphor and cognitive stylistics. Classroom-based research has focused on developing the pedagogical applications of cognitive stylistics as a discourse-grammar, specifically Text World Theory (Giovanelli 2017; Cushing 2018a, 2020). The relatively low amount of research investigating Cognitive Grammar as an L1 pedagogy is a motivating factor for the work presented here, especially in how clause-level concepts from Cognitive Grammar can be integrated into discourse-grammars.

4. Clause patterns in Cognitive Grammar

This section outlines how Cognitive Grammar treats clause structure, given that this was the focus of the classroom research. For many L1 English teachers, clauses are one of the more difficult aspects of grammar to teach (Myhill 2018) with teachers often over-relying on schematic or proxy definitions which can lead to conceptual confusion in students. Aside from inadequate training in grammar, which I discussed in Section 2, I suggest that another inhibitor to metasyntactic understanding can be the terms themselves. Clausal terms such as 'subject', 'object' and 'adverbial' are not particularly intuitive labels, and when coupled with a teacher's low grammatical knowledge and high grammatical anxiety, it is perhaps easy to imagine why confusion and misunderstandings can arise.

As an alternative framework, Cognitive Grammar offers a description of linguistic form that is motivated by correlations between grammatical concepts and embodiment, and so immediately forges a connection between language and experience. Grammatical notions such as 'subject' and 'verb' are simply manifestations of *image-schemas*, which are derived from repeated embodied experiences in the world (Langacker 2008b: 32–5). For example, transitive clauses with verbs denoting action and movement are seen to be encodings of one thing affecting another thing, such as fingers pressing computer keys, people pushing doors open, people kicking balls and so on. These kinds of structures – whereby energy is transferred from one thing to another thing – are called *action chains* (Langacker 2008b: 355), represented schematically in Figure 13.1.

In an action chain, circles represent the participants (prototypically nominals) involved in the events. Double arrows represent the transfer of energy. Figure 13.1 represents a schematic instantiation of a canonical transitive clause such as 'the students smashed the library', where a subject-agent (or *energy source*) transfers energy to an object-patient (or *energy sink*), whose physical state is affected as a result. In such canonical clauses, a subject-agent is most likely to act as the figure (hence the bold circle) or the 'head' of the action chain, since it is this nominal that our attention is first directed to. The ENERGY metaphor is fleshed out with the

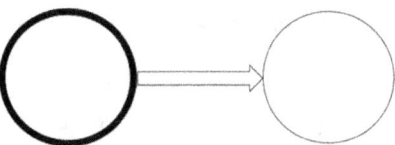

Figure 13.1 An action chain.

description of the 'billiard-ball model', whereby objects supply and soak up energy, and functions as a means to describe

> our conception of objects moving through space and impacting one another through forceful physical contact. Some objects supply the requisite energy through their own internal resources; others merely transmit or absorb it.
> (Langacker 2008b: 355)

Cognitive Grammar's treatment of clause structure is thus heavily metaphorical, relying on both linguistic metaphor ('energy'; 'billiard balls') and visual metaphor (diagrams; see Giovanelli and Harrison, this volume) to explain how CLAUSE STRUCTURE IS ENERGY TRANSFER (see Roche and Suñer 2016 for an extended discussion of this metaphor in relation to pedagogy). While the above has been a simplified description of clause structure in Cognitive Grammar (see Langacker 2008b: 354–405 for a detailed account), I show in the following sections how the concepts that underpin this kind of grammatical construction – the transfer of energy from one thing to another thing – can be exploited and used as a teaching tool.

5. Methods and approaches

This section outlines the methods and approaches in assessing the potential of Cognitive Grammar as a pedagogical tool with young learners and with teachers who identified as 'non-experts' in linguistics. The data from this chapter is taken from two one-hour lessons, taught by two different teachers, with Year 8 (age 12–13) students in a secondary school in London, UK. The teachers (Rosie and Daisy, both pseudonyms) were participants in a larger study looking at the application of cognitive stylistics and Text World Theory (Werth 1999; Gavins 2007) as a pedagogical tool for teaching poetry (see Cushing 2018a, 2020). The research included a number of lessons which featured concepts from Cognitive Grammar, namely construal, action chains and energy transfer. These were used alongside the concept of 'text-worlds' from Text World Theory. Text-worlds are mental representations of language, triggered by linguistic content and elaborated on by individual knowledge and memories (see Gavins 2007: 35–52). The teaching materials were informed by a series of pedagogical principles, part of which framed grammar as inherently meaningful and as a series of choices. Both participant teachers came from literature specialist backgrounds and had received very little training in grammar, stylistics or linguistics prior to their involvement in the project.

In Section 2, I discussed how teachers' typically low linguistic knowledge can serve as a serious barrier to developments in grammar pedagogy, and so a key part of the research was the training of participant teachers. Over a process of eighteen months, I trained Rosie and Daisy in key aspects of Text World Theory and Cognitive Grammar and we collaborated together by designing a series of lessons informed by these ways of thinking about language and experience, constructing a pedagogical grammar which cut across clause and discourse-levels of language description. This training took place in a series of formal workshops and informal conversations, and both teachers read some of the more accessible literature in cognitive stylistics and Cognitive Grammar (e.g. Gavins 2007; Giovanelli and Harrison 2018).

Rosie and Daisy delivered the lessons with their respective classes, and these were filmed and then transcribed by myself. There were twenty-five students in Rosie's class, and thirty-four students in Daisy's class, all of whom were native speakers of English. The data from the lessons which inform this chapter constitutes two hours of video recordings which resulted in 12,133 transcribed words and copies of all students' written work that took place during the lessons. Transcribed data was then thematically coded using NVivo software, using an inductive approach. The codes that are relevant for this chapter are *metalinguistic discourse* and *literary linguistic interpretation*, which steer the structure of the analysis section that follows. The two lessons of interest for this chapter were based on the poem *Dawn* by William Carlos Williams (Williams 1917), which is shown here and followed by a brief stylistic analysis (line numbers have been added):

Dawn

1 Ecstatic bird songs pound
2 the hollow vastness of the sky
3 with metallic clinkings -
4 beating color up into it
5 at a far edge, - beating it, beating it
6 with rising, triumphant ardor, -
7 stirring it into warmth,
8 quickening in it a spreading change, -
9 bursting wildly against it as
10 dividing the horizon, a heavy sun
11 lifts himself - is lifted -
12 bit by bit above the edge
13 of things, - runs free at last
14 out into the open -! lumbering
15 glorified in full release upward –
16 songs cease.

Dawn features three entities involved in an action chain: the 'birds', 'the sky' and 'the sun'. The first transferal of energy is airflow from the lungs of the birds to the surrounding atmosphere, a transferal which is not textually marked but is implicated metonymically, given that 'bird songs' are an entity which cannot function as an energy source by themselves. The noun phrase 'ecstatic bird songs' functions as a subject-agent and transfers energy to the noun phrase 'the hollow vastness of the sky' which functions as direct object-patient, via the verb 'pound'. The verb is a 'change of state' process (Taylor 2002: 414) given that 'pounding' something changes its shape or form. 'With metallic clinkings' has an adverbial-instrument function/theta-role, adding a sense of sound to the text-world of the poem, especially given that the sky is described as 'hollow', which generates a rather resonant and reverberant cognitive-acoustic effect. The object changes form to a pronoun, 'it', in Line 4, which is repeated five times, the last reference being on Line 9. In Lines 4, 8 and 9, 'it' is not a direct object of the verb, but of a preposition ('into', 'in' and 'against', respectively). The texture of the poem is, to an extent, weaved out of these multiple references to the same object, constructing a dynamic text-world with a repeating motion, and a high transferal rate of energy source to energy sink. The choice of verbs increases this sense of dynamism, with the *-ing* non-finite participle clauses such as 'beating', 'stirring' and 'bursting', contributing to the energetic fictional world. In Cognitive Grammar, non-finite participles invoke an *immediate scope* (Langacker 2008b: 120), whereby the viewing frame does not include the beginning or end point of the activity denoted by the verb, and so can make the events depicted feel close and intimate (see Giovanelli 2014b: 150–2). In Line 10, 'a heavy sun' becomes the subject, after having received the sonic energy from the bird songs in the previous nine lines. This first appears in an active construction as an agent – 'lifts himself' – and then switches to a passive construction as a patient – 'is lifted' – with the by-phrase omitted grammatically, but marked semantically by the previous presence and resonance of the 'bird songs'. Gradually, the sun takes on the role of energy source, although this is only fully realized in the final line, when the bird songs end and have zero energy, marked by the intransitive verb 'cease'. The 'lag' of the sun fully becoming the new energy source here is marked by the initial toggling between active and passive voice, the noun phrase 'bit by bit', the adverbial in the clause 'runs free at last' and the verb 'lumbering'. All in all, the image is one of the sun slowly waking, groggily at first, but finally released. Clause structure is a particularly important textual pattern in achieving such an effect.

There are, of course, other things to say about the poem but this is not the place nor focus of this chapter. The next section explores what young readers have to say about the poem in light of a Cognitive Grammar pedagogy, and so combines my own introspective analysis with reader-response data, as per the principles in much recent work in cognitive stylistics (e.g. Nuttall 2017).

6. Cognitive Grammar in the classroom

The participant teachers and I collaborated on the design of the teaching materials, with an aim to apply the concepts of construal and energy transfer as a contextualized, semantically motivated grammar pedagogy which was sensitive to the nature of personal literary responses. The lesson content was as follows:

1) Students read a copy of the poem and discuss their initial responses to it, including the kind of text-worlds (Werth 1999; Gavins 2007) that the poem triggered for them. This is explored in section 6.1.
2) A discussion of energy transfer in the poem, exploring the various energy sources, trajectories and sinks, how these correlate to clausal elements such as subject, object and adverbial, and how these patterns contribute to the meaning of the text. This is explored in section 6.2.
3) Exploration and application of a taxonomy of verbs based on systemic functional linguistics (material, cognition, verbal) (see Halliday and Matthiessen 2004). This is explored in section 6.2.
4) A 'textual intervention' (Pope 1995) activity: in small groups, creating short movement pieces or 'kinegrams' (Lapaire 2007) to represent the different grammatical entities in the poem and the nature of energy transfer, embodying aspects of the clause. This is explored in section 6.3.

Step 1 was designed to provoke an initial, personal response to the text, whereby students' accounts of text-worlds were shared in an act of collaborative reading. Steps 2–3 were designed to provide students with a conceptual understanding of 'energy' and its relation to language before looking in detail at the syntactic patterns responsible for the transferal of energy. Step 4 is an instance of textual intervention (Pope 1995), whereby new texts are created as part of a stylistic analysis.

At first glance, it may appear that the tasks above are linguistically complex and require a thorough understanding of cognitive-functional grammars, being perhaps more reminiscent of university stylistics seminars. However, I suggest that it is important not to see these activities as 'watering down' Cognitive Grammar theory but simply adapting it to suit the needs of a different context, providing young readers with investigative opportunities to talk about the language of literary texts. Given their inclusion on the primary curriculum, students were familiar with grammatical terms such as subject, verb, object and adverbial, and both teachers felt confident in the Cognitive Grammar concepts that we had discussed in reference to the poem. The following sections explore textual traces of the Cognitive Grammar pedagogy, which occurred in the classroom as a result of teachers and students engaging with the activities above.

6.1 Subjective construal, text-worlds and reader-response

An important part of any pedagogical stylistic is to first establish student responses to a text, and so I begin my analysis of the classroom data here. After reading the poem, students were invited to share the text-worlds that the poem had constructed for them in their mind, and the kind of affective and personal reactions they had experienced during reading it. In Cognitive Grammar terms, students became conceptualizers who jointly attended to a conceived scene (Verhagen 2007: 60, see also Nuttall 2017: 167). Initial responses were geared around the vivid text-worlds of the poem, for example:

> Well I just saw one still image like it was a painting almost (.) and there's a flock of birds with really sharp pointed wings and pointed beaks flying against the sort of silvery gold and background somewhere in the Amazon rainforest and it was just very (.) it looks almost like an oil painting (Felix)

> I don't know why but I saw it like a cartoon world and the sun is like kind of like growing and growing and then there's like loads of trumpets (Gabby)

> I think it starts with just the birds singing but then you see somebody open their window and then you just see everything start to change around them and then you see the sun and you hear the metallic clinkings and you see the metallic sky just crack with colour and all the heat and all the warmth and the colour just blend into it and at the end it's describing how (.) it might be that (.) I think the end it really tells me that this is about freedom not anything else because runs free it's about freedom it's not just about the sun (Oscar)

Grammatical construal is not just a sentence-level process, but a way of understanding responses to whole-text meaning (Popova 2002: 52; Stockwell 2009: 171; Nuttall 2017: 166). Put this way, responses (or construals) to literature operate as the 'negotiated conceptualization of the situations presented in literary texts' (Nuttall 2017: 166). The adjective 'negotiated' is especially important here, given that the reader-response data I am working with is multi-participatory in nature, with text-worlds being negotiated and built collaboratively in a social reading space. Felix and Gabby's turns construe the same state of affairs (the poem) in differently linguistically encoded ways – comparing their mental image to another visual modality ('an oil painting'; 'a cartoon world'). Although these construals are both triggered by the same text, they are fleshed out by their own background knowledge of birds, rainforests and other entities from their own experiences of the world. The Cognitive Grammar notion of encyclopedic/conceptual semantics is clearly applicable here, something advocated by Langacker in his rationale for a pedagogical Cognitive Grammar:

> Words are merely prompts for an elaborate process of meaning construction that draws on the full range of our mental resources. An appreciation of their richness and flexibility would seem essential for effective language instruction.
>
> (Langacker 2008a: 73)

More specifically, responses to the poem in the classroom were instances of subjective construal, since the conceptualizers were voicing their own personal responses. Textual traces of subjective construal are apparent in a number of different forms, such as I-predicate statement + cognition verb structures (e.g. 'I think'; 'I just saw'), negation (e.g. 'I don't know why') and modality (e.g. 'it might be that (.) I think the end it really tells me that this is about freedom'). When subjectively construing the poem, students placed themselves 'on stage' as part of the conceived scene, which presented their ideas to be assessed by others in the environment. Subjective construals are highly personal responses to literary texts, which for many students runs a risk of their ideas being assigned a 'wrong' answer by their teacher or peers. The Cognitive Grammar pedagogy promoted and legitimized personal responses in the sense that readers were encouraged to talk about the world-building process, relate this to their own subjective experiences and memories, and ultimately engage in what Giovanelli and Mason (2015) describe as 'authentic' reading, where responses to texts are not heavily refereed by teachers.

Incorporating the notion of construal into a grammar pedagogy frames grammar as a series of choices and options, much in the same way that systemic functional linguistics treats language as a semiotic resource for making meaning (Halliday and Matthiessen 2004: 31–48). During the training, participant teachers were encouraged to think about grammar in terms of construal, patterns and choices rather than rules and constraints. For both Rosie and Daisy, this was a radical re-conceptualization of what grammar is, and something that they both talked positively about during the fieldwork. For example, after the lesson on energy transfer, Rosie said:

> I've never thought about clauses that way before (.) when I was teaching clauses before I'd always just done it like rules and would say you have to have a subject here and verb here and so on (.) but I think that way of looking at it is just fantastic because it gives it meaning and they just instantly apply it to a piece of literature that they are looking at and the grammar just sits so nicely into that (.) it's like it's not this separate thing it's just part of reading and enjoying the poem and thinking about word choices and that's what I want to do with my grammar teaching.
>
> (Rosie)

6.2 Energy transfer and clause analysis

During the exploratory discussions of the poem, some students picked up on the high sense of dynamism, energy and movement in the poem, discourse which served as a primer for the introduction of the energy transfer concept. For instance:

> at the beginning I sort of imagined like the birds are caged up and then and then as it moves they are freed (Millie)
>
> I think it's starts off like the sky is quite dark (.) but as the birds start singing it says like after a few minutes it says the they run free at last and I think that's talking about the sun so I think it's about a sunrise so then all of a sudden it's like there's an orange sky and loads of lights (Leo)
>
> ok well I think (.) it starts quite static and then you get lots of (.) bursting singing and rising and beating which is all very like (.) 3D kind of action (.) very big and loads of motion (Louisa)

At this point in the lesson, the teachers started to introduce the concept of energy transfer, shifting the discourse towards a discussion of clausal elements such as subjects, verbs and objects. Importantly, this only happened once students themselves had started to touch upon the idea of energy themselves, and so the introduction of the grammatical concept only happened once there was a 'clear motivation for it' (Stockwell 2007: 20). This order is in line with Giovanelli (2014a: 8), who argues that a cognitive approach to grammar teaching is 'concept-led'. In this approach, the conceptual or embodied basis of grammar (e.g. energy transfer) provides an ideal starting point for the exploration of grammatical form (e.g. clause structure), because it grounds students' interpretation of grammatical form in conceptual ways, drawing on what they already know about the world (e.g. movement, force and energy).

New information added into a discourse event is a process of incrementation (Werth 1999: 289), whereby knowledge that was previously private becomes shared or mutual. In Cognitive Grammar terms, the introduction of the ENERGY concept into the classroom discourse is an instance of *grounding* (Langacker 2008b: 259), whereby participants are prompted to establish 'mental contact' (Langacker 2008b: 83) between two entities. The particular construal that was used by the teachers to ground the concept of ENERGY was metaphorical. Cognitive Grammar makes extensive use of metaphor in its description, and the ENERGY TRANSFER metaphor served a 'pedagogic metaphor' function (Boyd 2002, see also Semino 2008: 134) in that it was used to help explain and describe theories or concepts. Given that grammar and aspects of grammar are abstract, complex systems, they are perfect candidates to be construed metaphorically. The concept of energy transfer was incremented in three modes of metaphor: linguistic, visual and gestural. Linguistic metaphors were used by Rosie and Daisy in their first explanation of the concept:

> so who is doing (.) who or what is exhibiting or carrying out the action of the energy (.) and who or what is receiving the energy of each verb?
>
> (Rosie)

As is popular in Cognitive Grammar descriptions, teachers also made use of visual metaphor to explain the concept, shown in Figure 13.2, which is a PowerPoint slide used in the lessons.

Figure 13.2 shows a version of the typical 'billiard ball' diagram used throughout descriptions of Cognitive Grammar (e.g. Langacker 2008b: 356) and explained in Section 4, applied to Lines 1–2 of the poem. Diagrams in Cognitive Grammar are schematic and image-metaphorical representations of linguistic concepts,

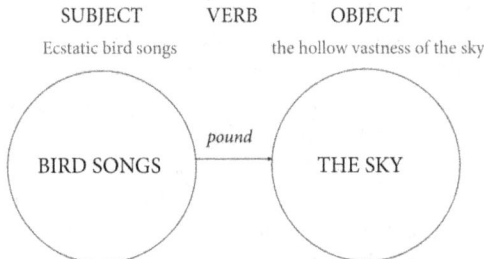

Figure 13.2 The CLAUSE STRUCTURE IS ENERGY TRANSFER visual metaphor.

represented spatially through the use of conventional symbols (e.g. arrows and shapes). Descriptions of Cognitive Grammar are heavily multimodal in this way, and so it made sense for a Cognitive Grammar pedagogy to do the same. In educational contexts, a typical pedagogical function of visuals and diagrams is to provide students with variable representations of abstract concepts, in order to develop understanding (Kress et al. 2001; Eilam and Gilbert 2014). The diagram helped to make explicit the ENERGY TRANSFER metaphor, building on student discourse about energy, dynamism and movement.

Students discussed the choice of verbs and their textual qualities, picking up on the foregrounded material processes and distribution of *-ing* forms. For instance, from Daisy's class:

> Daisy: so what do you notice about the types of verbs that the writer has decided to use? (.) and how would you describe those verbs? Minnie?
> Minnie: I think they are quite fast-paced like beating and stirring and dividing (.) they're all happening quite quickly and incredibly fast (.) and it gives the whole poem a kind of fast kind of energy
> Felix: they have (.) they pack some punch and power into them
> Daisy: ok so why do you think that is? why do you think there are so many action verbs?
> Harry: well probably because they're describing like physical things (.) like with the birds and how the birds move against the sky

And from Rosie's class:

> Rosie: and what else do you notice about the verbs? is there a pattern you can see?
> Grace: they all end in ing so it's like something that is happening right now (.) like it's now (.) as if we're seeing it happen
> Rosie: right excellent (.) like we're there and it's happening live as we read

In previous lessons, students had been introduced to a version of Halliday's verb processes taxonomy (Halliday and Matthiessen 2004) and drew on the metalinguistic label of 'action verb' in order to help qualify their responses about 'energy' with close reference to the text. Similarly, Grace's idea about the conceptual and deictic immediacy of the '-ing' forms ('it's like something that is happening right now') touches on the Cognitive Grammar notion of immediate scope, legitimatized by Rosie's response ('like we're there and it's happening live as we read'), which in turn draws on the READING IS TRANSPORTATION metaphor (Gerrig 1993; Stockwell 2009: 80–1). Although neither teacher nor student uses Cognitive Grammar terms at this point, I suggest that the underlying idea of immediate scope is apparent in the discourse. Immediate/maximal scope and the textual effect of progressive versus perfect forms of the verb had been discussed during the teacher training, and we spoke about the significance of these choices as a stylistic device. The extracts above are an example of this linguistic knowledge manifesting itself in classroom discourse, albeit in subtle ways, to support literary interpretations in metalinguistic discourse, much in the way that Langacker's original vision for a pedagogical Cognitive Grammar is laid out (Langacker 2008a).

Steps 2–3 of the lesson design focused on nominal and adverbial groups in the poem and the role that these played in action chains. Students were able to apply their existing grammatical knowledge of subjects, objects and adverbials with relative ease, marking up the text and discovering clausal patterns in the process. After this, they were encouraged to use the ENERGY TRANSFER metaphor to help validate and supplement their findings. For instance:

> Daisy: ok so can somebody explain the process they went through thinking about energy transfer and these parts of the clause? go on Ava
> Ava: well at the beginning it's the bird songs who are the subject and the sky is the object (.) and the bird songs are beating against it (.) the sky keeps being repeated (.) the whole thing is about the birds like hitting against that and giving it the energy (.) and then later the sun becomes the subject when it says a heavy sun lifts himself as that's now the thing that has the energy and that's where the energy ends up
> Daisy: ok good (.) so we have this transfer of energy from the bird songs to the sky to the sun and that's mirrored in the way that the clause structure changes

Here, Ava and Daisy blend 'traditional' metalinguistic terms (subject, object) with a Cognitive Grammar term (energy transfer) in order to arrive at a text-driven, stylistically sound interpretation of the clause structures in the poem. Of the repeated object-energy sink, rendered as the pronoun 'it' (where the subject-energy source is 'ecstatic bird songs') in Lines 4, 5, 7, 8 and 9, Finn suggested that:

> it's quite repetitive (.) it's all one subject so at this point there's not really any transfer of energy [...] it keeps on going it's like they're doing it and doing it and doing it and not stopping.
>
> (Finn)

Importantly, the metalinguistic discourse helped students to arrive at a whole-text meaning of what they thought the poem was about, meaning that the grammar pedagogy was embedded into a discussion of literary reader response, in line with the principles that pedagogical stylisticians generally argue for (e.g. Cushing 2018b):

> Ava: it's like we said at the beginning (.) I think the poem is all about energy and how things in nature are wanting to burst out but they need energy to do that (.) it's kind of a poem about life and how life is always changing
> Daisy: ooh I like that (.) it's about life cycles lovely idea

Ava's conclusion of poem being about 'life cycles' is stylistically sound – a response shaped not by vague impressionism but by close attention to how an author's syntactic patterns and lexical choices construct meaning in the mind of a reader, and showing awareness of grammatical patterns at clause and discourse-level.

6.3 Embodying the clause

This section is based on classroom discourse and events as a result of step 4 of the lessons. In this step, students performed an instance of textual intervention (Pope 1995), a critical-creative pedagogy for engaging with the language of texts. To investigate the significance of energy transfer in the poem further, students completed a movement activity, where they physically represented aspects of clause structure. Given that Cognitive Grammar rests on the fundamental principle that linguistic forms derived from embodied perceptions and physical experiences, it makes sense that a pedagogical Cognitive Grammar should make use of physical movement in some way or another (see also Giovanelli 2014a). Embodiment is a special type of construal (Littlemore 2009: 127), which, in this context, allows humans to use their bodies to represent a linguistic idea or concept, to make explicit and deepen their understandings of abstract concepts. Students were placed into groups of two or three, each of these groups given a line from the poem and asked to simply 'recreate the movement and energy in the poem through a physical interpretation' (Rosie). After a few minutes of group work, the class then performed the poem alongside the teacher reading it out.

As an illustration of the kind of work students engaged in, Figure 13.3 shows two images of three students' reconstrual of Lines 1–3. From left to right, the image shows Jonny, Felix and Miles, each standing in for a different grammatical function and a different role in the action chain. The reconstrual makes use of metonymy, namely PERSON FOR CLAUSAL ELEMENT. This applies Lapaire's (2007) *Grammar in Motion* project and the use of 'kinegrams', where students substitute their bodies for aspects of grammatical form or function. Kinegrams are 'postural and gestural analogues of core grammatical phenomena' (Lapaire 2007: 7; see also Giovanelli 2014a). Felix, in the centre, is the agent-subject-energy source, assuming the participant of the 'ecstatic bird songs'. He holds Jonny's arm and repeatedly strikes it, in a physical enactment of the verb 'pound', a word which invokes a high degree of force. These physical strikes

Figure 13.3 Energy transfer embodied.

transfer kinetic energy to Jonny, who assumes the role of the patient-object-energy sink, rendered as 'the hollow vastness of the sky'. As a result of this energy transfer, Jonny repeatedly moves both arms in an up-down motion to signify the change of state. To the right is Miles, who assumes the role of the instrument-adverbial ('with metallic clinkings'). Miles uses a prop in his metonymic role, repeatedly tapping a pen against a metal bottle which represents the sound marked in the text.

The kinegram then shows students reconstruing the grammatical structure and meaning of a literary in a highly engaged and creative way. This active, student-centred, participatory approach to grammar teaching allowed students to physically experience the significance of clause patterns, using gesture and their own bodies as a symbolic resource to explore how grammatical structures are not semantically empty but encode dynamic connections between language and physical experience. In a conversation I had with Tim, a student in Rosie's class, he suggested that thinking about energy and clauses was both different and interesting, when compared against previous experiences of grammar teaching:

> IC: have you ever thought about subjects and objects like that before in terms of energy?
> Tim: not really
> IC: and what do you think about that way of thinking about it?
> Tim: I think it's quite interesting because it's usually just like what types of words are used verbs adjectives or whatever (.) but this is a lot more like what's <u>happening</u> then and what that word does to other things

This section has argued for the place of embodied learning within a Cognitive Grammar pedagogy, which I suggest is a natural aspect to include given the embodied basis of Cognitive Grammar theory. Although explored in relation to prototypical subject–verb–object clause structures in literary fiction, the same principles might be applied to other aspects of the clause in a range of different text types, in considering how grammar is more than a set of disembodied structures (also see Harrison 2018).

7. Conclusion

This chapter has presented the first classroom-based study to explore the value and suitability of Cognitive Grammar as a pedagogical grammar in L1 English education, building on theoretical work from recent years (e.g. De Knop and De Rycker 2008; Langacker 2008a; Giovanelli 2014a). It also builds on a growing interest in using cognitive stylistics within schools (Giovanelli 2017; Cushing 2018a, 2020).

As demonstrated throughout this chapter, Cognitive Grammar provides a way of thinking about language which is radically different to the traditional grammatical models which dominate curriculum policy in England, and so requires teachers to reconceptualize what they think and know about grammar. I would like to foreground that in the pedagogy discussed above, Cognitive Grammar terms were not intended as a replacement set of metalinguistic labels, but provided an additional level of description, and these terms appeared to be useful because they are (a) inherently meaningful and (b) conceptually grounded. The 'success' of the Cognitive Grammar pedagogy, then, was demonstrated in the students' responses, where they blended new and existing metalinguistic concepts as a way of deepening their understanding of how literary language constructed a reading experience in their own minds, and explored the embodied nature of grammar as a gestural resource.

While this chapter has been limited to a relatively small dataset and selected aspects of Cognitive Grammar, it nevertheless demonstrates the potentiality of Cognitive Grammar as a pedagogy which teachers may draw on in their planning, thinking and classroom talk. Although the teaching materials used in the research were based on a literary text with canonical clause structures, it seems to me that the Cognitive Grammar notions of construal and energy transfer are applicable to a wide range of teaching contexts, including other literary texts, non-literary discourse and creative writing. The scope for exploring other aspects of Cognitive Grammar in various pedagogical settings is expansive and exciting, especially when combined with compatible discourse-grammars such as Text World Theory, to build pedagogies which offer English teachers an accessible, meaning-driven model of language concerned with both clause and discourse. Perhaps most importantly, these kinds of pedagogies, with stylistics at their heart, reject reductive and false divisions between 'language' and 'literary' studies and emphasize descriptive, exploratory linguistics rather than the narrow, clause-level version of grammar as contained within current education policy in England.

Nonetheless, the success and nature of any grammar pedagogy are defined by the socio-cultural context in which it is delivered. Within English education, certainly in England, this context is politically complicated. Variables such as teacher knowledge, professional identities and world-views about the place of language study in the curriculum result in a challenging context in which to conduct grammar pedagogy research. The teachers involved in this study were part of a collaborative research project which was sensitive to the contextual conditions of their professional identities and subject specialisms. Such contextual concerns should be very much part of the design of any pedagogical grammar. Because Cognitive Grammar – and even stylistics in general – is unlikely to be part of prototypical English teachers' repertoire, teachers must have access to training if they are to develop their subject knowledge in these areas (Cushing 2018b). This is a systemic, policy-level issue, and an increasing concern amidst government cuts to school funding which has a serious impact on training opportunities. I also argue that English teachers who identify as 'literature specialists' must be willing to engage in developing their own knowledge about language, in the same way that 'language specialists' must do for literature (see, for example, Giovanelli 2015). In short, any limitation of a Cognitive Grammar pedagogy is a result of systemic issues related to teacher training and teachers' linguistic knowledge, rather than the framework or the pedagogy itself.

References

Achard, M. (2008), 'Teaching Construal: Cognitive Pedagogical Grammar', in P. Robinson and N. Ellis (eds), *Handbook of Cognitive Linguistics and Second Language Acquisition*, 432–55, London: Taylor and Francis.

Bernstein, B. (1990), *The Structuring of Pedagogic Discourse: Class, Codes & Control Vol IV*, London: Routledge.

Bielak, J. and M. Pawlak (2013), *Applying Cognitive Grammar in the Foreign Language Classroom: Teaching English Tense and Aspect*, Berlin: Springer-Verlag.

Blake, J. and T. Shortis (2010), *Who's Prepared to Teach School English?: The Degree Level Qualifications and Preparedness of Initial Teacher Trainees in English*, London: Committee for Linguistics in Education.

Boyd, R. (2002), 'Metaphor and Theory Change: What Is "Metaphor" for?' in A. Ortony (ed.), *Metaphor and Thought*, 481–531, Cambridge: Cambridge University Press.

Cienki, A. and C. Müller (eds) (2008), *Metaphor and Gesture*, Amsterdam: John Benjamins.

Cushing, I. (2018a), '"Suddenly, I Am Part of the Poem": Texts as Worlds, Reader-response and Grammar in Teaching Poetry', *English in Education*, 52 (1): 7–19.

Cushing, I. (2018b), 'Stylistics Goes to School', *Language and Literature*, 27 (4): 271–85.

Cushing, I. (2019), 'Resources Not Rulebooks: Metaphors for Grammar in Teachers' Metalinguistic Discourse', *Metaphor and the Social World*, 9 (2): 155–76.

Cushing, I. (2020), 'A Textured and Sensory Grammar for the Experience of Reading', *English in Education*, 54 (2): 131–45.

De Knop, S. and T. De Rycker (eds) (2008), *Cognitive Approaches to Pedagogical Grammar*, Berlin: Mouton De Gruyter.

Department for Education (2013), *English Programmes of Study: Key Stage 3*, London: DfE.

Eilam, B. and J. Gilbert (eds) (2014), *Science Teachers' Use of Visual Representations*, London: Springer.

Ellis, V. (2003), 'The Love That Dare Not Speak Its Name? The Constitution of the English Subject and Beginning Teachers' Motivations to Teach It', *English Teaching: Practice and Critique*, 2 (1): 3–14.

Gavins, J. (2007), *Text World Theory: An Introduction*, Edinburgh: Edinburgh University Press.

Gerrig, R. (1993), *Experiencing Narrative Worlds: On the Psychological Activities of Reading*, New Haven, CT: Yale University Press.

Giovanelli, M. (2014a), *Teaching Grammar, Structure and Meaning: Exploring Theory and Practice for Post-16 English Language Teachers*, London: Routledge.

Giovanelli, M. (2014b), 'Conceptual Proximity and the Experience of War in Siegfried Sassoon's "A Working Party"', in C. Harrison, L. Nuttall, P. Stockwell and W. Yuan (eds), *Cognitive Grammar in Literature*, 145–59, Amsterdam: John Benjamins.

Giovanelli, M. (2015), 'Becoming an English Language Teacher: Linguistic Knowledge, Anxieties and the Shifting Sense of Identity', *Language and Education*, 29 (5): 416–29.

Giovanelli, M. (2017), 'Readers Building Fictional Worlds: Visual Representations, Poetry, and Cognition', *Literacy*, 51 (1): 26–35.

Giovanelli, M. and C. Harrison (2018), *Cognitive Grammar in Stylistics: A Practical Guide*, London: Bloomsbury.

Giovanelli, M. and J. Mason (2015), '"Well I don't Feel That": Schemas, Worlds and Authentic Reading in the Classroom', *English in Education*, 49 (1): 41–55.

Halliday, M. and C. Matthiessen (2004), *Halliday's Introduction to Functional Grammar*, London: Arnold.

Harris, A. and M. Helks (2018), 'What, Why and How – the Policy, Purpose and Practice of Grammatical Terminology', *English in Education*, 52 (3): 169–85.

Harrison, S. (2018), *The Impulse to Gesture: Where Language, Minds and Bodies Intersect*, Cambridge: Cambridge University Press.

Harrison, C., L. Nuttall, P. Stockwell and W. Yuan (eds) (2014), *Cognitive Grammar in Literature*, Amsterdam: John Benjamins.

Holme, R. (2009), *Cognitive Linguistics and Language Teaching*, Basingstoke: Palgrave Macmillan.

Kress, G., C. Jewitt, J. Ogborn and T. Charalampos (2001), *Multimodal Teaching and Learning: The Rhetorics of the Science Classroom*, London: Bloomsbury.

Langacker, R. (2008a), 'Cognitive Grammar as a Basis for Language Instruction', in P. Robinson and N. Ellis (eds), *Handbook of Cognitive Linguistics and Second Language Acquisition*, 66–88, London: Taylor and Francis.

Langacker, R. (2008b), *Cognitive Grammar: A Basic Introduction*, Oxford: Oxford University Press.

Lapaire, J. (2007), 'The Meaning of Meaningless Grams – or Emptiness Revisited', in W. Oleksy and P. Stalmaszczyk (eds), *Cognitive Approaches to Language and Linguistic Data*, 241–58, Frankfurt: Peter Lang.

Littlemore, J. (2009), *Applying Cognitive Linguistics to Second Language Learning and Teaching*, London: Palgrave.

Myhill, D. (2018), 'Grammar as a Meaning-making Resource for Improving Writing', *L1 Educational Studies in Language and Literature*, 18: 1–21.

Niemeier, S. and S. Reif (2008), 'Making Progress Simpler? Applying Cognitive Grammar to Tense-aspect Teaching in the German EFL Classroom', in S. De Knop and T. De Rycker (eds), *Cognitive Approaches to Pedagogical Grammar*, 325–56, Berlin: Mouton de Gruyter.

Nuttall, L. (2017), 'Online Readers between the Camps: A Text World Theory Analysis of Ethical Positioning in *We Need to Talk About Kevin*', *Language and Literature*, 26 (2): 153–71.

Pope, R. (1995), *Textual Intervention: Creative and Critical Strategies for Literary Studies*, Oxon: Routledge.

Popova, Y. (2002), 'The Figure in the Carpet: Discovery or Re-cognition', in E. Semino and J. Culpeper (eds), *Cognitive Stylistics: Language and Cognition in Text Analysis*, 49–71, Amsterdam: John Benjamins.

Pütz, M., S. Niemeier and R. Dirven (eds) (2001), *Applied Cognitive Linguistics II: Language Pedagogy*, Berlin: De Gruyter.

Robinson, P. and N. Ellis (eds) (2008). *Handbook of Cognitive Linguistics and Second Language Acquisition*, London: Taylor and Francis.

Roche, J. and F. Suñer (2016), 'Metaphors and Grammar Teaching', *Yearbook of the German Cognitive Linguistics Association*, 4 (1): 89–112.

Semino, E. (2008), *Metaphor in Discourse*, Cambridge: Cambridge University Press.

Stockwell, P. (2007), 'On Teaching Literature Itself', in G. Watson and S. Zyngier (eds), *Literature and Stylistics for Language Learners*, 15–24, London: Palgrave.

Stockwell, P. (2009), *Texture: A Cognitive Aesthetics of Reading*, Edinburgh: Edinburgh University Press.

Taniguchi, K. (2018), 'MAP Grammar: A Cognitive Grammar Perspective', in A. Tajino (ed.), *A New Approach to English Pedagogical Grammar*, 51–62, London: Routledge.

Taylor, J. (2002), *Cognitive Grammar*, Oxford: Oxford University Press.
Trousdale, G. (2016), 'Cognitive Linguistics', in M. Giovanelli and D. Clayton (eds), *Knowing about Language: Linguistics and the Secondary English Classroom*, 114–24, London: Routledge.
Tyler, A. (2012), *Cognitive Linguistics and Second Language Learning: Theoretical Basics and Experimental Evidence*, London: Routledge.
Van Rijt, J., P. De Swart and P.A. Coppen (2018), 'Linguistic Concepts in L1 Grammar Education: A Systematic Literature Review', *Research Papers in Education*, 34 (5): 621–48.
Verhagen, A. (2007), 'Construal and Perspectivization', in D. Geeraerts and H. Cuyckens (eds), *Oxford Handbook of Cognitive Linguistics*, 48–81, Oxford: Oxford University Press.
Verspoor, M. and N. Huong (2008), 'Cognitive Grammar and Teaching English Articles to Asian Students', in J.R. Lapaire (ed.), *From Grammar to Mind: Grammar as Cognition*, 249–68, Bordeaux: Presses Universitaires de Bordeaux.
Watson, A. (2015), 'Conceptualisations of "Grammar Teaching": L1 English Teachers' Beliefs about Teaching Grammar for Writing', *Language Awareness*, 24 (1): 1–14.
Werth, P. (1999), *Text Worlds: Representing Conceptual Space in Discourse*, London: Longman.
Williams, W.C. (1917 [2017]), *Al Que Quiere!*, New York: New Directions.

14

Towards a concept-driven pedagogy: A model of linguistic knowledge

Sally Zacharias

1. Introduction

Learning a new subject involves learning unfamiliar, discipline-specific, abstract concepts. In science, for example, students are expected to acquire and apply the concepts of power, life and energy. These discipline-specific concepts can be challenging for students to learn as they often differ from how the concept is used in everyday language (Scott et al. 2006). Furthermore, students' understandings of these concepts are expected to develop and change, often quite radically, as they progress through a unit of work or through school, college or in Higher Education. Equally challenging is the task of teaching these concepts, and evaluating students' conceptualizations, as evidence of a student's understanding of any new concept is primarily evaluated indirectly from their writing, speaking or from visual representations. These can be produced either in formal test situations or in during day-to-day classroom activities and interactions, which form part of a teacher's formative practices during which they evaluate their students' conceptual understandings. The language students use in these situations can seem, however, very 'messy' and difficult to interpret, since, as noted by van Lier:

> speakers, in their use, give evidence of the mental life behind their utterances, by using words such as 'I believe that.. ', 'it's like x,' 'that reminds me of ... ' as well as in a myriad of more covert and subtle ways .
>
> (1996: 174)

Thus, evaluating a student's conceptual understanding is essentially interpreting language in use. Current practices in formative classroom assessment in all contexts have been critiqued in that they lack theoretical foundations (Taras 2010) and, more specifically, they are not based on any reliable models of cognition of situated learning in a classroom (Black and Wiliam 2009). Many teachers' judgements of their students' ideas and concepts are therefore often based on their own inferences during ongoing classroom situations. Such judgements are not generally open to scrutiny from others and may indeed be open to bias. Further still, teachers just starting out have little experience of evaluating their students' work and may be uncertain of how to form reliable judgements. As succinctly expressed by Perrenoud:

> Without a theoretical model of the mediations through which an interactive situation [in the classroom] influences cognition, and in particular the learning process, we can observe thousands of situations without being able to draw any conclusions.
>
> (Perrenoud 1998: 95)

This issue also faces the educational researcher who is interested in the effect that discourse and the social and physical environment of the classroom have on the development of conceptual thinking, as well as what Knowledge About Language (KAL) (Carter 1982) is required by teachers to support conceptual development in their learners. Without a suitable analytical framework, there exists no means of being able to systematically track how learners construct and represent their conceptual thinking during a learning episode or lesson.

This chapter proposes that such a framework needs to be based on a model of language and cognition that recognizes that language reflects how we conceptualize the world. This view of language is best articulated in the field of cognitive linguistics that includes Cognitive Grammar (henceforth CG). The aim of this chapter, therefore, is to present a framework of linguistic knowledge based on a cognitive view of language, that has the potential to form the basis of KAL professional development sessions for teachers, and for researchers interested in classroom dialogue, especially in a secondary context. This is part of a concept-driven approach to pedagogy, first outlined by Giovanelli (2014), which places meaning, language and conceptual understanding at the heart of learning and teaching. Thus, it offers a principled approach to using students' language as evidence of their conceptual thinking which is of value not only to the teacher but also to the researcher interested in the role of language in conceptual development. The model I propose draws on principles from CG and other cognitive linguistic frameworks, most notably Text World Theory (TWT) (Werth 1999; Gavins 2007).

The structure of this chapter is as follows: first, I provide a brief overview of some key research milestones that have led to a cognitive linguistics-informed view of the connection between abstract concepts, learning and language. After detailing how the empirical data used in the analysis of this chapter was collected from a secondary school, I will outline some key tenets of CG and TWT that underpin this chapter's theoretical framework and model of linguistic knowledge. By applying CG's and TWT's respective approaches to an analysis of spoken discourse, I will propose a model of linguistic knowledge that draws on principles of both CG and TWT, with Langacker's (2008a: 55) concept of *construal* positioned at its core. This model of linguistic knowledge will be applied to the analysis of two episodes of classroom discourse taken from one science lesson and a student interview, whereby a number of construal operations, shown to be significant for the interpretation of the learning process, are explored.

2. Abstract concepts, learning and language

Through language we refer to things that we can directly perceive either through our senses (e.g. book, table, dictionary) or to entities that are not directly available to us as they are more abstract. We are able to think and talk about internal states (love, motivation), social constructs (institution, school), human born creations (theory, argument), ethical values (social justice, morality) (see Bolognesi and Steen 2019: 1) and abstracted constructs of our perception and understanding of the physical and living world (energy, life). Establishing a sense of shared consensus in a classroom of what concrete entities are is generally far more straightforward than coming to an agreement on what is meant by an abstract concept. Current research on how children and young adults acquire conceptual thought can be traced back to Piaget (1926, 1932, 1985), who prefigures a central concern of successive research, namely, how humans are capable of constructing knowledge of the world by observing and acting in the physical world around them. He focused on how conceptual reasoning is represented in propositional structures in children's language. Consequently, much empirical research that is directly based on his work focuses on the logical reasoning of children and tends to be carried out in interviews away from the classroom (e.g. Tao et al. 2012). In contrast, influenced by the work of Vygotsky (1978), socio-culturalists focus on the social dynamics of the classroom and have noted the type of interactions that favour a convergence in understanding between the participants involved. While research based on Piaget and Vygotsky's work frequently uses language data, it generally does not involve a linguistic analysis of the language patterns used by learners to represent their conceptual thinking. One notable exception to this is Seah et al.'s (2011) study which draws on Halliday's notion of social genre and register (Halliday 1994). It concludes that a group of middle school learners' conceptual understanding of heat expansion is directly influenced by their use of lexico-grammatical resources (Seah et al. 2011). The study notes that the more 'expert-like' their use of the scientific language after a period of instruction, the clearer their understanding of the scientific concepts seems to be. While this study is useful in that it focuses on the students' use of different academic registers, it is vague in how it determines the nature of students' conceptual understandings of the concept of heat expansion.

One important research project that does explore the learners' conceptual thinking is Deignan et al.'s (2017) recent study. This project is an investigation of secondary school students' understandings of the abstract concept of climate change and analyses students' use of domain-specific metaphors in group interviews. It then compares these findings to metaphor use in educational materials and specialist texts written by scientists. The study concludes that the students' use of metaphors tends to be more creative than its use in the other two sources which sometimes led the students to have inaccurate understandings of the science. This study is clearly significant and demonstrates how important it is for teachers to understand how metaphors work in their discipline. However, although metaphors play a key role in how scientists do and communicate science (Brown 2003; Reynolds 2018), I have recently shown that it is not the only cognitive process that is involved in the development of abstract thought in a naturalistic setting such as a classroom (Zacharias 2018, 2019). Indeed, as noted by Langacker (2008a), the metaphorical process is just one of several possible cognitive processes that are involved in the creation and use of abstract thought. Put simply, a linguistic expression imposes just one of many possible ways to conceptualize and represent a situation (Langacker 2013: 4): in other words, it may be construed in one of several different ways. Furthermore, as abstract concepts develop over time as a series of reconstruals within any learning situation, it is necessary to examine this phenomenon by exploring it at a discourse level to appreciate both the social and cognitive processes at work during their development.

3. Methodology

The linguistic model presented in this chapter developed as part of a cognitive discursive exploration of the development of abstract scientific concepts of heat energy in a secondary school science class (Zacharias 2018). More specifically, the context for the study was a first-year (11–12-year-olds) secondary class in an urban, state-maintained school in the UK. The class consisted of twenty mixed ability students from various socio-economic, cultural and linguistic backgrounds, representative of many city schools in the country. As the study aimed to understand the complex world of human mental experience and the role of discourse in the development of abstract concepts in a learning situation, a longitudinal case study design was adopted to gain close proximity to the conceptual world of the students. The data examined in this chapter focuses on an episode from one lesson and a student interview, which form part of the wider four-month study (Zacharias 2018). Confidentiality was ensured throughout the analysis by referring to the students with pseudonyms.

The learning events in this chapter were video recorded and later transcribed using Conversation Analysis notation (ten Have 2007) in order to represent the spoken interactions in a form that was close to their original. This process included transcribing, reading the transcripts after the events took place, reconstructing the events from fieldnotes, observing the video recordings and discussing the findings in interviews with small groups of students and the class teacher during the study. These activities revealed aspects of the learning situation, most notably socio-interactional ones and the possibility of alternative interpretations that would have been otherwise difficult to detect (ten Have 2007). Thus, although the main cognitive linguistic analysis results from my response to reading the transcripts after the events took place, my interpretation of these transcripts was strongly influenced by a deep immersion and re-construction of the events made possible by my fieldnotes and recordings.

4. Theoretical framework

Originally, Werth draws on Langacker's CG for TWT's grammatical basis (1999: 43, 199). This was subsequently replaced by systemic-functional grammar terminology and description, reflecting the fact that both grammars are considered to be usage-based systems that share many key principles (Gavins 2007: 56). Recently, however, there have been calls to re-examine Werth's original inclusion of Langacker's CG system. As Nuttall (2018: 55) claims, a '(re) adoption of Cognitive Grammar as the grammatical basis for close stylistic analysis enhances our ability to account for the experiential effects of specific stylistic choices during the text-world construction'. In this chapter, I demonstrate that although the TWT model, with its rich discourse-world account of context, offers a suitable overarching framework for conceptualizing the development of abstract thought amongst the participants in a classroom situation, the re-introduction of the CG model into the linguistic knowledge component of the TWT framework does indeed allow for a more fine-grained analysis of the cognitive effects of the linguistic structures at work during a learning episode. The relative affordances of each model will be outlined briefly in the following section, thus highlighting the need to integrate the two models.

As previously mentioned, it is important to examine the phenomenon of conceptual development in the classroom at the discourse level. According to Langacker, during any usage event, the speaker/hearer conceptualizes the immediate situation or the *ground* (Langacker 2008a: 78): this includes the speaker and hearer and where the event takes place and what is being said between them. To interpret this, the speaker/ hearer also needs to conceptualize a separate mental space to the ground, the *current discourse space* (CDS), which carries all the information needed to interpret what is being said (Langacker 2001: 145). Langacker acknowledges that in order to interpret the language, the speakers require support from the context of speech that includes 'the physical, mental, social and cultural circumstances' (Langacker 2001: 145). However, he is somewhat vague in what this entails, and he does not elaborate on how an individual speaker is able to conceptualize the ground in their own unique way. Langacker tends to explain the conceptualization process using a set of universal principles, ignoring the potential variation involved in how this process is experienced by individuals.

Moreover, Giovanelli and Harrison (2018) point out that although this structure provides a useful means to conceptualize a speech event and its surrounding context, it ignores how an onlooker might conceptualize the relationship between the two speakers and mentally respond to the exchange. In contrast, the TWT model allows for a multi-layered analysis that includes both participants and onlookers (e.g. researcher) and provides opportunities to account for individual variation in how the events are experienced both during and after the event has taken place by analysing transcripts of the dialogue.

Some key features of the text-world framework will now be described before highlighting why and how elements of the TWT framework can and should be integrated into Langacker's CG. TWT is a cognitive discourse grammar that provides a model of how language in use can be experienced and understood. It is based on the premise that in order to understand any form of language, we construct mental representations, or text-worlds, in our minds to achieve this. Text-worlds are similar to mental models (Johnson-Laird 1983) which emerge in the minds of the participants (e.g. teacher, learners and/or on-looker) and are 'the conceptualization of that part of the discourse-world which is "in focus" for that part of the discourse [...] it is the situation depicted by the discourse' (Werth 1999: 86–7).

One distinctive feature of the TWT model that makes the ability to conceptualize possible is what TWT terms the principle of 'text-drivenness' (Werth 1999: 140). This accounts for how elements from the text trigger only the schematic knowledge of the receiver, required by him or her, to make sense of the situation. This knowledge is part of the discourse-world, which Werth defines as 'the situational context surrounding the speech event itself' (1999: 83). Comparable to Langacker's concept of the immediate situation or ground, the discourse-world is made up of the participants, the text, all the elements that the participants can perceive. It also includes all the knowledge and beliefs about the world and identities that the participants bring to a situation. However, in contrast to Langacker's ground, Werth's discourse-world model provides a more elaborate account of how the text and visible objects evoke 'a whole range of experience' by drawing on Fillmore's notion of 'frames' (Werth 1999: 43). The discourse-world consists of not only sense input but also 'what the participants can work out from their perceptions' (Werth 1999). This implies that the participants draw from their knowledge frames in order to conceive of (perceive, remember or imagine) a coherent 'state-of-affairs' (1999: 84), when either producing or interpreting a given discourse. The crucial point is that the discourse-world, in contrast to Langacker's ground, accounts more convincingly for the individual variation in how various events are experienced, making it ideally suited for analysing how individuals construct meaning in group settings such as a classroom. Figure 14.1 illustrates a generic discourse-world

---

Participants: teacher, 20 pupils, researcher (onlooker)

Texts and objects: spoken discourse (teacher- and learner-led interactions), written classroom materials; notebooks, booklets, textbooks, wall posters, videos, whiteboard notes and illustrations, tables, chairs, whiteboard, classroom equipment.

Background knowledge (from prior learning experiences that took place both inside and outside the classroom)

(Assumed) Teacher's background knowledge: (knowledge about science, knowledge about teaching science, linguistic knowledge, beliefs about how pupils learn etc.)

(Assumed) Pupils' background knowledge: (knowledge about the world, knowledge about science and learning science, linguistic knowledge, ontological and epistemic beliefs etc.)

Researcher's background knowledge: knowledge about learning and teaching science, knowledge about language and classroom discourse, beliefs etc.)

Figure 14.1 Generic discourse-world of the classroom.

of the classroom that I observed. The discourse-world of the classroom consists of not only the physical objects, such as tables and chairs, but also less tangible entities, such as mental states of the participants as they engage with the learning tasks.

Relevant to any classroom event is the background knowledge of prior learning experiences that the teacher and learners have as part of this discourse-world. This shapes their expectations, their ontological and epistemic beliefs, the power dynamics between them and the social interaction patterns that characterize classroom practice. The teacher will have accumulated over time knowledge about science and knowledge about how science can be learned, which automatically places the teacher in a privileged position relative to his or her learners. Accompanying this is how scientific knowledge can be constructed, represented and communicated in and through language; in other words, drawing on linguistic knowledge.

5. A model of linguistic knowledge

This section presents a model of linguistic knowledge (Werth 1999: 98) that borrows Werth's concepts of the discourse-world and text-world but places Langacker's concept of construal at its core. The model includes an elaborated and extended version of Werth's original model of linguistic knowledge with a re-introduction of CG (1991, 2008a), and Croft and Cruse's (2004: 46) synthesis of different kinds of construal phenomena, as the model's grammatical basis.

Werth's concept of linguistic knowledge is interlinked with other cognitive systems. In other words, linguistic knowledge, memories and experiential knowledge 'may all provide input for each other' (Werth 1999: 98). The meanings that the students ascribe to the words and structures they use have arisen from how they experienced the words previously either during the lesson or before: these words and structures 'propose a mode of construal of that entity' (Holme, 2009: 161). Fillmore already notes that our knowledge of lexis and grammar depends on 'contexted experiences; that is, the contexts within which we have experienced the objects, properties or feelings that provide the perceptual or experiential base of our knowledge of the meaning of the word (or phrase, or grammatical category) may be inseparable parts of those experiences' (1976: 24). Linguistic knowledge consists of not only knowing about lexis and grammar, but also what Fillmore terms as cognitive or interactional frames: a type of linguistic knowledge 'in which the language user interprets his environment, formulates his own messages, understands the messages of others, and accumulates or creates an internal model of this world' (1976: 23). This knowledge is essentially experiential, the kind of knowledge that exists as memories of prior experiences and is necessary if a concept is to be attained. Thus, learners acquire experiential knowledge of how lexical items and syntactical patterns have been used in context but also an inter-subjective understanding of the referents of those units by members of the discourse community to which they belong. The flipside of this is that by observing the students' language choices, it becomes possible to observe which part of the learning context they are choosing to foreground and attend to. This close relationship between thought and language in online situations is noted by Slobin (1996), in his 'thinking for speaking' conception, which claims that the language we use while speaking directs our attention to certain ways of filtering our experiences of the world. The educational practitioner interested in observing and examining their learners' conceptual development requires a means of detecting, however, how their learners gain this experiential knowledge.

Thus, Langacker's CG system offers a set of principles and concepts for the educational practitioner or researcher to explain how this experiential knowledge might be attained during a learning event in the classroom by providing a means of analysing the learners' lexico-grammatical resources in a systematic way. It enables the practitioner and researcher a means to explore how learners develop abstract concepts by critically examining how particular events are construed in language during a learning event.

Langacker identifies several distinct construal phenomena that enable the speaker to conceptualize and portray a situation in several different ways (Langacker 2008a: 55). However, although Langacker's concept of construal is the key focus to this chapter's model of linguistic knowledge, this chapter uses Croft and Cruse's (2004: 46) topology of construal operations. This includes not only Langacker's proposal but also other key cognitive phenomena (e.g. image schemas and epistemic modality) that have been shown to play a significant role in the learning process (Zacharias 2018, 2019). Thus, the analysis in this chapter will focus on the following construal operations: schematization categorization, image-schemas (SOURCE-PATH-GOAL; CONTAINER) and Hart's (2011) classification of epistemic modality.

By analysing the learners' output, then, it becomes possible to observe how the learner construes the learning event through the different lexico-grammatical structures he or she uses. These structures are not produced in isolation but are part of different rhetorical acts in the classroom (e.g. descriptions, explanations). These rhetorical acts or 'formal knowledge structures' (van Dijk 1980; Fillmore 1985) are a crucial part of the linguistic knowledge framework, as they serve an important organizational function in the knowledge building process. Such cognitive frames are strongly associated with the notion of prototypicality in that the receiver or producer of the knowledge structure needs to be able to categorize it according to the schema with which it corresponds. More recently, from the field of English for Academic Purposes, Bruce (2008) identifies these as 'cognitive genres' as they reflect how the mind organizes information to carry out these different rhetorical purposes. To summarize, the context of any classroom interaction will include knowledge about how language is used, knowledge of the ways in which learning can be presented and knowledge of particular rhetorical strategies to do so.

To illustrate the key features of this model, Table 14.1 shows the component parts of the linguistic knowledge framework that forms part of a participant's discourse-world during a learning event.

It is worth noting that this linguistic knowledge is not a closed-off unit in the mind but part of an ongoing, dynamic system. Although Table 14.1 represents the component parts of this model as discrete entities, it is important to remember that in

Table 14.1 The Linguistic Knowledge Framework

Component Part	Details
Lexical and syntactic constructional knowledge. Experiential knowledge (Fillmore 1976)	Knowledge of how lexical items and syntactic patterns are used in context. Shared understanding of what these items and patterns refer to within a discourse community
Construal operations (based on Croft and Cruse 2004: 46; Langacker 2008a) For example, schematization, categorization, epistemic modality, image schemas.	Ability to recognize item's structure as an instance of a prototypical schema (categorization) Recurrent dynamic pattern of perceptual experience (image schema)
Formal knowledge structures (Van Dijk 1980; Filmore 1985) **Cognitive genre** (Bruce 2008)	Knowledge of rhetorical purpose

the context of a classroom interaction they work together with each other and other elements of the discourse-world to create meaning and new knowledge.

6. Application of model of linguistic knowledge: Analysing classroom discourse

The following section exemplifies this framework in more detail by looking at how language is used in a specific educational setting. Although I primarily focus on the language of science I start by looking at how concepts develop across the disciplines. I will then demonstrate how the model of linguistic knowledge (as shown in Table 14.1) can be applied to students' language output to evaluate their conceptual understandings. I present episodes of transcribed spoken discourse from a biology lesson in addition to an interview with two first-year secondary science students. During these episodes, the learners' understandings of the scientific abstract concepts of living and insulation are explored. The learners' conceptual knowledge is analysed and evaluated by considering schematization, categorization, image schemas and epistemic modality, all construal operations (Croft and Cruse 2004: 46) that are found to play a key role in the development of conceptual thought in learners. Although the focus in the following section is on how these construal operations play a role in conceptual development, it should be noted that the learners' output triggers the formation of a text-world by the practitioner, researcher and/or text analyst. Therefore, references to relevant aspects of TWT are made throughout.

6.1 Schematization

Langacker (1987a: 371) refers to experiential knowledge as:

an abstract characterization that is fully compatible with all the members of the category it defines [...]; it is an integrated structure that embodies the commonality of its members, which are conceptions of greater specificity and detail that elaborate the schema in contrasting ways.

Thus, an important aspect of linguistic knowledge is our ability to recognize the various symbolic units in our language as instances of abstract categories or schemas. Langacker refers to this ability as *schematization* (2008a: 17). For example, during a school day a learner may encounter the word 'water' in any number of different subjects that then activate various different knowledge frames associated with water. In geography, the focus of a description or explanation might be on the formation of rain clouds during an explanation of the water cycle or how the erosion of rocks can be brought about by the freezing of water. In art, the focus would be on the aesthetic features, in a physics lesson on its physical properties, such as that it boils at 100 degrees Celsius and freezes at 0 degrees Celsius. The point is, the learner encounters multiple experiences that vary in detail and content for the concept of water but extracts out of these experiences a conception of water at a higher level of abstraction: 'a liquid I see every day that may form ice or snow when cold'.

6.2 Categorization

Closely related to this is the ability to recognize that a symbolic unit is a typical example of a schema, in other words, the ability to see the symbolic unit as an instance of a prototype. This is referred to in CG as *categorization* (Langacker 2008a: 17). A young learner may have the following schema of METAL, which has developed and acquired associations over time with other words such as shiny, hard, cold, gold, silver, iron and so on. However, on first encountering a metal such as mercury, a silvery, shiny metal that is, unlike many other metals, a liquid at room temperature, this learner may place mercury on the periphery of this category of 'METALNESS'. As this learner encounters further examples of metals in class and continues to explore their properties, these new set of metals may be categorized according to a refined set of core features. In other words, what the learner first thought to be a typical feature of a metal (hard) may become less important as the learner encounters further examples of metals that are soft or liquid at room temperature. What the learner first considered to be a non-prototypical metal may gradually shift to a prototypical metal. The teacher plays a crucial role here in developing the concepts specific to the lesson, by foregrounding the associations appropriate to the focus of the lesson at the expense of others.

However, as noted by Sutton (1992), dismissing and ignoring the peripheral more idiosyncratic associations entirely may have undesired consequences in a school context. First, only giving prominence to the scientific meanings, the learner may soon feel alienated from the discipline as often the peripheral associations carry more emotive and personal associations. In terms of developing conceptual understanding, it might be beneficial also to see how the scientific meanings stand in relation to more idiosyncratic meanings held by the learner.

In contrast to the above example from the physical sciences, the following section will examine how learners might categorize the abstract concept of 'living' from the biological sciences. In the following episode, the teacher and learners each build their own mental space, or text-world, of the situation being discussed, namely, how to provide a scientific definition of living. The spoken discourse, that is part of the shared social space or ground, triggers text-worlds that are fleshed out by each participants' own discourse-world, including memories, beliefs, imagination and linguistic knowledge that they bring to the situation. Interestingly, here the learners chose to define 'living' by referring to real-world examples of living and non-living things they had encountered previously. In other words, they define living in terms of category membership either according to what it needs or how it behaves.

Episode 1: Abstract concept of 'living'
Mr D: ok boys and girls (.) that's fine thank you very much (.) we go around a find out how you would define living (.) shall we start over here (.) go on then someone
Kate: we didn't know how to define it (.) so we thought about something that all living things need like every single thing that is living is water
Mr D: good that's ↑brilliant(.) one thing that living things do need is moisture dampness and water (.) brilliant fantastic do non-living things need that sort of thing I talked about? a pair of scissors(.) a pen well a pen? doesn't really need water(.) a pair of scissors doesn't really need water plastic doesn't really need water right anything else
Kate: um um like err they all they grow

In the above example, the learners are drawing on their well-established encyclopaedic stores of experiential knowledge about living and non-living things that are accessed through the words 'all living things need', 'water' and 'grow'. Thus, by observing the learners' own language choices, it becomes possible to understand their conceptual understanding of the abstract concept of 'living' according to conventional norms of category membership.

6.3 Epistemic modality and image schemas

The following episode exemplifies how the construal operations of epistemic modality and image schemas play a crucial role in the development of abstract thought in social setting. It demonstrates how, by examining how these construals operate during a learning event, the teacher or researcher is able to provide strong linguistic evidence for their learners' conceptions.

Episode 2 is an interview between the researcher, Sally, and two first-year secondary students, Sanja and Rose, that took place one week after a physics lesson on the abstract concept of insulation. In the lesson, the students carried out an experiment to find out whether a snowman with a jacket would melt faster than a snowman without a jacket. The purpose of the interview was to probe the students' reasoning further and to examine, using principles from CG and TWT, the students' understanding of the concept of insulation.

Episode 2: Abstract concept of 'insulation'
Sally: u-huh ok can you explain your reasoning? why did you think that at the time?
Sanja: because I thought (.) like the jacket would ↑melt the snowman because it would bring a lot of heat to the snow (.) which would make it melt
Sally: yeah and Rose and you thought something slightly different didn't ↑you so can you remember what you thought at the time?
Rose: like if you put on a jacket it's not like (.) instantly warm (1.0) the body heat needs to heat up the jacket.
Sally: u– huh
Rose: so the jacket hadn't been on a radiator (.) or near any heat so if you put it on the snowman it wouldn't make any difference (.) and there's no like source of well there's the cold of the snow but it wouldn't keep him cold like
Sanja: at first I thought like (.) the cardboard would melt the ice (.) the snow it's trapped (.) and it has no way of like cold air to keep it (.) to keep it to keep it a ↑solid so I thought the heat would go to the snow
Sally: m-mh have you changed your view?
Sanja: yeah
Sally: and how have you (.) how do you think differently how would you explain that now?
Sanja: I think (.) I thought like the cardboard would melt the ice first (.) but when I saw the experiment I was actually quite ↑surprised
Sally: u huh?
Sanja: that the heat from the ↑sun would melt it first
Sally: ok
Sanja: not the one without the cardboard
Sally: so (.) the cardboard (.) what is it doing what would you say its function is?
Sanja: I think it's trying to keep the cold (.) inside the space it's in.

Not unsurprisingly, a strong feature of the discourse in this episode is the participants' use of epistemic modality to express their certainty and beliefs. Epistemic modality is classified in this chapter as a type of deictic construal operation which places propositions on a reality-irreality continuum. Both Langacker and Werth suggest that instances of epistemic modality are located by the conceptualizer at different points on this continuum (Langacker 1991; Werth 1999). Langacker (1991: 242) proposes a cyclical structure (see Figure 14.2).

In Langacker's model, 'known reality' is what the conceptualizer accepts as real and is generally what the conceptualizer (C) has perceptual access to at the time of the discourse event, or within 'immediate reality'. 'Irreality' is everything other than this known reality.

There are varying degrees of reality known to the conceptualizer who is most likely to accept whatever he or she has perceptual access to at the time of speaking. What is accepted to be true by the conceptualizer grows during the discourse event, and that which lies beyond what is accepted to be true is irreal. This model is helpful as it provides a clear, visual aid (see Figure 14.2) to show how certain propositions are accepted to be more real than others by an individual speaker. What this model does

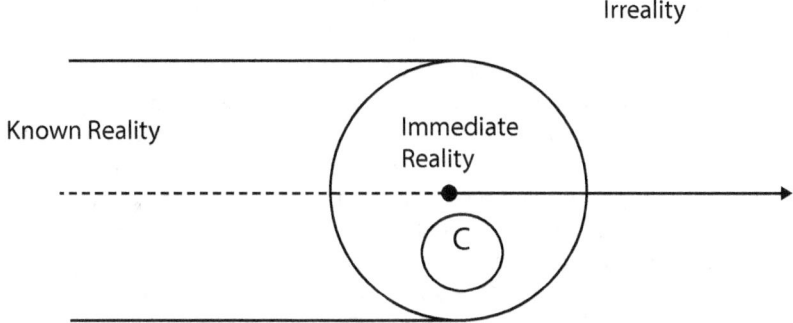

Figure 14.2 Langacker's reality-irreality continuum (based on Langacker 1991: 242).

not show, however, is how speakers draw from their own knowledge frames to assess the propositions as real or not. The TWT model offers a means to do this, in that it accounts for how a number of epistemic modal verbs (e.g. suppose, believe, think), modal adverbs (e.g. perhaps, maybe) and modalized questions 'can you explain?' can trigger the formation of an epistemic modal-world. Into this conceptual space the conceptualizer draws on their own knowledge frames to assess the evidence of a situation (Gavins 2007: 110).

During Line 6 in Episode 2, Sally establishes an epistemic modal-world with the question: 'can you explain your reasoning?' This modal-world is initially situated in the present time of the interview but shifts to a past time frame with: 'why did you think that at the time?' According to the reality-irreality continuum, the speaker does not have direct perceptual access to the past event and should therefore be less likely to accept the propositions pertaining to the event to be true. However, a past text-world can be experienced as a text-world aligned with the present, in that it can be compressed (Fauconnier and Turner 1998), together with any text-worlds formed at the time of the interview, into a single continuous time-zone. It can therefore trigger the knowledge frames of the discourse-world of the interview to assess its credibility.

The students' responses describing their inner thoughts during the discussion (Lines 7–32) are detailed and indicate a strong willingness to talk about their initial ideas. Sally's question, in Line 6, triggers an epistemic modal-world in the past from Sanja. This co-constructed text-world becomes a shared conceptual space for Sanja and Rose to describe and assess their mental representations of the learning situation with the researcher Sally. What can be gleaned from Sanja and Rose's responses is that they draw from their own CLOTHES schema. Here, the students draw on experiential discourse-world knowledge to evaluate the propositions within the epistemic modal-world set up by the question. They apply this knowledge to the everyday situation depicted in the task. In Sanja's response in Lines (7–8): 'the jacket would ↑melt the snow because it would bring a lot of heat to the snow', the agency of the jacket is instantiated by its subject position. In this context, this implies that it causes the snow to melt and is the source of heat; it would bring heat. If this is interpreted literally, it might imply that the jacket generates heat energy.

The choice of the epistemic modal 'would' (Line 7) can be explained by referring to the context. First, the scene is removed from the interview in both time and space and, therefore, is deictically removed from the learners' immediate surroundings. According to Langacker (1991), it will be experienced as less real than if the situation took place in the interview room. However, this explanation does not take into account the social dimension of the situation. Sanja and Rose have been asked to put forward opinions which might turn out to be wrong in front of the researcher, Sally, and the other participant. Therefore, the establishment of a more tentative, remote text-world to express their evaluations offers the participants a safe haven during the discussion. A language-aware teacher may be less inclined to interpret this hedged language as the learner simply not knowing or understanding as they would also take the social dimensions of the exchange into account. Accounting for the cognitive and social forces at play during problem-solving activities like this enables the teacher or researcher to systematically analyse and interpret the claims learners make, thus making the task of evaluating their conceptual understanding more robust.

During Sanja's response, it appears that two image schemas from her experiential discourse-world knowledge are employed to structure her reasoning. Briefly put, an image schema is 'a condensed redescription of perceptual experience for the purpose of mapping spatial structure onto conceptual structure' (Oakley 2007: 215) They are, as Langacker describes, 'preconceptual' structures that give rise to more sophisticated abstract concepts (Langacker 2008a: 32). First, Sanja uses the SOURCE-PATH-GOAL image schema (i.e. heat comes from the jacket and goes to the snowman), and second the CONTAINER image schema ('at first I thought like (.) the cardboard would melt the ice the snow it's trapped (.) and it has no way of like cold air to keep it to keep it to keep it a solid') Here, the jacket is construed as a CONTAINER. Although there is no clear referent for 'it' in 'it's trapped, from the co-text it might be assumed to be the warm air inside the jacket.

When Rose is asked to describe her inner thoughts, the SOURCE-PATH-GOAL image schema, which Sanja initiated with her implication that the jacket was a source of heat, appears to structure her reasoning too. Rose, however, contributes to the dialogue her knowledge that it is the human body which is a source of heat and not the jacket. In other words, Rose's schema of putting on clothes and understanding why they make you warm has a different and possibly more elaborate structure to Sanja's as it acknowledges the role that body heat plays. Furthermore, Rose demonstrates a willingness to consider factors that either she had stored in her own schema before the lesson, or she had accreted (Stockwell 2020: 79) into her existing schema during the classroom discussion (see Lines 14–16). For example, she mentions alternative sources of heat (e.g. radiator) that have not been mentioned previously in the interview.

In Lines 24–5, Sanja describes the surprise she felt when observing the result of the experiment that the snowman without a jacket had melted first. On comparing the responses of Sanja, when she describes her initial ideas with those she had after observing the outcome of the experiment (Line 27), she clearly demonstrates the need for an alternative explanation for what she has seen. In Line 32, she provides a revised explanation for the phenomenon that she saw. Still using the CONTAINER image schema to structure her thoughts, she describes how the jacket traps the cold air on the inside thus maintaining a low temperature: 'I think it's trying to keep the cold (.) inside the space it's in' (Line 34). This analysis has demonstrated how the both the SOURCE-PATH-GOAL and CONTAINER image schemas structure Sanja and Rose's mental images during a problem-solving task. Both image schemas are essential to understanding the concept of insulation, yet this passage has shown that it is how they are aligned and positioned in relation to each other that matters.

7. Understanding and evaluating learners' responses

This chapter has argued and demonstrated that an approach to understanding language that is informed by principles from cognitive linguistics can provide both teachers and researchers a means to unpack learners' understandings of discipline-specific abstract concepts. The question remains, however: what are teachers and researchers evaluating their students' conceptual understandings against? To claim that they are simply assessing their students' conceptions against what has been written in the syllabus or against the assessment criteria does not highlight the role the teacher or researcher plays in interpreting their students' responses. A more accurate description of the process, that this approach affords, is that teachers and researchers understand and evaluate the effect the students' language has on their own minds against their own prototypical understandings of what they think the students' conceptualizations are and should be. These knowledge structures develop much in the same way as the linguistic knowledge structures that the students are developing through the verbal and non-verbal interactions they have with their social and physical environment during any learning event.

By comparing their students' responses with these 'idealised models of reality' (Gavins 2007: 5), teachers are in a position to develop their classroom practice, which includes being able to formatively assess their students' work. For example, with the case of the snowman problem-solving task a teacher could assess a students' work against their own prototypes of CONTAINER and SOURCE-PATH-GOAL image schemas, and possibly additional structures, such as a BLOCKAGE or RESTRAINT image schemas that represent the jacket as an insulator that slows the movement of heat entering the space inside the jacket with the snow. These knowledge structures underpin aspects of cognition that govern the production of both written and spoken language, as well as visual representations. Teachers equipped with the knowledge of how these image schematic structures shape and are shaped by language during learning events in their classroom, for example, would therefore be in a position to harness the visual aspect underpinning their learners' language choices, use this to negotiate meaning, as well as better understand and interpret their learners' responses during classroom activities.

Although our knowledge structures may resemble each other, I have demonstrated in this chapter that they also vary between individuals. Classroom dialogue affords the possibility both to communicate the features of our mental models to each other and to fine-tune our own mental models in response to comparing ours to others. I argue that this emphasis on observing the cognitive effects of the language in the classroom, as opposed to focusing simply on the form of the language, allows teachers to place meaning in a more central position, thus opening an opportunity for undertaking a more critical and principled approach to teaching, learning and formative assessment.

8. Conclusion

Since CG is a usage-based approach and places meaning as central to language, it has the potential to offer teachers, students and researchers a powerful set of concepts and tools to analyse language-in-use (Langacker 2008b). This chapter tests this claim by applying the concept of construal to a series of learning episodes from a science lesson and a researcher-student interview, thus illustrating how, by analysing students' classroom language, it is possible to make useful inferences into the learners' conceptual processes, and therefore a means to systematically evaluate students' understandings of disciplinary-specific abstract concepts. One important aspect of cognition that has not yet been addressed in this chapter, but one that plays an important role in the development of abstract thought, is that of memory. Linguistic and experiential knowledge structures used to construct and represent concepts draw from different levels of memory (van Dijk and Kintsch 1983; Macnamara and Magliano 2009; Steen 2017). The level of memory these structures are accessed from will influence the degree of understanding of the abstract concepts displayed in the learners' language. Although Werth acknowledges that both memory and linguistic knowledge are interlinked, a more feasible account of how these two aspects of cognition are related would be welcome. Understanding this more fully would be a fruitful area for future research.

In this chapter, I have argued that, despite the CG model offering a plausible explanation for the experiential effects of language, it does not provide a clear account of the individual variation involved. Drawing on Werth's notion of discourse-world, I have proposed a model of linguistic knowledge that merges in elements of the TWT framework, thus extending Langacker's model to make it more suitable for analysing dynamic, socially embedded patterns of language-in-use, such as those found in a classroom context.

Transcription conventions:

↑↓   Arrows indicate marked shifts into higher or lower pitch after the arrow
(.)   Short pause
(3.0) Pause of 3 seconds

References

Black, P.J. and D. Wiliam (2009), 'Developing the Theory of Formative Assessment', *Educational Assessment, Evaluation and Accountability*, 21 (1): 5–31.

Bolognesi, M. and G.J. Steen (2019), 'Introduction', in M. Bolognesi and G.J. Steen (eds), *Perspectives on Abstract Concepts: Cognition, Language and Communication*, 1–13, Amsterdam: John Benjamins.
Brown, T. (2003), *Making Truth: Metaphor in Science*, Illinois: University of Illinois Press.
Bruce, I. (2008), *Academic Writing and Genre: A Systematic Analysis*, London: Continuum International Publishing Group.
Carter, R. (1982), *Linguistics and the Teacher*, London: Routledge.
Croft, W. and D.A. Cruse (2004), *Cognitive linguistics*, Cambridge: Cambridge University Press.
Deignan, A., E. Semino and S.A. Paul (2017), 'Metaphors of Climate Science in Three Genres: Research Articles, Educational Texts, and Secondary School Student Talk', *Applied Linguistics*, 40 (2): 379–403.
Fauconnier, G. and M. Turner (1998), 'Conceptual Integration Networks', *Cognitive Science*, 22 (2): 133–87.
Fillmore, C. (1976), 'Frame Semantics and the Nature of Language', *Annals of the New York Academy of Sciences*, 280 (1): 20–32.
Fillmore, C. (1985), 'Frames and the Semantics of Understanding', *Quaderni di Semantica* VI (20): 222–53.
Gavins, J. (2007), *Text World Theory: An Introduction*, Edinburgh: Edinburgh University Press.
Giovanelli, M. (2014), *Teaching Grammar, Structure and Meaning*, London: Routledge.
Giovanelli, M., and C. Harrison (2018), *Cognitive Grammar in Stylistics: A Practical Guide*, London: Bloomsbury Publishing.
Halliday, M.A.K. (1994), *An Introduction to Functional Grammar*, 2nd edn, London: Edward Arnold.
Hart, C. (2011), 'Moving beyond Metaphor in the Cognitive Linguistic Approach to CDA: Construal Operations in Immigration Discourse', in C. Hart (ed.), *Critical Discourse Studies in Context and Cognition*, 171–92, Amsterdam: John Benjamins.
Holme, R. (2009), *Cognitive Linguistics and Language Teaching*, Basingstoke: Palgrave Macmillan.
Johnson-Laird P.N. (1983), *Mental Models*, Cambridge: Harvard University Press.
Kövecses, Z. (2015), *Where Metaphors Come From: Reconsidering Context in Metaphor*, New York: Oxford University Press.
Langacker, R.W. (1985), *Topics in Cognitive Grammar*, Series of workshops at Universitaire Faculteit Sint-Aloysius, Brussels.
Langacker, R.W. (1987a), *Foundations of Cognitive Grammar, Volume I: Theoretical Prerequisites*, Stanford, CA: Stanford University Press.
Langacker, R.W. (1987b), 'Nouns and Verbs', *Language* 63: 53–94.
Langacker, R.W. (1991), *Foundations of Cognitive Grammar, Volume II: Descriptive Application*, Stanford: Stanford University Press.
Langacker, R.W. (2001), 'Discourse in Cognitive Grammar', *Cognitive Linguistics*, 12, 143–88.
Langacker, R.W. (2008a), *Cognitive Grammar: A Basic Introduction*, Oxford/New York: Oxford University Press.
Langacker, R.W. (2008b), 'Cognitive Grammar as a Basis For Language Instruction', in P. Robinson and N.C. Ellis (eds), *Handbook of Cognitive Linguistics and Second Language Acquisition*, 66–88, New York: Routledge.
Langacker, R.W. (2013), *Essentials of Cognitive Grammar*, Oxford: Oxford University Press.

McNamara, D.S. and J. Magliano (2009), 'Toward a Comprehensive Model of Comprehension', *Psychology of Learning and Motivation*, 51: 297–384.

Nuttall, L. (2018), *Mind Style and Cognitive Grammar: Language and Worldview in Speculative Fiction*, London: Bloomsbury Publishing.

Oakley, T. (2007), 'Image Schemas', in D. Geeraerts and H. Cuyckens (eds), *The Oxford Handbook of Cognitive Linguistics*, 214–35, Oxford: Oxford University Press.

Perrenoud, P. (1998), 'From Formative Evaluation to a Controlled Regulation of Learning Processes. Towards a Wider Conceptual Field', *Assessment in Education: Principles, Policy and Practice*, 5 (1): 85–102.

Piaget, J. (1926), *The Language and Thought of the Child* [*Le Langage et la pensée chez l'enfant* (1923)], London: Routledge and Kegan Paul.

Piaget, J. (1932), *The Moral Judgment of the Child*, New York: Harcourt Brace.

Piaget, J. (1985), *The Equilibration of Cognitive Structures: The Central Problem of Intellectual Development*, trans T. Brown and K.L. Thampy, 36–64, Chicago: University Chicago Press.

Reynolds, A.S. (2018), *The Third Lens: Metaphor and the Creation of Modern Cell Biology*, Chicago: University of Chicago Press.

Scott, P., E. Mortimer and O. Aguiar (2006), 'The Tension between Authoritative and Dialogic Discourse: A Fundamental Characteristic of Meaning Making Interactions in High School Science Lessons', *Science Education*, 90: 605–31.

Seah, L.H., D.J. Clarke and C.E. Hart (2011), 'Understanding Students' Language Use about Expansion through Analyzing Their Lexicogrammatical Resources', *Science Education*, 95 (5): 852–76.

Slobin, D. (1996), 'From "Thought and Language" to "Thinking for Speaking"', in J. Gumperz and S. Levinson (eds), *Rethinking Linguistic Relativity*, 70–96, Cambridge: Cambridge University Press.

Steen, G (2017), 'Attention to Metaphor: Where Embodied Cognition and Social Interaction Can Meet, but May Not Often Do So', in B. Hampe (ed.), *Metaphor: Embodied Cognition and Discourse*, 279–97, Cambridge: Cambridge University Press.

Stockwell, P. (2020), *Cognitive Poetics: An Introduction*, 2nd edn, London: Routledge.

Sutton, C. (1992), *Words, Science and Learning*, Milton Keynes: Open University Press.

Tao, Y., M. Oliver and G. Venville (2012), 'Chinese and Australian Year 3 Children's Conceptual Understanding of Science: A Multiple Comparative Case Study', *International Journal of Science Education*, 34 (6),879–901.

Taras, M. (2010), 'Assessment for Learning: Assessing the Theory and Evidence', *Procedia Social and Behavioral Sciences*, 2, 3015–22.

Ten Have, P. (2007), *Doing Conversational Analysis: A Practical Guide*, London: Sage.

van Dijk, T. A. (1980), *Macrostructures: An Interdisciplinary Study of Global Structures in Discourse, Interaction and Cognition*, Hillsdale, NJ: Lawrence Erlbaum.

van Dijk, T.A. and W. Kintsch (1983), *Strategies of Discourse Comprehension*, New York: Academic Press.

van Lier, L. (1996), *Interaction in the Language Curriculum: Awareness, Autonomy and Authenticity*, Harlow: Pearson Education.

Vygotsky, L.S. (1978), *Mind in Society: The Development of Higher Mental Process*, Cambridge: Cambridge University Press.

Werth, P. (1999), *Text Worlds: Representing Conceptual Space in Discourse*, London: Longman.

Zacharias, S. (2018), 'The Linguistic Representation of Abstract Concepts in Learning Science: A Cognitive Discursive Approach', Doctoral dissertation, University of Nottingham.

Zacharias, S. (2019), 'The Development of the Abstract Scientific Concept of Heat Energy in a Naturalistic Classroom Setting', in M. Bolognesi and G.J. Steen (eds), *Perspectives on Abstract Concepts: Cognition, Language and Communication*, 263–85, Amsterdam: John Benjamins.

15

Coda

Marcello Giovanelli, Chloe Harrison and Louise Nuttall

This book marks the next chapter in the stylistic application of Cognitive Grammar. The research showcased here demonstrates again and again the productive (and sometimes surprising) ways in which generalized concepts from cognitive linguistics can be applied to describe specific effects and issues resulting from our engagement with texts. It seems to us that the analytical apparatus developed through such applications has become increasingly refined over the past five years, with certain concepts (e.g. construal, action chains, simulation, scanning) emerging as key across different contexts, and other, peripheral or adapted aspects of the theory becoming established as significant for a cognitive grammar of style. At the same time, the range of text- and discourse-types to which Cognitive Grammar has been applied has broadened considerably. This evolution of the framework is exciting to see.

One significant concern for Cognitive Grammar and style is the question of scalability. While the basic principles of Cognitive Grammar are theoretically as applicable to an entire discourse as they are to individual clauses (Langacker 2008: 457), this discourse-level application has yet to be fully worked out in the framework itself. Stylistic adaptation of these principles to consider the different contextualized ways in which we think about whole texts and utterances is arguably the best possible means of developing the theory in this respect. The chapters in this book represent the current stage in this 'ongoing project' (Voice, this volume: 135), which promises to consider not only texts-as-wholes, but also the communicative exchanges they are a part of (e.g. between this teacher and that student, this reader and that reader) and the wider social systems (e.g. educational and political) in which they operate.

One effective scaling-up seen in the present volume is in consideration of the multi-levelled, dynamic 'viewing arrangements' that evolve during our comprehension of discourse, in interaction with (and to an extent resulting from) those that are coded clause-by-clause. Exploration of the complexity and variation with which viewing arrangements are attended to in novels, where further narrator or character levels are present (Stockwell, this volume), or in comics, where multiple modalities interact in our 'viewing' (Finn, this volume), are just two of the complex ways in which these arrangements are seen to operate within discourse. Closely related to this, the studies in this volume share attention to the minds of the individual 'conceptualizers' involved in each case. In a stylistic context, these abstract subjectivities may be fully fleshed-out human beings, or vague fictional projections; and our tracking and simulation of these other consciousnesses is a crucial – not to mention fascinating – part of our engagement with language. As Langacker (2014: xiv) emphasizes, '[b]ased on our ability to simulate the experience of other conceptualizers, each with their own perspective, speaking (or writing) is an intersubjective process aimed at negotiating a shared contextual awareness'.

Like the scalability mentioned earlier, this social process of meaning-making, or 'interactive cognition' as Langacker (2012) has called it elsewhere, is loosely outlined in more recent versions of the theory:

> Both interlocutors engage in coding. Ideally they activate the same units and impose the same structural interpretation. While this is seldom if ever fully achieved in actual practice, reasonably close approximations are usually enough for successful communication, discrepancies not even being noticed. It is important to resist the simplistic notion that the speaker merely encodes (going from meaning to sounds) while the hearer merely decodes (going from sound to meaning). For one thing, using an expression requires that both interlocutors activate all the units involved – semantic, phonological, and symbolic – whether the meanings evoke the sounds or conversely. Moreover, each interlocutor partially simulates the other's role: the hearer anticipates what the speaker might say, and the speaker estimates how the hearer will apprehend it. Coding is thus an intersubjective process in which (ideally) the interlocutors converge on the same interpretation.
>
> (Langacker 2012: 105)

The nature of this intersubjective negotiation of meaning is another significant concern for researchers in this book. An increased utilization of reader-response data in stylistics has facilitated analysis of the construals that readers (or listeners) carry out as separate to the construals coded by writers (or speakers). In the classroom, this distinction allows students' personal responses to texts to be understood (and valued) as subjective and valid construals (Cushing, this volume), and teachers' evaluations of them to be viewed as a further comparison with their own construal of what is a prototypical or 'correct' conceptualization (Zacharias, this volume). Respondents are seen to be highly creative in their 'reconstrual' of a political speech in line with their pre-existing beliefs (Browse, this volume), while other researchers consider the different ways in which the construals coded by text-producers may either invite or defy familiarization as part of a reader or listener's construal. While offering a 'more readerly' account of meaning construction (Hart, this volume: 111), this is still only a partial window onto the complex interpretative exchange described. The writerly side of this exchange and larger questions surrounding authorial creativity are perhaps in need of equal treatment (West 2017; Giovanelli 2019). The nature of the convergence between interlocutors and the shared contextual understanding that emerges (or fails to emerge) in practice remain areas for future stylistic research.

In their attempt to understand these socially situated interactions, researchers now draw increasingly on a range of empirical data, obtained through both naturalistic and experimental methods (Swann and Allington 2009), as a basis or sounding board for Cognitive Grammar analyses. In line with recent trends in stylistics, this development seems natural for further applications of Cognitive Grammar, given its requirement of 'psychological plausibility' (Langacker 2008: 14). For cognitive linguists, the idea of psychological plausibility is centred on a principled application of concepts externally validated in other cognitive scientific disciplines. For stylisticians, this explicit requirement is what sets apart cognitive stylistic research from analyses utilizing other established discourse frameworks (e.g. systemic-functional grammar). By making clear the psychological basis for our claims regarding interpretation, and supporting or scrutinizing this in context using empirical evidence, we stand a better chance in our future work of understanding the reality of these experiences, above and beyond what is 'plausible'.

References

Giovanelli, M. (2019), 'Construing and Reconstruing the Horrors of the Trench: Siegfried Sassoon, Creativity and Context', *Journal of Literary Semantics*, 48 (1): 85–104.

Langacker, R.W. (2008), *Cognitive Grammar: A Basic Introduction*, Oxford: Oxford University Press.

Langacker, R.W. (2012), 'Interactive Cognition: Toward a Unified Account of Structure, Processing, and Discourse', *International Journal of Cognitive Linguistics*, 3 (2): 95–125.

Langacker, R.W. (2014), 'Foreword', in C. Harrison, L. Nuttall, P. Stockwell and W. Yuan (eds), Cognitive Grammar in Literature, Amsterdam: John Benjamins, xiii–xiv.

Swann, J. and Allington, D. (2009), 'Reading Groups and the Language of Literary Texts: A Case Study in Social Reading', *Language and Literature*, 18 (3): 247–64.

West, D. (2017), 'Book Review: *Cognitive Grammar in Literature* Edited by Chloe Harrison, Louise Nuttall, Peter Stockwell and Wenjuan Yuan, 2014', *Language and Literature*, 26 (1): 66–8.

Index

action chain 3, 66–7, 97–108, 122–3, 126–8, 138–9, 184–6, 244–5, 247, 253–5
action discourse 148–50
active audience 118–21
agency 136–8, 273
  agent 3, 43, 66–7, 79–82, 86, 95–111, 122–3, 126, 136–47, 184, 244, 247, 254, *see also* patient
  agentless passive 94–6, 102–4
  agent-oriented strategy 101
Aldiss, Brian and Roger Penrose 30
ambiguity
  interpretive 182–8, 190
  literary 143
archetypal roles 3, 100, 104, 184. *See also* agent, patient
atemporal relation 61–2
attention
  attentional focus 3, 29, 45, 54–8, 65–6, 70–1, 79, 80–4, 98–104, 109–10, 123, 163, 205–7, 210, 215
  attentional shift 80–2, 84, 111, 165, 209
  attentional window 23, 26, 32, 55, 71, 109, 212
  auditory 205, 211, 213
  scope of 101–2
attenuation 161, 174
Austen, Jane 28–9
autobiography 164–6

backtracking 80–2, 84
Bechdel, Alison 157–9, 165–77
Blending Theory 51–4
  blend 22–3, 42, 55–8, 60–72
Bouchardon, Serge 210–13

canonical alignment 101
canonical event model 98, 137–9, 141–2, 184. *See also* action chains
categorization 270

causal listening 205–6
clause structure 98, 244–5, 251–5
coded listening 205–6
cognitive model 81, 86
compositional path 203, 125–6
compression 53, 127
conceptual substrate 122, 140
conceptual understanding 261–2, 275
conceptualization 37, 39–40, 101–2, 123, 157, 161, 165, 174, 177–8
  conceptualizer 82–3, 158–65, 170–8, 187–8, 229–30, 272–3, 281–2
construal 2–3, 36, 39–40, 54–5, 78–80, 97–100, 122–4, 131, 138–9, 144–5, 149–50, 157, 163, 172–7, 183, 187, 202–4, 208, 212, 249–68, 282. *See also* objective construal, reconstrual, subjective construal
construction 2–4, 97, 230
conventionality 78, 87
Corbyn, Jeremy 121, 128–31
Critical Discourse Analysis 94, 96–7, 111, 117–18, 120
cross-world identification 161–2, 164
Cummings, E.E. 75–8, 80–6
Current Discourse Space 159–61, 229

defamiliarization 42, 79, 197
default coding 98
definiteness 79–80
deixis 204
  audio 211, 213–14
  deictic centre 213
  empathetic 213
deliberate ambiguity 182
deviation 181, 196–7
diagrams 230–3
digital texts (second person address in) 204–5

Index

discourse participant 118–20, 124–5, 131, 159, 163–5
discourse-world 265–7
domain 207
  mapping 188–9, *see also* frame, schema
dominion 60
dual voice 22–4
dynamicity 36–47

elaboration sites (e-sites) 54
embodiment 1–2, 35–9, 183, 188–9, 244, 254
  embodied action 38
  embodied imagery 41–2
emotions 77, 84–6, 182, 205, 210–3
empathetic recognizability 79–80
enactment 38–9, 41–2, 44, 46, 77–8, 85, 207, 254
enactor 8, 25, 27, 29, 85, 160, 170
energy sink 3, 98, 184, 244, 253, 255
energy source 3, 98, 244, 247–8, 253–4
energy transfer 5, 66, 106, 122, 184, 198, 245, 247–8, 250–6
event-frame 109
experiencer 3, 42, 137, 184–6

face threatening act 129
fictive motion 38, 81, 203
figure 56, 79–80, 112, 160, 186, 244
  figural 79–80, 82, 175
figure/ground 121, 184, 203, 224. *See also* trajector/landmark
Flaubert, Gustave 17–18
focalization 177, 230
focusing 3, 25–6, 54–6, 60–2, 66, 99, 102, 122–3, 125, 159, 202–3
  refocusing 71, 125–6, 128
force dynamics 2, 23, 174
foregrounding (in stylistics) 76–8, 188. *See also* deviation, parallelism
frame 52–3, 71, 120–2, 124, 131, 207, 266–8, 270, 273. *See also* schema
free indirect discourse 17–32

The Guardian 95, 100–1, 109–10
generic space 52, 56, 61–3
Gestalt psychology 203
graphology 76, 81

ground 159–65, 171, 174, 176–7, 229, 265–6, 271
  surrogate 161, 163–5, 174
grounding 39, 159, 161–4, 170–3, 175, 177, 229, 251
  elements 83, 160

Hamid, Mohsin 35–45
harmonic processes 189–95
Harvey, Francis 51, 58–72
hedging 129–30

iconicity 77–8, 84–5, 233
idealised model of reality 275
ideology 31, 93–5, 100, 106, 112, 117–21, 124, 128, 131
image schema 1, 81, 93, 100, 183, 189, 191, 198, 203–4, 209, 269, 274–5
imagery. *See* embodied imagery, mental imagery
immediate scope 54, 60–1, 64, 70, 122–3, 128, 138, 141, 146, 247, 252
immersion 21, 31, 201, 205–6, 209–10, 213–14, 216
imperfective verbs 186, 234
indirect speech 18–19, 26
input spaces 52–5, 60–7, 71, 160
intentionality 53, 135–51
  bias 140
  unintentional actions 136, 148
interactive cognition 282
intransitive verb 94, 100–2, 112, 184, 247
irreality 272–3. *See also* reality

Joyce, James 27–8, 30–1

kinegram 248, 254–5
knowledge
  background 96, 120, 140–3, 145, 249
  cultural 120, 145
  experiential 2–3, 61–2, 81, 120, 122, 188–9, 207, 266–76
  Knowledge About Language 262
  linguistic 227–8, 242, 244, 253, 256, 262, 265, 267–76, *see also* frame, schema

linguistic exclusion 96–7, 111
linguistic rank scale 228
lyric narration 39–42, 44–7

mapping 36–7, 40, 43, 54, 63, 67, 215, 274
   cross-space 52, 57, 62, 70–1
   reverse 57–8, 61–2, 70. See also domain mapping
material process 136–8, 248, 252
maximal scope 54–5, 60, 63–4, 122, 252
May, Theresa 121, 124–8
memory 4, 35, 37, 45, 98, 207, 276
mental imagery 36, 38–9, 41–2, 46, 108, 202, 207, 209, 249, 275
mental spaces 52, 141, 159, 203
metaphor 2, 35, 147, 202, 263
   conceptual 35–8, 51, 55–8, 60–72, 189, 224, 244–5, 251–3
   Dynamic Life Story 40, 42–3, 45–6
   grammatical 231–3
   megametaphor 46
metonymy 43, 46, 94, 104, 112, 174–5, 247, 254–5
mind-modelling 84, 87, 125, 129, 144–5, 151, 160, 164, 174, 176–7
mindcast 25, 27
modality 41, 47, 83, 96, 110, 160, 225, 230, 234, 249
   epistemic 268–9, 271–2
   modal shading 129–30, 145, 230
   modal-world 25, 69, 273
moral judgement 84–7, 136, 147, 263
multimodal 108–10, 157, 178, 197, 201–8, 210–16, 252
Musical Grammar 188–90, 206, 210
mystification 94–7, 111
   agent-based 100, 102–4
   multimodal 108–10
   patient-based 100, 104–8

Nabokov, Vladimir 29
narrative urgency 40–1
natural path 79–80, 82, 165
neglect 56
New York Times 101, 103, 105–6, 111
nominalization 40, 94, 96, 99, 102, 103–4, 106, 109

objective construal 39, 42–4, 55, 82–4, 123–4, 160, 165, 173–4, 205, 229–30
objectification 159–60, 163, 165–6, 171
occlusion 56

parallelism 41, 45, 47, 76, 189, 193. See also deviation, foregrounding
   intersemiotic 108, 110
passive voice 44, 55, 61, 66, 79–80, 94–6, 99, 101–3, 112, 123, 163, 185, 247. See also agentless passive
patient 3, 55, 6–7, 71, 79–80, 86, 98–100, 101–2, 104–5, 107–9, 126, 139, 141–2, 184, 194, 244, 247, 255
pedagogy
   L1 5, 224–5, 241–2, 244, 248, 250, 252–6, 262, 275–6
   L2 5, 224, 243
pedagogical stylistics 5, 221, 226–7, 235, 241–2
perceptual symbols 207
perfective verbs 186
perspective 3–4, 6–7, 23, 39, 55, 82–5, 96, 122–3, 144, 165, 169, 187, 202, 207
   perspective-taking 84–6
preferred meaning 119
prepositions 81, 106, 139–40, 225
   directional 107–8, 204
profiling 26, 54–5, 80, 99, 101, 102, 104, 109, 123, 126, 160, 209, 212, 214
   agent-instrument 105
   agent-process 106
   and construal 124, 144, 171
   profile/base relations 54, 98, 174
   profiled relationship 71, 82, 100, 102, 202, 205
   relational 183–7
   shifting 29
projection 46, 177, 204
   fictive 170, 282
   modal 171
   text-world 69, 85–6
prominence 54–5, 78, 83, 97–9, 106, 122–3, 186, 207
psychoanalysis 160, 166
psycholinguistic methods 86
psychological plausibility 86, 283

Radiohead 8, 181–2, 189–90, 198
reality
   conception of 171, 174–8
   and irreality 272–3
   models of 8, 120, 131, 275

notion of 117, 166
psychological 225
reception 3, 5, 8, 131
    CDA of 117–18, 131
    of television discourse 118–19
reconstrual 111, 118, 124, 125, 128, 147
    and metonymy 254
    resistant 147
    subjective 130
recontextualization 95
    of grammatical theory 227, 231, 243
reference points 143, 149, 170, 177, 186–7, 234
    global 149, 151
    intentions as 150
reification 96
rhythmic processes 190

scanning
    sequential 40, 102–3, 186–7
    summary 40, 102–4, 186, 232
schema 2, 76, 86, 100, 102, 203, 244, 269–70, 273–4. *See also* image schema
    ACTION 103, 105
    BLOCKAGE 275
    CONTAINMENT 7, 60, 66–8, 70, 189, 203, 268, 274–5
    CYCLE 189, 191–3, 197
    ENTER 203
    FORCE 37, 98, 105
    PATH 36, 45–6
    SOURCE-PATH-GOAL 109, 189, 209, 268, 274–5
schema theory 76, 224
schematization 93, 100, 104, 111, 268–70
simulation 36, 39, 47, 78, 81, 82, 84, 86, 162, 173, 201, 282
    of bodily-perceptual experience 38–9
    of energy transfer 5
    multisensory 207–11, 214–15
    and recall 40
    speech and thought 170
    and writing design 203
social agency 140
sound
    ambient 211, 214–15
    and construal 207, 209, 211, 213, 215
    design 202, 206, 208, 210, 216

    and multimodality 209–10, 213–14
    patterns 41, 188, 247, 255
    perception 163
    source 205–6, 209, 213
source space 55–8, 61–3, 65–7, 69–70
specificity 3, 44, 54, 70, 99, 122, 185, 187, 202, 207, 209, 211, 270
    respecifying 126–7, 130
Stainton, H.H. 140–1, 144
sub-world 69. *See also* modal-world
subject-object relations 79, 99
subjectification 159–63, 177
subjective construal 44, 83, 160–1, 188, 207, 211, 213, 234, 248–9. *See also* objective construal
subjective movement. *See* fictive motion
supervention process 136–7
symbolic assembly 54, 97
syntax 1, 60, 76
    iconic 77, 81
Systemic Functional Linguistics 108, 136–7, 248
    and pedagogical grammar 224, 250

target space 7, 51, 56–8, 61–3, 66–7, 70–1
Text World Theory 7, 9, 20, 23, 69, 85, 118, 120, 122, 131, 146, 160, 262
    as pedagogical grammar 223–4, 229, 235, 244–6, 256
textual intervention 248, 254
text-drivenness 132, 265
theme-orientation 101
theory of mind. *See* mind-modelling
think-aloud protocol 8, 118, 121
trajector/landmark alignment 7, 25–6, 55–6, 58, 61–3, 65, 67–8, 70–1, 78–82, 98–9, 101–2, 106, 111, 184–6, 203, 209, 215
transitive clause 95, 98–9, 138, 244
transitive verb 100–1, 110–11
transitivity relations 3, 108, 139, 224

usage event 159, 161–5, 169–70, 177, 265

VanderMeer, Jeff 208–9
vantage point 6, 25–8, 30, 39, 46, 82–4, 158–9, 163, 165, 167, 172–5, 177, 202–4, 209, 211, 213–14, 233

viewing arrangement 8, 39, 47, 60, 83–4, 86, 157–9, 162–4, 173, 202–5, 207, 213, 216, 281
Volckaert, Vincent 210

Warsop, A.C. 144–6
well-formedness 78, 87
world-building elements 69–70
world-repair 146

www.ingramcontent.com/pod-product-compliance
Lightning Source LLC
Chambersburg PA
CBHW072125290426
44111CB00012B/1776